AFRICAN RIGHTS

FOOD AND POWER
IN SUDAN

A CRITIQUE OF HUMANITARIANISM

May 1997

A Publication of African Rights

11 Marshalsea Road
London SE1 1EP

Tel: 0171 717 1224
Fax: 0171 717 1240

Published by African Rights, May 1997

Copyright © African Rights

ISBN 1 899 477 13 6

Printed in the U.K.
Cover photograph: Child at food distribution, el Geneina, 1985.
Photo: Alex de Waal.

AFRICAN RIGHTS

African Rights is an organisation dedicated to working on issues of grave human rights abuses, conflict, famine and civil reconstruction in Africa. The urgent motivation for setting up African Rights is that we have become acutely aware of the limitations upon existing human rights, humanitarian and conflict resolution approaches to Africa's most pressing problems.

Any solution to Africa's problems—the emergency humanitarian needs as much as the long-term demands for political reconstruction and accountability—must be sought primarily among Africans. International organisations should see their principal role as primarily facilitating and supporting efforts by Africans to address their own problems. It is Africa's tragedy that the existing institutions for addressing these problems have not looked to the African people for answers. African Rights tries to give a voice to Africans concerned with these pressing issues, and to press for more accountability from the international community.

Rakiya Omaar   Alex de Waal

African Rights

11 Marshalsea Road, London SE1 1EP
Tel: 0171 717 1224, fax 0171 717 1240

TABLE OF CONTENTS

i

ACKNOWLEDGEMENTS

This book draws upon research conducted by African Rights during 1995-7, in addition to material previously obtained by African Rights and the contributors. The following people have contributed to the research: Michael Medley, Yoanes Ajawin, Hamdan Mohamed Goumaa, Ordesse Hamad and Chol Gakmar. The comments of a number of others were extremely helpful. The project was made possible by funds generously provided by the J. M. Kaplan Foundation. The book was edited by Alex de Waal, co-director of African Rights, who takes responsibility for the claims made and any errors of fact or interpretation.

LIST OF ACRONYMS

ABS	Agricultural Bank of Sudan
ACORD	Agency for Co-operation in Research and Development
Anyanya	Southern rebel forces in the first civil war
Anyanya II	Various non-SPLA rebel groups, 1983-7
ARS	Agricultural Rehabilitation Scheme (UNDP)
CART	Combined Agencies Relief Team (Juba)
Cdr	commander (SPLA)
COR	Commission of Refugees
CRRS	Cush Relief, Rehabilitation and Development Society
CSI	Christian Solidarity International
DHA	UN Department of Humanitarian Affairs
DUP	Democratic Unionist Party
Da'awa al Islamiya	Islamic Call (NGO)
Da'awa al Shamla	Comprehensive Call
EPLF	Eritrean People's Liberation Front
FAO	UN Food and Agriculture Organisation
FIB	Faisal Islamic Bank
IARA	International African Relief Agency
ICBP	Institution and Capacity Building Programme
ICRC	International Committee of the Red Cross
IGADD	Inter-Governmental Authority on Drought and Development
IIRO	International Islamic Relief Organisation
IMF	International Monetary Fund
intifada	popular uprising
JEO	Jonglei Executive Organ
khalwa	Koranic school
LWF	Lutheran World Federation
MFC	Mechanised Farming Corporation
MSF	Médecins Sans Frontières
Murahaliin	Baggara Arab militia
NCA	Norwegian Church Aid
NDA	National Democratic Alliance
NDF	National Development Foundation
NEC	SPLM National Executive Council
NIF	National Islamic Front

NPA	Norwegian People's Aid
NRRDS	Nuba Relief, Rehabilitation and Development Society
NSCC	New Sudan Council of Churches
OFDA	US Office of Foreign Disaster Assistance
OLS	Operation Lifeline Sudan
PDF	Popular Defence Forces
RASS	Relief Association of Southern Sudan
RRC	Relief and Rehabilitation Commission
SCC	Sudan Council of Churches
SCF	Save the Children Fund
SEOC	Sudan Emergency Operations Consortium
SIB	Sudanese Islamic Bank
SINGO	Sudanese indigenous NGO
SPLA	Sudan People's Liberation Army
SPLA-Mainstream	SPLA headed by Dr John Garang, post 1991
SPLA-Nasir	SPLA headed by Dr Riek Machar 1991-2
SPLA-Torit	SPLA headed by Dr John Garang
SPLA-United	SPLA headed by Dr Riek Machar, 1992-4; by Dr Lam Akol post 1994
SRRA	Sudan Relief and Rehabilitation Association
SSIM	South Sudan Independence Movement
SSU	Sudan Socialist Union
TMC	Transitional Military Council
TPLF	Tigray People's Liberation Front
Umma Party	Political party headed by Sadiq el Mahdi
Umma/Ummah	community of all Moslem believers
UNDP	UN Development Programme
UNHCR	UN High Commissioner for Refugees
UNICEF	UN Children's Fund
USAID	US Agency for International Development
USAP	Union of Sudan African Parties
WFP	UN World Food Programme
zakat	Islamic tithe

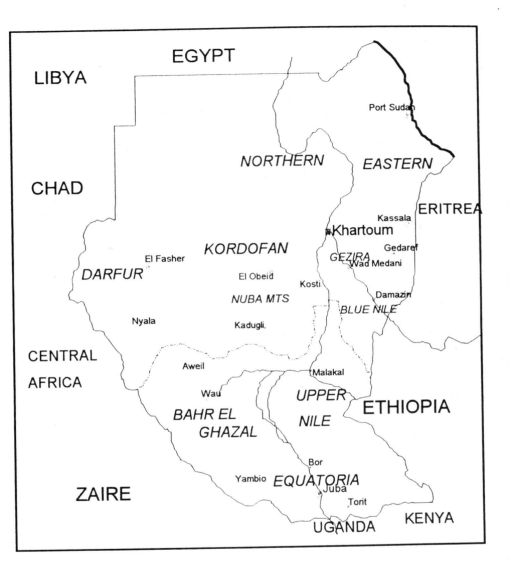

MAP OF SUDAN

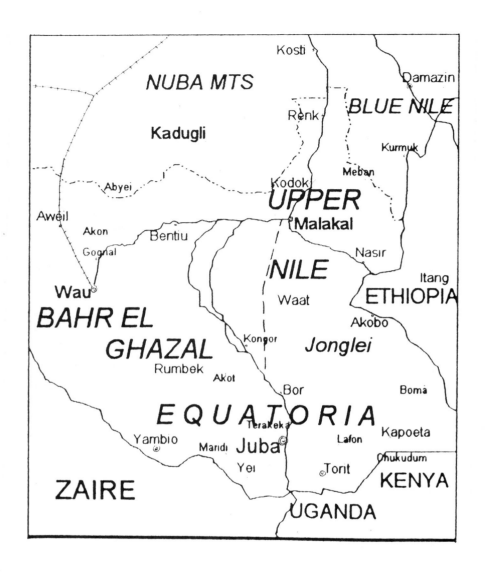

MAP OF SOUTHERN SUDAN

1.

INTRODUCTION

Famine is a gross infringement of the rights of ordinary Sudanese to live an acceptable life, or indeed live any life at all. Hundreds of thousands of Sudanese, very many of them children, have died from hunger and disease in the last fifteen years. The blame for this lies squarely at the door of Sudanese politicians and military commanders, who by their abuses and inactions have created these human tragedies.

The purpose of this book is partly to document some of the famine crimes committed in Sudan. Partly it is to evaluate relief programmes, not in detail but more generally with respect to their success or failure in fighting Sudan's chronic vulnerability to famine. More fundamentally it is to identify the political conditions that create famine or make its prevention possible.

The decline of Sudan is incontestable. Nearly a decade ago, a prominent Sudanese scholar and educationalist wrote:

> In three decades the Sudan has lived through two tragic civil wars. We are now more than a match for the Lebanese and the Irish. During these wars we have destroyed immense wealth, lost valuable opportunities for growth, and inflicted permanent injury to the national psyche with nothing to show for our deeds.[1]

In retrospect, the time when these words were written—1988— appears as a time of relative optimism. Sudan still had an elected government with a vibrant opposition, there were hopeful peace talks with the rebel Sudan People's Liberation Army (SPLA), and

---

[1] Abdul Rahman Abu Zayd Ahmed, 'Why the Violence?' in Panos, *War Wounds: Sudanese People Report on their War*, London, 1988, p. 14.

government and international donors were collaborating on programmes for reconstruction and development of areas stricken by drought and famine a few years earlier.

Things have got worse. Within a year, the military had seized power on behalf of the extremist National Islamic Front (NIF) and inaugurated Sudan's worst-ever wave of domestic repression, human rights abuse and militarism. The prospects for a negotiated end to the war have all but vanished. The NIF is implementing a gargantuan programme of social engineering intended to create an extremist state in its own image; at times the ruthlessness with which this is implemented has bordered on the genocidal. The SPLA has split (several times) and internecine warfare within the South has witnessed appalling human suffering. In 1996-7, the war has come North, with new fronts in Southern Blue Nile and Eastern Region to add to the longstanding armed resistance in the Nuba Mountains.

AID AND DECLINE

During the fifteen-year period this book is concerned with, Sudan has been one of the world's major recipients of international aid, especially humanitarian relief. While Sudan has changed from being one of the west's most favoured countries in Africa to being an international pariah, a constant factor has been the intimate involvement of international aid providers in the country's affairs. Sudan has also been a laboratory for humanitarian ideas. The series of aid and relief experiments includes:

- An extraordinarily high level of western aid to sustain a client regime, notably U.S. assistance to President Nimeiri, 1978-84, followed by a cut-off in almost all official development assistance following the 1989 coup.

- The deregulation and privatisation of relief work, starting with refugee programmes in 1980 and extending to general famine relief in 1984-5.

2

- Operation Lifeline Sudan (OLS) and the establishment of the principle of 'humanitarian access' in wartime in 1989.

- 'Islamic relief' and the rejection of western secular models of humanitarianism, especially pronounced since the 1989 coup brought the NIF to power and the 1992 adoption of the 'Comprehensive Call'.

- Various initiatives to assist and protect internally displaced people, including the mandate of the UN Department of Humanitarian Affairs, established in 1992.

- The initiation of 'capacity building' and 'humanitarian principles' within OLS-Southern Sector, with the aim of establishing a new humanitarian culture and humanitarian institutions in SPLA-controlled South Sudan.

Contrary to the assertions of many humanitarian advocates, Sudan *has* received its share of international attention and resources (at least compared to other countries in Africa). Sudan is rarely out of the news for long. Almost every major relief agency has an operation in Sudan. The UN has been deeply involved. Western governments, led by the Netherlands, have been consistently engaged in a range of initiatives.

There have been some successes. At one level, relief workers can point to achievements: nutrition rates improved in such-and-such a community, distress migration prevented somewhere else. (There are also relief programmes that cannot demonstrate any benefits at all.) But, more broadly, the massive investment of resources and effort seems to have had singularly little success. Sudan is worse off than it was fifteen or twenty years ago.

So, if the problem is not lack of resources, concern or goodwill, what has gone wrong? There are no simple answers. But in an important way, the remedy has become part of the problem: aid has been part of Sudan's decline.

Much of this book is concerned with the unanticipated (and often unobserved) outcomes of international involvement. One area of impact is allowing the belligerents to pursue the war through the simple provision of resources. The second area of impact is changing the direction of political accountability. Aid flows and the demands of external donors change internal political processes. Most obviously they may undermine democratic accountability in favour of external dependence, allowing dictators to resist pressures for democratic reform, but the relationship is often more complex. Finally and most insidiously, aid can influence political ideologies. Humanitarianism exercises its subtle tyranny over thought and speech.

FOOD AND POWER

Control of food, and by extension a range of aid resources, has become an intrinsic part of taking and wielding power in Sudan. Alongside the aid innovations mentioned above, Sudanese politicians have used food and famine for both democratic and authoritarian ends. This holds for successive governments in Khartoum, for the SPLA and for breakaway rebel factions, and for various coalitions of democratic or progressive forces.

As an account of the history of colonial famine relief shows, state security and food security (especially in the towns) were always linked. But in the early years of Independence, the politics of the food economy had become relatively benign. Until the 1970s, the safeguards against famine rested on a combination of robust local government, professional administration and a growing economy. Under the rule of President Jaafar Nimeiri (1969-85), these structures were swept away, to be replaced by much more fragile ones based upon a single party (the Sudan Socialist Union) and the promise of accelerated economic development.

By the early 1980s, Nimeiri's rule rested on a massive subsidy from international donors, primarily the U.S. This inflow of money made possible his authoritarian rule. Food aid was at first a relatively small part of this (and most of it was directed to the cities). This aid created a pattern of dependence upon—and accountability to— foreign donors. Without foreign aid, the Sudan Government would

4

not have been able to fight the civil war. Since Nimeiri, subsequent governments have been compelled to find more creative ways of financing themselves and their war efforts, as Sudan has gradually become more and more isolated internationally. To a remarkable degree, they have succeeded.

In 1984/5, a democratic coalition was formed against Nimeiri's aid-subsidised dictatorship. It mobilised people on several issues including opposition to the war, to human rights abuses, and to an Islamic state. Among these issues was famine: the famine then raging in western Sudan and the Red Sea Hills became a political scandal that discredited the government, while famine victims themselves became a small but important part of the coalition protesting on the streets. The 1985 Popular Uprising remains a model for how famine became part of a citizens' movement for democracy. Unfortunately, this democratic politicisation of famine was not sustained after the Uprising achieved its aim of removing Nimeiri. Control of food was re-captured by government and technocratic institutions.

The period 1985-9 saw the intensification of the war in the South, between the elected government of Prime Minister Sadiq el Mahdi and the SPLA headed by Dr John Garang. The most intense famine of the whole period under analysis occurred in Bahr el Ghazal at this time, as a direct result of the war strategies carried out by both sets of belligerents, but particularly because of the 'militia strategy' used by the government. Both sides were trying to deny food to the other and neither expressed much concern with providing for civilians under their own control. Both diverted food aid to their armies.

The liberal political institutions in Khartoum (such as the press and parliament) proved unable to halt this disaster. There was a succession of attempts, by *ad hoc* coalitions of concerned citizens, politicians, churches and relief agencies, to bring relief to the South, but all failed in the face of intransigence by one side or the other. Only in 1988-9, with the combination of a strong domestic peace process and heightening international concern with the blockage of relief, was there a breakthrough, which created Operation Lifeline Sudan (OLS) in April 1989.

5

The formation of OLS, followed by the resumption of the war, marked an important change in the way that food relief was integrated into the war. Rather than only trying to blockade their adversaries (although that continued), both sides became active in trying to manipulate relief deliveries to their advantage.

For the military-NIF government, humanitarian assistance came to assume greater importance as other sources of foreign aid were gradually cut off. For this reason it tolerates OLS, even though it regards it as an insult to national sovereignty. The famine of 1990-1 in northern Sudan (which even threatened an unprecedented food shortage in Khartoum) revealed the importance of food to national security. Taking control of food aid, and directing it to the most politically significant constituencies (such as the northern cities) became a government priority. Having established this, the NIF then moved on to using food, and humanitarianism more widely, as an integral part of a far-reaching programme of social, economic and political transformation: the 'Comprehensive Call' or *Da'awa al Shamla.*

Islamic humanitarianism under the aegis of the Comprehensive Call is one of the most important developments in contemporary Sudan. It is also one of the least understood. Islamic relief draws upon elements in the Islamic tradition of humanitarianism, which differs from the Christian and secular traditions in important respects. Some of its elements (for example regarding alms-giving as a duty rather than merely an act of charity, and certain forms of small-scale credit) are both politically progressive and remarkably effective. Islamic relief agencies have succeeded in channelling the energies of many committed people and reaching the poor. But overall, the Comprehensive Call is a project for the NIF to achieve a very high degree of domination of all aspects of Sudanese society. In the war zones of the South, the NIF is implementing an ambitious counter-insurgency strategy through the Comprehensive Call. It is a political project that serves the aims of an authoritarian, exclusivist and warlike party, and as such, it is not a protection against famine.

Although the Comprehensive Call, as actually implemented, contradicts many of the principles of humanitarian action, the government has succeeded in obtaining a high degree of compliance

6

from western relief agencies and donors. Several UN agencies are active partners in government-sponsored schemes for 'pacification' and social transform-ation, and some NGOs have also willingly collaborated.

One of the central theses of this book is that aid has supported the authoritarian tendencies of successive governments. For the SPLA, the story is more complicated.

In its early days, when based in refugee camps in western Ethiopia, the SPLA received a large subsidy of foreign aid, which it used to establish its control over the refugees. Since relief began to flow into SPLA-held areas of the South in 1989, and after the SPLA was forced to flee from Ethiopia in 1991, it has sought to recreate these conditions inside Southern Sudan, but with little success. On the whole, SPLA commanders and officials of the Sudan Relief and Rehabilitation Association (SRRA, its humanitarian wing), have seen relief flows as simple flows of material resources. The leadership has also used aid for diplomatic and propaganda purposes. But the SPLA has not had a practical social programme, into which foreign aid could be integrated, so that it might serve *both* the immediate needs of civilians and the political agenda of the Movement. As a result, the SPLA has not turned aid to its best advantage.

The internal weaknesses of the SPLA were dramatically revealed, and then exacerbated, by the splits in the Movement that began in 1991. Foreign aid, while it did not cause the splits, certainly helped to shape them: access to relief supplies was one factor in making some factions sustainable. The SPLA-Mainstream of John Garang (which has always been dominant) then recognised the need for internal reform, and permitted some liberalisation (for example allowing indigenous Southern Sudanese NGOs) and institutionalisation (in the form of a Convention in 1994 and a Civil Society Conference in 1996). Foreign humanitarians, led by OLS-Southern Sector's programmes for capacity building and 'humanitarian principles', have been intimately engaged with the SPLA's reforms. There have been some successes, but they are modest. The humanitarians have been handicapped by their own interests and preconceptions, and the opulence of expatriate lifestyles and the apparent waste of resources in international aid programmes has proved a constant source of irritation to Southern Sudanese. Meanwhile the SPLA leadership has always kept the issue of political power firmly in its sights.

International agencies enjoy a remarkably free hand in SPLA-held Southern Sudan, and their aspirations have been publicly embraced by the leadership of the SPLA to an unprecedented degree. There is a powerful coalition in favour of international humanitarian action in the South: but this is *not* the same thing as an anti-famine coalition. There is a need for Sudanese democrats to restore the taint of scandal to famine: it should be an issue that forces politicians from power, rather than only a malfunction that demands technical capacity and charitable giving.

AIMS OF THIS BOOK

This book follows the official review of OLS, led by Dr Mark Duffield of the University of Birmingham.[2] The *OLS Review* was required to aim its recommendations at the international humanitarians, specifically the UN Department of Humanitarian Affairs and other UN agencies. It provided an opportunity for those who were dissatisfied with the way in which OLS had been manipulated by the Sudan Government to seek a way out, by imposing the same standards of neutrality and accountability on the Northern Sector operations as were required in the Southern Sector. (This opportunity was lost.)

Food and Power in Sudan is different in several respects: primarily in its wider and longer scope, and its focus on the domestic political ramifications of humanitarian programmes. It is intended to be complementary to the official *OLS Review*, and to refocus attention on some of the main issues highlighted by that Review, in particular the way in which relief programmes have been co-opted

---

[2] Ataul Karim, Mark Duffield *et al.*, *OLS: Operation Lifeline Sudan: A Review*, University of Birmingham, July 1996.

by the Sudan Government in pursuit of its own political, military and social agenda.

It is customary for reports on human rights or humanitarian crises in Sudan to bemoan the lack of international (i.e. western) attention to the country. This book does not. The problem is not lack of attention, it is lack of knowing what can be done. Almost every international instrument of pressure has been applied to Sudan except military intervention or all-out trade sanctions. They have simply failed to work. The second reason is that responsibility for resolving the crises ultimately rests with Sudanese. Leaders of the opposition may call for international action, but they often have no clear idea of what that action might achieve and how it is linked to domestic initiatives. Beyond serving short term political interests, crying out for international action is not very helpful.

By contrast, the primary audience for this book is Sudanese. It aims to influence Sudanese citizens, including politicians and humanitarian workers, to adopt a different approach to preventing and mitigating human disasters such as famines. The key to this is building a democratic anti-famine politics.

2.

ORIGINS OF THE DISASTER: 1978-84

The people who own the country ought to govern it.

John Jay, First Chief Justice
of the U.S. Supreme Court

To understand the contemporary crisis in Sudan it is necessary to look at the extraordinary if little-understood transformation of Sudanese politics and economics that took place between 1978 and 1984, the second half of the regime of President Jaafar Nimeiri. This period saw the undermining of the key institutions that had anchored protection from famine in Sudan, alongside far-reaching political and economic changes. It is no coincidence that, simultaneously, new forms of aid intervention in Sudan began to be pioneered. The second part of this chapter looks at the history of protection from famine in Sudan and the growth of a new kind of deregulated humanitarianism that took hold in development activities in the South and refugee programmes in the east.

INTERNAL CRISIS IN SUDAN

Before the 1969 'May Revolution', the Sudanese state was founded on an enduring if unstable political dispensation. The state was dominated by two major families (Mahdi and Mirghani) each with their sectarian followings, in uncertain coalition with each other and with secular professional and military elites. The Mahdist Umma Party had its base in the central and western regions, and was led by large landowners and the chiefs of Arab tribes. The unionist bloc led by the Mirghani family was based in the north and east, had its economic base in trade, and was strongly pro-Egyptian. The 'modern forces' included civil servants, industrial workers and a growing professional class. Trade unionists and tenants in the Gezira irrigated scheme were the backbone of Africa's strongest Communist party. This dispensation excluded large sections of the Sudanese populace. From 1955, the South was in rebellion against northern Arab-Moslem domination, and large sections of the northern populace, such as the Nuba, west African immigrants and inhabitants of other peripheries were also marginalised. There was little populist rhetoric or commitment to social welfare, partly because the nationalist movement had been both divided and elitist, and independence had been achieved through political and diplomatic intrigue rather than popular mobilisation.

On 25 May 1969 a group of radical officers headed by Jaafar Nimeiri seized power, and promised a radical transformation of all aspects of society. In his sixteen years in power, Nimeiri proved a master of political survival, allying himself successively with the communists (until their failed coup in 1971), secular modernisers and Southern non-Moslems, the same conservative sectarians who had been overthrown in 1969, and finally the extremist Moslem Brothers. Sudan was indeed transformed, but not in the ways anticipated. One prominent critic dubbed it the 'Revolution of Dis-May.'[1]

Rejecting sectarian Islam, Nimeiri sought legitimacy by a promise of economic development. Sudan seemed ripe for rapid growth, especially after the Addis Ababa Agreement brought peace in the South in 1972. Sudan attracted an unprecedented amount of external investment, and the government borrowed extensively to finance ambitious development plans. These included a project to turn Sudan into 'the breadbasket of the Middle East', oil exploration, digging the Jonglei Canal to exploit the Nile waters better, and a range of industrial and agro-industrial projects such as the giant sugar factory at Kenana. For the first time, there was both a broad coalition that included the South and marginalised northerners (such as the Nuba) and a strong governmental commitment to welfare. The colonially-inherited system of native administration, based on village

---

[1] Mansour Khalid, *Nimeiri and the Revolution of Dis-May*, London, Kegan Paul, 1985.

11

sheikhs and tribal paramount chiefs, was abolished and replaced with elected councils, an expanded civil service and a single party, the Sudan Socialist Union (SSU). This era of optimism contained the seeds of its own demise: the debts would become due, the progressive coalition proved unstable, and the populist rhetoric failed to conceal deepening authoritarianism.

Political Instability and the Turn to Islam

Starting in 1977-8, President Nimeiri began to reverse his political direction and unpick the achievements of his early years in power. It is tempting to blame the President's personal weaknesses for this regression, but there were strong political and economic influences at work. A succession of coup attempts led Nimeiri to declare 'national reconciliation' with his former sectarian adversaries and the Moslem Brothers. Conservative political exiles and former Mahdist guerrillas returned to Sudan, and the National Assembly and SSU broadened to include many critics of the government. This coincided with a full alignment with the West in the Cold War, completing a shift away from the Eastern Bloc begun in 1971.

The opposition party that used National Reconciliation to best effect was the Moslem Brothers. They decided to take what was initially a small stake in government, compromising in the belief that they would be able slowly to expand their influence. This proved correct: the return of political Islam had profound consequences that would become evident much later. Dr Hassan al Turabi, leader of the Moslem Brothers, took the post of attorney general, and embarked upon Islamising the legal system. He also demanded that Islamic banks (which charge no interest and instead enter a partnership with their clients) be allowed to operate, with tax privileges. The civil service, army and financial sector became dominated by Islamists. The social base of the regime narrowed: the prominent secularists and regional leaders left one by one, and the South returned to unrest and finally war. Nimeiri explicitly sought legitimacy in political Islam, declaring Islamic law in September 1983 and proclaiming himself as Imam and demanding an oath of unconditional allegiance from all members of the civil service and judiciary. The President claimed he was accountable solely to Allah: any enforceable commitment to social welfare was jettisoned.

The Islamisation of political life in Sudan antagonised the South. By 1983 Nimeiri calculated that he no longer needed Southern support; his alliance with the Moslem Brothers was bringing him sufficient political and financial capital, and the U.S. was ready to tolerate almost any domestic political gambits in order to keep a faithful ally in power. Nimeiri sought to placate his northern coalition partners at the same time as practising divide-and-rule on the South. He interfered repeatedly in internal Southern politics, violating the Addis Ababa agreement, and in 1983 divided up the single autonomous Southern region into three parts. This was welcomed by some Southerners, but drove others towards revolt.

Economic Transformation

In the first half of Nimeiri's rule, the sectarian capitalists' domination of the economy was challenged with the growth of a new class of entrepreneurs, exploiting the state's commitment to rapid development and the inflow of foreign aid and investment. In the second half, a more radical change occurred. The twin motors behind this transformation were the migration of most of Sudan's professional class to the Gulf states, where the oil boom provided lucrative employment, and their remittances fuelled the growth of new economic sectors at home, and the government's foreign debt, which reached $12 billion by the end of this period, and which represented part of a chronic crisis of state financing.

The finances of Sudan during 1978-84 were quite extraordinary,[2] and go a long way to explaining why the President appeared oblivious to any domestic political accountability by the end of his rule. Although the government was almost bankrupt, the country was awash with hard currency remitted by the Sudanese expatriates in the Arab states. An estimated 350,000 expatriates earned about $5.5 billion per year, equal to fully three quarters of Sudan's gross

---

[2] Richard Brown, *Private Wealth and Public Debt: Debt, Capital Flight and the IMF in Sudan*, London, Macmillan, 1992, Chapter 4.

domestic product of $7.5 billion. The inflow of remittances, mostly through informal channels, did not appear in Sudan's official economic statistics, but was ten times greater than the next highest source of exchange, cotton exports.

In the mid-1970s, there was a marked capital migration within Sudan. Capitalists were trading in the regions but investing their profits in the main towns of the North, especially Khartoum.[3] As always, human migration followed capital. Skewed investment combined with the first remittances from the Arab states to finance a real estate boom in major cities, a lucrative market in consumer goods, and an explosion of the informal sector. Then, as the economic crisis deepened, capital flight from the country itself followed. The remittance system provided the hard currency to finance Sudanese capitalists' export of about $10 billion in capital flight, which, when combined with accumulated savings abroad, more than outweighed the national debt: Sudan was actually a creditor country.

The political repercussions of this transformation were profound. The government could abandon most of its internal tax base (and tried to, when an Islamic commercial code was introduced in 1984) and instead rely on the Islamic tithe (*zakat*) and the apparently magical liquidity of Islamist financiers who had their hands on much of the remitted money. Meanwhile, as sectarian and secular capitalists divested, the Islamic banks and Islamist merchants were investing, exploiting their tax privileges, political connections and access to hard currency. The Faisal Islamic Bank (FIB) was the first Islamic bank, and enjoyed spectacular growth. It targeted the expanding niches of the remittance-based economy (chiefly small businesses) with small-scale loans, and also bought up farms, transport companies, and former state assets that were being sold off. It is not a major exaggeration to say that Sudan was sold and bought in these years. Having become the 'owners' of Sudan, the Moslem Brothers concluded (in accordance with the U.S. 'Founding Father' John Jay) that they were entitled to govern it.

---

[3] Fatima Babiker Mahmoud, *The Sudanese Bourgeoisie: Vanguard of Development?* Khartoum University Press, 1984.

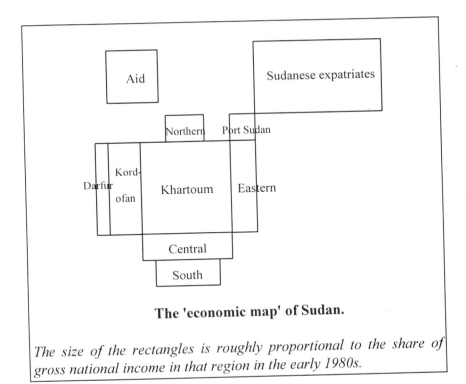

The 'economic map' of Sudan.

The size of the rectangles is roughly proportional to the share of gross national income in that region in the early 1980s.

The economic transformations wrought changes in income distribution. Sudan divided into two classes: the opulent who had access to remitted hard currency, and the rest. The income of the privileged few, chiefly in Khartoum, Port Sudan and a handful of other towns, was equivalent to the income of the entire rest of the country. It followed that it was possible to achieve economic domination of Sudan while ignoring the vast majority of the people, notably those in the far west and the South. The urbanisation of economic power also underpins continuing mass migration to Khartoum, the ability of the urban economy to sustain millions of displaced people, and the efforts of subsequent governments to maintain the social and ethnic 'purity' of the main towns by removing migrants to the margins.

The private wealth held by parts of the Sudanese expatriate and merchant classes contrasted with the bankruptcy of the state. From

15

its adoption in 1971, Sudan's 'open door' strategy for foreign investors did not lead to accelerated development. Money was borrowed recklessly, but much of it went into private consumption and greasing the wheels of Nimeiri's corrupt patrimonial system. When the debts became due in 1977-8, Sudan could not pay. This economic crisis pushed Nimeiri to turn to the IMF, USAID and 'national reconciliation'. A succession of stabilisation, austerity and adjustment packages followed, all of which failed to halt Sudan's accelerating inflation, mounting indebtedness and economic disequilibrium. This failure can be attributed both to the inappropriate design of economic policies and the failure of the government to adhere to the policies it formally agreed to, compounded by the willingness of the western donors (especially the U.S.) to continue to provide aid money nonetheless.

Sudan's renowned local government rapidly decayed in the late 1970s and early '80s. Inflation eroded the value of governmental salaries, and many civil servants joined the mass migration of Sudanese professionals to the Gulf. Corruption became endemic and local government budgets dwindled. Experiments with regionalisation fostered factionalism in local government and further lowered morale. After 1981, members of rural councils were appointed rather than elected.

External Orientation and Aid-Dependence

The early 1980s were years of Cold War confrontation. Having abandoned his Eastern-Bloc leanings, Nimeiri and his right-wing domestic allies (including the fanatically anti-communist Moslem Brothers) were attractive to the U.S., and Sudan became a key piece of the pro-western strategic jigsaw. Though massively in debt to the Paris Club of western creditors and the IMF, Nimeiri exploited his strategic advantages to the maximum. Sudan became the largest recipient of U.S. foreign assistance in sub-Saharan Africa, including both financial aid, development assistance and a large programme of food aid (most of which was wheat, destined for subsidised sale in the politically important urban market). The official debt was rescheduled no fewer than eight times. This slowed but did not prevent deepening economic crisis and Nimeiri's insatiable demand for foreign finance to stay afloat.

A routine became established in which: the IMF recommended a package of economic reforms; the Sudan government agreed; the IMF duly issued its 'seal of approval'; the Paris Club met and provided generous funds (supposedly on the basis that Sudan honoured its agreement and repaid its debt); Khartoum made symbolic gestures towards reform and debt repayments, but in reality the money disappeared into the vortex of corruption around Nimeiri; the Ministry of Finance then ran out of money and came back to the donors for bailing out; and the U.S. State Department contacted the U.S. Treasury and IMF and began the process all over again. By 1983 Nimeiri's treasury was living from hand to mouth, and the U.S. State Department was obliged to conspire with the Sudanese Ministry of Finance in various financial contortions to keep the routine going. By July 1984 the donors began to balk at providing 'the extraordinary levels of foreign aid that [were] necessary to maintain some semblance of stability in an otherwise explosive environment.'[4] A major complication was that Sudan was now defaulting on its debt to the IMF itself. The IMF is constitutionally debarred from dealing with a defaulter, and getting round this required great ingenuity. (At one point the U.S. State Department took out a commercial bridging loan, repaid the IMF, and was then reimbursed by the Sudanese Ministry of Finance when the Paris Club aid tranche was unlocked. When Congress discovered this trick it prohibited it.) The day-to-day ins and outs of these financial conjuring tricks and the accompanying negotiating manoeuvres took up a formidable amount of time and energy at high levels of government. They also changed the nature of political accountability: Nimeiri was reporting to his financiers in Washington D.C. before all others. When in December 1984 the IMF

---

[4] Richard Brown, 'A Background Note on the Final Round of Economic Austerity Measures Imposed by the Numeiry Regime: June 1984-March 1985,' in T. Barnett and A. Abdelkarim (eds.) *Sudan: State, Capital and Transformation*, London, Croom Helm, 1988, p. 73.

17

and State Department finally withheld their money and insisted on severe austerity measures, Nimeiri could not survive.

Nimeiri had other financial strings to pull. One was investment in the 'breadbasket' plan; chiefly Arab finance to develop mechanised agriculture. Nimeiri's fear of discrediting the breadbasket scheme and thereby stopping investment was one of the motives for concealing famine in 1984. A second string was the Falashas (Ethiopian Jews), who were being clandestinely evacuated from Ethiopia to Israel through Sudan. Over $300 million was spent on this operation by the U.S. and Jewish charities, an undisclosed amount of which was paid to Nimeiri and leading security officers.

The Slide to War

Another financial string was oil. The oil company Chevron invested over $1 billion in drilling for large high quality oil deposits in Sudan. Nimeiri expected that oil revenues would solve his demand for easy money. Southern anticipation of this contributed to the war, which began with attacks on Chevron's operations. Nimeiri tried various gambits, including forming militias and buying off fragments of the rebel forces, to buy enough time for the oil to flow—expected in 1986. These were instrumental in the descent into war in Southern Sudan.

Chevron's principal oilfield was at Bentiu, just south of the internal frontier. The political tussle for control of the oilfield, the oil refinery and its revenues between Khartoum and the Southern Regional Government in Juba was one of the key sparks to the outbreak of the war. In order to deprive Juba of control over the oil revenues, Nimeiri had to undo the 1972 Addis Ababa agreement that had brought to an end the first civil war, redivide the South into three regions, and then create a new 'Unity' region specifically for the oilfields.

But by 1983 Bentiu was already a war zone, and in February 1984 the SPLA attacked Chevron's headquarters at Rub Kona, forcing the company to suspend its operations. Vice President Omer al Tayeb immediately promised troops to protect Chevron and large military operations began so that by June the government could claim to control the area. This provided only brief respite, and in September a pro-SPLA faction of Anyanya II attacked a mission near Bentiu and took three priests as hostages—creating a fear that the SPLA could attack the oil installations again. Nimeiri was anxious not to admit that Sudan was at war, so rather than mobilise the army and negotiate with the SPLA, he embarked upon the 'militia strategy'. (Conscription, canvassed as an option in September 1984, was so politically unpopular that Nimeiri quickly dropped it and turned to less politically costly ways of mobilising forces.) In Bentiu and the nearby oil field of Heglig, this had two components. One was negotiating with Nuer rebels, all of whom called themselves 'Anyanya II', and the second was arming and organising militia from the Baggara Arabs immediately to the north. The militia strategy was to be at the heart of the creation of famine in Bahr el Ghazal and parts of Upper Nile during 1986-9. In the meantime, Nimeiri was simply playing a convoluted political game, hoping to gain enough time for the oil to flow, at the cost of plunging the South ever deeper into war.

The causes of the outbreak of war in 1983 are complex and will not be detailed here. Some, referred to above, include the redivision of the South, the imposition of political Islam, and disputes over economic resources such as the Jonglei Canal and the Bentiu oilfields. Internal differences among the Southern political class also played a key role: from its inception the Southern Regional Government was dependent on foreign aid and grants from Khartoum, and Southern politicians spent much of their energies trying to secure their access to these funds, and placing their friends and kinsmen in governmental posts. Such patrimonial politics were open for manipulation by Nimeiri, master of the game in Khartoum. When the SPLA went to war, one of its early slogans was opposition to the older generation of Southern politicians who were seen as corrupt placemen.

The mishandling of the national army provided the final spark for war. The army too was brought into the vortex of corruption, notably with the creation of the Military Economic Board in 1982, which formalised officers' role in commerce. The Addis Ababa agreement had provided for the reintegration of former Anyanya fighters into the national army, police, prisons and wildlife. But many absorbed Anyanya were unhappy at their treatment, and in two cases in 1983 unhappiness turned to mutiny when it appeared that Southern units were to be transferred North, in abrogation of the agreement. Colonel John Garang, a PhD holder working in the army's research department, joined the mutineers in Ethiopia and the SPLA was formed shortly afterwards.

HUMANITARIAN TRANSFORMATION

Overall, during the period 1978-84, western interest in Sudan was strategic and commercial rather than humanitarian. Relief policy was made with other aims in mind. Later, international policies driven by concern with human suffering were to become prominent, when these more substantial interests had evaporated. But in the meantime, humanitarian policy and practice had rapidly evolved; protection against famine had been weakened and new and less effective relief mechanisms had been introduced.

The History of Protection against Famine in Sudan

Until the 1970s, rural food security was founded on a robust administrative system and a migrant labour economy. Sudan had a civil service well-known for its professionalism, which retained an ethos of safeguarding local food supplies. This functioned alongside the native administration of village and sub-district sheikhs (chiefs), most of them (in the North) members of either the Mahdist or Mirghani sects. They ensured a basic level of accountability: loyal supplication by these men did not preclude them from making representations on behalf of their people when scarcities threatened. Village sheikhs were also a reliable and timely source of information about scarcities—an early-warning system that no amount of technical information can replace.

The formal centrepiece of protection against famine was the 1920 Famine Regulations,[5] introduced by the British administration as a response to political pressure from two sources. One was discontented Sudanese. The government's main concern was with urban food supplies (a serious problem in 1919 and intermittently over the following decades), but drought relief was also used to assist pacification in remote areas such as the Nuba Mountains. The second concern was to quell Egyptian agitation for the unity of the Nile Valley: the Egyptians used every pretext to claim that the British were inflicting misery on the Sudanese, who would therefore be better off under Egyptian rule. This was the spark for the introduction of the Regulations in 1920, but they were effectively abandoned when the threat had passed.

When political pressures heightened, the Regulations were re-introduced. The spark was a political controversy surrounding the Funj famine of 1930-2, when official relief was niggardly. Most help for the hungry came in the form of donations from the Sudanese public and the Egyptian royal family (always eager to show that they were more concerned with Sudanese welfare than the British) and above all, free distributions of grain by the local paramount chief, Sheikh Yousif el Aggab, from his own stores. After the famine, the government reneged on its promise to reimburse the Sheikh (disputing his accounts) and removed him, now-bankrupt, from his chieftancy. Sheikh Yousif protested by fasting (Ramadhan-style) for twelve years until he was reinstated. The British, recognising the Funj famine as a political disaster, resolved that more effective measures be taken thereafter.

The Sudan Famine Regulations were modelled on the famous Indian Famine Codes, specifically the Madras code of 1905 with virtually no alterations except to make provision for irrigated agriculture along the Nile. But Sudan was very different from south India: it lacked the same level of infrastructure and local administration. As a result, the Regulations could not be

---

[5] Alex de Waal, 'The Sudan Famine Code of 1920: Successes and Failures of the Indian Model of Famine Relief in Colonial Sudan,' London, ActionAid, 1989.

implemented exactly as prescribed: instead they were a symbol of administrative obligation to prevent hunger and general guidelines for action. They were used intermittently and occasionally effectively during British rule, notably in response to the droughts of 1941-2 (when famine relief labour schemes constructed airfields for the war effort) and 1948 (when the British distributed free train tickets as a relief measure, and also included coffee in labourers' rations in the Beja hills). Most of the time, however, famine relief was seen as unnecessary because of the high availability of work for migrant labourers.

Most of Sudan's economic development was concentrated on the Gezira and adjoining areas. The irrigated schemes, and later the mechanised farms of eastern Sudan, had an enormous appetite for labour that was rarely fully met. Labour was provided, successively, by west African migrants, and by labourers from Darfur and the Nuba Mountains. For the scheme managers and tenants, drought in remote rural areas was a boon, because impoverished rural people became seasonal labourers. Migrant labour was the first and most effective coping strategy for those facing hunger, and the need for drought relief measures was reduced.

The South was extremely lightly administered during the colonial period. For the first two decades of the occupation, the British did not take any anti-famine measures, largely because they were busy inflicting famine using punitive patrols and mass confiscation of cattle. Even after the 'pacification' was complete, the South received virtually no economic development or social services, and the collection of taxes was nominal—undertaken largely to assert the authority of the government rather than to raise revenue. Famine protection and relief measures were extremely modest, focusing on encouraging drought-resistant crops such as cassava and on food-for-work schemes building roads and river embankments. One district commissioner pointed out the inappropriate-ness of the detailed provisions of the Famine Regulations, which he dryly noted, 'may have not been drafted with an eye to Dinka districts.'[6]

---

[6] Sudan National Archives, Khartoum, File Civsec 19/1/2, 'Famine'.

The Famine Regulations were dropped at Independence but some of the basic ethos lived on, in particular the local administrative obligation to safeguard food supplies and the governmental obligation to maintain rations to the towns. In 1971, the system of native administration was replaced by elected local councils, but in much of rural Sudan there was some continuity, as the old sheikhs were elected. The growth in seasonal employment on irrigated schemes and mechanised farms rendered much of the regulations redundant anyway by the early 1970s. Meanwhile the increase in national grain production and the post-independence expansion of the railway system to the west and South helped to even out regional fluctuations in food supply. These were the conditions under which Sudan faced the drought of 1972-4 and the Eritrean and Ethiopian refugee inflows of 1975-8. It coped with both in a manner that appears in retrospect as exemplary. For the drought, the SSU, local councils and Red Crescent Committees organised food distributions, food supplies for towns were transported from the surplus-producing east to the deficit-struck west, and labour migration to the cotton schemes was encouraged. The government encouraged commercial farmers' labour recruitment efforts in Kordofan and Darfur. No international relief was requested, as none was needed. The response to the refugee influx will be considered below. But all this was to change by the early 1980s.

The Changing Context

In the 1970s the world-wide emergency relief system appeared to be fast developing a new order of professionalism. The system was dominated by governments, acting in partnership with official multilateral agencies such as the UNDP and WFP. But relief NGOs were rapidly emerging from relative obscurity to become important players in the system.

The first major NGO-dominated relief programme was the Biafra operation of 1968-70, where official agencies were wholly absent and there was considerable antipathy between the official and NGO networks. In the 1970s, NGOs were involved in a series of relief operations, including Bangladesh, Ethiopia, the Sahel, and a number of refugee crises, in which they came to a rapprochement with official agencies. Emergencies were still dominated by governments and UN agencies, which retained the power to regulate the NGOs, often strictly. Meanwhile, the NGO world was relatively small and clubby, and the leading relief NGOs were dedicated to collaboration and the pursuit of professional standards. This, the 'normal' period in which most modern senior aid officials came of age, can now be seen as an anomaly: a time of relative stability and optimism.

It did not seem particularly 'normal' at the time: there was outrage at what were seen as needless crises, and the complacency and ineffectiveness of major relief bureaucracies. Many leading NGO humanitarians saw these official obstacles as the main constraint on effective relief work, with the result that they advocated expanded roles for NGOs. Overall, however, relief practitioners believed in progress, including the professionalisation of their work. There was a common belief that shortcomings could be blamed on failures of technology and management. Specifically, there was said to be a lack of 'early warning information', poor co-ordination of activities by different agencies and lack of the necessary logistical and technological capacity.

At an official level, the response was to set up new institutions such as the UN Disaster Relief Organisation, with special responsibilities for information collection and dissemination, and to give certain agencies enhanced powers (UNDP took on the lead role). Much energy was also put into the development of special technologies such as emergency sanitation and nutrition, early warning systems to monitor rainfall, crop production, prices etc. For example, the late and inefficient response to the 1984 famines in Ethiopia and Sudan were blamed (incorrectly) on lack of prior warning and the low profile of relief agencies. In consequence, new UN emergency offices were established and expensive early warning systems established.

At an NGO level, the consensus was that higher technical standards could be achieved through specialisation and collaboration. Thus Oxfam concentrated on emergency water supplies, Save the Children Fund on child nutrition, etc. There was also a widespread belief that failures at a higher level were caused by the political constraints on official agencies, in particular the geo-strategic imperatives of the U.S., and the lack of clout of the NGOs *vis-à-vis* their official counterparts. The flexibility and relative informality of NGO operations were identified with sensitivity to local concerns and efficiency.

The late 1970s and 1980s saw a number of significant changes. The first was the increased size and influence of NGOs, which began to obtain significant governmental funding for emergency programmes and to become formal partners with official agencies. This began with refugee programmes. For example the Lutheran World Federation was a signatory of tripartite agreements with UNHCR and Tanzanian authorities to provide assistance for Burundi refugees in Tanzania. At the 1979 International Conference on Assistance to Refugees in Africa (ICARA I), UNHCR and its major donors granted NGOs a major role in refugee assistance. This role was soon to spread to all relief operations.

The second change was the deregulation of the aid system, with western donors (particularly the U.S.) supporting private contractors and international NGOs in preference to host government structures. Some large NGOs took on a role as public service contractors, bidding for contracts from major donors. NGOs with their own funds became more and more free to run programmes as they wished with little official oversight. International NGOs became much more assertive with respect to host governments, and foreign donors and diplomats became much more protective of them.

Sudan was a key locus for the deregulation of aid. Two areas in particular were affected: the reconstruction of the South after the 1972 peace agreement and assistance to refugees from Eritrea and Ethiopia.

Aid and Development in the South after 1972

The story of the dashing of the hopes of the 1972 Addis Ababa Agreement is a long one and cannot be detailed here—though it prefigures many of the problems of Southern politics during the war. Instead, this section will focus on how aid and development in the

25

South during the decade of peace helped establish a set of expectations and power relations that have remained very important.

At first, proposals for the rehabilitation and development of the South were dominated by multi-year development plans. This reflected conventional development thinking at the time, and Sudan's socialist orientation. It was envisaged that the Southern Regional Government would take the lead role in centralised aid planning. This was undone by several factors. One was the lack of finance in the Southern government departments. The local tax base was small and very slow to expand. The commercial sector was dominated by Northern traders, who preferred to pay taxes in the North and invest their profits in the North. Local scarcity left the Regional Government dependent on subventions from Khartoum. In 1973/4, over 90% of regional government expenditure was provided by central government grants, and though this proportion declined over the following years, the 1977/8-82/3 six year development plan still envisaged a mere 17.5% of expenditure being met from the local revenue base.[7] Central government subventions were inflexible and rarely provided in full—on average 20-25% of the original allocation.[8] This not only led to perpetual fiscal crisis, but also meant that ordinary Southern citizens had virtually no influence over government in their capacity as taxpayers. Autonomy for the South was a mere dream.

A second factor in the crisis of development in the South was the way in which external agencies began to substitute for the state. This took several forms and was not planned. In Upper Nile, for example, the Jonglei Executive Organ (JEO) took responsibility not just for building the canal—a classic aid megaproject—but also for development projects and service delivery in the area. Financed jointly by Sudan and Egypt, its main aim was to provide water for irrigation in the Egyptian Nile. Locally, the JEO's mandate was so

---

[7] George Tombe Lako, *Southern Sudan: The Foundation of a War Economy*, Frankfurt, Peter Lang, 1993, pp. 57-9.

[8] B. Yongo-Bure, 'The Underdevelopment of the Southern Sudan since Independence,' in M. Daly and A. A. Sikainga (eds.) *Civil War in the Sudan*, London, British Academic Press, 1993, pp. 56-7.

broad that it 'led many people to assume that it was a substitute for other government departments, when in fact it could only supplement their services.'[9] In the event, the JEO concentrated on research and planning and its Commissioner remarked in 1981: 'the Canal Zone lags far behind in development and its citizens do not appreciate long scientific research which does not provide them the benefits they firmly believe they should receive.'[10]

In fact, *all* the South was lagging behind. By 1983, transport and communications had more-or-less returned only to the state they were in at Independence.[11] The South was littered with uncompleted, abandoned or inappropriate development projects. Regional and central government were notorious for their failures to consult the people before implementing their plans, an attitude summed up in a remark by Abel Alier, President of the Southern Regional Government, that, 'If we have to drive our people to paradise with sticks, we will do so for their own good and the good of those who come after us.'[12] There were popular protests against the Jonglei Canal, and well-articulated critiques of the Southern development process were circulated in the newspapers and at the Universities of Khartoum and Juba. But no alternatives were forthcoming. Although few in absolute terms, posts in government were the main source of employment for educated Southerners. They became disillusioned and frustrated by lack of resources, but still needed to obtain and hold on to civil service posts. Much of the Regional Government became a patronage machine. It is unsurprising that after a decade of

---

[9] Paul Howell, Michael Lock and Stephen Cobb (eds.) *The Jonglei Canal: Impact and Opportunity*, Cambridge University Press, 1988, p. 432.

[10] Quoted in Howell *et al.* (eds.), 1988, p. 433.

[11] Elias Nyamlell Wakoson, 'The Politics of Southern Self-Government 1972-83,' in M. Daly and A. A. Sikainga (eds.) *Civil War in the Sudan*, London, British Academic Press, 1993, p. 44; Howell *et al.* (eds.), 1988, p. 436.

[12] Quoted in: George Tombe Lako, 'The Jonglei Scheme: The Contrast between Government and Dinka Views on Development,' in T. Barnett and A. Abdelkarim (eds.) *Sudan: State, Capital and Transformation*, London, Croom Helm, 1988, p. 88.

peace, Southerners were scarcely more impressed with government than during the first civil war.

A third factor was the shortage of educated Southerners: both a severe handicap and a source of frustration. The Southern Regional Government was chronically understaffed.[13] Only 1051 administrators were available for the whole South, out of a national total of 92,000. By 1976, only about half the required posts were filled, and as the years passed, shortages of staff grew more, not less, acute. Southern secondary schools and Juba University were turning out a tiny fraction of the graduates required.[14] In 1972, 48 students from the South were awarded university places, as against 1,768 from the North; in 1978 the figures were 50 and 2,511, and in 1984 24 and 2,878. In 1980, the South had only fifteen secondary schools, the North had 199.

The prominent role of aid, and especially NGOs, in the South came about by default rather than imposition. The Southern Regional Government did not plan to be aid-dependent. As late as 1977, it envisaged that external aid would provide no more than 7.5% of regional expenditure.[15] But, as local taxes and central government subventions failed to appear, and local government came to a standstill, international agencies came to take on a more and more prominent role.

After the 1972 peace agreement, international agencies rushed in to take charge of returnee and rehabilitation programmes. Many contemporary problems of competence and co-ordination were prefigured in the agencies' rush to Juba and other Southern towns. The 1972 rehabilitation conference in Juba was attended by no fewer than 38 NGOs—more than were present in the whole of Northern Sudan at that date. At that time, 'Hilary Logali, the Regional Minister of Economic Planning, was working from three offices with a staff

---

[13] Terje Tvedt, 'The Collapse of the State in Southern Sudan after the Addis Ababa Agreement: A Study of Internal Causes and the Role of NGOs,' in Sharif Harir and Terje Tvedt (eds.) *Short-Cut to Decay: The Case of the Sudan*, Uppsala, Scandinavian Institute for African Studies, 1994, pp. 73-5.
[14] Yongo-Bure, 1993, pp. 68-72.
[15] Lako, 1993, p. 57.

of five people, including a filing clerk and a typist.'[16] NGO numbers increased over the following years, but the Southern regional capacity did not. Several NGOs, such as ACROSS, first emerged from these rehabilitation efforts, while others, such as ACORD, were profoundly shaped by them. Some donors, such as Britain's Overseas Development Administration, also became semi-operational by providing finance, personnel and planning assistance to special quasi-governmental development units. There was a new influx after 1979 in response to the exodus of refugees from Uganda. A disproportionate number of projects were in Equatoria.

The level of NGO competence and professionalism in the South was heavily if unsystematically criticised.[17] Some of the criticism is fair, but there were also some effective programmes. Large parts of Equatoria enjoyed unprecedented prosperity and service provision, in part because of these projects. A more serious problem was the wider political impact of the privatisation and internationalisation of responsibility for public services in the South.[18] Foreign agencies took over many of the functions of local government, including education, health, veterinary care, water provision, agricultural extension, road building and the like. These agencies enjoyed far greater levels of resourcing than government departments and undermined the legitimacy of local government. In time, the only services provided by the Regional Government were security and law enforcement, and even then only intermittently.

Aid agencies attracted the best staff to their programmes, where they could offer high and regularly-paid salaries, good working conditions and job satisfaction. The Norwegian Church Aid programme in Eastern Equatoria (where Torit was dubbed 'little Norway') was a prime example of this. By contrast with the Regional Government, agencies such as NCA never had problems with recruiting. The high educational standards of their staff (and the fact that many were Equatorians who had obtained an education in

---

[16] Wakoson, 1993, p. 43.
[17] Barbara E. Harrell-Bond, *Imposing Aid: Emergency Assistance to Refugees*, Oxford, Clarendon Press, 1986.
[18] Tvedt, 1994.

Uganda during the civil war) made for troubling comparisons with local government.

Aid agencies undermined the principle of local accountability. They did not aim to do so, but by creating high expectations and unsustainable social and administrative structures, they implicitly mocked the capacity of the Southern state. As Terve Tvedt has noted in his study of NCA, their philanthropic culture aggravated this impact:

> For some of the NGOs money was not the deciding constraint on their scope of activities. What affected the project size and the project components was in general not the purse, but arguments about what was morally right and conducive to local development. Generally, the NGOs acted within a culture of absolute affluence, where services and goods were not priced. . . . It was difficult to question the principle that aid was free and in some mysterious way outside the realm of economic realities.[19]

As economic crisis gripped Sudan after 1978, compounded by political paralysis in the South with the undermining of the Regional Government in 1981 and redivision in 1983, local government became paralysed. While the government's commitments, in terms of services, projects and staff, increased, its finance did not. Salaries were paid late or not at all, and the only way that civil servants could obtain the resources they required was often to travel to Khartoum and lobby directly with central government. All the three Southern regions set up liaison offices in Khartoum, and by 1984, many—perhaps even most—of the administrative staff were to be found there rather than in post in the South. (The JEO had established its headquarters in the capital at its creation in 1975 precisely so as to have ready access to where real power and money lay.) Local government had become a structure for begging resources from a faraway patron, and competing for this consumed much of the energies of educated Southerners.

Meanwhile, aid agencies were left providing services in a patchy and arbitrary manner in the South. NGO-state relations were

---

[19] Tvedt, 1994, p. 97.

formally characterised by co-operation; in reality local government officers became dependent upon NGO resources for transport, telecommunication and many other essentials, while the NGOs circumvented much of the state bureaucracy in search of quick answers to pressing needs. The NGOs helped to foster an administrative ethos of personal connection and arbitrary decision, at the cost of rule-governed behaviour.

Aid agencies' allocations of resources raised the question of bias. Residents of Bahr el Ghazal and Upper Nile challenged their MPs: why had they allowed most NGOs to go to Equatoria? Some agencies provided favours to politicians serving in government. One former parliamentary candidate in Bahr el Ghazal commented:[20]

> As the election of 1979 was approaching, I asked an NGO representative to give me a lift to my constituency. He declined to do so. But when a government minister who had just completed his term came to him, he gave the minister a car with a few cartons of medicine, which he claimed [to the people] to be able to provide more if he was elected.

Another source of complaint was the appointment of unqualified relatives and associates of ministers to positions in aid agencies. The same politician remarked on the exchange of favours between agencies and ministers:

> A convoy of [aid agency] cars came to our area, being headed by one of the officials who used to work in the same ministry where my contender was working. Upon his arrival he told people that if it was not for this man [the minister], who had good relations with the khawajat [white people] , these services wouldn't have come to you. As a result, people voted for him.

Deliberate or not, the agencies' activities supported the minister's electoral campaign, while the minister gave the impression to local people that unless you work with foreign agencies, you cannot provide development or services.

---

[20] Interviewed in March 1997.

The undermining of the Southern Regional Government had many facets, of which the role of NGOs was only one, and not the most important. (Interference from Khartoum, corruption and the 'casual way in which [the regional government] was prepared to act outside the law and constitutional prescriptions' were much more crucial.[21]) But many NGOs slipped readily into their role as service-provider in the absence of the state, and by their actions helped erode the state. The benevolent functions of the state became privatised and supplied by external organisations. The only functions left to the state were coercive law-enforcement and patronage: it is little wonder that its legitimacy foundered. Southern citizens were left marginalised and frustrated, and subject to arbitrary abuses such as the mass expulsions of labourers from Khartoum in 1981-2 and the restrictions on Dinka cattle owners in and around Juba the following year.

New Forms of Refugee Aid in Eastern Sudan

If peacetime development in the South was a case of foreign agencies taking over governmental services because of the failures of the state, refugee aid in eastern Sudan was a case of foreign donors foisting international NGOs on a capable and reluctant government.

In 1967, 30,000 Eritrean refugees crossed the border into the Eastern Region, the first of more than a million. The government created a small office within the Ministry of the Interior, the Commissioner of Refugees (COR) to deal with the protection and assistance. The COR was small but efficient, and the resources for refugee assistance were mobilised from within the country.[22] For more than a decade, in contrast to the situation in the South, the model of refugee response reinforced the legitimacy of the state.

These refugee flows did not challenge the prevailing developmentalist optimism of the 1960s and '70s. On the contrary,

---

[21] Abel Alier, *Southern Sudan: Too Many Agreements Dishonoured,* Exeter, Ithaca Press, 1990, quotation from p. 166.
[22] Ahmed. A. Karadawi, 'Refugee Policy in the Sudan, 1967-1984,' DPhil thesis, University of Oxford, 1988.

the Sudan government did its best to fit the refugees into development planning, by creating agricultural and wage-earning settlements. Two years after the first influx, refugees from the reception centre at Wad Sherifei near Kassala were moved to a permanent agricultural settlement at Qala en Nahal, south-east of Gedaref in the main mechanised farming zone of Sudan. After another two years, when each family had cleared its four hectare plot, rations were cut. Thereafter, Qala en Nahal was administered under the local rural council, supervised and funded by COR. Sudan government policy depoliticised the refugees, treating them as a social and economic problem, and removing them from the context of the Ethiopia-Sudan mini-Cold War. While relations with the Eritrean and Tigrayan liberation fronts were the concern of external security and foreign relations, refugees fell under the remit of Sudanese domestic institutions, which were concerned with social control and local prosperity. The refugee settlement policy was a disservice to the political mobilisation of the fronts and rarely achieved the aim of economic self-reliance. But it assisted the Sudanese authorities to control the refugees and attract foreign aid. There is some evidence that the government exaggerated refugee numbers in order to attract more assistance: donors were certainly suspicious of most figures produced by COR. However, in general aid donors and UNHCR supported the settlement policy (although the restrictions on freedom of movement it entailed contradicted UNHCR's legal obligations) because it helped make the refugee 'problem' visible and measurable, and thus aidable.[23] Meanwhile, the labour force provided by the refugees played an important role in the rapid expansion of commercial agriculture in the Eastern Region.

The COR was briefly active in Southern Sudan after 1972. In the east, it was anxious to avoid a repeat of the NGO competition it had witnessed there, and pressed for a single indigenous NGO to take the lead role in providing services to the refugee camps and settlements. The Sudan Council of Churches (SCC) was awarded this position,

---

[23] Tom Kuhlman, *Asylum or Aid? The Economic Integration of Ethiopian and Eritrean Refugees in the Sudan*, Leiden, African Studies Centre, 1994, pp. 125-8.

33

and was able to work in liaison with the Eritrean Relief Association (ERA) and the Relief Society of Tigray (REST), the relief arms of the Eritrean and Tigrayan rebel movements, with international agencies restricted to narrow specialist programmes such as supplementary feeding, some aspects of curative medical care and some development programmes.

As the burden of refugees inexorably grew, along with social and economic strains on the Sudan government, the COR began to agitate for more international assistance. In 1979-80, the Commissioner, Dr Abdel Rahman al Bashir, repeatedly compared levels of international expenditure on refugees in south-east Asia with those in Africa: the former received about twice as much per head. Sudan was receiving only about $2 million in aid per year for assistance to Ethiopian refugees, and the outlay for creating refugee settlements and building up services fell largely on the Sudan Government. This campaign led up to the convening of a conference in Khartoum in June 1980, intended to pressure the UNHCR and its donors to pledge more funds. (It was the second such African initiative, following the Arusha Conference hosted by the Tanzanians a year earlier. These two conferences were the last occasion on which African governments set the agenda for international agencies operating on the continent.)

The Khartoum conference succeeded in attracting funds, but at a cost. UNHCR supported the conference but pursued a different agenda: it suspected COR of inefficiency and corruption, and wanted to take greater control of the programmes itself, and use international NGOs as implementing partners. Some NGOs used this opportunity to entrench themselves: for example ACORD, which had been having difficulty funding its programme in Qala en Nahal, now approached international donors direct for support, bypassing COR. The regulated twin control over relief work by COR and SCC was broken, and replaced with free competition under the sponsorship of UNHCR plus direct political bargaining between UNHCR, USAID and high levels of the Sudan Government.

Eastern Sudan in 1980-81 was an inauspicious place and time to launch such an initiative. The austerity measures and conservative ideology of the incoming Republican administration in Washington

34

D.C. entailed the privatisation of relief contracting, by-passing host government institutions. A big element of USAID policy was to identify commercial contractors and foreign NGOs to take on relief work. This was combined with a new hawkish foreign policy which included what might best be called 'assertive containment' of communist Ethiopia, which led to constant and high level interference in Sudanese relief policy. Hence, the increased assistance that flowed to Sudan in 1981-4 was paid for in ever-closer political control. One of Washington's interests was in trying to find and sponsor a conservative Ethiopian opposition movement (it tried the Ethiopian People's Democratic Alliance but it proved a military and political failure; the leftist EPLF and TPLF only received diplomatic support from the U.S. in the dying days of the war against Mengistu). Another was extracting the Falashas (Ethiopian Jews) from Ethiopia to Israel through Sudan.[24] In this it succeeded. When the Falasha deal was made public the credibility of COR in Sudan was badly damaged. The relative international importance of the Falashas is highlighted that $300 million was raised to finance 'Operation Moses' in 1984 and care for its 8,000 beneficiaries, compared to overall expenditure of $30 million on the remaining 600,000 refugees in eastern Sudan. The Falasha evacuation was also one of the main items on the agenda of Vice-President George Bush when he visited Sudan in March 1985.

More generally, UNHCR saw its opportunity to further its institutional interests in Sudan. Most of the funds unlocked by the Khartoum Conference and the subsequent Geneva Conference were captured by UNHCR, contrary to COR's original aim. UNHCR expanded its presence in Khartoum and the major refugee centres of eastern Sudan. Senior UNHCR officials became adept at playing institutional politics, running from COR to the Ministry of the Interior, Ministry of Social Welfare, Ministry of Foreign Affairs and Regional Government in order to find ways of establishing its power. A succession of UN missions visited to assess projects for funding, consuming a large amount of time and resources on the part of the

---

[24] Ahmed Karadawi, 'The Smuggling of the Ethiopian Falashas to Israel through Sudan,' *African Affairs*, 70, 1991, 23-49.

COR, and requiring the Sudan government to rewrite its refugee policy three times in as many years. Hence the Sudan government rapidly forfeited control over the refugee programmes in eastern Sudan. The number of NGOs working with refugees in Sudan rose from seven in 1978 (most of them indigenous agencies) to 23 in 1981 and 57 in 1985. The role of SCC also dwindled as UNHCR preferred dealing with international NGOs rather than local ones.

One result of the higher profile of UNHCR, and the way in which its priorities were driven by the availability of funds, was that during 1980-4 it actively promoted repatriation to Ethiopia, despite overwhelming evidence that the refugees still remained in fear.[25] On several occasions this policy led UNHCR into connivance with serious human rights violations by the Ethiopian government, such as the forced repatriation of refugees from Djibouti and their subsequent deaths at the hands of Ethiopian security. The repatriation of refugees from Sudan was prevented by lack of co-operation from COR and the refugees themselves, and by the embarrassment that an investigatory mission by UNHCR arrived in Sudan in January 1984 just the defeated Ethiopian garrison at Tessenei arrived in Sudan asking for refuge. This was, however, an ominous sign of how humanitarian priorities would be set in the future.

In late 1984, the inflow of Ethiopian refugees—almost all Tigrayans whose exodus was organised by the TPLF—into eastern Sudan was the occasion for an important expansion of UNHCR's mandate. Until November 1984, UNHCR's mandate was based upon the 1951 Refugee Convention, which defined the agency as responsible for protecting those with 'a well founded fear of persecution', and giving such people necessary assistance. In 1984, many of the Tigrayans crossing into Sudan were perceived to be famine refugees who did not fit that definition (ironically, they could have legitimately been considered war refugees). On those grounds, as the influx gathered pace in October, UNHCR refused to consider the Tigrayans for assistance. The situation was complicated by

---

[25] Africa Watch, *Evil Days: Thirty Years of War and Famine in Ethiopia*, London, 1991, pp. 99 and 120-2.

President Nimeiri's refusal to ask for assistance, and the fact that the TPLF—which was the representative of the refugees' political interests—was not recognised as a legitimate intermediary by the UN. For two critical months the UNHCR did not appeal for assistance. Nor, despite entreaties from COR, did it supply any. The additional relief needs were left to COR, REST, SCC, other agencies and the refugees themselves.

In November 1984, the Ethiopian famine had at last become world news. At this point it was embarrassing for both President Nimeiri and UNHCR not to appeal for emergency assistance to the Tigrayans in Sudan. Hence Nimeiri made an appeal, and the UN General Assembly voted that UNHCR could make the Tigrayans a 'special case' in which it expanded its mandate to deal with people who had fled across an international border on account of acute distress. The Tigrayans were 'people of concern to UNHCR.' Shortly afterwards this formulation of the expanded mandate became permanent.[26]

Meanwhile, the resources available to feed and house the refugees increased hugely, but the high-profile programmes and the open door to international agencies after April 1985 meant that the process of loss of control by COR and SCC already under way was greatly accelerated. Hence by 1985, emergency refugee programmes in Sudan were irretrievably internationalised.

Three consequences of the 1980-84 internationalisation of refugee relief are particularly important. One is expense. The internationalised programmes proved vastly more expensive than the domestic-run ones of earlier days. Though new technologies were provided, the level of professional competence was not necessary

---

[26] In fact, in the 1990s, most of the people routinely referred to as 'refugees' who receive UNHCR assistance in Africa and elsewhere have not been through the formal procedures of registering as a refugee and proving their 'well founded fear', but are treated *en masse* as 'people of concern to UNHCR.' In former Yugoslavia, UNHCR has used this formula to assist people who have not even crossed an international frontier. The exception has become the rule. In countries neighbouring Rwanda in 1994, fugitives from justice were counted as 'refugees' in this sense.

any higher. Secondly, given the mixture of motives of the international players—particularly clear in the case of the Falashas—frank evaluation became impossible. Thirdly, the host government not only lost control over the operations of foreign aid agencies on its territory, but was encouraged to look to external sources for resolving its social welfare problems. These all added up to a loss of domestic political accountability for humanitarian action.

IMPLICATIONS

Sudan's aid dependence had a profound impact on its internal democracy. The government was accountable on a day-by-day basis to its foreign donors, not to domestic constituents. Meanwhile the aid itself immunised the government—to a degree—from the implications of its authoritarianism. It made possible the war. Echoing what was already emerging in the South and with refugee assistance, this relationship was later to be recreated in a different form, this time using humanitarian resources.

3.

NIMEIRI'S FAMINE AND THE POPULAR UPRISING

The situation with respect to food security and health is reassuring.

President Jaafar Nimeiri, 5 November 1984

Famine and the fact that there were Sudanese who could not find food in this land that Nimeiri had called 'the breadbasket of the Arab world' was an insult to the sensibilities of many Sudanese. This spread by word of mouth, by noticing that Sudanese were coming knocking on doors asking for food. This was pivotal in making people feel committed to a process that something must change.

Dr Taiser Ahmed Ali, democracy activist

One of the main themes of this book is the manner in which international relief operations have undermined domestic political accountability, encouraging the authoritarian tendencies of successive governments in Sudan. Famine and other extreme human suffering has become the subject of international charity rather than being a domestic political scandal. There is one important exception to this trend, however: the famine of 1984-85 in Northern Sudan, which directly contributed to the overthrow of President Nimeiri through popular protest. The democratic coalition that emerged for a few months in early 1985 included the fight against famine as one of its central elements, and shows how political action against famine can work, and perhaps provides a model for building future protection against famine.

FAMINE CONCEALED

In 1983, drought threatened hunger in north Kordofan, north Darfur and the Red Sea Hills. The Ministry of Agriculture's routine assessment of food production in these provinces was 25% of normal. To have admitted such a widespread food shortage would have conceded the failure of the breadbasket strategy.

Local government was poorly placed to respond. In 1981, regional governments had been established in Darfur, Kordofan and the Eastern Region. This led directly to intra-regional power struggles. In Darfur, for example, inter-ethnic rivalry between the Fur and the 'Arab alliance' emerged for the first time, while in Kordofan one of the main issues was the level of Nuba representation. Hence regional politicians were less well-placed to represent their constituents to Khartoum. At the same time, elected rural councils had been replaced by appointed ones. The flow of information from villages to the government deteriorated. Most significantly, regional governments' budgets were extremely tight, even non-existent.

In response to the drought of 1983, local government officers made attempts to distribute some relief, but the amounts distributed were meagre. Requests for assistance from central government met with no response: Khartoum simply banked upon normal rains returning the situation to normal in 1984. The Governor of Darfur, Ahmed Diraige, was increasingly hostile to Nimeiri for a range of reasons, but chose to make Khartoum's inaction on the drought the spark for his public departure from office. In December 1983 he resigned, denouncing Nimeiri's indifference to impending famine, and went into exile. This did not change Nimeiri's stand: it became clear that the President himself was the chief obstacle to relief. In early 1984, the FAO sent an assessment team to estimate the relief needs of Darfur. The mission's original figure of 39,000 tonnes of food aid needed was cut down to 7,000 tonnes by central government. There was no appeal for international assistance, and in the end, only 5,400 tonnes was delivered, late. Nothing was sent to Kordofan.

When the rains failed again in the summer of 1984, conditions became more desperate in Darfur and Kordofan. Grain production in the whole of Darfur and Kordofan was 37% of the average over the previous five years, falling to as little as 18% in northern Kordofan. The harvest was due only in November, but by July the devastating implications of the drought were clear. On 31 July, Nimeiri was forced to declare Darfur a 'disaster region.' This declaration amounted to a command to all local government staff to direct their efforts towards famine relief; it was not an appeal for international assistance. No mention was made of Kordofan, where conditions were equally bad, but where breadbasket investment was targeted.

Nimeiri was determined to avoid having to declare a famine, which would jeopardise breadbasket funds and raise further questions among the Paris Club and IMF about Sudan's economic future. If western assistance were switched from government-to-government support to emergency aid, Nimeiri's financial games would come to an abrupt end. The U.S. State Department was also anxious to play along, and in September it released 82,000 tonnes of emergency food aid for Sudan, hoping that this would be enough to provide for food needs in Darfur and Kordofan. USAID had a more astute perception than Nimeiri of the destabilising potential of the famine.

Until August 1984 the famine was exclusively a rural affair, below the horizon of national and international politics. This situation was transformed by the famine victims themselves. Several thousand drought-stricken farmers and herders began abandoning their villages in Kordofan and migrating to Omdurman, twin city of the capital Khartoum. Other displaced people congregated in all the major cities of the north. The famine came to town. It could no longer be ignored by the government.

Dr Taiser Ahmed Ali, a human rights activist who played an important role in the popular uprising that was to bring down Nimeiri's government, commented on the impact of the famine on wider Sudanese society:

What made the famine issue very felt in society was the number of young kids moving in the residential areas asking for food. This

41

was very shocking to people. It was pivotal in mobilising people, better than distributing one million leaflets.[1]

Yoanes Ajawin, another activist during this period, concurred: 'Begging became a common phenomenon. Sudanese felt their own culture of charity was being challenged.'

In the closing months of 1984, there was much anti-government agitation, led by the trade unions, but it was diffuse and had yet to find a common set of themes or forum for co-ordination. The Bar and the judiciary had started agitation in September 1983, with a four month strike. The doctors also independently organised a strike. As the professional protests grew, several things happened. One was that the opposition learned and applied the major lesson of the fragmented actions during 1983 and 1984: future action should be taken in unison. A second was that protest moved from purely professional issues to wider political demands. Since Nimeiri had dismantled the railways and workers' unions, formerly the most radical trade unions, political leadership was now passing to the professional associations. Thirdly, as government repression intensified, the opposition demands hardened. Many activists no longer believed that it was possible to reform the regime: it had to be removed.

In the last months of 1984, some opposition groups began to mobilise around the famine. But there were obstacles. Famine was a general social concern, rather than an issue that immediately lent itself to a particular trade union, and there were few organised links between the professionals leading the opposition and the famine victims themselves. Dr Taiser explained:

[In late 1984] we began feeling pressure from Nimeiri's security, which was one of the most developed organs of the state. It was not easy to organise.

The people in the Ministry of Agriculture were leaking figures to us in the University about the famine. Students and some members of the faculty were producing papers and pamphlets that said that this famine is not the will of God, as Nimeiri would have

---

[1] Interviewed in February 1997.

us believe, but is the outcome of the policies of the government. Doctors were also working as individuals, reporting on conditions from the camps, such as Muwelleh [in Omdurman].

Nimeiri's domestic political strategy was based upon divide and rule, switching alliances to keep the opposition off balance. He wanted to avoid coalitions being built up. At this point he was trying to cultivate the urban constituency: he had just rescinded a proposal for universal conscription to the armed forces in the face of urban opposition, and was trying to pre-empt rural-urban solidarity. It did not succeed. *Ad hoc* private and communal relief activities in Omdurman became a focus for opposition mobilisation. Ordinary citizens began to go to the displaced camps on Fridays to distribute food. The Khartoum University Students' Union organised its members to donate a day's food each. On 2 November, the Omdurman branch of Sudan Socialist Union (SSU) asked for the citizens to give help to the drought migrants encamped around the city. This was the first sign that national institutions were at odds with the President, and the first split in the SSU.

The Secretary General of the SSU, Mohamed al Tayeb, contradicted the Omdurman branch and ordered the removal of the migrants by force. He ordered that transport be made available, but was unable to enforce the order. By this time, President Nimeiri's statements bore less and less relation to reality. On 3 November, Nimeiri said: 'The situation with respect to food security and health is reassuring.'[2] A week later, he personally ordered the forced return of all the drought migrants around Omdurman to their rural homes.[3] Some were forcibly removed from the city, but the Omdurman SSU failed to co-operate and it also proved impossible to prevent the human tide of displacement. Instead, the security forces tried to contain the famine migrants within outlying parts of Omdurman.

Dr Taiser explained the obstacles the government was creating for citizens' charitable efforts.

---

[2] BBC, *Summary of World Broadcasts*, ME/7792, 5 November 1984.
[3] BBC, *Summary of World Broadcasts*, ME/7799, 13 November 1984.

But very quickly the security made it very difficult for us to penetrate [to the displaced camps]—they set up roadblocks and unless you had permits you could not go there. Suleiman Baldo was among the first people to begin to go there. But we did not go regularly, because then the security would take notice of you and it would be difficult [to continue to organise].

At that time we were in the Trade Union Alliance trying to organise. There was no organised movement among the famine victims, but there were linkages with us, flows of information. My sense is that the activity was mostly spontaneous. When Omer al Tayeb tried to send them back to their villages, and prepared the transport, the resistance was mostly spontaneous, popular resentment against this regime.

The displaced were kept in Omdurman beyond Suq al Sha'abi. At first there was a sort of self-help; families went to take food to them on Fridays, that sort of thing. But people started to realise that this was a larger phenomenon than could be treated by self-help. Then the security forces made it impossible for famine victims to move, they could not even visit downtown Omdurman, let alone cross the bridge to Khartoum. And even professional and people who were taking food to them on Fridays were turned back, prevented from going.

The attempts to deny the famine and remove the migrants crystallised outrage among leading professionals and trade unionists. Government ministries were soon blatantly contradicting the President. On 26 November a group of leading doctors in the Ministry of Health published a report on famine conditions. This unilateral initiative was a test of the ability of civil groups to mobilise politically against Nimeiri. Shortly afterwards the Ministry of Agriculture released its estimate that 160,000 tonnes of food relief was needed for Kordofan and Darfur.[4] Connections with international agencies provided some guarantee of the veracity of the officials' claims, and some protection against reprisal by the government. Moreover, Nimeiri's opponents were attacking him where it hurt most—in his relations with aid donors, at a time when,

---

[4] *Africa Economic Digest*, 23 November 1984.

44

because of BandAid, famine in Africa was becoming a domestic political issue in Europe and America.

The emergent steering committee for the Popular Uprising also took note, as explained by Yoanes Ajawin:

> There were already some elements among the trade unions— especially the doctors—working among the famine victims. They were giving us feedback about the sentiments of discontent among them against the government. This was also confirmed by some representations from the Ministry of Agriculture trade union, giving their findings from visits to the affected areas. It was all these situations that made people feel that famine is not only a card to be played but also an essential part of the disenchantment of the people with the government.

For Nimeiri, scapegoating drought migrants had not worked, and he now tried to blame refugees from Ethiopia and Chad, for whom he at last authorised an appeal for international assistance. Following the public estimates for food aid needs, 'President Nimeiri confirmed . . . that Sudan had not asked for aid from anybody but it welcomes assistance in order to combat drought, particularly as Sudan bears the burden of being host to thousands of refugees from neighbouring states.'[5] This was the official government line: no national food problem existed. Thus Sudan remained off the FAO's list of drought-affected African countries. But meanwhile the Ministry of Agriculture was collaborating with the FAO to contradict this line, and they jointly published an estimate of national food import needs of 288,000 metric tonnes.

In December there was a shift in the balance of power in Washington D.C.: the (hard-line) Treasury briefly gained the upper hand over the (conciliatory) State Department. As a result, the U.S. insisted on major economic reform, freezing $190 million worth of aid until austerity measures were introduced. This, combined with the apparent inability to contain urban opposition, led to a change in Nimeiri's strategy. On 19 January he belatedly admitted the existence of the famine and appealed for food aid.

---

[5] BBC, *Summary of World Broadcasts*, ME/7804, 19 November 1984.

The same day Nimeiri executed the renowned Islamic scholar and moderate political leader Ustaz Mahmoud Mohamed Taha. The execution of Ustaz Mahmoud shocked the entire Sudanese community: it was symbolic of the depths plumbed by the regime.

THE APRIL 1985 POPULAR UPRISING

The execution of Ustaz Mahmoud was also the spark for the civil opposition to organise to try and bring down the regime, as detailed by Yoanes Ajawin.

In January 1985 we felt aware that the *Intifada* [Popular Uprising] was likely , specifically after the execution of Ustaz Mahmoud Mohamed Taha. By that time, most of the trade unions came together in a show of solidarity to oppose, and later on mourn, the execution of Mahmoud. Various options for toppling the government were discussed. Two things were apparent. One, the execution of Mahmoud could be extended to any other individual or group of individuals in the name of apostasy. Secondly, it became apparent that the only backers of Nimeiri, after he had been losing all his allies, were the Moslem Brothers under Dr Turabi, then the Political Advisor to Nimeiri.

The Islamic State which was started in 1983 became more apparent in January 1985. Although a year earlier the Islamic constitution was aborted in the National Assembly by an alliance of secular groups in the SSU with Southerners. In 1984, people saw different signals about the Islamic state, but in 1985, through the execution of Mahmoud Mohamed Taha, it was clear that steps towards an Islamic state were going faster.

Within discussions, the option that was possible was civil disobedience. By that time there was no military component of the underground trade unionists and activists. This was due to the insecurity prevailing in the military. 1983 and 1984 saw a sequence of crackdowns—unannounced—on attempted military coups, which scattered the sympathetic officers. By January 1985 it was difficult to figure out who is who in the army. Therefore an Intifada with military backing was not envisaged. It became apparent later, in March, that there were some army officers who could support an

46

uprising, provided that they were put in a situation of choice between the regime and the people.

This meant to us the option of a successful civil disobedience campaign that would bring the machinery of state to a halt. Some areas of action were mapped out by marking roles to specific trades unions. Engineers and technicians, especially for the service sectors light and water, were targeted. Doctors, lecturers and lawyers were also given specific assignments to pioneer civil disobedience. By March, it was clear that the doctors, lawyers (both the Bar and the judiciary), engineers, university lecturers would be the 'steering committee' for the uprising. Every trade union had its own steering committee, two in fact, both an official one and an alternative, so if the members of the main one were arrested, the alternative would continue. It happened that on 1 and 2 April, most of the steering committees were arrested, so that it was the second layer in most unions that took over. I personally became part of the White Nile Steering Committee in Kosti with my colleagues Abdel Mahmoud Haj Saleh, Dr Fatah Rahman Hamoda and others.

[In February-March] we were writing and distributing leaflets against the government, stressing the economic deterioration, the war in the South, famine in the west and the oppressive apparatus of state security, and the threat of an Islamic state due to the influence of the Islamic Charter group (later the National Islamic Front), led by Hassan al Turabi. All were policies which were not acceptable to us and should be opposed by the Sudanese people.

Meanwhile the call for famine relief was rightly seen as an act of desperation by a government that had lost legitimacy and any political initiative. Only the opposition could now capitalise on the famine issue. Dr Taiser explained:

There were leaflets and short essays trying to expose Nimeiri's policies that were responsible for the famine. They were widely photocopied and circulated. They were passed around the University and in the evening if you went to a wedding you would find people talking about them.

A typical leaflet said the following:

47

Because of the negligence of the government and lack of concern about the welfare of the people in the west, a famine that could have been avoided was allowed to take its toll on the people.

Nimeiri's attempt to terrorise and split the opposition could work only if he had enough money to buy support, and at the end of March he flew to the U.S. in a last bid to obtain aid. It worked: the State Department promised assistance and did not insist on pushing through the austerity package. But it was too late. The Popular Uprising steering committees organised widespread non-violent protest against the regime, bringing the country to a halt. Yoanes Ajawin continues:

> When demonstrations started on 27 March against the prices, the price rises, the main targets were the Nimeiri Co-operative Society, along with the Islamic banks. Then options were explored: what specific demands do trade unions and activists have to raise? At that time, Nimeiri was going to America. By 2 April the demand of handing over power to the people was articulated by the leadership of the steering committee—the representatives from the trade unions. The message was sent to the grassroots to decide in what form to present that demand. In some places it was presented through slogans and petitions to the government representative in the localities. For example in Kosti the demonstration ended up handing over a written petition to the representative of the government—the assistant commissioner— requesting him to pass it to the government, to hand over power. In some places, there were demonstrations with slogans demanding the handing over of government to the people, but no petitions were organised.

Meanwhile, the famine victims themselves were becoming active in opposing the government. In provincial towns such as el Fasher, el Obeid and Kosti, they played an important part in anti-Nimeiri demonstrations. In Kosti, Yoanes Ajawin witnessed them turn out in force.

> In many places, famine-affected people—though not the majority— were part and parcel of the larger crowd that came out against the government. Most of their leadership, in the form of elders, were

48

already frustrated by the lack of response from the government to their demands for food, shelter, etc.

In Khartoum, the clampdown by security and restrictions on movement (especially crossing the bridge from Omdurman into Khartoum) made it difficult for many of the famine displaced to play an active part in the demonstrations. But, as Dr Taiser explained, some of the urban poor and dispossessed made their frustrations felt, while the scandal of the famine resonated more widely:

> Street kids were not necessarily part of the famine victims community. They were growing in numbers but not necessarily to the extent that they could make a big difference.
>
> The first protest took place as Nimeiri was leaving to the United States. His motorcade was intercepted by young students, and among them were a number of street kids who started throwing stones and things like that. Some were from the famine-affected communities but not in large numbers.
>
> At the famous demonstration on 4th [April] in which people declared a national general strike, it was mostly trade unionists and professionals and women, people like that, there were few street kids.
>
> My perception is that famine and the fact that there were Sudanese who could not find food in this land that Nimeiri had called 'the breadbasket of the Arab world' was an insult to the sensibilities of many Sudanese. This spread by word of mouth, by noticing that Sudanese were coming knocking on doors asking for food. This was pivotal in making people feel committed to a process that something must change.

A key moment in the uprising was the failure of the SSU counter-demonstration on 2 April in support of the government. The SSU turn-out was small—one of the reasons was the dispute over how to handle the drought migrants in Omdurman. The failure of this demonstration illustrated the government's dwindling support and gave a big boost to the opposition. Dr Taiser suddenly saw the reality change:

I can remember very graphically the time when we knew we were going to make it. It was 4 April, when the call for a general strike went out. That morning I went to the University. Our colleagues were being arrested, we were surrounded by security people. The idea was that the University people would have our own demonstration, but the security people came to the Staff Club, where we were preparing our slogans. So we decided to go individually and join the demonstration at the Faculty of Medicine. I went in the car of Suleiman Baldo and as we were driving there we saw the bank employees coming out on strike, the banks were closing. At that moment I knew we were going to succeed, because if the banks closed, the markets would close and economic activity would come to a halt. At that moment we knew the regime was going to fall.

Before that, even that morning, my personal feeling—we did not discuss it but there was a silent consensus among us—was that it was going to be a long struggle. We could look around and see that in Africa, struggles were always a long haul. We were aware that every year, for the last few years, there was an [attempted] coup, and the security forces were spreading rumours that if we attempted to challenge the regime there were going to be rivers of blood in the streets of Khartoum.

Also at that point there was the beginning of a sense that we had an alliance.

The next day, 5 April, the steering committee declared a 'dead city': the streets of the capital and other major towns were entirely deserted. Meanwhile, intense discussions went on among senior army officers. On 6 April, as the demonstrations resumed, the army stepped in and took power.

THE ANTI-FAMINE ALLIANCE FALLS APART

If the broad democratic alliance had been sustained over the following decade, the history of modern Sudan would have been very different. But in fact the opportunity was lost. The problems began with the way in which the Uprising was hijacked at its moment of success by the Transitional Military Council (TMC), as Yoanes Ajawin explains:

> After April, the steering committee disintegrated. The common solidarity was undermined by three elements. One was that the political parties came in. At the eleventh hour, the parties became part forcefully of the Intifada steering committee. Second, the TMC succeeded to arrogate to itself the power of legislation and some executive powers, therefore determining the agenda for the transitional period. Third, there was disagreement among the trade unions in the Council of Ministers. Political parties and the TMC exploited these disagreements. The agenda that was planned by the trade unions was completely ignored during the transition, and only the issues considered important by the political parties and the TMC were addressed. The main victims of this neglect were famine and peace.

The TMC 'solved' the famine issue by depoliticising it: handing relief over to technical organisations and then ignoring it. General Suwar al Dahab took personal responsibility for making sure relief provision was expedited—a symbolic act assisted by the fact that he visited Kordofan and Darfur just as the rains came, early and heavy, raising (justified) hopes that the end of the famine was in sight.

Two simultaneous initiatives were to have longer-term consequences. One was setting up the Relief and Rehabilitation Commission (RRC), a technical government department set up to co-ordinate relief activities. One of the RRC's main tasks was to design and run a Famine Early Warning System (FEWS) with international donors support, which gathered information about rainfall, crops, market prices etc. This was premised on the erroneous belief that the problem in 1984 had been lack of information about the impending famine rather than lack of political will to prevent it. (Detailed information had certainly been scarce, but enough was known to make an effective response possible.) The RRC was partnered with a newly-established UN office, the UN Emergency Office for Sudan (UNEOS), which had a similar brief.

The second initiative was delegating responsibility to international agencies, which were given unprecedented autonomy.

This was another stage in humanitarian deregulation. In late-1984, USAID had carved up Sudan between international NGOs, each of which was contracted to monitor food distributions in a different region. Darfur was awarded to the Save the Children Fund (UK), Kordofan to CARE, the Central Region to World Vision and the Red Sea Hills to Oxfam (UK). Transport contracts were given to Sudan Railways and private hauliers, while distribution itself was (somewhat ambiguously) to be done under local government authority. Now the international NGO role was strengthened. The NGOs took over needs assessment, transport and distribution itself, all of which they could do with scant reference to the local authorities. Foreign NGOs became the largest hauliers in the country; their staff could travel anywhere without travel permits; they could make food allocations on their own criteria without reference to government at all.

The handover to international NGOs was a vital step; in effect it removed famine from being the political property of Sudanese people to being 'owned' by international agencies. Henceforth, famine could be blamed on the failures of these foreign agencies, rather than the government itself. Before the Uprising, the Sudanese media had given prominent coverage to U.S. food aid, especially during the visit of George Bush, so there was a widespread popular feeling that U.S. aid would solve the problem. In time, however, the prominent role of foreign NGOs came to cause no little resentment among local government staff and politicians. In the 1986 ceremony at which the Governor of Darfur distributed awards to the agencies that had contributed to relieving the famine, Save the Children Fund (which had run 140 trucks and distributed over 130,000 tonnes of food) was pointedly put at the back of the queue, behind a range of small local initiatives and gestures of solidarity from Arab countries.

The failure was one of the democracy activists also. For a start, they were over-optimistic, as Dr Taiser explained:

People felt that with the change there would be immediate solutions to everything—to the war, to the economy, to all the problems. The change came too soon, too quickly after the organisation and the structure were formed. People didn't have time to ask, how are

52

things going to be after Nimeiri goes? Instead they were just concentrating on getting rid of Nimeiri.

Second, they were divided. Dr Gizouli Dafallah, who had led the Doctors' Association protests over the famine, became transitional Prime Minister. But, as Yoanes Ajawin explains,

> Once Dr Gizouli became Prime Minister, all his agendas were compromises with what the TMC wanted. In the middle of the transition, Gizouli lost touch even with the trade unions.

General Suwar al Dahab maintained that the famine issue was resolved (and by November 1985, an excellent harvest began to be gathered in), and the political parties were not interested. Ahmed Diraige remained in exile and did not return to mobilise his people. The democratic forces that soon found themselves in opposition concentrated their energies on constitutional issues and the question of peace. A coalition calling itself Rural Solidarity was formed from many of those who had taken a leading role in the Uprising, but this was thwarted by internal divisions and the arrest of leading Nuba members of the coalition on charges of plotting a military coup.

Interest in famine and relief continued, with some organisations set up to address the issue. But they did not go far, as explained by Dr Taiser:

> The Trade Unions formed their own relief agency in the first week after the *Intifada*, it was called the Trade Union Relief Association. It held its meetings in the Staff Club of the University of Khartoum. The Trade Union Alliance also formed several committees—for the economy, for foreign affairs, for education, for peace, and one was in charge of studying the famine. It remained just a talking shop.

A Rehabilitation Programme Committee was also established by the trade unions, to draw up plans for the rehabilitation of the drought-affected regions and the resettlement of displaced people who had come to the towns. Despite the fact that prominent trade unionists and the Minister of State for Finance served on the committee, it took no active role in the politics of the transitional period and its findings were never made public.

No party made efforts to keep the displaced mobilised. On the contrary, most townspeople lost sympathy with the famine migrants, especially when relief distributions began. No such alliances between the democratic forces and the displaced were to arise again.

The SPLA made an opportunistic use of the famine issue. In late 1984 in its radio broadcasts, the SPLA had complained about famine in both North and South and chastised the government for its inaction:[6]

> The price of food continues to rise day by day. Famines mow down thousands of lives in many areas of Sudan and government forces are plundering the livestock of our countrymen. The Khartoum government is paying no attention to any of these problems. . . . The ruling regime has proved its failure once again on the death through hunger of these countrymen without taking any action on this issue.

These broadcasts found a responsive chord among the northern urban population, who were in most respects unsympathetic to the rebels. But, as later openly admitted by John Garang (see Chapter 4), SPLA military strategy itself was not only creating severe hunger in Southern garrison towns, but was precisely designed to do this. The SPLA could not continue to play the famine card.

There were two notable exceptions to the depoliticisation of famine and humanitarianism. One was the a criminal investigation into the actions of the Faisal Islamic Bank. The FIB had bought up large stores of grain before the famine, either for speculation or export, and in contradiction to the stated government grain marketing policy. The FIB's hoarding was popularly blamed for much of the shortage in the eastern and central regions. Though its impact was probably exaggerated, its role was certainly scandalous. This investigation dragged on until 1988, when the very first act of the newly-appointed Attorney-General, Dr Hassan al Turabi, leader of the National Islamic Front (NIF), was to remove the file and close

---

[6] BBC, *Summary of World Broadcasts*, ME/7804, 19 November 1984.

the investigation. This thwarting of accountability can stand as a symbol for the wider failure of the TMC and the subsequent elected government to address the fundamental reasons for Sudan's famine, with disastrous results for the Sudanese people.

The second investigation was into the Falasha affair, which was seen as an outrageous intervention in Sudanese sovereignty by an international conspiracy of Zionists, CIA agents and humanitarian agencies. The Falasha hearings, held in late-1985, caused considerable stir in Khartoum. Several leading members of the security services were convicted and imprisoned. The trials were largely ignored by foreign agencies, who were therefore unaware of the haze of suspicion that was descending upon them.

There was no commission of inquiry into the famine itself, and hence no thorough-going revisions of national food relief or emergency planning. The urban wheat subsidy remained sacrosanct.

Subsequent governments have learned many lessons from the Popular Uprising. One is that rural-urban coalitions should be suppressed at birth. Much of the political strategy of successive regimes has been aimed at preventing hunger becoming a political issue, and dividing the opposition. Democratic activists have been slower to learn their lessons.

A DOMINANT ROLE FOR THE INTERNATIONAL AGENCIES

The relief operation for western Sudan and the Red Sea Hills in 1984-5 was one of the largest peacetime emergency food delivery programmes ever mounted. Despite a late start and major logistical obstacles, over 250,000 metric tonnes of sorghum was transported and distributed. Subsequently, western donors poured enormous resources into a famine 'early warning' system, rehabilitation of infrastructure, agricultural planning and the like. Sudan was one of the donors' favourites. In 1985 it received over $1 billion in foreign aid, including over $350 million from the U.S., which hoped that generous and effective assistance to Sudan would demonstrate the value of being a member of the western alliance—and stand as a contrast to Ethiopia.

But did this massive aid operation achieve its stated objectives? There is remarkably little evidence to go on.

A newspaper reader might conclude that millions of lives were saved. This is not correct. At the beginning of 1985, when the international media 'discovered' the Sudanese famine, journalists and NGOs made extremely pessimistic predictions for imminent famine deaths. They confidently asserted that hundreds of thousands, even millions, would die in the coming months, if there was no massive food relief programme.[7] The quantities of food delivered during those months were meagre. But the numbers who died were far, far fewer: the best estimates put the figures in the tens of thousands. The level of deaths was shocking, but far from the predicted apocalypse. The reason for the survival of such large numbers of people was their own food and economic resources, notably the reliance on wild foods such as berries and grasses during the critical months.

There is an extraordinary lack of systematic studies of famine mortality in Africa.[8] Western Sudan in 1984-5 is fortunate that one of the few was carried out there (by one of the authors of this book).[9] Although its sample is very small by European or Asian standards,[10] the sample total of over 6,000 people in eight sites is much larger than almost any other study done in recent decades in Africa.

The principal findings of this research were, first, that total excess mortality in Darfur during the famine period was an estimated 105,000 people. Given that conditions in Kordofan were broadly comparable, and that a smaller population was also stricken in the Red Sea Hills, this implies a total famine mortality in the region of 250,000. Secondly, the mortality followed a characteristic seasonal

---

[7] See: Alex de Waal, 'The Perception of Poverty and Famines,' *International Journal of Moral and Social Studies*, 2, 1987, 251-63.

[8] John Seaman, 'Famine Mortality in Africa,' *IDS Bulletin*, 24.4, October 1993, 27-32.

[9] Alex de Waal, 'Famine Mortality: A Case Study of Darfur, Sudan, 1984-85,' *Population Studies*, 43, 1989, 5-24.

[10] Tim Dyson, 'On the Demography of South Asian Famines,' *Population Studies*, 45, 1991, 5-25.

pattern: it rose during the second half of the dry season (largely associated with diarrhoeal diseases and outbreaks of measles) and remained high during the rains (with malaria entering the picture), dropping away during the 1985 harvest season. It displayed a 'lag': the death rate remained higher than normal after the food situation returned to normal. Thirdly, as expected, children between the ages of one and five were most vulnerable, with raised mortality among older children and elderly people as well. Men were more likely to die than women, in common with all recorded famines.

Fourthly, and most controversially, the research found that death rates did not vary according to occupational group or socio-economic status. There was spatial variation—some villages were worse hit than others—but it did not appear that poorer members of any community were more likely to die than richer ones. Bringing other evidence to bear, this was interpreted to mean that the chief reason for famine deaths was a deteriorating public health environment rather than undernutrition. Mass migration, poor sanitation, unclean water and the rapid spread of communicable diseases meant that there was far more disease around, a fact that alone could account for the raised death rates. Within a particular village, rich and poor alike suffered from communicable diseases. In this 'health crisis' model of mortality, undernutrition was not recognised as a major factor, let alone starvation.

This hypothesis was subsequently examined in more detail, and significantly revised.[11] Later research has shown how levels of undernutrition have a different significance, depending on the environment. If people remain in their home villages, nutritional state can deteriorate sharply without bringing with it an increased risk of death. But if people move to a new environment, especially a degraded public health environment such as a relief shelter or displaced camp, then that poor nutritional condition brings heightened risks of fatal diseases.

The 'health crisis' model of famine deaths remains controversial, but its main contention is widely accepted, at least in the basic form

---

[11] Helen Young and Susanne Jaspars, *Nutrition Matters: People, Food and Famine,* London, Intermediate Technology Publications, 1995.

that mass migration and changes to the health environment are critical factors in raising death rates. This has important implications for the assessment of the impact of relief programmes. In particular, in peacetime famines where people can follow coping strategies, food relief alone has only a marginal impact on death rates: medical and public health interventions are more significant. Food relief can in fact have a negative impact if it helps to draw people into overcrowded and unsanitary relief camps, where health crises kill more people.

The life-saving impact of the western Sudan relief operation is further reduced when the poor quality of targeting of assistance is taken into account. During the critical period of the famine, relatively small amounts of the relief food actually reached the intended recipients: the very poorest.[12] There were four main reasons for this. One was that, because of the insistence by USAID that food aid should be 'monetised'—a certain proportion of the cost of distribution should be recovered from consumers by asking them to pay—some of the poorest villages received nothing. Secondly, commercial contractors were hired with very poorly-drafted contracts, that allowed them to deliver food to the most accessible locations first, leaving remote villages for later (or leaving them out entirely). Thirdly, regional governments tried to use food relief to pressure some villages to pay their tax arrears: villages that did not pay received nothing. Finally, regional governments also prioritised urban consumers and civil servants. Later, the main international NGOs (notably SCF-UK) brought in their own trucking fleets and delivered food directly to villages that were, according to nutritional and socio-economic surveys, identified as most in need.[13] (Interestingly, as more and more detailed surveys were done, the level of perceived need for food aid diminished. At the beginning of 1986, the estimated food needs for Darfur were 121,000 tonnes. By

---

[12] David Keen, 'Targeting Emergency Food Aid: The Case of Darfur in 1985,' in S. Maxwell (ed.) *To Cure all Hunger: Food Policy and Food Security in Sudan,* London, Intermediate Technology Publications, 1991.
[13] Ruth Buckley, 'Food Targeting in Darfur: Save the Children Fund's Programme in 1986,' *Disasters,* 12, 1988, 97-103.

August, after five months of survey work, the estimate for needs had been reduced to 61,000.[14])

The economic effects of food aid were more significant. It acted as an income transfer to its recipients, albeit not a very efficient one. It enabled poorer farmers to spend more time preparing their own farms, to avoid having to sell livestock and other assets, and to conserve more seed. The prolongation of food aid into the post-famine period, when it coincided with the good harvests of 1985 and 1986, was also widely criticised for having undermined the profitability of surplus-producing farms in more fertile areas.[15] This is a variant of the much-cited 'dependency' argument. The adverse economic effects of an oversupply of food aid are real, but in remote rural areas such as western Sudan they should not be overstated. It will take more than one season of (unexpected and modest) free food distributions to entice sceptical peasants to abandon their own cultivation in favour of the uncertainties of relief aid.

There were some serious attempts to learn from the shortcomings of the 1984-5 relief programmes. The more careful targeting of relief in 1986 is one example. Another is the way in which SCF-UK put more emphasis onto public health type interventions in its ongoing programmes. The people of Darfur and Kordofan themselves undoubtedly learned, as manifest in their actions during the 1990-1 crisis, when mass migration to towns and relief shelters was avoided, with rural people explicitly saying that they had learned from their previous experience.

Unfortunately, the main donors did not appear to learn lessons with anything like the same alacrity. For example, when drawing up transport and distribution contracts in 1987 and then again in 1990-91, the European Community made exactly the same mistakes as in 1984: the contracts did not specify intermediate targets for delivering food to specific locations, and known logistical bottlenecks were not circumvented. There was no donor-led evaluation of the appropriateness of the aid effort: it remained an unspoken

---

14 de Waal, 1987, p. 260.
15 Mark Pearson, 'Household Returns to Grain Production,' Zalingei, Jebel Marra Rural Development Project, 1986.

assumption that the direct delivery of food aid was the correct response, and should remain so in the future. This model has remained, unchallenged, in Sudan and elsewhere. For example, it has been consistently the chief model for aid intervention in Southern Sudan.

Beyond superficial observations that the attitude of the Nimeiri government was unhelpful, none of the donors or humanitarian agencies examined the political context and implications of the famine and relief effort. But, arguably, these political consequences were the famine's most significant legacy. Some of these have been alluded to above: responsibility for famine relief was shifted towards a rather intangible 'international community' and away from Sudanese politicians. International agencies tended to hold that, with greater logistical and managerial expertise, and better preparation, the job could have been done 'properly'. Sudanese—in government, relief agencies and elsewhere—were more sceptical about the foreigners' contributions, but tended to focus their criticisms on competence and efficiency, rather than the basic technocratic model of relief itself. They argued that Sudanese institutions could have done an equally good or better job more cheaply. Much of the subsequent argument between the Sudan Government and foreign NGOs has been precisely over who should manage technocratic assistance programmes; there has been much less discussion over whether assistance programmes are the answer at all, and virtually none at all over whether technocratic approaches are appropriate.

A second political implication of the relief programme was that, for the first time ever in Sudan, mechanisms were set up that could distribute to almost every village. There had never before been a patronage structure that could reach so far. Far-sighted politicians could appreciate the possibilities of using such distributional structures—either the same ones or newly-built ones—for other ends. The NIF was the only political organisation that recognised this possibility. Islamic humanitarian agencies and the NIF were later to create a comparable nationwide network that has become an integral part of the project of creating an Islamic state (see chapter 9).

4.

LIBERATING AREAS, EXPLOITING PEOPLE: THE 'OLD' SPLA

We did not start as a Movement in the classical way of Latin American liberation movements with a small group of men. We started as a mob. We have been in a series of reforms, reforming a mob.

Dr John Garang[1]

There are those who feel that it is hardly conceivable for a guerrilla unit to exist for a long period behind enemy lines. This is a viewpoint based on ignorance of the relations between the army and the people. The popular masses are like water, and the army is like a fish. How can it be said that when there is water, a fish will have difficulty in preserving its existence? An army which fails to maintain good discipline gets into opposition with the popular masses, and thus by its own actions dries up the water. In this case, it naturally cannot continue to exist. All guerrilla units must thoroughly understand this principle.

Mao Zedong.[2]

---

[1] Opening address to SPLM Conference on Civil Society and the Organisation of Civil Authority of the New Sudan, New Kush, 30 April 1996.

[2] Quoted in 'Mao's Military Principles,' in L. Freedman (ed.) *War*, Oxford University Press, 1994, p. 321.

THE EARLY ORIENTATION OF THE SPLA

The humanitarian policy of the SPLA must be seen in the light of its political orientation and practical approach to the liberation of Sudan.

For the first six years after its inception in 1983, the SPLA was an unusual guerrilla army in that it could readily outnumber its opponents in the field. Until 1989 the Sudan Armed Forces numbered about 65,000, of which no more than half could be deployed in the war zones at any one time.[3] Most of the latter were Southern, former Anyanya forces. Most of the government's fighting was done by militias, notably Anyanya II, the *Murahaliin*, the Mandari and the Murle. By 1989 over 70,000 SPLA troops graduated from training camps in Ethiopia. The SPLA forces were more numerous, better armed, often better trained, and had a more formal command structure than many of the pro-government forces they fought against.

The SPLA's de facto military philosophy was derived less from the principles of Mao Zedong and Che Guevara than the practice of Colonel Mengistu Haile Mariam, President of Ethiopia. Mengistu fused traditional Ethiopian doctrines of massed armies with Soviet belief in the power of numbers. Massive, forced conscription and rudimentary training was the characteristic of the revolutionary Ethiopian army.[4] This force, that numbered over 400,000 at its peak, aimed to conquer territory metre by metre, mile by mile. Mengistu's generals mounted 'human wave' attacks against the Somalis and Eritreans that have been compared to the Somme and the North Koreans. Foot soldiers were regarded as expendable: Mengistu believed that with forty million Ethiopians (as against six million Somalis and three million Eritreans) he had demography on his side.

---

[3] International Institute for Strategic Studies, *The Military Balance 1988-1989*, London, Brassey's, 1988; also see 1992 edition. Some estimates for the government military strength are slightly higher.

[4] Africa Watch, *Evil Days: Thirty Years of War and Famine in Ethiopia*, London, 1991, chapter 17.

(History proved otherwise.) The aim was to control territory, not to win the willing support of the people.

Sadly for thousands of Southern Sudanese young men, the Ethiopian element was prominent in SPLA military doctrines. In early assaults on the small border garrison of Jekau, SPLA soldiers did not even take cover, but simply rushed the Sudanese army machine guns.

The early political orientation of the SPLA reflected both the experience and outlook of the younger generation of Southern Sudanese radical politicians, and Ethiopian influence. The SPLM Manifesto of 1983 was unlike party manifestos in liberal democracies. It was not a detailed outline of proposed policies, such as providing services and guaranteeing rights: the single objective was to achieve 'a united socialist Sudan'. What the content of socialism in the Sudan might be, was not set out. This was a question which was deferred until such time as the war had been won. The SPLA strategy was not to mobilise the people in pursuit of a political aim, so much as to capture state power, and then use that power to effect a radical transformation of Sudanese society. This reflected the state socialist (or, less kindly, 'Afro-Stalinist') approach of Mengistu. While Mengistu ruled Ethiopia, the SPLA used Ethiopian state power as part of its structures of control and transformation. In the Ethiopian refugee camps, the SPLA was a government. In rebel-held areas of Sudan it sought to recreate these conditions, and since the defeat of Mengistu, it has sought an external backer prepared to play the same role.

Hence, the SPLM 'Manifesto' is a different kind of document. It is an interpretation of Sudanese history, concluded with a summary agenda for winning state power with the aim of a radical transformation of the state. It uses historical-determinist language. The greatest weakness in the Manifesto was the gap between establishing the validity of the cause and a realistic political strategy for realising its goals.

The Manifesto makes an interesting contrast with many Southern Sudanese presentations of their case (and indeed speeches and writings by Dr John Garang), which argue that Southern Sudan has historical grievances and a powerful case for justice, concluding with constitutional proposals to guarantee rights. The trajectory of the argument is similar—from history to the current struggle—but the Manifesto is not founded on the human values of redressing wrongs.

The Manifesto introduced the war plan as a 'strategy to transform the Southern Movement into a genuine liberation movement', but here 'liberation' is used only in the sense of 'conquest'. Mostly it is about building the army. The one clause which treats the relationship between the Movement and its local populations runs:

> Politicization, organization and militarization of the peasantry shall follow as areas become liberated.

This was the liberation of areas, not of people. People—here reduced to the category of 'peasantry', which has uncertain relevance to Sudan—were seen as the means, rather than the purpose, of the struggle. Even disabled veterans of the struggle were rarely cared for.

Ethiopia and Sudan: A History of Antagonism

Ethiopia and Sudan had supported each other's rebel movements in the 1960s; mainly on the one hand the Anyanya guerrillas, and on the other the Eritrean Liberation Front (ELF) which was later superseded by the Eritrean People's Liberation Front (EPLF). The Ansar opposition to Nimeiri also fled en masse to Ethiopia in 1970 after Nimeiri's assault on the Ansar stronghold of Aba Island: some military camps close to the border remained until 1985. After the settlement of the Anyanya war in 1972, this antagonism by proxy was subdued for a while, but when the Dergue took power in Ethiopia, the hostility re-ignited. The Sudan Government warmed again to the Eritrean fronts and, most significantly, supported the conservative Ethiopian Democratic Union (EDU) in its military struggle against the Dergue. The EDU proved militarily ineffective.

By 1977 the antagonism between Sudan and Ethiopia had become part of the Cold War line-up. The Soviet Union began supplying large quantities of arms to Ethiopia: Cuba sent military, ideological and technical trainers and advisers. Sudan meanwhile began to receive economic and military support from the United States. One of the particular U.S. aims was to assist President Nimeiri in his resistance to Gadaffi's unpredictable ambitions in the region. Later, Sudan's support was mobilised for the Camp David accords between Egypt and Israel.

After the Dergue's failure to dislodge the EPLF in the huge 'Red Star' offensive of 1982—despite Nimeiri allowing it to send its tanks through Sudanese territory to outflank the rebels—relations again deteriorated. President Mengistu assumed that the Sudanese President had the power to choke off the Eritrean supply lines—a misreading not only of the EPLF's capacity for self-reliance but the deep pro-Eritrean sentiment in Eastern Sudan, which the government could not override. Hence Mengistu began a strategy of destabilising Sudan. Ethiopia gave shelter to remnants of Anyanya and other dissidents that came its way.

Drawing up the Manifesto

In May 1983, when Battalions 104 and 105 of the Sudanese army mutinied in Bor, Pibor and Ayod, it was natural for them to flee to Ethiopia. The Dergue was already assisting Anyanya II fighters, though it was becoming frustrated by military shortcomings and political incoherence. The newcomers presented a better opportunity: they themselves were determined not to repeat the mistakes of the past. A former Ethiopian official recalled collecting Garang and others from the border.[5]

> We took them to Gambela. Then we had a meeting with security from central government and the Vice-President [of Ethiopia]. We asked them to explain their objectives. Then we sent them to Itang and analysed their political consciousness. The standard of their consciousness was better than Anyanya II and the situation of the [Southern Sudanese] people was so desperate as to [make us] actually act on the matter. We decided: now we have to use these people as the yolk and core of the Movement.

---

[5] Interviewed by African Rights, June 1996.

There was a meeting of minds between the Ethiopians and the nascent SPLA leadership. They agreed that the Anyanya had failed to achieve its potential in the first civil war. The Manifesto stated:

The jobbist[6] character of Anyanya I forms an important experience from which the present Movement (SPLM) has a great deal to learn. During Anyanya I there was a proliferation of Governments and political parties such as SANU, SSLF, Southern Front, Sue Republic, Nile Provisional Government, the State of Anyidi and many others. Each of these 'governments' was complete with its Western-type cabinet. The bourgeoisified Southern Bureaucratic elite of Anyanya I were quite content with these job titles even though most of these titles carried no functions. . . . The SPLA will never allow such fake governments and parties to exist.

Note 'SPLA': it was to be the Army not the Movement that was in ultimate control. The leaders recognised that it was only when the Anyanya had finally achieved centralised military command that it could begin to achieve its aims. That centralised command had come about through Joseph Lagu's control over arms supplied from abroad (Israel via Ethiopia and Uganda).

The 'Manifesto' was also tilted against old-style civilian politicians and the trappings of democracy. It referred to:

Early determination of the correct leadership of the SPLA and SPLM so that the movement is not hi-jacked by counter revolutionaries.

This reflected Southern experience during the Anyanya war, when governments in Khartoum had considerable success in dividing Southern politicians by offering them, as individuals, senior posts or other inducements. These failings were also reflected in the decade of Southern Regional Government, when Southern politics was again beset by factionalism, personal ambition and manipulation by Khartoum. Many younger Southerners came to believe that the older generation of Southern politicians had failed them—even betrayed

---

[6] I.e. overly concerned with members' jobs; individualistically self-serving.

them. Better-educated and more radical than their elders, they longed for a new start.

In Sudan in 1983, there was widespread belief that Nimeiri's days were numbered, and that a decisive military blow could be struck that would topple the regime. Hence the SPLA—in common with the civil opposition in the North—did not feel obliged to undertake the slow and painstaking process of mass mobilisation, but instead planned a quick strike. This analysis proved tactically correct-as the events of March-April 1985 showed—but strategically inadequate, in that the fall of Nimeiri did not resolve the basic problems of Sudan.

Given these political circumstances, the nature of the SPLM Manifesto had logic behind it: it was highly centralist, was based on an overall analysis of the nature of the Sudanese state, and put military victory above political organisation. It also converged with the interests of the Ethiopians. By 31 July, eleven weeks after the Bor mutiny, an SPLM Manifesto was in circulation.

The Supremacy of Garang

Dr John Garang was the personification of someone determined to overcome the shortcomings of the past. As a young Anyanya officer in 1972, he had made astute and prophetic criticisms of the Addis Ababa Agreement. By 1983, Garang had been a lecturer at the military academy in Khartoum and a director of research at army headquarters. A colonel, he held the most senior rank among the first rebel leaders who assembled in Itang in mid-1983, although he had less military experience than some of the less senior officers present. Garang was a leading choice as head of the military wing, but he was not named as Chairman of the SPLM. The political leadership of the Movement was divided among the former ministers present: Akuot Atem, Samuel Gai Tut and Joseph Oduho. But differences over seniority among the leaders resulted in the withdrawal of Akuot Atem and Samuel Gai Tut to join the bulk of their supporters from Anyanya II.

The disagreement was resolved by military means. Garang's forces, under Kerubino Kuanyin, drove the Anyanya II out of

67

Ethiopia, and killed Samuel Gai Tut. John Garang then took the title of Chairman of the SPLM as well as Commander-in-Chief of the SPLA. This marked the ascendancy of the military over the political.

Many threats to the 'correct' running of the liberation movement still existed. Based in Upper Nile, and supplied by the Sudan Government, Anyanya II continued to resist the SPLA until 1987. Another Anyanya II group in Bahr-el-Ghazal, led by Kawac Makuei, was also discontented. Makuei was angry at being denied a high position in the SPLA: Garang had him imprisoned from 1984 to 1992. Lakurnyang Lado, the Chairman of the Front for the Liberation of South Sudan (which captured Boma independently from the SPLA in the early days of the war) was detained and publicly executed after refusing to be absorbed. There are many allegations of other extra-judicial killings.

Southern intellectuals and politicians who wanted to join the SPLM were subordinated to the military. Most were required to become soldiers and thus be ruled by command, before any responsibility was given to them. Then they were given assignments which tested their loyalty. Even then, some of them were arrested and detained without trial.

In the vocabulary of the Manifesto, these were counter-revolutionaries who threatened to take over the Movement, and men who threatened a disunity that would jeopardise the SPLA's ability to forge unified and progressive political force. According to a liberal-democratic view, they were victims of human rights abuses because they challenged autocratic leadership. The shadow of these early violations still hangs over the Movement.

The SPLA and the End of Nimeiri

During the last months of Nimeiri's rule, the SPLA's political analysis had wide appeal in Sudan. The prospect of a unified and powerful force representing not just the South but also the other marginalised areas was something radically new and extremely attractive to a broad spectrum of Sudanese, disillusioned with both Nimeiri's dictatorship and with the corrupt and indecisive 'democratic' politics that had preceded it. Political decay had marked the South after 1972. As well as articulating the first clear radical vision for Sudan for over a decade, the SPLA was also the first genuine threat to Nimeiri's rule for almost a decade: it showed that he was not invulnerable, and gave an enormous boost to the internal opposition.

But the SPLA was not part of a wider Sudanese coalition. Members of existing clandestine political organisations were absorbed as individuals only. There was no broad front: the Movement was resolutely centralist. The SPLA had not decided whether it could achieve the liberation of the country alone or if it needed civilian allies in the North. By leaving this question unanswered, it made only opportunistic and tactical alliances with northern groups, rather than developing a common political strategy. It was caught out by the April 1985 Popular Uprising.

The uprising did not end the war. Nimeiri had disregarded popular opposition, but—as Garang quickly pointed out—the old sectarian families merely took over, with a similar agenda of northern domination. However, the trappings of liberal democracy and the political openings that existed presented a severe challenge to the Movement. Having achieved its stated goal of removing Nimeiri, should the SPLM join the government or not? Garang decided not. This decision was made at the top without widespread consultation. Political discussion within the SPLA was curtailed. The two remaining civilian politicians on the SPLM's original Provisional Executive Committee (PEC)—Joseph Oduho and Martin Majier—were imprisoned from 1985 to 1992. (Majier was later re-imprisoned and died in detention; Oduho consorted with another faction and was killed by the SPLA in a commando strike.) The PEC was turned into a 'Political-Military High Command' (PMHC) composed only of soldiers. Two of the five original members of the PMHC (Kerubino Kuanyin and Arok Thon) were then incarcerated because they acted independently of Garang.

THE HUMANITARIAN STRATEGIES OF THE SPLA

Military centralism was not the way to maximise a respect for humanitarian values. At the outset, the SPLA had three priorities which governed its attitude to humanitarian relief.

Firstly, it wanted to be able to train soldiers systematically. This was no light matter. The aim was to create an army capable not only of harassing the enemy with guerrilla raids, but of defeating the Sudanese Government forces in conventional engagements. A raw recruit would need a course of at least six months. And in order to build up a force of sufficient size, successive batches of trainees would have to be graduated for several years. Initially the training was applied to men who had already come to join the SPLA in Ethiopia. After them, a stream of new recruits was required. A second requirement was that this process of recruitment had to be managed.

Thirdly, the SPLA needed to supply its soldiers in the field. This was partly a matter of arms and ammunition. There was also a requirement for food, domestic utensils and medical supplies.

These three priorities roughly corresponded to three unwritten relief strategies. First: the international system for relief to refugees was to be exploited in order to sustain people while many of them were undergoing military training in Ethiopia. Second: people were to be discouraged from staying in Government-held areas. (Humanitarian activity was one of the things that kept them there.) Third: if possible, relief was to be mobilised in the SPLA-held areas which would ease the problems of provisioning the rebel soldiers.

Refugees and Trainees

A few Southern Sudanese refugees had been present in Ethiopia before 1983, but no internationally-recognised relief camps had been set up. From May 1983, the numbers of refugees grew rapidly, and by the end of 1987, four camps had been established. These were related to SPLA bases and training centres.

The main refugee camps and SPLA centres were:

- Itang, situated about 30 k.m. west of Gambela town, and 50 k.m. east of Jekau on the Sudan border. This is where the rebel Sudan army soldiers were first brought, when they crossed to Ethiopia in May/June 1983, and where the SPLM/A was first constituted. An official refugee camp was established there at the same time, in June 1983. It remained the largest of the camps for Sudanese refugees until all the camps were evacuated, in May and June 1991. At that time, the camp population was between 100,000 and 250,000.

- Bilpam, about 40 k.m. south-west of Itang. In May 1983, this was already the base of the Anyanya II guerrillas. Later in the year, the forces of John Garang chased out those who had not been absorbed. Bilpam became the headquarters of the SPLA, and the site of a military training camp.

- Bonga, about 40 k.m. east of Gambela town, is the site of an Ethiopian military training school. This was shared with SPLA. The SPLA managed its own section and was allowed to administer its own internal discipline there on its own authority.

- Zinc training centre, near Gambela Town. This was an Ethiopian training centre for signallers, intelligence work and ideological instruction, shared with the SPLA. It was attached to a barracks. Senior officers of the SPLA would sometimes stay there, for security.

- Dima is about 100 k.m. south-east of Pinyudo and 100 k.m. north-east of Boma. A refugee camp was opened there in August 1986, when the official number of Sudanese refugees in Ethiopia had topped the 100,000 mark.

- Pinyudo (alternatively spelled Panyido, Panydiu, Pignudo or Fugnido) was on the Gilo river, about 100 k.m. south of Gambela town, and 50 k.m. north-east of the border town of Pochala. A refugee camp was opened there in December 1987, to relieve the pressure on Itang after an influx in the middle of that year.[7]

• Tsore refugee camp was near Asosa town (about 200 k.m. north of Gambela town) in Welega Province. It was opened in May 1987 and housed mainly Uduk people. The camp population had reached about 40,000 by the end of 1989, when Tsore was attacked and destroyed by the Oromo Liberation Front (OLF). The people set out on a long flight down the Sudan-Ethiopia border to Itang. The camp was not re-opened.

• Boma base. Inside Southern Sudan, Boma became the main centre for the SPLA. It is situated in hills near the Ethiopian border.

Relief commodities officially destined for Itang served also the SPLA training centres and headquarters at Bonga and Bilpam. When Dima camp opened, it became a source of supply for the base at Boma. Tsore was a depot for the SPLA units in Blue Nile and Welega Province, where the Ethiopian Government was using them to fight the OLF (which was being supplied from Sudan).

Between 1983 and 1991, almost all the SPLA's regular troops—roughly 110,000 men and boys[8]—were trained using these centres. This included training of trainers, of senior officers, of radio operators, of intelligence personnel and other specialists. The SPLA was essentially created in these places.

A senior SPLA officer later told African Rights[9] that the trainees had been entirely dependent on relief food from the camps. This is not strictly accurate—the soldiers also fed themselves with food from the local populations—but certainly a large proportion of their consumption was food aid. Sudanese who were in Itang during that period later reported that they routinely saw trucks being re-loaded

---

[7] Radda Barnen, 'The Unaccompanied Minors of Southern Sudan', 1994.

[8] A rough figure. A former official of the Dergue estimated that Ethiopia had provided for the training and full equipment of 120,000 soldiers. In fact many of the supplies came originally from Soviet bloc countries and Libya. The Sudan Armed Forces numbered about 75,000 by 1991, augmented by a rapidly growing PDF.

[9] Interviewed in November 1995.

was publicly commended by John Garang for doing so. At the same time, it was common for SPLA soldiers to gain cattle and other commodities by extortion and looting from the local Anuak and Gaajak Nuer.

For much of the time, in accordance with Ethiopian policy, the SPLA restricted private trade. Individuals were forbidden to engage in anything except small-scale local commerce. This had the rationale of stopping intelligence passing to the enemy or foreigners, and of preventing the growth of a bourgeois sector. This placed the trade monopoly in the hands of the SPLA itself, and those officers who could bend the rules. Allegations have been made against specific officers and ethnic groups. In March 1989, when a meeting was held to resolve many complaints by local Ethiopians against SPLA lawlessness in the border region, unauthorised trading by SPLA commanders was one item of contention.

In 1990, Ethiopian policy on domestic trade was liberalised. SPLA policy in the adjoining region also changed: some attribute the loosening up to the posting of Riek Machar as the main commander in western Upper Nile, others to the SPLA's consolidation of most of the east bank of the Nile in 1989. Of all the SPLA economic initiatives, this was the most systematic and sustained. It involved a truce with the Misiriya and opening up of markets for North-South trade, encouraging businessmen to trade with garrison towns, and a friendly attitude towards foreign relief agencies. By 1991, refugee relief was a large component of a widespread trade revival in Upper Nile.

> Itang camp became a centre for commercial activity. During the dry season the people of the Sobat and Pibor rivers came to Itang with their cattle and canoes, sold their cattle for Ethiopian currency, bought food in large quantities (larger than could be carried overland), and brought it back by canoe to their homes in the Sudan. Small markets grew up inside the Sudan, especially at Jokau and Nasir, where goods from Ethiopia and Itang were sold for Ethiopian and Sudanese currency. Relief supplies from Itang were

dispersed over a wide geographical area through kinship networks which straddled the international border.[16]

Commerce was good for the economy of Upper Nile, and for the food security of its inhabitants. However, in Itang, the main beneficiaries remained those who controlled the allocations of relief. The SPLA was acquiring some of the characteristics of a centralised state, allocating the resources it controlled for its own policy ends, while certain individuals extracted benefits from their positions.

Social Change among the Refugees

Exile is an important experience. Depending on circumstances and leadership, it can radicalise people or depoliticise them; it can make them more assertive or more obedient. In the 1960s, many Southerners in exile in Uganda had acquired a good education and returned to Sudan with high career aspirations; in the 1970s Ansar exiles had nurtured their neo-Mahdist ideology and plotted an armed return. The unique conditions in the Gambela refugee camps had their own implications. Normal family life was rare: more than ninety per cent of the refugees were boys and men (while a majority of the Southerners displaced to the North were female). The MDTM noted:

> It is obvious that this is a period of great social change and transition for the Southern Sudanese in these camps. Different ethnic groups are now living closely together cultural norms and traditions are changing and new skills and innovations are being developed and implemented. The implications of all this are not lost on the refugees who are very aware that once they return to Sudan they will have to start from zero to rebuild their societies. There is a strong feeling that the reshaping of society here, in a way is making them into an 'avant garde' group.[17]

---

[16] Douglas H. Johnson, 'Increasing the Trauma of Return: An Assessment of the UN's Emergency Response to the Evacuation of the Sudanese Refugee Camps in Ethiopia, 1991,' mimeographed paper, 31 October 1992.
[17] MDTM *ibid.*

In fact, many of the real social and political implications of exile are not apparent at the time: refugee camps are an artificial environment in which myths and hopes may appear as realities, while many latent allegiances and aspirations are not evident—there is never a reduction to complete 'zero'. Many of the former refugees have indeed become a vanguard of social change in Southern Sudan, but not always in the ways anticipated.

One of the most significant social changes was the spread of church affiliation. Several Christian groups were active in the camps in Ethiopia, some with small-scale aid projects, while relief sacks bore the marks of agencies such as Catholic Relief Services. Many of the refugees had come to Ethiopia seeking an education. With many of the traditional restraints on culture-change missing, Christianity was easier to accept. Many converts were won. When the refugees returned to Sudan they provided an impetus for the dramatic increase in church membership which happened during the war. This boom was especially notable after the SPLA gave clergymen greater freedom to work in 1989. That year saw the beginnings of the New Sudan Council of Churches (NSCC), one of whose important origins was a committee in Itang, set up to attract aid resources for the indigenous Sudanese church organisations.[18]

In 1991, when the camps were disbanded, many new Christians returned to Sudan and founded churches where none had existed before. Perhaps as many as sixty Roman Catholic congregations had appeared by late 1994 in areas of Upper Nile where previously the only Christians had been Presbyterians. This posed a problem for the Catholic authorities, who were almost completely unable to provide trained priests or lay workers, and thus ensure that orthodox doctrines were being followed. The Protestant churches, also, have been, faced with grave questions about the nature and sustainability of the Christianity that has been propagated.[19]

---

[18] Interviews with Church leaders, January and July 1995.
[19] See African Rights, 'Great Expectations: The Civil Roles of the Churches in Southern Sudan,' Discussion Paper No 6, April 1995.

In the camps, church groups were usually active in the field of education—a traditional focus of missionaries. By the late 1980s, Southern boys had very few alternatives for obtaining an education. There were no schools in the SPLA-controlled areas of the South, but in the camps, rates of school enrolment were much higher than they had been in most parts of Southern Sudan before the war.[20] Church membership and education became virtually inseparable.

Since the evacuation of the camps in 1991, education provision has improved in SPLA-held Sudan, though it is still tiny compared to need. Aid agencies have begun supporting institutions inside the country, but there are acute problems in obtaining teachers of commitment and quality, in organising curricula and examinations, in escaping insecurity, in receiving and holding on to the necessary supplies and equipment. In 1995 only four secondary schools existed in the SPLA areas, all of them in Western Equatoria. Becoming a refugee has remained the best choice for many young people wanting an education: there are better chances of schools in Uganda and Kenya, and the more ambitious strive for sponsorships outside north-east Africa.

The effects of the refugee bias in education have yet to be fully seen. It may well widen the gap between the elites and the poor in Southern Sudan, and increase the tendency for the better-educated people to be resettled eventually in industrialised countries.

Many of the children who came to the camps in Ethiopia did so without a responsible adult from the family. The great majority of these were boys. They became known among humanitarian agencies as 'the unaccompanied minors'. There has been controversy about the reasons for their arrival, and the extent and nature of their exploitation by the SPLA. The SPLA has said they came because of the desire for education and the need to flee from enemy raiding. Human rights and humanitarian organisations have compiled sufficient evidence that many of them were deliberately recruited from villages, marched to Ethiopia, given military training, and even deployed in battles.[21] The refugee camps certainly acted as a magnet

---

[20] MDTM *ibid.*
[21] See, e.g., Human Rights Watch/Africa, *Children of Sudan*, 1995.

for boys, many of whom wanted to be armed and trained, as well as educated. This combined neatly with the SPLA's early policy of developing youth cadres. Many of the unaccompanied minors went on to die or suffer extremes of hunger and other privation. As with the refugee phenomenon in general, the final impact on Southern Sudanese society has yet to be assessed. But there are fears that many of the survivors, having grown up without the normal socialising experiences of family and community, will add to the instability of Sudanese society.

Recruitment and the Military Ethos

The priority of the SPLA was to build a strong army. The emphasis was on numbers. Particularly in the early years, many recruits were driven by personal experience of exploitation or discrimination. Often these young men (and a few young women) had a specific desire to reclaim their land or 'drive out the Arabs.' Others joined up, inspired by solidarity and the noble cause of fighting for liberation. Some were defecting army units or locally-mobilised self-defence or militia groups, wanting to join the struggle. One of the problems for the SPLA was that it was unable to offer an immediate, tangible realisation of these recruits' aspirations: social liberation would have to wait until the war was won. In the meantime, the bonds of solidarity that grow among fellow fighters could not serve indefinitely.

The SPLA was not organised as a liberation movement, merging with the people and carrying out social reform. It was organised as a hierarchical army, broadly on the model of its opponent. But it did not provide a formal system of wages for its soldiers. The SPLA told its recruits that, as guerrillas, they needed to be very tough and self-reliant; they would have to fend for themselves. The message to graduating soldiers was:

You must live through the barrels of your guns. Food, wife and property wherever you find them are to be acquired through your might.[22]

All military training is, in a sense, dehumanising. It prepares people to kill others. But the SPLA took this to an extreme. It inculcated a callous attitude towards civilians, not only in order to help its fighters to survive, but to spread the idea that the only option for a self-respecting man was to join up.

[Military training] changed a human being's mind. Untrained people seemed inferior. 'Civilian' became an insult. 'You don't know what people are doing' [a common phrase to dismiss someone as incapable] meant you don't know what the soldiers are doing.[23]

At times, the elevation of the military verged on a nihilistic attitude towards civilians and existing social structures. Many cases of abuse by SPLA soldiers against civilians have been documented.[24] The list includes extortion, destruction of assets, looting, murder, abduction, forced labour and rape. Of course atrocities happen in many wars. But from the beginning, the SPLA failed to show a determination to eliminate such actions. True, they were included as offences in the 1984 SPLA Disciplinary Code, but implementation of the code was always haphazard. Usually it depended on the attitude of the local commander, and while some

---

[22] Variants on this theme are commonly recounted now by former trainees including some who still belong to the SPLM. This particular wording is quoted from a tract by a group of former political detainees: 'For a Strong SPLM/A: What is to be Done?' (Amon Mon Wantok and others, 11 June 1992).

[23] Former SPLA solder, interviewed in April 1996.

[24] Collections and summaries are included in, for instance: Amnesty International (1989) 'Sudan: Human Rights Violations in the Context of Civil War'; Africa Watch (1990) 'Sudan: Denying the Honour of Living'; Human Rights Watch/Africa (1994) 'Sudan: Civilian Devastation'; Human Rights Watch/Africa (1996), 'Behind the Red Line: Political Repression in Sudan.'

were strict and respectful of the law, too often others were tolerant or complicit in the crime.

Before 1995, the only documented cases of the SPLA High Command punishing serving officers on the grounds of offences against civilians occurred in Ethiopia. The regional authorities in Gambela delivered stern warnings about the SPLA's failure to stop its soldiers abusing the local people.[25] After the killing of over twenty Ethiopians and the burning of the houses of many more in September 1989, 25 SPLA soldiers were arrested and four executed.

This was exceptional. Southern Sudanese civilians were not so fortunate. This can be attributed partly to the fact that soldiers had been told to fend for themselves in the first place. The High Command was prepared to forgo disciplinary control in order to maintain a basic level of loyalty.

As the war progressed, ethnically-driven mobilisation persisted and even increased. John Garang is probably sincere in saying that he did not want to create a tribally-divisive army. But the dynamics of recruitment, training and provisioning made it hard for him to avoid doing so. Recruits came to Ethiopia in ethnically-homogenous groups, and were enrolled in the same manner. An ethnically-driven mobilisation was also forced upon the SPLA by the divisive strategies pursued by the government, and the ethnic labels carelessly or deliberately used by some Southern intellectuals in Khartoum. While the leadership disavowed tribalism, SPLA units in the field often pursued ethnically-specific agendas. For example they took the side of the Bor Dinka in dispute with the Murle (who were armed by the government) in 1983-4 and the side of the Shilluk against the Nuer-dominated Anyanya II in 1985-6.

The SPLA's use of land mines reflects the same ethos. As might be expected, the Sudanese army, as an occupation force in much of the South, has made wide and indiscriminate use of land mines, causing many civilian casualties. The SPLA, claiming to represent

---

[25] 'The Joint Declaration made by the Gambella Adm. Region and the SPLA to Improve the Relations Prevailing Between the Ethiopian Masses and the SPLA,' 27 March 1989, points 1.5-1.10; 'Nekempte Declaration', September 1989.

the people, might be expected to be more restrained in its mine warfare—the inhabitants of the South will have to live with mines for years, perhaps decades, after the end of the war, when they will continue to cause loss of life and limb and keep roads, fields and pastures out of use. In 1985, when the SPLA first received land mines from the Ethiopians, one senior commander suggested keeping careful maps of where mines were laid. His advice was not followed, and the locations of mines are known only to those who laid them—and many have since died or have forgotten where they were placed. Both sides are continuing to use mines to this day.

In summary, despite the aspirations of its political agenda, and the personal motives and qualities of very many of its officers and rank-and-file, the SPLA was not set up to be 'the fighting vanguard of the people' as envisaged by Che Guevara[26] and other practitioners of revolutionary warfare. It was established as a conventional military force, aiming to seize power. When it failed to do that, it lost its way.

The SPLA's Blockade on Relief

[The] garrison towns in the South are famine-stricken and are real disaster areas, and this is good; our military strategy is working.[27]

Like other guerrilla armies, the SPLA counted on moving through rural areas to cut government supply lines and overrun small garrisons. By 1986, it was making travel and transportation very difficult to many major towns, by means of landmines, ambushes, shooting at barges and aircraft, and damaging the Lol bridge on the single rail link to the South. At the same time, military activity had meant that many of these towns now contained populations displaced from the surrounding countryside. Officially, the SPLA wanted these people to go out from the towns, so that they could join the struggle,

[26] Che Guevara, *Che Guevara Speaks,* London, Pathfinder Books, 1967, p. 75.
[27] John Garang, in Mansour Khalid (ed.), *John Garang Speaks*, London 1987, p. 71.

and leave the government forces in an exposed position. But this did not often happen, due largely to fear of both the SPLA and government forces. In addition, while the SPLA often called upon civilians to leave the towns, it rarely provided safe passage through the battle lines, and still more rarely did it provide any sustenance to those who arrived in the 'liberated' area.

The siege tactics cut normal urban-rural links. Before the war, large parts of rural Southern Sudan were dependent on regular interaction with towns for economic survival. Rural people sold cattle, fish and produce in towns, and many depended on seasonal labour, in order to buy grain and consumer goods such as salt, soap and clothes. As these links withered, economic life in the villages stagnated.

The combination of siege and swollen populations began to create severe shortages of food and other commodities in the government-held towns. Humanitarian agencies responded by trying to arrange special access for relief supplies. In response, the SPLA took a hard line on relief. In February 1986 it refused a specific request from the UN to allow relief trucks access to Juba. Four months later, it turned down the idea of a 'food truce' put forward by a consortium of NGOs. And on 16 August, two days after the ICRC had started airlifting supplies to Wau, it shot down an airliner near Malakal, killing sixty people and also putting an end to the Red Cross operation. 'We are not repentant' said John Garang, 'We warned that the airspace over War Zone I is closed.'[28]

The SPLA defended this policy publicly by alleging that relief operations had been abused in order to assist Khartoum's military activities. It claimed that a 1985 relief convoy to Shambe and Yirol by barge and truck had provisioned the garrison in Yirol. Supplies destined for Lakes Province in September had been commandeered by the Military Governor in Juba. A UN-flagged barge convoy to Malakal in February 1986 had carried equipment and food for the army. One NGO's vehicles and fuel had been used for military

---

[28] Blaine Harden, 'Sudan Rebel Leader "Not Repentant" Despite Famine, Downing of Aircraft,' *International Herald Tribune*, 19 September 1986.

purposes in Eastern Equatoria.[29] Some of these allegations were true, though they were made to justify a harsh policy that was causing many Southern civilians to suffer.

These policies remained essentially unchanged until 1989. Interviewed by Arop Madut, Dr John Garang admitted that he was blocking food supplies, and responded to the proposal of allowing free passage: 'that would be a very simplistic way of dealing with a rather complex situation.'[30] He argued again that relief agencies working in the North were subject to governmental manipulation, and that food destined for displaced Southerners was being stolen by traders and the army.

Humanitarianism in SPLA Areas

In its early years, the SPLA helped create famine and did very little to relieve it. One of its most serious omissions was the neglect of protecting civilian populations at risk of raiding by militias. As the following chapter documents, massive and repeated raiding by pro-government militias during the years 1985-8 was the prime cause of the disastrous famine in Bahr el Ghazal, and to a slightly lesser extent Upper Nile. These raids were foreseeable and were indeed foreseen. As early as 1984, when the SPLA recruited 10,000 soldiers in Bahr el Ghazal, large-scale assaults were expected. A relatively modest force of trained soldiers could have protected the thickly-populated areas of northern Bahr el Ghazal from the militias' onslaught. It was requested but not sent.[31] SPLA forces moving through Upper Nile also refused to engage with militias attacking defenceless villagers, on the grounds that they had not been ordered to do so. When the SPLA besieged garrison towns, it did not help civilians to escape, or provide escapees with assistance.

The second major omission was to organise an effective structure for delivering services. By 1986, the SPLA could also

---

[29] SPLA/SPLM Newsletter, 1 August 1986.
[30] *Sudan Times*, 29 November 1988.
[31] The SPLA force that first arrived in the area in 1985 was locally known as 'the human locusts'.

86

claim that a large proportion of the needy people in Southern Sudan lived in its territory. A communiqué stridently asserted that 95% of the population in Southern Sudan was under rebel administration, and that any relief must be allocated accordingly.[32] The stated figure of 95% was a huge exaggeration; but it made a point that was hard to ignore.

Once again, there was a gap between stating the justice of the case and making realistic proposals to solve the problem. The Sudan Government was determined to maintain its sovereignty, and not cede legitimacy to any cross-border assistance to rebel-held territory. Even more importantly, the *Ethiopian* Government agreed: it was determined not to cede the precedent of such an operation, for fear of legitimising the operations into rebel-held Eritrea and Tigray. The SPLA was in a trap. Its solution was to ask for assistance delivered outside Southern Sudan, some of which could be taken inside by the SPLA itself. In March 1984, Col. Garang wrote to several agencies, telling them that the SPLA was not anti-Western, and that its overseas representatives would 'receive any non-military material assistance that you may offer to the SPLA/SPLM and to the South Sudanese Refugees.'[33] (No assistance for civilians *inside* Southern Sudan was requested.) The agencies did not respond. In March the SPLA was contacted by a representative of BandAid to discuss the possibility of setting up a programme in its areas, but no agreement was reached.

In November 1984 an agency was formed with an express mandate to obtain and deliver supplies: the Sudan Relief and Rehabilitation Association (SRRA). In its registered constitution, the SRRA first took the form of an association of refugees, deriving its authority from the Refugees' Council based at Itang. When the SRRA became more active in 1986-7, it became clear that the senior officers of the organisation were chosen directly by the High Command. Assertions that SRRA was independent were enough to

---

32 'The SPLM/SPLA's Position on the Relief Situation in Sudan', 26 August 1986.
33 Letter to various agencies from John Garang, SPLA, 15 March 1984.

87

get it registered as an NGO in Kenya, but did not succeed in convincing anyone.

This fact need not, in itself, have been an insurmountable obstacle to external aid. In fact, in different circumstances it could have helped. ERA and REST were also tied to their respective guerrilla armies. But those organisations each took a place within a liberation economy founded on the promotion of local democracy and development, that attracted solidarity and support from certain western humanitarian agencies which admired the Eritrean and Tigrayan struggles. Being attached to the SPLA was no advantage for the SRRA. Early experiments by NGOs in giving funds or supplies to SRRA showed that it could not account for the assistance. BandAid, Oxfam and SCF provided some support to test its capacity and willingness, but it failed the test. In the words of one of the foreign donors involved, the SRRA headquarters staff 'just ate it. . . . By that casual act of peculation they set back [the cause of their people] for years.'[34] Its reports and monitoring were not credible, and foreign aid workers came to believe that it could not implement its stated programmes.[35]

Some of the people who worked for SRRA were intelligent, hard-working and sincere. But the agency suffered from the absence of a strong mandate or genuine humanitarian strategy within the Movement as a whole. Civilian work had little place within the SPLA; local commanders would see the job of an SRRA official as being about the administration of supplies, not community work. Any attempts to build a grassroots organisation or generate extra discussion about social conditions would have been treated with suspicion and hostility. In fact the SRRA officials were all named from amongst the soldiers anyway and retained their military rank. They received no salary and usually no instructions from the head office. Without supplies, they had nothing to do except other military

---

[34] Interviewed in August 1995.

[35] Such perceptions are recorded in notes on an informal opinion-gathering exercise among UK NGOs by Anthony Ratter, a consultant working with SRRA, when he visited Britain in October/November 1988.

duties. If aid did materialise, the first human needs to be served would naturally tend to be those close to the army.

How far the SRRA was purposely designed for provisioning fighters is open to debate. At the time, the SPLA was already meeting its material needs 'at source' and an organisation like the SRRA would have been superfluous. Like many institutions set up by the SPLA, it might not have been thoroughly discussed by the leadership, and so it could have been adopted without a practical strategy so that it served an array of miscellaneous ends.

Meanwhile, the SPLA was prepared to bargain tough. It maintained its opposition to relief in government-held areas except as part of some deal by which a greater—or at least comparable— quantity would be delivered in rebel territory. In late 1986, some United Nations agencies tried to appease it with a smaller amount to be sent as part of 'Operation Rainbow' (see chapter 5). The SPLA rejected the offers that were made through secret contacts. The UN went ahead and announced the operation anyway. The SPLA promptly called its bluff, by declaring that airspace in Southern Sudan would remain closed, contributing to the failure of the initiative.

Although by 1986 the SPLA could claim to hold a lot of territory, not much of it was suitable for relief access. Either the place was dangerous or the route was very difficult. The area of greatest need was northern Bahr el Ghazal, roughly 1,000 k.m. from the Kenyan border overland, even by routes passable in peacetime. The small consortium led by BandAid gave £20,000 to SRRA to take relief there, but never received evidence that anything was delivered. Until 1989, almost the only externally verifiable aid activities took place around Narus, just 30 k.m. from Kenya. (Ironically this was in an area where at the time the SPLA had extremely poor relations with the local population; the greatest relief needs were caused by its own fighting against the Toposa.) Church-related organisations would sometimes transport relief to the border where it was handed over to the SRRA to be carried on army lorries. The Médecins Sans Frontières agencies started small programmes. In 1988, UNICEF did the same, though this stopped immediately when the Sudan Government objected.

89

A different approach was taken by Norwegian Peoples' Aid (NPA), an approach very much determined by a single individual, Egil Hagen. Hagen was a former soldier who came to identify himself closely with the SPLA. Having worked for NPA previously in Lebanon, he persuaded the organisation to back him in creating a Southern Sudan programme. He worked not with the SRRA, but directly with the army, a fact which encouraged rumours that he was deliberately providing military assistance under the cover of humanitarianism. The more dramatic rumours—about supplying guns and ammunition—have never been substantiated. NPA often took food near to the war front. Most likely, Hagen was motivated by political solidarity and personal empathy with some of the SPLA leaders, and liked dealing with military men who had the power to make local decisions and stick to them. Hagen was afflicted by cancer, and died in 1991.

These relief initiatives were all small, late and far from the areas of greatest need. Most importantly, they were an afterthought in the SPLA's military and political strategy. The most telling verdict on the SPLA's humanitarianism comes from the fact that hundreds of thousands of Southern civilians preferred the trek north, into the heartland of the northern militias, to trying to survive in areas controlled by the SPLA. The story is much more complicated than the 'northern hospitality and SPLA abuses' repeatedly cited by the Sudan Government, but the simple fact remains that huge numbers of Southerners fled from their supposed liberators. The SPLA's failure to provide for them was not only an abuse, it was a blunder, as large areas of the South were deprived of the 'water' on which the rebel 'fish' depended, and many of the displaced subsequently returned to the warfront, conscripted by the Sudan armed forces and militias.

Disabled Veterans and Families of the War Dead

One of the Sudan Government's major humanitarian initiatives is to provide for the families of 'martyrs'. The SPLA, in common with other liberation struggles, also speaks of its 'martyrs', but unlike them, its provision for their material needs is modest and haphazard.

In the Nuba Mountains, some widows and orphans have been cared for and there have been attempts to put this welfare duty on a more systematic basis. (Captain Miriam Yohana was placed in charge of their welfare.) Elsewhere, most widows and orphans have had to rely on the goodwill and generosity of relatives or have fended for themselves. There is a similar story for those left physically disabled by the fighting. Very few are given non-combatant positions where they can still make a useful contribution despite their handicap. Many disabled veterans remain bitter at their neglect. Their plight was recognised at the SPLM Convention of March-April 1994, which resolved to create 'A department for wounded heroes and families of martyrs,'[36] but nothing has been set up at the time of writing.

CONCLUSIONS

In the first years of the war, the SPLA took a very hard view of relief: it was something to be manipulated as an immediate tool for fighting the war, and not allowed to get in the way of that purpose. International relief agencies failed to mount an effective opposition to this policy. The SPLA attitude of non-humanitarianism—like the fact of war itself—caused a great many deaths and a great deal of suffering; but such a stance can be explained by the origins and early priorities of the rebellion. The SPLA failed to win a quick victory, and later its circumstances changed. The relief policy had to be softened and in many ways reversed, as will be seen in the following chapters.

The position taken by the SPLA also had important implications for the failure of the anti-famine coalition to re-emerge in Sudanese national politics. In the last months of Nimeiri, the SPLA radio broadcasts denouncing the Government for ignoring the famine had helped mobilise civil resistance in Khartoum and other cities. After the Popular Uprising, the SPLA radio fell silent on this issue—

---

[36] SPLM/SPLA First National Convention, 'Resolutions, Appointments and Protocol,' March/April 1994, Article 14.1.5.

because the SPLA was itself guilty of the same crime. Progressive and Southern forces in Khartoum tried to push the Government to respond to the human crisis in the South, but they were unable to make any sort of alliance with the most powerful Southern force—the SPLA—and their efforts failed.

The authoritarianism of the SPLA also has implications for the central contention of this book: that external aid abets authoritarian tendencies. It is hard to see how the SPLA could have become *more* authoritarian than it was in the 1980s. What happened when the centralist and authoritarian SPLA began large-scale dealings with international relief agencies will be discussed in later chapters.

5.

THE COALITION FOR FAMINE IN THE SOUTH

[A] variety of powerful Sudanese interests helped create the famine. The apparent 'failure' of the Sudanese government and international donors to relieve this famine cannot be understood without comprehending how these 'beneficiaries'—at the local level and in the central government—were able (and permitted) to manipulate famine relief for their own purposes. For the donors, although the famine itself was not functional, the pursuit of narrowly defined relief agendas served important functions, even as it tended to allow the creation and perpetuation of famine.

David Keen[1]

The invisibility of famine in Sudan's democratic politics after April 1985 had enormous ramifications. One result was that the next military government was able to survive an even more scandalous nationwide famine in 1990/91 unscathed. More immediately, it meant that famine rapidly developed in the South on account of the war and how it was fought. While a powerful coalition of interests emerged behind the creation of the Southern famine, there was little democratic mobilisation against the famine. This was particularly ironic because at the time Sudan was experimenting, for the third time since independence, with a form of liberal democracy in which a wide range of civil and political rights were granted to citizens. But these rights did not extend in full to Southern Sudanese, and those who·were able to exercise their rights did not do so on behalf of the Southern victims of famine.

---

[1] David Keen, *The Benefits of Famine: A Political Economy of Famine in South-Western Sudan, 1983-1989*, Princeton University Press, 1994, p. 3.

93

By contrast, the government *did* hold itself accountable to the Northern urban populace and the western donors. Unlike 1984, there was no effective political coalition between the famine-affected people (or their leaders) and city dwellers. An assault on the famine began only when foreign journalists, relief workers and diplomats began to take the famine seriously. The Sudanese famine became a political issue through international pressure. As a result, the politics of famine changed in important ways that undermined the viability of anti-famine strategies.

THE SOUTHERN FAMINE AND ITS BENEFICIARIES

Famine conditions existed in some Southern garrison towns as early as 1984. Localised famines in besieged towns and enclaves has remained a feature of the war, alongside massive displacement and chronic impoverishment of the rural population. An exceptionally severe famine that was to belatedly spark an international response was centered in northern Bahr el Ghazal and reached its nadir in 1988.

The military means of famine creation deployed in Sudan were elementary but devastating. Many of these methods have been documented in detail elsewhere[2] and will only be summarised here. The SPLA's role has been described in chapter 4, so this chapter will be concerned solely with the government and its proxy forces. The main mechanism for creating famine was the militia, specifically the Baggara *Murahaliin* militia that raided the Dinka of northern Bahr el Ghazal starting in earnest in late 1985. The militias originated in a number of local and national factors, including the poverty of Baggara herdsmen following the 1984/5 famine and government attempts to protect Chevron's oil concessions.[3] Both the Nimeiri and Sadiq el Mahdi governments were keen not to have to resort to

---

[2] Keen 1994; Alex de Waal, 'Starving out the South,' in M. W. Daly and A. A. Sikainga (eds.) *Civil War in the Sudan*, London, British Academic Press, 1993.

[3] Alex de Waal, 'Some comments on militias in contemporary Sudan,' in Daly and Sikainga (eds.), 1993.

conscription in the Northern towns, and recruiting rural militiamen was thus an attractive alternative. Finally, playing the ethnic card—a divide-and-rule strategy—was a tradition for both colonial and Northern governments in Khartoum, whose effectiveness had repeatedly been demonstrated.

The *Murahaliin* raids were frequent, widespread and devastating. The raiders stole livestock, destroyed villages, poisoned wells and killed indiscriminately.[4] Some women and children were taken into captivity for forced labour or slavery. As early as May 1986, reports in the international press told of 600,000 people driven from their homes by militia activities in Bahr el Ghazal alone.[5] The mainly-Nuer force Anyanya II was also active in raiding Dinka and Shilluk communities. From 1984 until 1987, there was a large Anyanya II force operating in Upper Nile, receiving arms and logistical support from the government. After the majority of the force defected to the SPLA in 1987, a rump based among the Bul Nuer remained loyal to the government, and operated at different times in the succeeding years in Bentiu and Mayom, Abyei and Kadugli.

The militia raids alone were enough to create severe famine in northern and eastern Bahr el Ghazal. Their effects were compounded by abuses against the displaced. In the garrison towns, Dinka were forced to sell their cattle and other assets cheaply. They had to work for little or no pay; they were prohibited from moving outside camps to gather firewood or straw; and they were often prevented from moving further north to places where work or charity might be available. Prohibiting movement and wage earning amounted to a sentence of death by starvation.

The cumulative effect of the raiding and these restrictions was to starve people to death. In the summer of 1988, death rates in el Meiram and Abyei reached the unprecedented levels of one per cent per day—far higher than any levels recorded before or since for famines in Africa. By comparison, these levels of mortality were

---

4 Amnesty International, 'Sudan: Human Rights Violations in the Context of Civil War,' London, December 1989.
5 Sheila Rule, 'Khartoum Suspected of Role in Raids on African Tribesmen', *International Herald Tribune*, 7 May 1986.

more than fifty times higher than those suffered in Kordofan and Darfur during the 1984-5 famine. As well as the familiar health crises—measles and diarrhoeal diseases were major killers—outright starvation claimed many lives. The contrast between the death rates in the two famines indicates how much more severe war-famines can be, the different treatment of Dinka displaced compared to drought migrants from north Kordofan and north Darfur, and how starvation is a crime: it does not just happen, it has to be deliberately inflicted on people. Over 30,000 displaced people, almost all Dinka, are known to have died in camps in southern Kordofan alone in 1988.[6] However, the oft-cited figure of a total of 250,000 famine deaths for the whole of Southern Sudan in 1988 is purely speculative.

Army commanders and local government officials also prevented relief assistance from reaching the displaced. There are innumerable examples of the blocking of relief, on different pretexts. In one instance, relief food donated by the European Community sat for a year in wagons in railway siding in Babanusa, just a few hundred yards from a displaced camp where Dinka were starving. Excepting Juba, it is hard to find a single instance in which relief was delivered and distributed as planned.

More widely, localised famines were created by military tactics including raiding and requisitioning, scorched earth and sieges. The army and militias raided cattle and other movable goods and stole food on operations. Around garrisons the army prevented cultivation and cut down any cover, including standing crops, to give clear lines of sight.

These war tactics often coincided with the mercantile or power interests of the ruling elite. The raiding of cattle and depopulation of villages served economic interests as well as military ones. In 1982 the cross-over between military and commercial elites was formalised in the creation of the Military Economic Board, which comprised seven military corporations with extensive ownership and privileges across economic sectors.[7] The President, the Minister of

---

[6] Based on a compilation of aid agency reports.

[7] *Economist Intelligence Unit*, Quarterly Economic Report for Sudan, 1983, No. 2, p. 16.

Defence and the Commander in Chief of the armed forces were all on the Board. In 1985 the Board was formally disbanded, but the principle of military-commercial co-operation lived on. Military aircraft left the Southern garrisons laden with smuggled coffee, hardwoods and ivory, and looted or cheaply-bought household goods. Traders provided incentives for army commanders to capture or protect towns where they had shops and stores. Private fortunes were made on contracts for supplying the army. Military checkpoints levied taxes. Some commanders connived with SPLA sieges because they made profits from the high prices obtained by selling scarce goods to which they had exclusive access.

Meanwhile the Dinka themselves were left without political representation, exposed to 'raiding without redress and to famine without relief.'[8]

THE FAMINE IN SUDANESE POLITICS

Did the Sudan government set out to create famine in Southern Sudan, either with the intention of starving the SPLA into submission or depopulating the region for a take-over by northern ranchers and oilmen? This is probably not the right question to ask. Certainly *some* people within the government, army and militias had grandiose plans of this sort. A spirit of territorial expansionism probably motivated some militiamen; the idea of redrawing the internal frontier so as to include Bentiu in the North certainly figured in some political calculations; and the subsequent expansion of mechanised farming in Upper Nile and the Nuba Mountains indicates some of the commercial pressures behind the mass displacement. But there is no evidence that a deliberate programme of Southern genocide was pursued at the top of Sadiq el Mahdi's government. What is more likely is that the moral and political logic of the war as interpreted in Khartoum created a space where such near-genocidal motives and practices could flourish. The South was not only a war zone, it was a zone whose population had no political

---

[8] David Keen, 1994, p. 213.

clout either nationally and internationally, and it was increasingly an ethics free zone, where agents of the state could do exactly what they liked with impunity.

The abolition of restraint in the South did not happen automatically, and was refracted through complex local politics. Khartoum still had clients and allies in the South, whom it had to mollify and appease, and who had significant power bases in their own right. Displaced people came to the cities, and gained a little leverage through the electoral process. But in Khartoum politics, the famine was virtually invisible.

Failure of the Democratic Opposition

No anti-famine coalition emerged comparable to that of 1984-5. Some parliamentarians, churchmen and government officers took up the question of famine at various times, but it never became an issue of major concern in national politics. Bishop Paride Taban of Torit made many vocal appeals, and Bishop Joseph Nyekindi of Wau said, 'People are dying while looking at food. The market is the biggest gun in this war.'[9] A provincial governor described hunger as 'an atomic weapon'. Indigenous voluntary agencies made appeals. But all of these failed to generate any national political momentum. There were few Southern political leaders well-placed to take up the cause. Bahr el Ghazal and Upper Nile only returned sixteen MPs to parliament in 1986. The Union of Sudan African Parties (USAP), a coalition of Southern and Nuba parliamentarians, raised the issue publicly and in parliament. For example, in early 1988 they proposed a motion in parliament on the famine. The government response was that it was doing all it could to tackle the problem, by preparing relief barges and trains. In response to press conferences and newspaper articles (almost entirely in the Communist *al Meidan* and the Southern-oriented *Sudan Times*), the government repeatedly refused to answer questions or hold inquiries into famine and relief. It came out with reassuring but erroneous claims about dispatching relief, which were difficult to disprove.

---

[9] Quoted in the *Sudan Times*, 4 April 1989.

These obstacles were compounded by splits in the Southern leadership itself. Some Southern leaders opportunistically joined the government, and echoed the official line. Aldo Ajou, who comes from Aweil, the epicentre of the famine in northern Bahr el Ghazal, conspicuously failed to represent the interests of his people. He rose to become Deputy Prime Minister, and his support for the government over the famine proved a major obstacle to attempts to push for restraint on the militias or relief efforts.

The most important split was between the democratic opposition and the SPLA. The SPLA consistently betrayed the hopes of its potential allies in Khartoum by taking a hard line over famine and relief. In 1986, trade unions and some parliamentarians (including the small Southern representation) were seeking to form a strategic coalition with the SPLA, and were holding meetings to agree on common political demands. But instead the SPLA took the lead in blocking relief efforts, for example refusing to allow sixty relief lorries to travel freely to Juba in February, and threatening to shoot down relief flights to Wau in September. SPLA military strategy aimed at starving garrisons, and no concessions were made for the civilians who suffered as a result. The refusal of the SPLA to politicise the famine made it extremely difficult for the democratic forces to do so, while the SPLA's lead in obstructing relief allowed the government to claim the moral high ground—at this stage, it was permitting relief operations.

Another key reason why the Southern famine did not become politicised was that famine migrants did not emerge as a political scandal. Large numbers of famine displaced around Khartoum began to become an issue of concern to the government in 1987-8, which, as before, responded with proposals for forced removal. There was no opposition from the urban public; on the contrary, government plans met with a wide measure of popular support. The government line was that the displaced represented a security threat, a 'fifth column' of the SPLA. Although the removals were not implemented until several years later, the government did succeed in sowing political division between the displaced and the town dwellers. Most mainstream Arabic newspapers echoed the government's fears, or, in the case of the NIF papers, exaggerated them. Playing the card of 'security threat' worked.

At one moment it appeared that solidarity might emerge, when, following the August 1988 floods, there was criticism from all quarters over corruption and favouritism in the distribution of relief. Significantly, a wide spectrum of Sudanese were affected by this disaster, including politically-influential northern Arabs and Nubians. A USAP-sponsored motion on the floods and famine and relief attracted support. But just as protests were growing more vocal, the ruling coalition collapsed in a dispute over the issue of Sharia law, and the issue was taken no further.

The press never paid the famine much attention. During the parliamentary period, Sudan had a remarkably free press. Forty newspapers and journals were published more or less regularly, and expressed opinions with great freedom. Leader writers and cartoonists were often savagely critical of the government and the NIF, and political, commercial and sexual scandals were the daily fare of many. The war itself was covered as a political issue rather than a human one. There was no front-line journalism and few papers had correspondents with the troops. Partly this was through the difficulties and dangers of reporting from the South (one journalist was killed by a land mine in 1987), partly through restrictions on travel permits, and partly because the battlefront itself was of relatively little interest to the urban reading public. The government helped keep it that way. It was determined to keep Northern soldiers away from the front as much as possible, entrusting most of the fighting to militias and Southern units within the army. Between 1983 and 1988 less than 2,800 soldiers were killed, most of them Southern ex-Anyanya troops.

For similar reasons, the press gave virtually no coverage to the famine. In March 1986, Mike Kilongson, a Sudanese journalist who worked in Juba and who frequently provided material for the BBC filed reports on the developing famine. The Governor, Peter Cirillo, had repeatedly assured the press that there were no food shortages. Kilongson was immediately arrested and kept in prison in very poor conditions for two months.[10] Two Khartoum University lecturers, Ushari Mahmoud and Suleiman Baldo had a similar experience after publishing a report into the April 1986 massacre at ed Dai'en and the resurgence of slavery at the hands of the *Murahaliin*. After this, most journalists were deterred from any frank coverage of what was happening. Sadiq el Mahdi also issued a clear warning in a speech to parliament in June 1988, saying that 'elements in the Sudanese media, in co-operation with the foreign media, have been attempting to create an impression abroad that there is religious and racial conflict in the Sudan.'[11] Sadiq called for new regulations to control the press. They were never implemented: when the Minister of Information, Abdala Mohamed Ahmed, tried to impose very tight restrictions on reporting in the aftermath of the August 1988 Khartoum floods, he was forced to back down.

The most important constraint, however, was the solidarity and conformism of the mainstream newspapers, which catered for a reading public in Khartoum that was overwhelmingly concerned with the affairs of the capital, and who considered the war and famine, at worst, as embarrassing irritations. For example, when a train of some six thousand starving displaced Dinka arrived in Khartoum in April 1988, and six children died at the railway station, the only Khartoum paper to cover the incident was the *Sudan Times*. Even *al Meidan* did not report the story. Despite the fact that the famine had come to town, as the Kordofan migrants had in 1984, and no permits or dangers stood in the way of reporting, the Arabic language press, whether pro-government, independent or opposition, was simply not interested. Rural-urban solidarity never developed over the Southern famine, however briefly. Hence, remarkable government statements about the non-existence of the famine passed largely unchallenged in the mainstream press. In December 1988, the Minister for Relief and Refugees, Hassan Ali Shibu dismissed

---

[10] M. Griffin, 'The Case of Mike Kilongson', *Index on Censorship, 15.10,* 1986, p. 18.
[11] Quoted in: Moyiga Nduru, 'Reporting the Sudan,' *Index on Censorship, 18.1,* 1989, 11-14 at p. 13.

reports of famine deaths as a creation of the international media.[12] As late as March 1989, the official news agency reported that Dr Haj el Tayeb, head of the RRC, had 'dismissed as baseless reports about the existence of famine in the South.'[13]

Finally, Southern leaders concerned with the famine had no opportunity to make international allies. As detailed below, after a series of confrontations with the government in 1986, western donors and international agencies faithfully followed the government's lead. Only a handful of NGOs spoke out, but they too were fragmented and under pressure. The pro-famine coalition prevailed with the tacit support of the donors and the UN.

Domestic Accountability and the Urban Bread Subsidy

While the Khartoum government was oblivious to the deaths of Southerners, even in Khartoum central railway station, it was acutely sensitive to the demands of the northern urban constituency over food prices. The wheat subsidy was a political issue that the government was terrified to touch. The bread subsidy theoretically reached all consumers but in practice was confined to the 'planned' central areas of the main towns: it was economically regressive. It was also fiscally expensive: at a cost of $90-$100 million per annum it amounted to fully seven per cent of government revenue.[14] It rested on cheap sales of wheat from foreign donors, particularly USAID. In one form or another, the subsidy had existed since colonial times, and its partial removal at IMF insistence in March 1985 had contributed to the downfall of Nimeiri.

---

[12] Quoted in *The Guardian*, 7 December 1988.
[13] Sudan News Agency, quoted in BBC, *Summary of World Broadcasts*, ME/0419, 28 March 1989.
[14] Simon Maxwell, Jeremy Swift and Margaret Buchanan-Smith, 'Is Food Security Targeting Possible in Sub-Saharan Africa? Evidence from North Sudan,' *IDS Bulletin, 21.3*, July 1990; Suleiman A. Shugeiry, 'Wheat Subsidies in Sudan: Policy Implications and Fiscal Costs,' Washington D.C., International Food Policy Research Institute, Famine and Food Policy Discussion Paper No. 3, 1990.

Sudan's donors, notably the IMF, insisted that the subsidy should be cut or abolished. This was a prerequisite for making a firm deal with the IMF and hence with the main western donors. But Sadiq el Mahdi repeatedly stalled. In May 1987, the bread subsidy blocked the negotiation of an agreement with the IMF. In September, Sudan could only make a modest 'twelve month action plan' which involved cutting subsidies on sugar and fuel, but not bread. This was not enough to get the World Bank and other donors to disburse their frozen loans. Other measures that the government introduced on donor insistence included devaluation, spending cuts and the privatisation of nationalised corporations. But the bread subsidy was not removed. One donor representative explained, 'the current position may be 95 per cent of the way but the crucial five per cent is missing.'[15] This pushed the IMF to break off negotiations. When it resumed talks in April 1989, the bread subsidy again blocked progress.

The bread subsidy was perhaps the key factor in preventing Sadiq el Mahdi from achieving financial respectability in the eyes of the donors. It is arguable that the donors were politically insensitive to have insisted on this reform, but it is also remarkable how sensitive the government was to urban public opinion. Its accountability was such that it could not move 'the crucial five per cent' towards a key agreement with the donors.

The only conclusion that can be drawn from this is that the Sudan Government considered the Northern urban populace to be first class citizens, to whom it was answerable, whereas Southerners were second class citizens or not legitimate citizens at all, to whom it was not in the least accountable. Many Northern urban people appeared to agree. All the trappings of a liberal democracy counted for nothing in the face of such power relations.

---

[15] Quoted in: *Africa Economic Digest*, 14 August 1987.

THE POLITICS OF RELIEF

The basic elements of an effective wartime relief programme were established by March 1986, and have changed remarkably little over the eleven years since then. But by the end of 1986, the Sudan Government succeeded in subverting those principles and obtaining the acquiescence of the international community. A decade on, it is still playing essentially the same game.

CART and Principles of Neutrality

The Combined Agencies Relief Team (CART) in Juba was a model for impartial, accountable relief. It was established in March 1986, three years and many tens of thousands of lives before Operation Lifeline Sudan. CART grew out of a context of optimism: impending elections, the Koka Dam Agreement between the National Alliance (a coalition of democratic forces that included the Umma Party) and the SPLA, and a relief initiative by the UN. In February 1986, Winston Prattley, the UN Resident Representative in Sudan estimated that 960,000 people in Southern Sudan faced famine: 'I think a lot of people will certainly die' he said.[16] He appealed for a 'food truce' to allow relief to reach famine-affected civilians in the war zones. The appeal foundered on intransigence on both sides. Just two weeks later, Mike Kilongson was arrested for reporting on the food shortage. But there were hopes that the initiative could be revived. In the short term, it contributed to the creation of CART.

Several local and international agencies came together in Juba to agree to work as a consortium to meet the needs of poor and displaced people in Juba. They agreed that relief should be fully accounted for, and that it should be handled solely by civilian authorities, and transported without military escort. The latter was called the principle of 'neutrality': the architects of CART envisaged that although the immediate target population was entirely in

---

[16] *International Herald Tribune*, 28 February 1986.

government-held areas (and the SPLA was not in the vicinity of Juba at the time), cross-line access to SPLA-held areas was a future possibility. In the event no relief was provided to SPLA-held areas. One member of the consortium preferred the term 'integrity', saying that 'neutrality' implied dealing with both sides, in the manner of the ICRC.

At the time, CART appeared to be the model for how relief operations would develop across the South. The CART principles were taken on by the UN and the RRC in a meeting held on 25 June in Khartoum. A Technical Co-ordinating Committee (TCC) was set up to jointly co-ordinate relief operations throughout the South, and be a focal point for information, planning and agreement between the donors, the RRC and CART-type consortia. The government had signed on to the principles of neutrality, monitoring of relief and the de-militarisation of relief. At a TCC meeting on 29 July, a CART consortium for Wau was proposed and the details agreed. A coalition was emerging that included Southern-based organisations (primarily churches), liberal members of the RRC and civil service, and a few international NGOs (notably ACORD and Oxfam-UK). In the meantime, there were renewed calls for a 'food truce' in the South. A statement on 9 June was signed by a number of national and international NGOs, including CART members. In retrospect, a co-ordinated approach by relief agencies with strong donor backing could have set up an OLS-type programme at the time.

The Western donors were not ready for such an initiative. The U.S. Ambassador, Norman Anderson, has implied that he did not see the need: 'We all knew from 1983 on that the civil war was creating various states of famine, the surprise was only the degree.'[17] Anderson also argued that the U.S. had little 'leverage' over the Sudan government and could not press for humanitarian initiatives. The UN Under-Secretary General Abdulrahim Abby Farah later claimed that 'Politically the time was not ripe.'[18] Both the U.S. and

---

[17] Quoted in Larry Minear, *Humanitarianism under Siege: A Critical Review of Operation Lifeline Sudan*, New Jersey, Red Sea Press, 1991, p. 79.
[18] Quoted in Minear, 1991, p. 80.

the UN were simply covering up for their complete lack of action: the political opportunity had come and the donor leverage was there, but they chose not to use it.

Principles Abandoned

By the end of 1986, the key principles of CART were abandoned. The SPLA, the Sudan Government, the UN and the donors all played their role. The SPLA blocked relief initiatives, pushing the government to a hard line and providing the pretext that the pro-war interests had been seeking. The UN sought to set up Operation Rainbow, an international airlift to the South, but damaged it by inept handling: its leading proponents announced initiatives to the media before even informing the government. It was a humiliation to the government, and polarised the situation. CART was calling for equally radical measures but was politically more astute.

The Sudan Government then forced a confrontation with the relief agencies. Its first battle was with the UN. In October it not only prevented Operation Rainbow from proceeding (it flew just eleven times) but expelled Prattley himself. Under most circumstances the expulsion of the most senior UN representative in a country would have been considered a scandal. The donors did not protest. In fact it is possible that some of the donors privately welcomed the expulsion—the UN, EC and USAID were all competing for influence and programmes in Sudan. The contempt held by USAID for UN programmes was no secret, while the EC sought to exploit any opportunities opened by the government.

The expulsion of Prattley decisively gave the Sudan government the upper hand. The next stage was closing down the UN Emergency Office for Sudan (UNEOS) itself, on the grounds that the famine was over. The famine they referred to was of course the 1984/5 famine in western Sudan, rather than the developing famine in the South. Again, the donors did not object, and UNEOS began winding down and transferring its assets and responsibilities to the RRC.

The next battle was with the NGOs, and again the government won. At the final meeting of UNEOS, held in December 1986, a group of NGOs, Sudanese and international, presented an estimate that the relief food needs for the south for the first six months of 1987 amounted to 71,000 tonnes. Normal practice was for the RRC to endorse the figure, and use it as the basis of an appeal to the donors for food and resources to transport the food. On this occasion the RRC tried to discredit the figure, insisting that six thousand tonnes of relief food had been recently delivered to Juba,[19] and more was on its way to Juba and other famine-stricken areas. This was not true but served to undermine the agencies' contention that Juba was about to run out of food. Pretending that these fictional food deliveries were providing a 'breathing space', the RRC claimed that the South's need for relief would start in April at the earliest—four months after the relief agencies' estimate. The RRC also falsely said that a train of relief food was arriving in Wau.

At this time, the RRC also tried to set the precedent of consigning relief to military authorities, initially in Bahr el Ghazal. The EC complied promptly; it hired three trains for delivery of relief to the military governor of Wau (while it cut back on funding for CART). Bahr el Ghazal began to starve. Government promises of dispatching regular relief trains were not kept. In May 1987 the Minister of Transport, Fadallah Burma Nasir, promised to send three trains with 108 wagons of relief to Aweil each month. In fact, only nineteen wagons were sent between then and September; 600 tonnes of food consigned to Aweil was 'discovered' at Babanusa junction in Kordofan in September 1988, and no trains at all travelled between October 1987 and February 1988. In the following eleven months, relief was only 23% of three train loads sent.[20] Sending relief by road was no better: of 8800 tonnes despatched to Wau via Raja in April 1987, all but 131 tonnes never reached its destination, and all but 35 tonnes of the remainder was looted or destroyed in Raja.

The history of supplies by river to Malakal is a similar story of few and belated deliveries, containing little relief, followed by intense obstructions to relief distribution on arrival. In Juba, CART suffered in the crackdown. In November 1986 two expatriates working with CART were expelled. Without political backing from

---

[19] Technical Co-ordinating Committee, Khartoum, 15 December 1986.
[20] Keen, 1994, pp. 142-4.

donors (and regularly facing acute shortages of funds), CART had to take a much lower profile.[21] There were no more public calls for truces. As security deteriorated, the radius of operations contracted, and CART had to agree to having its food escorted by the military. (The later development of CART within the context of Juba will be examined in chapter 10.)

The donors abandoned the principles of neutrality and accountability. During 1987 and '88, each weekly TCC meeting consisted of a well-presented report from CART followed by obfuscation and lack of any solid monitoring from the military authorities in Bahr el Ghazal and Upper Nile. The implications of the donor surrender of December 1986 were evident on a week-by-week basis, but still the official line from the UN, USAID and the EC was that government claims were correct. Overall, Bahr el Ghazal received 2000 tonnes of relief in 1986, 4000 tonnes in 1987 and only 1300 tonnes in 1988.

In 1987/8, the 'Western Relief Operation' began to provide food for Darfur and Kordofan, which were once again stricken by drought. Only very small amounts were designated for the displaced people fleeing the Bahr el Ghazal famine, and most of this food never reached those for whom it was intended. Abyei—where thousands of Dinka displaced were crossing from Bahr el Ghazal— got the smallest allocations in 1987 and a zero allocation for 1988.

Not a single one of the main donors even considered providing relief to SPLA-held areas during 1987 and most of 1988. Finally, UNICEF opened a small 'co-ordinating office' in Nairobi to assist NGOs that were beginning small-scale operations in non-government held areas. But in a meeting on 3 October 1988, Dr Hussein Abu Salih, the Sudanese Foreign Minister objected to James Grant, Director of UNICEF, that this was a violation of Sudanese sovereignty—and Mr Grant replied that he had anticipated this objection and already closed down the operation. (Replying to a question from Grant about whether children were in need in the rural

---

[21] Richard Graham and John Borton, 'A Preliminary Review of the Combined Agencies' Relief Team (CART), Juba, 1986-91,' London, Overseas Development Institute, March 1992.

108

South, Dr Hussein mentioned 'since these problems have existed for months, either most of the children have moved or if they have not been able to move they must have unfortunately perished and therefore the aid may not really be used for them.'[22] Such statements were characteristic of the Sudan Government, just as Grant's docile acquiescence had characterised donor responses.) Only a few small NGO operations were mounted cross-border from Kenya, notably the efforts of Norwegian People's Aid, led by the buccaneering Egil Hagen. In 1987 the ICRC began slow, painstaking and fruitless attempts to gain air access to several places in the South. The ICRC efforts were obstructed by the government with complete impunity and the first aircraft flew only in December 1988.

FINANCING THE WAR

While the famine was developing, the government was engaged in prolonged and sensitive negotiations with other representatives of the same donors over official economic assistance, debt rescheduling and economic policy. Billions of dollars in debt, Sudan should have been very vulnerable to pressure from the donors. In important ways, the government's agenda was set by the IMF and the Paris Club, and this is the direction in which accountability flowed. Yet the relationship was far more complex than debtor-creditor might suggest.

The Sudanese Ministry of Finance had several assets. One was its supreme diplomatic skill that repeatedly charmed donors who might otherwise have remained sceptical. This skill was put to use dividing the donors against each other, and splitting the U.S. Treasury from the State Department—for example, hinting that hard-liners within the government were keen on closer ties with Libya if the U.S. did not play along with the financial technocrats. Cold War thinking still prevailed in Washington D.C. But the biggest asset was Sudan's very weakness: it could formally default on its debt to the IMF, becoming the first country to do so, and thus creating a

---

22 From UNICEF 'Note for the record' of the meeting.

precedent of 'moral hazard' for other much larger debtors, such as Mexico, whose formal default might rock the global commercial banking system.

In February 1986, Sudan was declared ineligible for IMF funds on account of its arrears to the Fund, which at that point stood at $220 million.[23] This should have spelled an end to any further IMF negotiations, debt rescheduling agreements, or Paris Club aid. It did not. International assistance continued at over $900 million per year, while Sudan actually paid only between five and twenty per cent of the almost $1 billion in debt service due each year. *I.e.* Sudan broke the rules but no penalties were enforced. In fact, the major donors went out of their way to find creative ways of continuing to do business with Sudan. The IMF invented a new form of agreement, for a 'shadow programme' of reforms, which had the Fund's implicit blessing and unlocked donor assistance just as if it had been a formal agreement. Meanwhile, the U.S. scheduled its assistance payments to slip through during the brief moments when Sudan was not ineligible under the Brooke Amendment, which mandates a halt to all U.S. non-emergency assistance to a country that is twelve months in arrears on repaying debts to the U.S.[24]

During the period 1986-9, the IMF needed Sudan almost as much as Sudan needed the IMF. The Fund needed to bring Sudan back from the brink; if possible it needed to get its money back and at the very least it needed to avert a formal default for as long as it took to rewrite its constitution so that countries like Sudan (and Liberia and Somalia) were no longer a threat to the 'grandmother' (its own term) of the international financial system. The game of keeping Sudan solvent needed great ingenuity on both sides: the Sudan government needed to display enough diplomacy and commitment to maintain the minimum of donor confidence. Financial and political decisions needed to be structured around the visits of IMF delegations and the timing of debt repayment schedules. As in 1983-

---

[23] The Fund's indifference to democratic credentials—the suspension was enforced two months before Sudan's first free elections for almost twenty years—should be a cause of concern among Sudanese democrats.
[24] *Africa Economic Digest*, 14 August 1987.

4, the machinations of the international financial system were the heartbeat of the Ministry of Finance, which was in turn the key to the political survival of the government.

By these means the donors were indirectly financing the war and famine. For the 1987/8 financial year, the Sudan government estimated its expenditure on 'security' to be $449 million and on the 'armed forces' $230 million.[25] The level was rising each year. The annual budget deficit amounted to about $600 million and the balance of payments deficit to $800 million. Official development assistance was about $950 million each year during 1986-8.[26] It was not difficult to come to the conclusion that foreign assistance was both financing the war and fiscal policies that were leading Sudan ever-deeper into economic crisis.

IMPLICATIONS

The Southern famine grew out of military strategies that reflected the interests of a political and commercial elite. It also reflected the disenfranchisement of Southerners within an ostensibly democratic state. It is one of the cruellest episodes in modern history.

David Keen has documented the extraordinary saga of the relief failures during this period.[27] He remarks on the donor strategies for justifying their inattention and inaction. Foremost among these was the consistent claim that famine victims were 'unreachable', without analysing how the (political) obstacles to reaching them could be overcome. A second problem was lack of attention to implementation of programmes once initiated; there was an assumption that unless hard evidence was received to the contrary, relief was reaching its target and doing what it was required to. Thirdly there was an unwillingness to address the conflict underlying the famine, and simply to treat symptoms rather than causes. It is interesting to note what has and has not changed. The 'right' of

[25] *Africa Economic Digest*, 26 June 1987.

[26] OECD, *Geographical Distribution of Financial Flows to Developing Countries*, Paris, OECD, various dates.

[27] Keen, 1994.

humanitarian access has been promoted (OLS was one of the pioneers); demands for monitoring have increased; but a reluctance to address the causes of crises has not changed.

Relief *failure* was part of the crisis, but subsequent relief 'success' did not resolve the crisis. In many ways, it compounded it. After 1989, humanitarian relief was to take over the role played by concessionary international finance in sustaining the war (albeit on a smaller scale), while it continued to assist the government in its headlong retreat from any form of democratic accountability.

6.

THE PEACE PROCESS AND THE CREATION OF O.L.S.

Two years after hopes were crushed in 1986, a coalition for relief in the South emerged again in 1988-89, associated with the peace process set in train by the 'November Accords' between the Democratic Unionist Party (DUP) and the SPLA. This coalition had important differences to the earlier peace-and-relief coalition: most importantly, its leading members were Sudanese political forces. Indigenous NGOs and a few international NGOs joined, though they were less confident and assertive than three years previously. The Netherlands was the principal donor to support the coalition; the U.S. and others joined slightly later, and the UN at the last moment. The peace process foundered with the 30 June 1989 coup in which Brigadier Omer al Bashir seized power on behalf of the NIF, severely weakening this relief coalition and changing the political complexion of relief activities.

This chapter looks at domestic and international political processes in Sudan in 1988-90 period, that led to the creation of Operation Lifeline Sudan (OLS) and its renewal—the period when the political character of the operation was determined.

THE MOMENTUM FOR OLS

The famine did not undermine the legitimacy of Sadiq's government at home, but ultimately it was to be devastating abroad. In September-October 1988, the famine simultaneously became world news and came onto the political agendas of the major donors.

The pressure had been building for some time. A group of NGOs led by Oxfam (UK) had been pressing the major donors in Khartoum. The inflow of displaced people from Bahr el Ghazal could no longer be ignored. The August floods in Khartoum attracted the international press, which, somewhat disappointed when the Nile did not break its banks, looked for and found greater disaster stories to the south. The famine had in fact been 'discovered' by the international media some months before. Deborah Scroggins of the *Atlanta Journal and Constitution* visited the area and covered the famine in a series of articles, and on 28 June 1988, the paper carried an editorial entitled 'Sudan hides its famine.' It was not press disclosure as such that spurred action.

At this stage the major donors still tried to pretend that the famine had no connection with the politics of the civil war. Charles LeMunière of UNDP visited Sudan to draw up a comprehensive plan for assistance to war-displaced. (The government's agenda was to minimise the threat and burden of these people, and if possible utilise them as cheap labour—see chapter 8.) Informed NGOs briefed LeMunière at length on the political, military, and human rights background to the famine. Yet the UN appeal document of October 1988 made no mention of the SPLA, nor of human rights.[1] This was a characteristic of western approaches to Sudan at the time—while domestic newspapers were carrying interviews with John Garang, foreign diplomats and aid workers avoided mentioning the SPLA at all. At the same time, the U.S. failed to make any public pronouncements that attached blame to the Sudan Government for causing the famine. The relief programmes that sprang from this policy of politically-naive humanitarianism quickly ran into insurmountable obstacles: the government appropriated the relief programmes for its own ends where possible, and obstructed the remainder.

The key to a more ambitious programme was political developments in Khartoum. In mid-1988 Sadiq el Mahdi achieved an aim for which he had been working for two years: the re-admission of the NIF to government. Hassan al Turabi was appointed Attorney General and drafted a revised version of Islamic Law. Sudanese politics polarised: any prospects for peace were dashed. Meanwhile

---

[1] United Nations, 'The Emergency Situation in Sudan, Urgent Humanitarian Requirements,' New York, October 1988.

114

the Umma-NIF alliance was marginalising the DUP, hitherto the main partner in government, and its patrons in Egypt. The DUP sought to make an opening towards the middle ground of northern Sudanese politics, by resisting the increasingly hard line taken by the Umma and NIF. Leading DUP members worked closely with the 'peace coalition' of trade unions and USAP. This coincided with an increasing awareness in the army that the war was unwinnable by conventional military means.

The Foreign Minister, a leading member of the DUP and a close protégé of Egypt, Sid Ahmed el Hussein, opened negotiations with the SPLA. Relief aid was one of the items tabled by the SPLA. The DUP, however, was reluctant to award it prominence: it feared that a re-run of Operation Rainbow would lead to an abrogation of Sudanese sovereignty. Meanwhile, the SPLA was itself under pressure from the Ethiopian government, which had the same concerns about sovereignty, reflecting its own war in Eritrea and Tigray. Hence the negotiations dealt almost exclusively with constitutional matters. These culminated in an agreement signed in Addis Ababa on 16 November, covering the main points of political disagreement. This was a major breakthrough—the most definite moves towards peace since early 1986. It transformed the political atmosphere in Sudan. The Accords were immensely popular—and it immediately became clear that the DUP stood to reap large rewards in the anticipated general elections.

The press conference that followed the Accords included an appeal for relief to all civilians in the South, the minimum that the signatories could agree upon:

> The two parties call upon the Sudanese nation and the international community to extend emergency relief to help save the lives of millions of people threatened with famine and disease in the Sudan.[2]

Some initiatives followed immediately. Within days, the Lutheran World Federation began flying aid to Juba and USAID started an

---

2 BBC, *Summary of World Broadcasts*, ME/0314, 21 November 1988.

airlift to Aweil, and within weeks the ICRC obtained agreement for an airlift to both government and SPLA-controlled areas .

Sadiq el Mahdi spent the next four months trying to undermine or derail the November Accords, in the hope of keeping the NIF in government and maintaining his own supremacy. But Sadiq's political manoeuvring helped to consolidate an alliance against him and a popular sentiment for peace.

The same NGO coalition for relief that had so nearly achieved a breakthrough in 1986 was instrumental in pushing the donors to review their policies in 1988. By August 1988, the consequences of the appeasement policies followed by the donors since late-1986 had become so gross that they could no longer be ignored. Persistent activism by Mark Duffield, country director of Oxfam, supported by SCF-UK and (intermittently) MSF-France, finally began to yield results. The major western donors in Khartoum agreed to regular meetings to monitor relief programmes. As accounts of blockage and diversion were received on a week-to-week basis, at last the ambassadors began to appreciate that their rosy assumptions that relief would reach its destination were completely unfounded. Attitudes began to shift.

After the November Accords, as the political space opened up again, the NGO coalition could have widened to include more international and national NGOs, as it had done in 1986. A genuine alliance for humanitarian relief could have become established. Unfortunately, just as the NGO activism bore fruit, this coalition fell apart. It had been sustained by the determination of just a few individuals, notably Mark Duffield, who left Sudan in late-1988 and early 1989. Their replacements were not only new to the country but also took a much more politically quiescent line, reflecting a wider conservative shift in NGO politics. The donors now took the lead.

After November, the mounting frustrations of the donors now had a point of leverage in what had hitherto been a united front among the northern parties on the issues of war and famine. Donors who had been extraordinarily anxious to avoid any confrontation with the government now no longer had any excuse for avoiding the issue. Two prominent Americans, Julia Taft of the Office for Foreign Disaster Assistance (OFDA), and Congressman Mickey Leland,

116

travelled to Sudan and became personally involved in the twin causes of peace and famine relief. OFDA initiated a review of U.S. relief policy towards Sudan, which reached fruition at the time of the inauguration of George Bush as President.

Disillusion with the Sadiq regime deepened with his resistance to the SPLA-DUP peace accords, overtures to Libya and the continuing refusal to come to an agreement with the IMF. In the December 1988 meeting of the Paris Club, the Netherlands insisted on action to end the war as a precondition for more economic assistance to the government. A momentum began to gather. The biggest failing of this coalition was its remoteness from the intricacies of Sudanese politics and the realities of famine, so that the weapons that were used were blunt, and the expectations of rapid change unrealistic. The question was whether the peace process would yield results faster than the disillusion of the donors could undermine them.

In January 1989, the incoming U.S. Administration spoke about the possibility of cross-border operations to SPLA-held areas, made public with a demand by the new Secretary of State James Baker that the government of Sudan should allow relief to go to all needy people. Meanwhile, the U.S. brought economic pressure to bear by suspending concessionary food sales to Khartoum. The lack of media interest, relative to comparable disasters elsewhere in Africa, undoubtedly facilitated the vigorous U.S. action. The U.S. was 'playing politics with food' and would have been pilloried in the media if Sudan had been under closer scrutiny. Indeed Turabi accused the U.S. of the politics of starvation.

Western—particularly U.S.—pressure had other goals than peace and facilitating relief. James Baker had just moved from the Treasury, where he had been frustrated at Sudan's unwillingness to agree to IMF conditions—economic reform was high on the agenda. A change in relations with Libya was another U.S. priority. Having been enthusiastic supporters of 'Africa's newest democracy' a year or so previously, the U.S. now began to hint at its support for a military government. A lengthy article by two of the best-informed U.S. journalists fleshed out the evidence:[3]

> [S]ome U.S. officials have begun speculating that a military coup in Sudan might be preferable to its current parliamentary government, which helped cause southern Sudan's deadly famine and continues to obstruct relief.
>
> 'We favor democracy over dictatorship,' said a senior U.S. diplomat. 'We can't be in a position of seeking an undemocratic government there. On the other hand, we have to treat the government on its merits, and its performance on the humanitarian tragedy has not been satisfactory.'
>
> Three U.S. diplomats who have had frequent dealings with Sudan have suggested to The Atlanta Journal and Constitution in recent weeks that—although they have not abandoned all hope for the government of Prime Minister Sadek Mahdi—they wonder if a transitional government under a military officer friendly to the West might be preferable.

The article continued, 'A military name sometimes mentioned these days in the State Department and in Congress is that of Gen. Abdel Magid Hamid Khalil, the defense minister.' This level of clumsiness helped to prevent the pro-peace and pro-relief elements in western policy from succeeding.

Sadiq el Mahdi's attempts to derail the peace process with NIF support collapsed in February. After parliament voted to reject the November Accords in December, the DUP withdrew from the government and formed a strong opposition bloc with the peace coalition (consisting of USAP and the Sudan Communist Party, and supported by extra-parliamentary groups such as the trade unions and the Union of the Northern and Southern Funj). Sadiq formed a new government with the NIF as his chief partners on 1 February. A week later, the DUP and the peace coalition met with the SPLA in Ambo, Ethiopia, and issued a joint communiqué detailing a wide-ranging plan for dealing with the constitutional, human rights,

---

[3] Colin Campbell and Deborah Scroggins, 'Officials: U.S. May Welcome Coup in Sudan; Military Rulers Might Improve Famine Relief,' *Atlanta Journal and Constitution*, 27 January 1989.

security and economic problems of Sudan. At the end of the month, a Memorandum from the office of the army chief of staff, saying that the war could not be won, undermined the hard-line stand of the government. Soldiers do not call for peace, but the manner in which the Memorandum—signed by an unprecedented number of army officers—put forward its demands made the army's position quite clear. It was a devastating blow to the hard-line military pretensions of the government. On 11 March, the government resigned. Four days later, parliament accepted the November Accords, and on 25 March a new government was sworn in, including the DUP and the peace coalition, and excluding the NIF.

When international pressure was added to the domestic process, it brought immediate results for the prospects of relief. On 8-9 March, a conference was convened in Khartoum and the government and the UN agreed to the principle of an ambitious relief programme.

The SPLA Position

The SPLA had most to gain from a relief programme that was to become OLS. But obtaining agreement was not straightforward. The SPLA leadership was still closely influenced by the Mengistu government in Ethiopia, which in February 1989 was fighting for its life. The TPLF had just captured the entire province of Tigray, leaving only one government outpost, and the Ethiopian air force was busy bombing cross-border relief convoys coming from Sudan. President Mengistu was absolutely intransigent on the principle of sovereignty and respect for international frontiers, and imparted the same attitude to Colonel Garang, reputedly telling the SPLA leader that he had to choose between the UN and him. Mengistu was also determined that the SPLA would not cease fighting at this critical juncture.

However, the SPLA had its own clear political and material interests in a UN-led relief operation. At the time of the 1985 Popular Uprising, the SPLA did not control any towns and had recently suffered its first significant military reverses, when the regular Sudanese army was deployed against it for the first time.

Hence it was in a weak negotiating position with the TMC. In 1989, Garang was determined to be in a far stronger position. Therefore, while the peace talks progressed in Ethiopia, the SPLA launched its largest offensive to date, and captured a string of towns including Kapoeta, Torit, Bor and Nasir. The SPLA New Kush Division also entered the Nuba Mountains and attacked close to Kadugli. For the first time, the SPLA was controlling recognised towns—and names on the map. The towns needed to be fed, and relief was the obvious way. After the capture of Kapoeta, the international agencies World Vision and Norwegian People's Aid rapidly provided assistance, some of it funded by USAID. At this time, the term 'New Sudan' was first used,[4] and John Garang spoke about forming an alternative government as soon as the SPLA captured all the territory east of the Nile and south of Malakal. His agenda was primarily to gain wider political recognition and help set the pace of national political events: he intended an alternative *national* government rather than an alternative local administration.

Never before in its history had the UN dealt directly with what would previously have been called a 'non-recognised entity' fighting against an independent African state. UN relief agencies had refused point blank to deal with the Biafran secessionists, the EPLF and TPLF, or similar rebel organisations.[5] For the UN to extend *de facto* political recognition to the SPLA was a political coup.

When the Khartoum Conference on relief convened, John Garang sent a message that he would co-operate, and invited the UN to meet with him at a location outside Sudan. But he was adamantly opposed to a ceasefire. He authorised Cdr. Lam Akol, head of both foreign relations and the Committee for Organising Production and Services, then in Addis Ababa, to negotiate on his behalf. On 9 March, the head of UNICEF and UN Special Representative for

---

[4] SPLM/SPLA Department of Information, 'On the New Sudan', February 1989.

[5] The UN had dealt with anti-colonial organisations and fronts such as SWAPO and the PLO, but had never provided them with relief resources, and had never recognised an insurgent fighting against a recognised independent African state.

120

Sudan, James Grant flew to Addis Ababa and met with Lam Akol. Grant came with a proposal for a six month ceasefire. Lam Akol rejected this and instead proposed 'corridors of tranquillity' down which relief could move. Grant accepted, and on 1 April, OLS started. There was no written agreement: rather a series of verbal commitments, and a pace of events that caught up the participants.

At the end of April, before flying to West Germany to address parliamentarians there, Garang announced a unilateral one-month ceasefire to begin on 1 May. This was a reversal of his previous position and came as a surprise to many (it called a sudden halt to a long-planned SPLA assault on New Fanjak, the last government outpost on the East Bank of the Nile south of Malakal). The Nuba Mountains were excluded from the relief programme and the ceasefire.

Garang's new-found enthusiasm for relief in part reflected his much enhanced status in the eyes of the west. But western concern with Sudan was limited. The Paris Club and Washington financial institutions gave no leeway to the Sudan Government on economic matters. The IMF and U.S. Treasury insisted on a tough line, and broke off talks in April without an agreement or further assistance. The economic situation worsened in Khartoum. Sadiq and the hard-liners within the Umma Party also remained conspicuously reluctant about the peace process, and equally overt about their continuing preoccupation with increasing the government's military capacity. Military spending was rising fast. In May, the Defence Council discussed the controversial proposal to legitimise militias in western Sudan under the Popular Defence Forces (PDF), and then withdrew the proposal in the face of parliamentary opposition. (Sadiq had introduced the PDF plan in March to circumvent the army's insistence in its February Memorandum that it would not tolerate irregular militias—so the Prime Minister proposed to regularise them.)

On 30 June, the day before the National Assembly was due to suspend Islamic law and four days before Sadiq el Mahdi was due to meet with John Garang, the government was overthrown in a military coup.

THE CHANGING INTERNATIONAL CONTEXT

Developments in the humanitarian international made the idea of OLS timely. The late-1980s were simultaneously a time of growing crisis in many parts of Africa and heightened ambition among international relief agencies to develop new tools for tackling these crises.

The concept of 'complex emergency' first emerged in Mozambique, reflecting the fact that the disasters in which relief agencies were being required to intervene were growing more complicated and intractable. Instead of a natural disaster such as drought or flood, the typical famine of the late-1980s was closely bound up with war, civil unrest or gross abuse of human rights. One particular obstacle was that nation-state sovereignty stood in the way of providing relief to the large numbers of famine-affected people beyond the reach of governments embroiled in civil wars. This was a particularly acute problem in Ethiopia, where the majority of those stricken by famine could not be reached from the government side, but the government was absolutely immovable on the question of sovereignty. This problem hobbled all agencies, but especially the official ones. The official system was increasingly unable to cope, and looked slow and inefficient compared to the NGO network, which obtained a consistently good press.

The NGOs often believed the praise that was heaped upon them. Since Biafra, generation of NGO aid workers had grown up believing that the main constraint on effective relief was the realpolitik of the superpowers (most strikingly manifest in the supremacy of state sovereignty) and the bureaucratic inertia of official agencies. It now appeared that these constraints were falling away and the benevolent instincts of NGO relief workers could be unleashed. In fact, a rather different set of developments were undermining this possibility. A crucial development was the use of aid as a strategic alibi by donors. After BandAid in 1984, western governments recognised that NGOs had the capacity to cause them domestic political embarrassment, and it became important to manage the public relations aspects of overseas emergency aid. This entailed supporting NGOs, or more specifically, being seen to support visible NGOs. Humanitarian action became more focused on the symptoms of crises and more averse to evaluation. Rather than crisis prevention or resolution, the main thrust of humanitarian policy has been crisis management, which entails containment.

The institutional response at the UN was inept. It proceeded as though the clubby world of the 1960s and '70s still existed, except that a greater concentration of humanitarian power was needed (located, or course, at the UN). Reforms concentrated on organisational proliferation and regulation, culminating in the creation of the Department of Humanitarian Affairs (DHA) in 1992. The head of this, the UN Under-Secretary General for Humanitarian Affairs, variously known as the 'humanitarian supremo' and 'humanitarian Czar', had wider powers than any other international humanitarian official. But DHA too failed to impose any greater order or professionalism, notably so in the first two major crises with which it was confronted: Somalia and Bosnia.

Meanwhile, the deregulation of humanitarianism proceeded much further than in the early 1980s. This had several important consequences. One was the abandonment of legal principle as a determinant of relief action. The Geneva Conventions lay onerous responsibilities on humanitarian organisations to ensure that their operations are neutral and impartial. The ICRC was loyal to these principles to a fault until the early 1990s, being famously discreet about its operations. Since the entry of a range of less legally scrupulous organisations into war-famines, legal principle has been eroded. Meanwhile, UN Security Council resolutions have significantly rewritten the articles in the Geneva Conventions that deal with humanitarian relief, in effect bestowing new legal privileges on relief workers and implicitly lessening their own legal obligations.

A second, related consequence was the deregulation of mandates: agencies became more ready to range beyond their core areas of providing material relief into issues such as human rights, conflict resolution and the like.

Thirdly, the era of deregulation saw a decline in inter-agency collaboration, and notably the demise of agency consortia. It became more important for NGOs and UN agencies to promote their individual 'brand names' through individual profile, at the expense of submerging identities in collaborative ventures, how ever more effective the latter might prove.

The OLS Model

Operation Lifeline Sudan was initiated at the crucial point where the humanitarian international began to free itself from the shackles of the Cold War, and was beginning to gain the confidence to try and set the agenda. OLS was the first-ever official programme in which a government conceded the right of relief agencies to provide relief to civilians in rebel-held areas. Sovereignty was breached. It pioneered the concept of negotiated access, which was later used (less successfully) in Angola, Ethiopia and Bosnia. One of the main attractions of OLS to James Grant and others was precisely that it set this important precedent.

The OLS model of 'negotiated access' represents the fusion of two approaches to disaster relief. One is the non-political natural disaster model, which assumes that civilians are innocent victims and that the governing authorities (government or rebels) are anxious to see them assisted. The second approach is the diplomatic and neutral humanitarianism of the ICRC. This is based on a similar assumption that the belligerents will fulfil their obligations under the Geneva Conventions to respect civilians and facilitate assistance.

The date of the launch of OLS is crucial to its character. A few years earlier, the donors would not have been ready to support an initiative that appeared to undermine the concept of sovereignty. A few years later, the deregulation of the industry would have proceeded to the extent that it would have been impossible to exercise the formal control over NGO activities that exists in OLS. The price of allowing the formal breach of sovereignty was a reversion to a more tightly regulated humanitarianism. The UN took the lead role in this regulation, with the Sudan Government closely scrutinising it. That regulatory framework has survived, and is the source of some of the important strengths and weaknesses of the operation.

OLS has not been subject to the rapid deregulation that has occurred elsewhere in the humanitarian business (for example Somalia and Rwanda). International NGOs can work independently of OLS in SPLA-held areas, but the costs are so high that few of them actually do so. In some respects, therefore, OLS is redolent of an earlier era of humanitarian action. In some respects it is like an agency consortium, with cooperation partly enforced and partly ensured by complementary interests. The leading role of the UN also means that legal principle has not been jettisoned, and the Geneva Conventions and the Rights of the Child can be brought into the humanitarian sphere. UNICEF's programme of 'humanitarian principles' in Southern Sudan would have been unthinkable in recent deregulated humanitarian emergencies such as Somalia and Rwanda.

But OLS and its affiliated NGOs still have to compete for humanitarian funds from western governments and publics, and work within the general context of contemporary humanitarianism. Systemic weaknesses have become more and more apparent. Both government and SPLA have exacted another price for permitting the programme to continue, by manipulating the programme to serve their strategic ends, and diverting aid resources to feed their soldiers. As the years have passed, OLS (along with other humanitarian activities in the war zones) have become closely integrated into the conflict itself.

DID OLS WORK?

Two major claims are made for OLS in 1989. One is that it halted the Southern famine, the other that it supported the peace process. According to Vincent O'Reilly of UNICEF, 'We've averted a repeat of the famine. . . . Yet Lifeline was not about the relief commodities moved but about peace, almost an accidental by-product.'[6] Both claims must be investigated more carefully.

---

[6] Quoted in Larry Minear, *Humanitarianism under Siege: A Critical Review of Operation Lifeline Sudan*, Trenton, N.J., Red Sea Press, 1991, p. 63.

There are two reasons why OLS cannot be credited with relieving the famine of 1988. One, it was largely over by the time that the operation began and two, the worst-hit areas received relatively little food. Of the 94,500 metric tonnes of food provided by OLS by the end of August 1989, a mere 17,700 tonnes had gone to Bahr el Ghazal (about two thirds of it to government-held areas). Equatoria received the single largest share of OLS supplies at 37,000 tonnes (again about two thirds to the government-held areas) and Kordofan was second with 22,500 tonnes.[7] One of the ironies of the operation was that the people whose suffering prompted the international outcry—the rural Dinka of northern Bahr el Ghazal—remained entirely cut off from assistance until early 1992, when SCF-UK sent a convoy, nearly a year in advance of the first OLS assistance.

In addition, the amounts of relief delivered were simply not enough to have prevented a slide towards famine, should the causes of severe famine have recurred. The first OLS evaluation came to this conclusion:

> By the time Operation Lifeline Sudan got underway in 1989, those who had survived the previous year were attempting to revive their local economies by relying on traditional networks of support and mutual assistance. In 1990 we found that most people were still recovering from the devastation experienced in 1988, and they were relying on their own networks of kinship and exchange.[8]

The ceasefire that was maintained from May until October 1989 (with the exception of the Nuba Mountains, where fighting was uninterrupted) was probably at least as important in material terms as any relief provided. There was no descent into comparable famine in 1989, because militia raiding into northern Bahr el Ghazal had

---

[7] Operation Lifeline Sudan, Situation Report No. 6, 14 September 1989, p. 18.
[8] United Nations/Operation Lifeline Sudan, 'An Investigation into Production Capability in the Rural Southern Sudan: A Report on Food Sources and Needs,' Nairobi, UNICEF, 1990, p. 5.

ceased and because sieges of garrison towns had been lifted or the towns themselves had fallen to the SPLA.

In 1989, according to official (UN) statistics, OLS cost between $200 and $300 million (depending on whether NGO initiatives are included) and moved just over 100,000 tonnes of food. This compares with expenditure of over $1 billion in 1984/5, when USAID alone provided 255,000 tonnes of food for Kordofan and Darfur. Between 1986 and 1990 the SPLA-controlled refugee camps in Gambela received over 50,000 tonnes of food aid per year; more than OLS provided to SPLA-held areas in the South.

OLS and the Peace Process

The parallel tracks of relief initiatives and the peace process in early 1989 seemed to indicate that OLS was accelerating the momentum towards peace. Vincent O'Reilly said explicitly that 'Lifeline was about peace.'[9] Humanitarian advocates hailed the agreement as a model for how relief could herald peace. Indeed, in a number of specific ways the relief negotiations speeded up the peace process. The demands for relief were instrumental in the SPLA ceasefire initiative. Lam Akol referred to OLS as the 'catalyst' for the ceasefire,[10] and the relief negotiations were undoubtedly important in breaking the SPLA's diplomatic isolation and dependence upon Ethiopia.

Meanwhile the peace process expedited relief. The limitation of hostilities made relief possible and allowed civilians to cultivate, herd cattle, trade and carry out other essential activities. At the time, with the expectation of an imminent end to the war, neither side had a strong motive for abusing relief for strategic military advantage. This did not prevent obstruction and diversion carried out by officers and government officials for a variety of motives, but the wholesale subversion of the entire operation did not occur.

The OLS initiative did not address the fundamental causes of the war. The basic political and economic problems remained. Some of

---

9 Quoted in Minear, 1991, p. 63.
10 Quoted in Minear, 1991, p. 130.

these were addressed in the peace negotiations. Others were not: notably the issues of land ownership and the continued political dominance of the pro-famine coalition in the North. The economic and political interests of some members of this coalition continued to subvert relief, notably along the railway line to Aweil and over the despatch of relief barges to Malakal.

During the 1984-5 famine, relief (initially) supported the democracy process by providing tactical allies for democratic activists in their struggle. Later, relief helped to depoliticise the famine. Comparable processes were at work in 1988-89. The international agencies helped boost the confidence of the peace movement in the early stages. But OLS then cut itself off from a domestic political base and depoliticised the famine: it became a technical and diplomatic exercise. There was a rationale for this UN strategy. The 1986-9 famine in Southern Sudan was arguably the most purely political famine in modern Africa. Despite the opening of a middle ground through the post-November peace process, there was still deep polarisation and mutual distrust between the belligerents. For the UN, it followed that the quickest way to overcome political sensitivities was to depoliticise the issue and involve domestic interest groups to the minimum. Taking such a stand was arguably the only way in which the UN agencies—constitutionally committed to a stand of neutrality—could enter such a political arena. As in so many decisions taken by international humanitarians, it was perfectly reasonable given their outlook and constraints.

Famine victims themselves were not consulted. This is unsurprising, given how humanitarian organisations operate. Sudanese NGOs were provided with only a minor role. This was perhaps more surprising, given their activism in the mid-1980s, but again is understandable within the context of UN modalities. There was no formal connection with the peace process or respect for human rights: the overwhelming concern remained purely access to Southerners. Within the context of an imminent peace treaty, these shortcuts were understandable, but in the event of renewed war they were missed opportunities.

OLS II

The successes of OLS in 1989 were largely due to its political context. When that context changed, with the NIF seizure of power and the return to war, OLS took on a different character. It became integrated with the political dynamics of war rather than peace. Problems with the model of negotiated access became increasingly apparent as OLS was renegotiated during 1990, twice coming to the point of collapse.

The success of negotiated access is predicated on the goodwill of the parties; their readiness to discharge obligations under international law. It becomes problematic when government and/or rebels are themselves creating famine, either deliberately as part of a military strategy, or for other reasons. In this case—which is in fact the norm—governments or rebels begin to try to extract military and political advantage from the access agreement. This is exactly what happened in Sudan. As relief became separated from the peace process, it led to different strategic calculations by the parties.

The original OLS agreement had a number of weaknesses, including the absence of a detailed memorandum of understanding. These would have mattered less if it had been, as initially envisaged, a strictly time-limited operation. But as the formal closure date of 31 October approached, and the need for a continued operation became apparent, these weaknesses became more problematic. No long-term plans were made. James Grant, the director of UNICEF who had headed OLS at its inception, handed over to Michael Priestley, the newly-appointed Special Representative of the UN Secretary General. Mr Priestley came to Sudan with a reputation for having been extremely compliant with government wishes in Ethiopia, and did nothing to sully his record while in Khartoum.

While in principle agreeing to the continuation of OLS, the government put it under severe pressure. On 2 November it closed its airspace to relief flights, and then sent bombing missions against relief centres, including Yirol, where the ICRC was operating. The

RRC was brought under tighter central government control. Government spokesmen made several accusations that OLS was smuggling arms, ammunition and spare parts to the SPLA. On 26 December, the Government announced that OLS would restart under government control.

There was intense fighting in the South, especially around Juba, in early 1990, and vigorous negotiations to restart the relief programmes. In a donor consultation on 26 April the Sudan Government formally agreed to the principle of neutrality as a means of restarting the operation largely under its control. The SPLA never actually signed the OLS II agreement, disputing the quantities that it awarded to the two sides. But it agreed in principle, and the operation restarted.

The SPLA leadership had by this time recognised the advantages of OLS. Lam Akol, now bestowed with the ad hoc title 'Head of Task Force on Relief', pushed for OLS to continue, even in the absence of a formal agreement—a decision the SPLA was later to regret. Other senior SPLA figures were determined to achieve more, and when Cdr Salva Kiir took over as Head of Task Force on Relief in August 1990, the SPLA took a harder line.

With the relaunch of OLS, the price of the Sudan Government's 1989 concession on sovereignty was now exacted: tighter regulation of the programme. According to Roger Winter of the U.S. Committee for Refugees, the new OLS framework appeared to amount to 'a paper chain of legalism which seeks to [establish government control of] OLS operations in the SPLM section.'[11]

The UN first asserted its dominant role in May-June, when Michael Priestley instructed MSF-Holland that its programme in Leer, Upper Nile, was 'illegal' and a threat to the whole of OLS. Somebody passed the MSF-H flight schedules to the Sudan Government, putting the programme in serious physical danger. Priestley accused MSF-H of 'transporting more than relief

---

[11] Quoted in letter from Roger Winter to Secretary of State Herman Cohen, 10 September 1990.

supplies.'[12] The SPLA quickly accused OLS of having lost its neutrality.

The government still saw OLS as a temporary arrangement that it would undo as soon as possible. In September, it made renewed threats against OLS, saying that it would be officially closed in October. In the last week of September there were two air raids on Bor and three on Leer, in which 23 people were killed and many wounded. Both towns were relief centres used by the ICRC and OLS.

In the end what saved OLS was the Sudan Government's desperate need for food to feed the Northern cities in the famine that struck in August 1990.

---

[12] *Ibid.*

7.

THE N.I.F. AND THE 1990-91 FAMINE

We will never accept any food aid, even if famine is declared.

Sudan Government statement, October 1990.[1]

The famine of 1990-91 in Northern Sudan is an event of great political importance as well as human tragedy. What began as a disaster for the NIF government, with many echoes of Nimeiri's famine and the potential of shaking the regime to its foundations, was transformed into an opportunity for the NIF. The ruling party entrenched itself in power, by monopolising the commodity vital for life, food. It was able to ensure that, in the long run, its favoured constituencies escaped the impact of the famine, while disfavoured groups bore the brunt. The famine forced the NIF into some compromises with the international donors, notably in allowing the continuation of OLS, but also led it into a successful strategy of co-opting the UN into its comprehensive plan for transforming Sudan.

OUTLINE OF THE 1990-91 FAMINE

The 1990-91 famine was unprecedented in independent Sudan in that it affected the central regions, including the towns, as well as rural areas in the east and west, not to mention the South.

There was drought in the western regions in 1989 and a poor national harvest.[2] Regional governments appealed for food relief, but Khartoum reduced the figures and the donors were complacent. For

---

[1] Col. Salah el Din Karrar, Chairman of the Economic Affairs Committee, quoted by Associated Press, 29 October 1990.
[2] Africa Watch, 'Nationwide Famine,' *News from Africa Watch*, November 1990.

132

example, Darfur had asked for 66,000 tonnes; the WFP assessed the needs at 3500 tonnes; the EC promised to cover this amount, but transported only 1000 tonnes and distributed none at all. The Islamic Development Bank, the government's chosen alternative for relief distributions, provided only 506 tonnes.

Overall, both government and donors were gambling that an adequate harvest in 1990 and villagers' reliance on coping strategies would be enough to avert disaster. As with Nimeiri in 1983/4, this did not pay off. Both government and agencies had failed to learn the lessons of the 1980s. The drought intensified and spread in 1990. The harvest shortfall in Darfur was estimated at eighty per cent, with a food deficit of 144,000 tonnes. The familiar market symptoms of high grain prices and a collapse in livestock prices were evident. The situation in Kordofan was even worse, but most serious of all was severe drought in the Eastern Region, where rainfall was about half of the long-term average.

In August 1990, the famine suddenly widened to the central regions and Khartoum. The vulnerability of these regions to famine was an outcome of the disruptions of the 1980s which had brought very large numbers of migrants to these areas. A food security study in 1988 found that the highest concentration of 'food insecure' people (1.32 million) was in and around Khartoum, with very large numbers of 'poor and vulnerable' in Gezira.[3] Some of the highest rates of malnutrition (16.1%) were found in Khartoum region.[4] The vulnerable people are a class that includes agricultural labourers, casual workers, low-level government employees, domestic servants and petty traders. Many of them are in female-headed households and many are squatters or displaced. These people do not own land on which to grow their own food and do not own assets such as animals, and are almost wholly reliant on food bought in the market.

---

[3] Simon Maxwell, 'Food Insecurity in North Sudan,' Institute of Development Studies, Sussex, Discussion Paper No 262, June 1989, Appendix 4.
[4] Sudan Emergency and Recovery Information and Surveillance System report 1987, cited in Maxwell, 1989, pp. 26-9.

The existence of such a large vulnerable class is unprecedented in Sudan's history, and extremely unusual in Africa.

There was an extremely sharp increase in food prices in July-September 1990. In Gedaref, the price of a 90 kg sack of sorghum rose by a factor of fifteen, from LS 80, in twelve months from mid-1989.

Grain prices in Gedaref during 1990 (in LS)[5]									
Jan	Feb	Mar	Apr	May	Jun	Jul	Aug	Sept	Oct
168	217	229	242	280	330	429	750	1300	1350

In Khartoum, prices were about fifty per cent higher, and in August and September 1990 frequently no grain was available in the market at all. The grain price hyper-inflation was totally without precedent, far more extreme than the 1984/5 famine, and comparable shortages in Khartoum markets had not been known since the great famine of 1888-92. Wage rates fell far behind the cost of basic provisions. For example, farm labourers who were fortunate enough to find work were earning about LS20 per day, enough to buy between one and 1.4 kg of sorghum per day, barely enough to buy sorghum for a family of four without any other expenditure at all. Prices fell back slightly at the end of 1990 but rose again in the first half of 1991.[6]

The reason for these extraordinary rises was panic. When President Omer al Bashir announced his support for the Iraqi invasion of Kuwait, Sudanese feared that remittances from the Gulf states and US food deliveries would be halted. Those with money rushed to convert it into food. In effect, middle class people and traders bought up all the available food on the market, laying in stocks against the feared disaster. This panic-driven spiral then developed a momentum of its own, with speculators and others joining in the buying spree, and in effect inflating the price of grain

---

[5] Source: RRC *Early Warning System Bulletins,* various 1990.
[6] Maresh Patel, 'An Examination of the 1990-91 Famine in Sudan,' *Disasters, 18,* 1994, 313-31.

beyond what 'natural' market forces alone would have created. For those who depended on buying grain on a day-to-day basis, the result was immediate hunger.

A well-managed national food policy could have prevented this spiral by releasing grain onto the market. But the government had exported the reserves. After the 1984 famine, stringent controls on food exports had been introduced, regulated by the Agricultural Bank of Sudan (ABS). In March 1990 the NIF reversed this. Leading cadres were brought in to manage the strategic grain reserve. The ABS had export contracts for 200,000 tonnes of grain but was deferring fulfilling these until after the harvest, in case the food was needed as reserves. This caution was abandoned and all the reserve was exported under the auspices of the Faisal and Baraka Islamic banks. A total of about 500,000 tonnes was sold to the EC and Saudi Arabia for animal feed. By October, the main government silo contained just 9,500 tonnes, most of it unfit for human consumption.

GOVERNMENT RESPONSE

Initially, the government's response to the August price hike was like its citizens'—bewilderment and panic. Rather than the Agricultural Bank or the RRC, the security services were put in charge of food security. The army was sent to markets in Khartoum to confiscate traders' stocks, a move that only undermined confidence. Traders responsible for 'smuggling' food were threatened with the death penalty. The movement of grain across regional boundaries was banned and the legal price of grain fixed at LS300 per sack. None of these measures worked.

Unable to manage the crisis with the resources available, and determined not to beg from international donors at the very start of its Islamist revolution, the government determined simply to ride out the crisis. Regional governments in the East, Darfur and Kordofan made statements of food need: they were ignored. The national early warning system did its job as required. It warned: 'immediate action is called for to avert the repetition of the 1985 catastrophe.'[7] Its bulletin included all the technical information a food security planner could ask for: updates on grain prices, livestock prices, wheat and wheat-flour supply, refugees, displaced population, and relief deliveries and stocks.

Between early warning and the necessary political action in Khartoum was a 'missing link'.[8] The official line from central government was that no famine existed, nor was imminent. No declaration of famine was made, nor any appeal for assistance. The official view was naively and aggressively optimistic. For example, the Minister for Agriculture described accounts of an impending famine as 'unfounded rumours' circulated by 'some malicious circles to serve their own political objectives.'[9] A release by the Sudan Embassy in London, dated 9 October, reads:

> The view of the government regarding aid is that relief work will be largely unnecessary in Sudan if the government's attempts to achieve self-sufficiency in food and to resettle the displaced people in suitable areas where they can support themselves are backed. Already the government, with little outside help, has managed to increase food production by 55% in some areas and achieve self-sufficiency in others. Those really interested in the welfare of the Sudanese people should support those efforts, instead of doling meagre rations that only enhance dependency and loss of dignity. Those who are not should keep their peace and leave us alone.

The government was not wholly united. Some regional governments and some departments acted in a more pragmatic way. The Regional Government in Darfur, for example, tried to facilitate relief organisations' work. But the resources that could be brought to bear without central authorisation were very modest. Policy was being made elsewhere.

---

[7] RRC, *Early Warning System Bulletin*, *5.10*, 15 October 1990, p. 1.
[8] Margaret Buchanan-Smith and Susanna Davies, *Famine Early Warning and Response—The Missing Link*, London, Intermediate Technology Publications, 1995, chapter 5.
[9] 'No imminent famine in Sudan', letter, *Daily Nation* (Nairobi), 15 October 1990; SUNA 12 October 1990.

Triage

Beneath the bluster, the NIF was developing a strategy of political triage: the limited grain supply was to be secured for politically vital constituencies. Khartoum was the priority. For the first time ever, sorghum—the staple food of the poor—was rationed. The ration was distributed through neighbourhood committees under the control of security and NIF appointees, set up by a special Food Security Council for the capital. The committees later evolved into permanent Popular Committees, some of which were explicitly dedicated to the 'defence of the nation' and which became one of the main instruments of surveillance and supervision in the cities. There was barely enough food for the committees to retain their credibility for the first few months, but nonetheless discontent was contained and the famine was turned to an opportunity for political control.

The relocation of squatters and displaced people was another priority for the Food Security Council. Their number had risen to an estimated 1.8 million, almost all from the South and the west. The government feared that food riots might make Khartoum ungovernable. The Food Security Council cut off water supplies to shanty towns and in October about 30,000 people had their houses demolished and were forcibly removed. It was not logistically feasible to remove all the displaced, but the show of force had the desired effect of intimidating them. The famine passed without serious disturbances and the relocations continued over succeeding years.[10]

In the 1980s, local and international agencies had enjoyed a great deal of independence in initiating relief allocations. This was taken away, and Regional (later State) Relief Committees were given full legal powers to determine relief allocations. Their power was constrained by their lack of resources vis-à-vis foreign agencies, but the balance of power was shifting.

---

[10] African Rights, *Sudan's Invisible Citizens: The Policy of Abuse against Displaced People in the North*, London, 1995.

Confrontation with the Donors

Foreign NGOs planned to distribute food in rural areas: the government wanted to divert it to the towns. In one instance, after a food riot in Um Ruwaba town, NGO relief food intended for displaced Southerners was commandeered at gunpoint and distributed to residents. The ban on food movement left 35,000 tonnes of USAID-donated food in warehouses. USAID suspected the government would redirect it from the western provinces to Khartoum.

This was the spark for a dispute with the U.S. government: the only serious political confrontation caused by the famine. On 2 October the U.S. took firm measures: it turned down a request for $150m of food aid (on concessionary sale terms), suspended all deliveries of food under the current food aid contract (these were worth another 55,000 tonnes), and diverted a ship carrying 45,000 tonnes of U.S. (concessionary sale) food aid destined for Port Sudan. The effect was immediate: two days later, the government unblocked the internal movement of relief food, thus exempting international relief from its strategy of triage. OFDA Administrator Andrew Natsios then spelled out stiff conditions under which Sudan would receive U.S. food, proposing also that all western donors put together a cartel to enforce the conditionality.[11]

The Sudan Government's negotiating position was not as weak as it appeared. USAID also wanted to continue to use Sudan for cross-border relief supplies to Eritrea and rebel-held parts of Ethiopia, and so needed co-operation from Sudan. Nonetheless, the confrontation was the sharpest to date between the U.S. and Sudan. These adversarial negotiations over international relief contrasted with the lack of any internal politicisation of famine.

In contrast to USAID, the UN took an extremely conciliatory line. Trevor Page, the WFP representative in Khartoum, never disputed the Government's analysis of the situation and its prescriptions. Trevor Page went on the record to say 'much of Sudan

---

[11] Andrew Natsios, Statement before the U.S. House of Representatives Committee on Foreign Relations Subcommittee of Africa, 25 October 1990.

faces food insecurity' but insisted that it was not 'famine' but 'food shortage.'[12] He also spoke to the magazine *Sudanow*:

> The food situation in the Sudan at the moment is difficult. The people of Sudan are facing an acute food scarcity but there is a big difference between food scarcity and famine. I do not believe that the Sudan is currently facing famine.[13]

In October, Page agreed to a government proposal that WFP take the lead with other donors to plug the 'food gap' in accordance with the government plan, which was that sixty per cent of international food aid be distributed on a food-for-work basis, twenty per cent be sold at a subsidised rate and only twenty per cent be distributed free. Page's willingness to co-operate with the government made him unpopular with other donors, who saw his stand as capitulation. Whether in response to U.S. threats or UN conciliation, or the combination of the two, the Sudan Government agreed to withdraw its threats against OLS, which was brought back from the brink of collapse and allowed to continue. Feeding the Northern cities on its own terms was a much bigger prize.

FAMINE AND REPRESSION

The military government had already launched a massive crackdown on any internal dissent before the onset of the 1990-91 famine. Immediately after the coup, political parties and trade unions were banned and strict censorship imposed. Hundreds of actual and suspected opposition figures were arrested and detained. The lengths to which the regime was prepared to go was demonstrated in December 1989, when a leading doctor, Mamoun Hussein, was sentenced to death for organising an illegal strike. A businessman was executed for allegedly trading in illegal foreign currency the same month. In April 1990, 28 army officers were summarily executed after a coup plot was uncovered.

---

[12] Quoted by Associated Press, 6 October 1990.
[13] *Sudanow*, interview with Trevor Page, November 1990.

The government used the famine to further entrench its repressive apparatus. The militarisation of food supply has been mentioned and will be a recurring theme in the following chapters. In 1990, even mention of the word 'famine' was close to a treasonable act: Sudanese journalists and local government officials who even hinted at the problems were intimidated.

Equally significant was the way in which, in an ideological sense, the famine was removed from the political sphere. Confronting its own people, the Sudan Government both denied that the famine existed, and did all it could to encourage an attitude of fatalism. One striking instance of this comes from drought-stricken Kordofan, where the NIF ordered villagers to organise the *istisga* rain prayer, 'to generate implicit public displays of the legitimacy of the regime.'[14] Placing the famine in a highly traditional context and playing on religious devotion was an attempt to negate ordinary people's anger and legitimise the government's denial of any responsibility. What blame could not be directed at metaphysical powers was laid on Western governments, which, the government said, were conspiring against Sudan. (Whether or not this succeeded in convincing rural Sudanese is another matter: most indications are that people had a good idea where blame lay.) Meanwhile the Western donors' main political concern was Sudan's stand *vis-à-vis* Iraq and Kuwait, not the establishment of a domestic coalition opposed to famine inside Sudan.

Citizens' Initiatives

One of the striking aspects of the 1990/91 famine and its aftermath is the absence of popular attempts to mobilise assistance for relief and rehabilitation. Many citizens' associations simply no longer existed. All formal professional associations and trade unions were banned at the time of the 1989 coup. These organisations not only had

---

[14] Michael Kevane and Leslie Gray, 'Local Politics in the Time of Turabi's Revolution: Gender, Class and Ethnicity in Western Sudan,' *Africa*, *65*, 1995, 271-96, at p. 282

important social and economic roles, but had been the focal point for democratic mobilisation against famine.

Some migrants' associations were allowed to continue in existence, either because of their close connections to senior politicians and civil servants, or because they kept a low political profile.[15] The most prominent Southern migrants association, the Fashoda Benevolent Cultural and Social Association, almost entirely confined itself to Shilluk cultural activities, only emerging to play a significant welfare role in the wake of the Jebelein massacre of January 1990, when it would have been politically embarrassing for the government to have impeded the Shilluk community's attempts to help their kin who had survived the atrocity. Connections with international NGOs helped these migrant associations in their service provision roles, but did not bestow immunity: connections with the state proved more important for that.

The northern riverain migrants' associations fared best. Some, such as the Kanar Union, became vehicles for implementing state-initiated development schemes. This is unsurprising: northern riverain people are generally well-educated and well-connected in the state apparatus. Before the coup, these same associations had shown far more independence of action, for example in response to the 1988 floods. In 1990-91, the northern Nile regions were least-affected by the famine, so these associations had least to do. Migrants' associations based in less influential rural areas had no political space in which to mobilise, and remained invisible.

To the extent that the famine sparked political resistance, it was symbolic only. Subversive jokes such as 'Omer [al Bashir] tea', i.e. tea without sugar, circulated. Dinka migrants in Gerief West, forcibly relocated to Suq el Markazi in October 1990, renamed their

---

[15] David Pratten and Suleiman Ali Baldo, '"Return to the Roots," Processes of Legitimacy in Sudanese Migrant Associations,' in Michael Edwards and David Hulme (eds.) *Non-Governmental Organisations—Performance and Accountability: Beyond the Magic Bullet*, London, Earthscan, 1995, p. 126.

new home 'New Sudan'—with provocative echoes of the SPLA's agenda.[16]

IMPACT

By September 1991, only about 200,000 tonnes of food aid—one fifth of the national deficit—had actually been distributed. No large-scale starvation was reported, and the government concluded that there had been no famine, as it had claimed all along. The donors and relief agencies were only marginally less sanguine. One assessment concluded that

> the major part of the impact of the food shortage was carried by the community who had, perforce, to resort to a range of traditional and non-traditional coping strategies, including reduced consumption, if the last can rightly be called a 'coping strategy.'[17]

The government allowed no systematic measure of mortality, and in the absence of any hard data, it is easy to infer from the absence of mass starvation in relief shelters that no excess mortality existed. This would be wholly wrong. Certainly the 'megadeaths' predicted by some relief workers did not materialise, as they never in fact do. Famine deaths were more insidious and less spectacular. Examination of what scraps of evidence are available combined with extrapolation from nutritional surveys provides very strong indications that child death rates were at least double normal levels in many parts of western Sudan.[18] In Darfur, after the 1990 harvest, malnutrition stayed high at hungry season levels; children approached the 1991 hungry season in an extremely vulnerable

---

[16] Yath Awan Yath, 'The Dinka Immigrants in Gerief West, Khartoum: A Study on the Local Participation in a Third World City,' PhD Thesis, Bayreuth University, 1994, p. 193.

[17] Patel, 1994, p. 317.

[18] Marion Kelly and Margaret Buchanan-Smith, 'Northern Sudan in 1991: Food Crisis and the International Relief Response,' *Disasters*, *18*, 1994, 16-33.

state.[19] There was indeed a killing famine, but the Sudan government was able to ride it out while entrenching itself in power.

Immediately after the 1990 crisis, the government began to draft a new relief policy with far-reaching implications. It was determined to gain the upper hand over western donors. The first stage was to tighten control of relief. Legally, this was implemented first with an act that asserted that all humanitarian supplies, once in Sudan, legally belonged to the government. Enacted in 1992, this is the foundation of the government's tight regulation of all relief activity since then. This was followed by a series of measures to regulate NGO activity. One senior UN official later commented: 'There is a big political backlash from the 1980s [when it seemed that] NGOs took over the country. The government feels that NGOs are a real threat to its sovereignty.'[20] The *OLS Review* noted that, 'In contractual terms, INGOs are little more than an extension of the state in Northern Sudan, and are bound by a code of conduct which defines humanitarian aid as a purely technical response blind to context or cause.'[21] Meanwhile, UN agencies were drawn into a closer relationship to government policies.

The second major development was the shift in emphasis of assistance from relief to 'development', made in 1992. This was one of the most astute moves by the Sudan Government. Western agencies and donors dislike long-term relief programmes and much prefer to 'do development' when possible. In a country afflicted by a chronic crisis (a civil war) it is highly questionable whether any sustainable 'development' is possible unless the basic reasons for the conflict have first been resolved. This is particularly the case in Sudan, where development policies implemented to serve the narrow interests of certain groups were a prime reason for the outbreak of conflict in the first place. Nonetheless, leading western agencies, notably UNDP, have embraced the idea that the 'emergency phase' is

---

[19] Young and Jaspars, 1995, p. 96.
[20] Interviewed in Khartoum, February 1996.
[21] Ataul Karim, Mark Duffield *et al., OLS: Operation Lifeline Sudan: A Review*, University of Birmingham, July 1996, p. 60.

somehow over, and that 'development' should follow. This will be examined further in the following chapter.

A third development was the intensification of policies aimed at the most disfavoured groups in Northern Sudan—the displaced people and the inhabitants of the Nuba Mountains. These people continued to suffer chronic famine conditions, as government policies focused the hardship upon them, while making them the raw material for thorough-going programmes of political and social transformation. The fate of these 'invisible citizens' is also examined in the next chapter.

Finally, the NIF provided a coherent overarching rationale for its new strategy: the 'Comprehensive Call' and Islamic social planning. Although its philosophy and practicalities are often obscure to those not steeped in an Islamist political culture, the NIF strategy for transforming Sudan is coherent and comprehensive. Chapter 9 analyses the 'humanitarian' instruments used for pursuing that transformation, specifically the Islamic agencies operating within the framework of the 'Comprehensive Call'.

8.

HUMANITARIAN CAPITULATION

'DEVELOPMENT' AND DISPLACEMENT IN THE NORTH

We have to take positive action to assist. We are not thinking about the reasons [for the suffering]. We are doing the work of the Government of course. But if we don't we are not able to do anything, we are not working.

International NGO director, Khartoum, February 1996.

The most extreme manifestation of the government's policy of triage have been the campaigns against the Khartoum displaced and in the Nuba Mountains, both of which intensified in 1990 and reached peaks in 1992. They continue at the time of writing. The latter includes the systematic denial of food relief and commercial food supplies, and an intensification of raiding by militia and army units. The government was expanding its arsenal of using food as a political and military weapon, selectively denying food relief to some people while incorporating it into a political and military strategy elsewhere.

These 'invisible citizens' dramatically illustrate the shortcomings of the international humanitarian response. The displaced are the most accessible of all the suffering people in Sudan, with over one million encamped within a few miles of the capital itself. Yet international agencies provided only modest assistance and virtually no protection. The Nuba Mountains are more remote, and here, OLS and international agencies were wholly inactive. The absence of foreign agencies and the restriction of indigenous secular or church agencies created an arena in which the government could impose its agenda unchallenged.

RELIEF, DEVELOPMENT AND DISPLACEMENT

The plight of Sudan's 'invisible citizens' reflects institutionalised discrimination and historical inequities of development. Their human suffering demands a humanitarian relief response. The Sudan Government, however, prefers to emphasise the 'developmental' needs and opportunities. This has become a pretext for denying these people basic relief, while forging ahead with programmes of economic and social transformation.

There are estimated to be well over two million displaced Southerners and Nuba in and around the cities of Northern Sudan: a dramatic manifestation of the economic and political inequalities of Sudan. Some Northern political leaders have said that the decision of famine-stricken Southerners to move North is an indication of sentiments of national unity. This is absurd: it would be more correct to see their need to move at all as a symptom of civil war, and their trek towards Khartoum as a reflection of the complete economic and political dominance of the capital. As discussed in Chapter 2, the period after 1978 saw an economic transformation in Sudan whereby Khartoum and a handful of other major cities came to control more than half of Sudan's gross national income.

An estimated 1.9 million people are currently in camps in and around the Three Towns of Khartoum, Khartoum North and Omdurman alone. Nearly half of these are war refugees from Southern Sudan; the remainder are drought migrants from eastern and western Sudan, and labour migrants. This represents an enormous internal movement. This internal displacement is not merely the result of the last decade of war and related disasters, but also has deeper roots in the long-term social, economic and political development of Sudan. Both the colonial and post-colonial governments in Sudan have built an economy based around a heavily-invested core and a wide periphery with negligible economic development acting as a labour reserve. The private sector has

146

followed a similar pattern: traders from the provinces have tended to reinvest their profits in Khartoum and other major cities. (While major businessmen have moved large amounts of capital out of the country altogether.) The Sudan government is now living with the inevitable result of this imbalance: the inhabitants of the periphery have followed the patterns of capital migration, and moved to the core.

When the rate of migration was relatively modest, the incomers could be economically absorbed. Some leading members of earlier waves of migrants, for example the West African Fellata who moved to the Gezira and parts of eastern Sudan during the colonial period, have since become prominent in the business classes and have joined major political parties including the NIF (although they have never been completely accepted as social equals by some of the ruling Sudanese Arab families). Recent waves of migrants, especially non-Moslems from the Nuba Mountains and Southern Sudan, have been both too numerous and too culturally distinct to be able to be absorbed. This has built up a massive tension at the heart of social and economic planning: the government does not want to alter the political and economic disparities that created the mass migration, and it still needs plentiful and cheap labour, but it is also deeply fearful of the migrants and what they represent.

Mechanised Agriculture and Displacement

The government has a slightly different attitude towards the displaced in the 'transitional zone' (the North-South borderlands). Here, the aim is to create 'development' by encouraging the rapid spread of mechanised agriculture. Since the 1970s, large-scale commercial farms have been spreading rapidly in the more fertile parts of Northern Sudan. By the 1990s, the main accessible reserves of the most productive clay plains in Gedaref, Blue Nile and central parts of Kordofan had been used up, and existing farms are becoming less productive as the soil becomes exhausted. Hence entrepreneurs have been looking further afield—further south—for new areas to exploit. Recent expansion of mechanised farming has been chiefly in Southern Kordofan, northern Upper Nile and

Southern Blue Nile, and to a lesser extent in Southern Darfur and Bahr el Ghazal—directly encroaching into areas inhabited by non-Arab minority peoples.

This expansion has been undertaken by various means. Sudanese land law has long favoured the government over indigenous people. The law recognises few customary claims to land rights. Moreover, successive governments have established a number of institutions dedicated to creating large-scale farms, which have in effect become instruments of land dispossession. The first and most important of these is the Mechanised Farming Corporation (MFC), established in 1968. The MFC demarcated areas of unregistered (but not necessarily unfarmed) land and gave 25-year leases on schemes of one thousand or 1500 *feddans*[1] to private merchant farmers. In theory, farming experience was a requirement for obtaining a lease; in practice any wealthy or well-connected merchant, civil servant or army officer could obtain a lease. Contrary to the MFC's stated policy, very few leaseholders were local 'small farmers.' According to a 1975 agreement, half the finance for the expansion of private mechanised farming was provided by the World Bank.

The MFC legally based its operations on the Land Registration Act of 1925, amended in 1961. This amendment awarded unregistered land to the government, subject to the approval of the Registrar of Lands. The key legal instrument is the remarkable Section 380 of the Sudan Penal Code of 1974, which concerned trespassing:

> Whoever enters into or upon property in the possession of another with intention to commit an offence or intimidate, insult or annoy any person in possession of such property, or, having lawfully entered into or upon such property, unlawfully remains there, with the intent thereby to intimidate, insult or annoy such a person, or with the intent to commit an offence, is said to commit criminal trespass.

The second part of this section means that any farmer whose land, owned in accordance with customary law, was expropriated, was

---

[1] One feddan equals 1.038 acres or 0.42 hectares.

guilty of criminal trespass if he or she should remain there with the intention of so much as 'annoying' the new owner. The MFC was aggressive in using the law to intimidate such smallholders. This section was retained in the subsequent 1983 and 1990 acts. The trespass provision was no mere piece of paper. Numerous smallholder farmers were prosecuted under this provision.

In the aftermath of the 1984-5 famine there was a vigorous debate on the merits of mechanised farming. Environmental studies indicated that large-scale farms were creating ecological devastation, including deforestation and soil erosion. The resulting loss of soil fertility meant that the farms themselves were rapidly becoming unproductive. Stated government policy, with the support of the World Bank, changed course: large farms were to be discouraged. In the event, nothing changed. Commercial grain farming was so profitable—especially during periods of food scarcity such as 1984-5, 1987 and 1990—that there were powerful commercial impulses behind the continued expansion. While the brake was put on the MFC, privately-owned mechanised farms continued to spread. It has become extremely difficult to keep track of the amount of land under cultivation in such schemes, because often the true areas of land are under-registered. By 1984, perhaps half of the total area of mechanised farmland in Southern Kordofan was in such private schemes.

By the mid-1980s, there was widespread discontent among labourers on mechanised schemes. Many were Southerners, Nuba and other marginalised people, who either sympathised with the SPLA or were widely believed to do so. Rural people were encouraged to become bolder in their challenges to commercial farms, and incidents of sabotage of tractors and stealing of crops became more common. In response, farm owners made deals with army units to defend the schemes, or hired their own private guards. Local government officials and magistrates were encouraged to take prompt action against intruders and punish them severely in the courts.

The present military government has been far more draconian in its land policies than any of its predecessors. The expropriation of land for mechanised farming has accelerated, based upon legislation

149

that gives the government almost unlimited power over land allocation. The 1990 amendment to the Civil Transactions Act has swept away *all* customary title to land. The first provision of the amendment states that 'All non-registered land should be considered as if registered in the name of the State.' It also decreed that all land cases before the courts were to be struck off, and prohibited judicial recourse against land allocation decisions made by the government. In a single legislative act, the Sudan Government took legal hold of all smallholders' land, throughout Sudan. Combined with the law against 'criminal trespass,' this is the legal foundation for the dispossession of peoples such as the Nuba.

The most draconian method of agricultural expansion involves creating vacant land by destroying villages. This is common in the Nuba Mountains and parts of Upper Nile, and is likely to become common in Southern Blue Nile as the war restarts in that region. Under the name 'combing', army units set out to destroy all human habitation in a certain area. Villages are burned, along with all property, including foodstores, that cannot be removed. Livestock are either looted or killed. The inhabitants of the villages are rounded up and taken back to the army garrison; those who try to escape are usually killed on the spot. Often, villagers have advance warning of attacks and run away. Troops have been known to pursue them to their hideouts, using tear gas to force them out of caves to surrender. But even when villagers escape completely, they find themselves destitute, and fear of further attacks is a powerful disincentive to rebuilding their houses.

Farmland in the North-South transitional zone has also become an important underpinning of the pro-war and pro-famine coalition held together by the Sudan Government. Government followers are rewarded with grants of land; indeed seizing farmland is one of the reasons for the continued war.

The transitional areas possess another strategic resource: oil. Sudan's major oil deposits are at Melut (northern Upper Nile), Bentiu (western Upper Nile) and Hajlij (Southern Kordofan). The proposed route of the oil pipeline from the largest oilfield at Bentiu also passes through the Nuba Mountains. Oil installations were one of the first targets of the SPLA in the war. The government has made one of its major medium-term aims the extraction of oil and its shipment to a new refinery located in el Obeid. To do this it needs to secure the routes.

In these circumstances, mass displacement is not a by-product of conflict: it is one of the aims of the conflict. Indigenous people stand in the way of agricultural expansion and oil extraction. Destroying their villages and relocating them to new, government-run secure sites enables the government to control the area, while also obtaining a labour force under military supervision. In pursuit of this, the government has revived the idea of 'peace villages', first used on a small scale during the first civil war, and made it into a central component of a comprehensive counter-insurgency plan. (The idea was first re-floated in early 1988 by the Sadiq government[2] but not systematically taken up until 1991.) 'Peace villages' or 'peace camps' are a version of the classic 'protected hamlets' used by western armies in South-East Asia and elsewhere: they are a means of maintaining strict military control of a civilian population. They also double as recruiting centres for the Popular Defence Force militia, labour reserves for mechanised farms, and centres for Islamic education and re-education. For the government, this is 'development'.

'Relief to Development'

At the centre of the government's relief policy is an insistence on the 'relief to development continuum'. Although the origins can be traced back to the 1980s, it was entrenched at the centre of government policy only in 1991. The RRC policy document for 1992 stresses that the priority for assistance should be rehabilitation and development. These concepts hold different meanings for the Sudan Government and the international donors, but the government's understanding is what prevails on the ground.

The *OLS Review* notes that for the Sudan Government, 'development is associated with the expansion of mechanised

---

[2] *Sudan Times*, 13 January 1988.

agriculture, and establishing the infrastructure for this to happen.'³ This kind of food production enriches the elite and is an essential component of the government's determination to break its dependence on the west. A commitment to 'development' also indicates an emasculation of the principle of providing free relief. A second component of 'development' is the establishment of peace camps. The internees in peace camps would under other circumstances be considered deserving of humanitarian assistance and small-scale rehabilitation aid such as seeds and farm tools. The Sudan government would prefer the internees to provide cheap labour, and hence portrays the assistance needs of the camps as 'developmental'. Providing tractors and other infrastructure for commercial farming takes the place of providing food and other basic services.

As a result, many people who are suffering malnutrition to a degree that would have warranted emergency food relief a decade ago have lost that entitlement. This enables the government to gloss over poor conditions in peace camps, inferring that they are a transitional phenomenon to be overcome by 'development', rather than admitting that impoverishment is in reality an integral component of war and a policy of social and economic transformation.

Humanitarian Accommodation with Government Strategy

In Northern Sudan, the UN specialised agencies are in an invidious position. On the one hand, their work in the war-affected regions is implicitly governed by the Operation Lifeline agreements (only one of which—the 1994 agreement—is actually formally on paper), which should provide for neutrality between the belligerent parties. But at the same time, UN agencies are expected to respect national sovereignty, and work within the general framework of government policy. All the UN agencies associated with OLS—UNICEF, WFP

---

³ Ataul Karim, Mark Duffield *et al.*, *OLS: Operation Lifeline Sudan: A Review*, University of Birmingham, 1996, p. 48.

and UNDP, which has the Northern Sector co-ordination role—also have large programmes in non-war affected areas of the North, quite separate from OLS. The problematic implications of this ambiguity are one of the central themes of the 1996 *OLS Review*.[4]

The division of OLS into separate Northern and Southern Sectors has been simultaneously a major reason for its survival and the cause of its deepest problems. The implicit pact with the Sudan Government has been that the UN will allow the Northern Sector to come under tight governmental regulation, in return for the government tolerating the continuation of the Southern Sector (punctuated by occasional demands for its closure). Hence, the Northern Sector operations have accommodated to government policies, while the Southern Sector ones have been marked by regulation by UNICEF and an abiding concern with neutrality and humanitarian principles. Aspects of the Southern Sector will be examined in later chapters.

Since 1992, the government's insistence that the 'emergency' is over and that 'rehabilitation' and 'development' should dominate in assistance programmes has gone down well with some international agencies. Examples of their readiness to become implementing agents for the 'developmental' aspect of government policy will be detailed below. At the outset, however, it should be noted that one central aspect of 'development', cited in all western agency literature, is conspicuous by its absence. There is *no* community participation in decision-making. One consultant commented, 'The Khartoum displaced must be the least consulted group in the history of humanitarian aid.'[5] But there is a fig leaf, as the UN Resident Representative has claimed:

> We are taking people out of the beggar mentality. People are proud to pay for themselves [i.e. not receive free food]. . . this is part of society building, enabling people to feel more consciously self-reliant. It is linked to democracy building because people have to elect a management committee.[6]

---

[4] *OLS Review*, pp. 31-3.
[5] Quoted in, *OLS Review*, p. 207.
[6] Christoph Jaeger, quoted in, *OLS Review*, p. 100.

Such is the powerlessness and sense of vulnerability among displaced people that it is highly unlikely that they would elect anyone prepared to enter a dispute with the authorities.

Another fig-leaf is the notion of a 'coping strategy'. This refers to the fall-back strategies used by destitute or famine-stricken households to try to retain an economic base and obtain food and other necessities. It has much applicability in drought-famines, such as that of 1984-5 in western Sudan. Study of coping strategies at this time revealed that the prime aim of affected households was to maintain their economic and social viability for the future, so that they would not be subjected to indefinite destitution by losing land or other vital assets.[7] In a war-famine such as in Southern Sudan and the transitional areas, the situation is radically different, because the war is in part targeted precisely at the asset base that makes coping strategies meaningful. When people have been dispossessed of their land, livestock and former economic activities by war, they can no longer be said to be following 'coping strategies' in the same sense: they are merely struggling for physical survival. Hence the OLS assertion in 1994 that it aims 'to assist the civilian population re-establish traditional survival and coping mechanisms'[8] is somewhat misleading: this cannot be achieved until the war is over.

In the meantime, the predominant survival mechanism for displaced people is wage labour, especially on agricultural schemes. In ed Da'ien district of Southern Darfur, displaced Southerners provide some 85% of the (waged) agricultural labour force: formerly they were agro-pastoralists relying on a broad base of economic activities.[9] This subjugation fits neatly with the objectives of both the government and the local militiamen and commercial farmers who were responsible for devastating the Dinka communities in the first place.

---

[7] Alex de Waal, *Famine that Kills: Darfur, Sudan, 1984-1985*, Oxford, Clarendon Press, 1989.
[8] *OLS Review*, p. 111.
[9] *OLS Review*, p. 199.

The government maintains that the war is essentially over; that the SPLA was defeated in 1991-2 and that its own initiative, 'Peace from Within', is efficiently sweeping up the disorganised remnants of the rebellion. A rhetoric of normality is used to legitimise talk of 'development' and social reconstruction. The UN appears to have succumbed to this too. A recent UNDP initiative, jointly with the UNESCO 'culture for peace' programme is called 'Peace, Culture and Development', and is based on the rationale that 'if you give people an alternative to war they will prefer peace.'[10] The implication is that the war is an outcome of ignorance or cultural predispositions among Southerners and Nuba, that can be overcome by offering them the benefits of civilisation and development. This is merely a secularised version of the philosophy underpinning the NIF's 'Comprehensive Call' (see next chapter).

It is not merely the UN that has been ready to make major ethical compromises—and justify them—in order to remain active in Northern Sudan. All the international NGOs that are operational there have come to similar positions. Some staff members are frank in recognising their position—such as the NGO director quoted at the head of this chapter. Others have become apologists for the Sudan Government, arguing that its record can be defended, or at least an effort should be made to accommodate it. The Khartoum director of a prominent NGO said:[11]

> You must recognise that the Government is not homogenous and give support and encouragement for those who are more internationally-minded. I have an awful feeling that we are walking into a position where the hard-liners may say, 'Look where you've got, bowing to your fancy foreign friends.'

On some occasions, the NGO attitude has appeared to become like the 'Stockholm Syndrome'—in which hostages come to identify psychologically with their captors. The director of GOAL, an Irish NGO, whose clinic in a displaced camp had just been destroyed by the government, told a human rights investigator that he did not want

---

[10] Senior UN Official, Khartoum, February 1996.
[11] Interviewed in Khartoum, February 1996.

to even whisper a complaint, in case his agency's access was jeopardised. In September 1994, Oxfam-UK refused to protest when three of its Sudanese staff were detained, fearing that this might 'endanger' them. In such circumstances, international NGO claims to be concerned with justice, or to be witnesses for human rights, are less convincing than the *OLS Review*'s remark that they are 'little more than an extension of the state in Northern Sudan.'[12]

OFFICIAL POLICIES TOWARDS THE DISPLACED

They don't care. They don't give a damn about those people.

International aid agency official, Khartoum

The characteristic government attitude towards migrants in the towns is to regard them as an economic burden and a security threat. When their labour is not needed, they are deported. On several occasions in the 1970s and early '80s, refugees and Southern migrants were expelled from the capital in campaigns known as *kasha*. By the mid-1980s, however, it was clear that a more comprehensive policy was needed, as the numbers had simply grown too large. In 1987 the government of Sadiq el Mahdi set up a committee to advise on the problem of the displaced. It drew up a key distinction, between 'squatters' (longer-term migrants, almost all Moslems from western Sudan) and the 'displaced' (recent arrivals, almost all Southerners). But before it could report, the question of urban planning was given a new salience by the 1988 floods, but the emerging plans were thrown into disarray.

Many of the policies of the NIF over the displaced have their origins in the proposals drawn up by the Sadiq el Mahdi government. Notably, the policy of 'peace villages' emerged in 1988. In January, Sadiq el Mahdi hinted at using 'successful' counter-insurgency strategies modelled on colonial anti-guerrilla tactics (i.e. the evacuation of civilians to protected hamlets).[13] The term 'peace

---

[12] *OLS Review*, p. 60.
[13] *Sudan Times*, 1 February 1988.

156

village' had already been resurrected in from the 1960s. In July, the Minister of Housing spoke of 'peace villages' for resettling the Khartoum displaced.[14] After a visit to Kordofan by Sadiq el Mahdi, the outlines of an official nationwide policy towards displaced Southerners began to emerge.[15] Short term policy was humanitarian assistance and putting the displaced to work as an agricultural labour force. Medium term policy involved setting up 'border reception centres' at inter-regional frontiers, and keeping the displaced as an agricultural labour force. Long term policy was envisaged in terms of establishing productive settlements close to the displaced people's home areas. Plans to resettle displaced people from Khartoum to 'peace villages' in Upper Nile were floated and then postponed.[16]

The Sadiq government was hostile to international aid agencies, accusing them of 'misreporting' government mistreatment of displaced and violating national sovereignty. But the government needed foreign aid if it was to actually implement the projects. Hence it reluctantly co-operated with international agencies. The Sadiq government also needed votes and was bound by constitutional niceties. It therefore negotiated with the leaders of the Khartoum displaced rather than summarily expelling them. This changed with the 1989 military coup.

Demolitions and Relocations

The weaknesses of the Sadiq government and the confusion during the first year after the al Bashir coup prevented the development of the comprehensive policy on the displaced. But by mid-1990, the government was back on track. On 20 May 1990, Decree 941 was passed, entitled 'Approval of Some Procedures to Contain Squatter Settlement.' Article (d) stated that the relevant authorities are 'to immediately demolish squatter settlements on planned residential

---

[14] *Sudan Times*, 6 July 1988.
[15] Ministry of Social Welfare, Zakat and the Displaced, 'Statement regarding the Government's general policy towards the displaced,' 22 September 1988.
[16] *Sudan Times*, 15 December 1988.

and agricultural land and are to immediately give the land to its rightful owners.' Also in 1990, Popular Committees (*lijan al sha'abiya*) were created in planned urban areas—but not in squatter settlements or displaced camps, thereby depriving the migrants of any formal voice in government. The Commission of the Displaced refused to meet formally with delegations that did not represent such committees.

Thereafter, the government began a programme of demolitions and relocations. The squatter-displaced distinction, with its political and racial implications, was retained. Squatter settlements were razed and the inhabitants relocated to 'peace cities' outside the Three Towns. Here, basic services were provided, usually belatedly, and the residents were given residence rights and the opportunity to form a neighbourhood Popular Committee. Community leaders needed to acquire some formal status *vis-à-vis* the government, but could only do it through forming Popular Committees, which entailed acquiescing in the relocations programme.[17] Leaders could also obtain political or economic reward through co-operation, which led some to support the relocations. But while gaining official recognition, the migrants were deprived of any rights of residence in the capital itself, including any theoretical voting rights.

Displaced camps were also destroyed, but in this case the inhabitants were moved to transit camps, temporary sites outside the city with few services, supposedly as a prelude to onward movement back towards their regions of origin. Some people were indeed returned southwards, to government-held areas of Upper Nile, to Juba and to Bahr el Ghazal. 'Peace caravans' of returning migrants to the Nuba Mountains were also organised. During the first fifteen months of the return programme in 1992/3, fifteen convoys transported nearly 28,000 people to the South and the transitional zone.[18] The principal vehicle for this was the Voluntary Return

---

[17] Yath Awan Yath, 'The Dinka Immigrants in Gerief West, Khartoum: A Study on the Local Participation in a Third World City,' PhD Thesis, Bayreuth University, 1994, pp. 208-11.

[18] Republic of Sudan, General Administration for Displaced Affairs, 'The Reallocation and Repatriation Convoys Carried out for the Displaced in 1992-1993,' Khartoum, 1993.

Programme of the Sudan Council of Churches, which assisted nearly 32,000 people during 1992-5 (many fewer than the projected 152,000).[19] Many of the return programmes were oversubscribed—return to the South is very popular among the Southern displaced. (Hope that relocation to transit camps was the first stage in an assisted return home was one reason for the widespread acquiescence in the programme.)

Other people have been moved to 'productive zones'—areas of large-scale mechanised farming suffering from labour shortages. Such operations were carried out in 1992 and 1995. When they returned to their home regions or nearby, these displaced people were often placed in peace camps, as part of the wider nationwide strategy.

The government plan is to relocate the entire displaced and squatter population of Khartoum. A quick survey of official statements reveals frequent claims that the job is almost done, or will be completed within the year. In fact, at the time of writing, relocations are still continuing at a rate of between 4,000 and 8,000 per month. By May 1992, over 600,000 people had been relocated. More recent overall figures are not available—perhaps because many of the people who are removed then trickle back into the city, and exposure of the disparities in the figures would prove embarrassing.

Demolitions are carried out using force and usually with little or no advance warning. Bulldozers, trucks and army units simply arrive at the chosen location and begin their work, leaving the residents to salvage what they can. Those who are absent at the time may return home in the evening to find their homes destroyed, their possessions lost or looted, and their families relocated. Among the demolitions were some long-established communities, such as Ishish Fellata (in this case, because of the political representation of the Fellata in the NIF and the sheer level of economic investment the residents had made in their semi-planned area, the site for relocation was relatively well-prepared).

---

[19] Sudan Council of Churches, 'Clarifications on VRP Operations: 1992-June 1995,' mimeo, Khartoum.

The abuses are compounded by the failure of the different government departments to co-ordinate properly. A UN official noted:[20]

There is mismanagement between the agencies responsible. The Ministry of Planning issues the orders. The Department of the Displaced [DoD] is supposed to screen the people, according to the time they have been in Khartoum, and their source of income, and whether they have another place to go. These criteria are unfortunately applied very individually [i.e. only exceptional individuals benefit]. If they have only been around a short time, they are supposed to get into the displaced camp, where they are officially only allowed to live in *tukuls* [huts] and *rakubas* [shelters]. But the DoD often takes months and months about it, and the people wait on their rubble.

In total, 39 people have been reported killed during the demolitions. This number is remarkably low given the scale of the programme, and is certainly due to the reluctance of the population to resist the massive police and army operations, as explained by one Dinka chief:

Fighting is not an issue that is tackled by women and old men like myself. There were no young men for the fight. The work of old men in war is to direct the strong ones, because old men have the experience. But when your flank is actually broken. it is the youth that secure the running [retreat] and safe return home of the old.[21]

At the outset of the demolitions in October 1990, the people of Hilat Shok resisted. The cost was three dead and all the squatters' property burned: this deterred further resistance from Southerners. Moslem westerners from Kordofan and Darfur were more ready to assert their rights, and at Kurmuta in December 1991, they resisted. Among them were a number of policemen, whose gunfire killed at least one soldier in the demolition squad. In three days of conflict, at least 21 squatters, including women and children, were killed. On the final

---

[20] Interviewed in Khartoum, February 1996.
[21] Quoted in: Yath, 1994, p. 209.

160

day, the army burned and bulldozed the entire settlement and removed the people. Among the casualties was a UNICEF water programme—whose destruction appeared to cause more outrage in the international agencies than any other abuse. A third major incident at al Kadier in Omdurman in October 1994 occurred when police shot into a crowd of protesters, leaving fourteen dead.

The displaced were unable to secure alliances with the democratic forces in Khartoum: they had few contacts with them, could not engage in strikes (because very few worked in the formal sector), and the government was successful in turning much of the city population against them.

The removals from Khartoum have several rationales. One was urban replanning (the official pretext for the entire programme) and implicitly maintaining the Arab-Islamic character of the city. The economic transformation of Sudan since the late 1970s, followed by the ideological triumph of extremist Islam, appeared to be threatened by the sheer weight of numbers of non-Arab and non-Moslem migrants to the capital. The government selectively cites a World Bank report that supported the principle of town planning, but not the practice forcible relocation, in support of its programme.

A second rationale was land speculation and dispensing land grants to civil servants, salaried workers, army officers and others as a reward. Unable to pay reasonable salaries, the government is trying to buy the loyalty of the urban populace through giving out land. It uses a complicated land classification system, with all plots graded according to location, size and desirability. Most middle class Sudanese families aspire to build themselves a town house, and one of the major obstacles they face is obtaining land. Government distributions of urban land to salaried employees and others proved extremely popular, and became an important means of dispensing patronage.

A third rationale is maintaining security in the capital. The Southern displaced have often been described as the 'fifth column' of the SPLA, and successive governments have been deeply fearful of the implications of having such a huge Southern population on the doorstep of Khartoum. The NIF is well aware that governments are made and unmade in Khartoum, and recalls the important role played by displaced people in the demonstrations that brought down the Nimeiri regime. Dr John Garang has occasionally spoken publicly of his 'cells' in the northern cities, and although there is no evidence for SPLA mobilisation among the displaced, the security services have taken the implied threat seriously.

In the new 'peace cities' and 'peace camps', security is tight. The same UN official quoted above continued:

> There is very tight control. They are registered for everything; jerrycans. . . . It is mass controlled so as not to be a threat to the Government.

More generally, the government and its sympathisers blame much of the crime in the city on the Southern population. A former advisor to the NIF's urban planning programme has written of the consequences of the collapse of order in the South and the mass migrations north:

> The orderliness and tranquillity of Khartoum is gone; it has become a wild, uncontrollable city full of crime, thieves, drunkards, whores, hustlers, homeless, shills and terrorists, which all of the various security organs and religious police are hard-pressed to 'tame.'[22]

The implications were made explicit by a prominent government magistrate: 'Perhaps all the wrong-doings in society come from the slums: wine-making, prostitution, and the handling of stolen property.'[23] Many of these acute social problems are indeed located in the camps, because of the extreme poverty and social dislocation to be found there. The NIF prefers to ascribe the problems to the allegedly backward practices of non-Moslems, implying that removal or conversion to Islam will solve the problems.

According to a survey in Gerief West and Suq el Markazi, most of the displaced themselves attributed the relocation programme to the social and cultural prejudices of the general population of

---

[22] T. Abdou Maliqalim Simone, *In Whose Image? Political Islam and Urban Practices in Sudan*, University of Chicago Press, 1994, p. 118.
[23] *Al Inqaz al Watani*, 10 December 1991.

Khartoum. Slightly fewer blamed the government—those who did believing that security concerns were paramount.[24] The relocations policy is indeed genuinely popular among much of the urban population, some of whom have provided generous support to the Commission of the Displaced and local agencies involved in the programme.

Finally, placing squatters and the displaced in peace cities and peace camps enables the government to exercise social and political control over a diverse population and where possible advance the cause of extremist Islam. This issue will be taken up in the following chapter.

Restriction, Repression and Neglect

Government policies towards the displaced have maintained them in a state of subjugation, deprived of services and economic opportunities.

Education is a major concern for the displaced. In the 1980s and early '90s, voluntary organisations, notably churches, established modest schools in the camps. By 1990, the Roman Catholic church had 66 schools. In July 1992, however, the government annexed or closed all the schools in displaced camps on the pretext that they were not properly licensed. This led to a major confrontation with the churches, and at the end of the year, the government partly backed down. A former journalist noted the unusual act of solidarity that made this possible:

> The government tried to take over the primary schools [saying] the curriculum and teachers must come from the Government. It wants the Christian children to be influenced at all costs. The church leaders stood together. They had help from the UN agencies. The U.S. ambassador and the U.K. ambassador and UNICEF went to quarrel. In meetings they talked, and saw results.[25]

---

24 Yath, 1994, pp. 204-5.
25 Interviewed in Khartoum, February 1996.

The government agreed that the church schools could reopen, but under strict conditions, one of which was that they could not provide meals to students. The lack of a meal made the schools far less attractive to impoverished pupils and their families. By 1994, out of a total of 300,000 displaced people, less than 9,000 children were in schools.[26]

Medical services are extremely restricted. The mainstay of the regular health service, the subsidised distribution of drugs to registered pharmacies, is limited to planned areas of the city (i.e. excluding displaced camps), and only those with identity cards (i.e. not the displaced) are entitled to make use of their services. In 1994, only 22 clinics operated in the official displaced camps. For serious illnesses, displaced people have to travel to the hospitals in Khartoum, where they routinely face discrimination.

Apart from Islamic agencies (see chapter 9), the main attempts to provide basic services to the displaced communities have been made by Sudanese church agencies. Their attempts to operate in the displaced camps have been met with official restrictions and a range of methods of harassment.

The government restricts the economic options for the displaced, to the extent that many people have no option but to turn to illegal activities. One of the main sources of income is brewing. Sharia law prohibits alcohol production for sale. In theory, non-Moslems can brew for their own consumption, but the law is enforced in a way that criminalises all alcohol production for whatever reason. All unlicensed trade is forbidden and petty traders are regularly arrested and detained. Restrictions on women's dress, specifically the requirement that women wear the veil, ensure that the poorest displaced women are unable to travel freely and hence cannot conduct trade.

The Public Order Courts, set up in 1991, dispense summary justice. Junior military officers, using elementary interpretations of the Sharia, pass judgement on minor offences. Displaced people, almost always appearing without any form of representation, are

---

[26] African Rights, *Sudan's Invisible Citizens: The Policy of Abuse Against Displaced People in the North*, February 1995, p. 24.

164

routinely sentenced to lashing, fines or prison terms for trivial offences.

One of the more remarkable legal provisions is the definition of prostitution. Under Article 154 of the 1991 Penal Code, 'They shall be deemed to commit the offence of prostitution whoever is found in a place of prostitution so that it is likely that they may exercise sexual acts or earn therefrom.' The act describes a place of prostitution as 'a place designated for the meeting of men and women between whom there are no marital relationships or kinship, in circumstances in which the exercise of sexual acts is likely to occur.' This provision gives such leeway for interpretation to a judge that it is extremely easy to convict women on the slenderest evidence, or no evidence at all.

Displaced people face great difficulties in obtaining accommodation. They are easily exploited or evicted by unscrupulous landlords. They enjoy no legal protection in the labour market, and can be dismissed by employers without notice or reason given, or exploited—for example, not be paid their full wages— without redress.

This litany of discrimination and abuse is no accident: it is a reflection of policy based upon economic and political interest. The displaced are wanted only insofar as they present a pool of cheap labour and the raw material for the NIF's programme of Islamic social planning: otherwise, the government would rather they did not exist.

Co-opting the International Humanitarians

The crisis of the displaced has coincided with international concern with finding a means for providing assistance and protection to internally displaced people. This has included the establishment of a special inquiry at the UN Secretariat,[27] a resolution at the UN

---

27 Francis M. Deng, *Protecting the Dispossessed: A Challenge for the International Community*, Washington D.C., The Brookings Institution, 1993.

Human Rights Commission,[28] and various other initiatives by governments and NGOs. So far, these have done rather little for the Sudanese displaced.

Since 1988, a succession of UN missions has visited Sudan with a view to finding solutions to the problem of the displaced. While providing remunerative employment for UN consultants, these missions have also had at best a modest impact. A consistent theme in UN approaches to the crisis in Sudan is to see the problems as technical and logistical, wholly ignoring the political dimensions. The crisis is envisaged as the outcome of managerial shortcomings, instead of being recognised as the result of policy. This has allowed the Sudan Government to neutralise the potential threat caused by international agencies, and even to obtain their blessing for its entire project of relocation.

In June 1990, a UNDP consultant's report recommended that a comprehensive socio-economic survey of the displaced settlements was needed before a policy could be formulated, and recommended that the migrants should be integrated into urban planning, and all relocation be done on a strictly voluntary basis.[29] Despite this recommendation, and evidence that only a minority of the displaced were ready to leave the Three Towns, the UN continued to toy with plans for large-scale relocation. An internal report by the UN Emergency Unit in November 1991 supported the establishment of 'zones of peace' in 'productive areas free from conflict' to absorb 200,000 displaced people.[30] It also echoed government policy with a proposal to move the displaced into former refugee camps in eastern Sudan. The same document deplored the fact that the government Commission on the Displaced was 'organisationally weak, disorganised and lacks resources', and mentioned the advantages of membership of the Squatter Settlements Abolishment Committee. In

---

[28] UN Commission on Human Rights, 'Forced Evictions,' (1993/77), 10 March 1993.
[29] UNDP, 'Relocation and Repatriation of Displaced Persons in Sudan,' Report to Minister of Relief and Displaced Persons, June 1990.
[30] UN Emergency Unit, 'Report on the Problems Facing the Khartoum Displaced,' 7 November 1991.

short, the UN accepted the government's policy priorities and worked with the avowed aim of trying to improve the programme.

In 1991-2, the UN role involved sending a series of consultants to Khartoum. A fact-finding mission from Habitat, the UN housing agency, in March 1992 met with government and UN representatives and concluded that 'with proper planning and professional guidance, the extensive economic costs of this program could be significantly reduced.'[31] The UN special emergency co-ordinator in Sudan also made an assessment. Neither assessment involved consulting the squatters or displaced themselves, nor indigenous or international NGOs. The most comprehensive UN investigation was carried out in April 1992. While not questioning the need for an ambitious and rigorous urban plan for Khartoum, the consultant recommended that the present relocation program be stopped. In his draft report, he stated that further UN assistance to the Sudan government should be conditional on the Government of Sudan accepting certain principles, notably (1) the right of Sudanese citizens to live where they chose; (2) the reality that most migrants in urban areas have come to stay, (3) the immediate halt to all relocations, and (4) the principle of volition and choice in all future programmes for urban planning and the displaced.[32]

The official version, dated 9 May, was significantly different. It contained the same four principles, but the conditionality has been removed, and the report stated that the government of Sudan 'has reiterated its commitment and acceptance of' the four points. Apparently, the government had told the UN that the relocation programme was now complete, so the demolitions would cease. The government, however, displayed no noticeable willingness to stop the relocations, which continued unchecked. Sharaf el Din Bannaga, the Khartoum State Minister of Housing, speaking at a government

---

[31] UN, 'Short and Medium Term Needs Assessment of the Displaced, Squatter and Urban Poor in Sudan,' Report of the UNHCS (Habitat) Fact Finding Mission, 20-27 March 1992, p. 7.
[32] UN, 'Needs Assessment of the Displaced and Squatters in Sudan, Technical Report,' Draft, April 1992. (Not made public.)

seminar on unauthorised settlement, angrily rejected any suggestion that voluntary relocation was a possibility:

> The squatters of Khartoum . . . are in most cases land speculators rather than people in need of shelter. Apart from government employees, the majority of the squatters are unemployed. . . Ideally the movement should be voluntary but this is not practical. Because, some occupy very expensive plots which they want to sell and not live in. The attitude of most squatters is to grab government land and when compensated he sells it and looks for another squatter site.[33]

Government maps of Khartoum circulated at the seminar clearly showed large areas of each of the Three Towns designated for demolition, and other areas marked 'pending.' The Minister also attacked western humanitarian organisations for 'becoming very aggressive for no reason' and spreading 'unfounded allegations' in the western media.

Speaking at the same seminar, Per Janvid, the UN Special Co-ordinator, mentioned only that the government had accepted *three* principles—halting the relocations was notable for its absence.[34] However, the UN's commitment to working with the government was unaffected. Mr Janvid said: 'The UN has embarked upon a process together with the Ministry of Housing to re-examine the problems and propose solutions which fall within the parameters of government policy and which will be addressed through a project proposal we are developing.'

The UN project proposal called for international assistance to fourteen sites in and around Khartoum, and was costed at US$11.5

---

[33] Sharaf el Din Bannaga, 'Unauthorized and Squatter Settlements in Khartoum,' May 20, 1992, pp. 27-8. Referring to the 'unemployed', the Minister chose to ignore the fact that 65% of the Khartoum workforce is employed in the informal sector, and that the city's middle classes rely on the cheap labor provided by the 'unemployed' squatters in their houses, offices and markets.

[34] Speech to the Ministry of Housing Seminar, May 20, 1992, p. 2.

million.[35] The concessions that the UN had wrung out of the government were (1) that there would be no more relocations to unprepared sites and (2) that the affected communities would 'participate' in the relocations—in all other respects, the government's 'action plan' was to go ahead. As before, the UN declined to invite NGOs to participate, and remained secretive in all its dealings with the Sudan government.

The government thereby succeeded in co-opting the UN. For several months, the UN consulted and negotiated, while the government went ahead regardless. By the time the UN had come close to adopting a position, the government presented the relocations as a *fait accompli*. Perhaps believing that there were no more relocations remaining to be done, the UN then pretended that the government had agreed to halt the demolitions. When this was proven false, the UN instead agreed to co-operate with the ongoing programme. Until his departure in 1995, Per Janvid remained wholly docile.

Since May 1992, the Sudan Government has maintained the upper hand over the western donors. While some donors (notably the U.S.) have tried to take a more vigorous stand, the supine position of the UN has thwarted this. A report by the UN Emergencies Unit in September 1994 contains the following passage, revealing for the extent to which the UN had been rendered powerless:

> Although two years ago an agreement was reached to allow UN monitoring of relocation procedures, communications have downgraded and the activities take place in a more clandestine manner. It is noted from previous observations that the relocations are a military maneuver involving considerable show of force, commandeering of civilian transport, and exercise of martial law. There are on record, 18 incidents of fatality resulting from forced relocation and perhaps more undocumented. As of late the relocations are reported to take place at night with the residents 'being forced from their homes at night by men with guns.'[36]

---

35 UN Project Proposal for the Urban Poor in Khartoum, May 20, 1992.
36 UN Emergency Unit, Khartoum, Sudan, 'Briefing Notes about the Khartoum Displaced Population,' September 1994, pp. 5-6.

Given that the main aim of UN policy was to 'humanise' the relocations policy by helping to provide services to the peace cities, another comment in the report is worthy of note:

> 396,000 [people] have been forcibly relocated to six official, but virtually unserved areas on the urban fringe.[37]

The total number of people in official camps at the time was estimated by the UN at 453,000. At the time, UNDP was circulating a project proposal, costed at $11.4 million, virtually identical to the May 1992 proposal. It even included the following item:

> The project seeks to reinforce the urban planning capacity of the Ministry [of Housing and Public Utilities] through technical training programmes, both in country and abroad. . . . The objective of the technical assistance and training is the strengthening of the managerial capacity of the Ministry regarding the implementation and the development [of] urban area planning, upgrading and land regulation procedures and policies, with an emphasis on community participation and the involvement of beneficiary households.[38]

After so many years of watching violent removals to unprepared sites, not as an outcome of accident but a matter of government policy, it is remarkable for the UN to believe that training government staff in 'community participation' and 'the involvement of beneficiary [sic] households' would make a difference.

The co-option of UNDP in Khartoum was unfortunate for a higher-level UN initiative, which was aimed at developing new international mechanisms to protect internally displaced people. For too long, internally displaced people had been denied the international assistance and protection that refugees are entitled to (although they do not always receive it). The proposal to create a new Department of Humanitarian Affairs (DHA) at the UN was an

---

[37] UNEU, 1994, p. 7.

[38] UNEU, 'Urban displaced squatter settlement project', project proposal, January 1994, p. 4.

attempt to address this problem. UN General Assembly Resolution 46/182 which authorised the creation of the DHA in March 1992 specifically mentioned 'complex emergencies', and one of the countries the drafters had in mind was Sudan. In his first year in office, the head of DHA, Ambassador Jan Eliasson, was given formal oversight of emergency programmes in Sudan, including OLS.

Unfortunately, internal UN politics hamstrung the DHA from the outset. Jealousies from other UN agencies prevented it in practice playing its wonted co-ordination role. The UN Secretary General undermined the DHA by giving the role of humanitarian co-ordinator in former Yugoslavia to UNHCR and by failing to award it a lead role in Somalia. On the issue of internally displaced persons, the Secretary General set up his own commission to investigate the problem, and sent the eminent Sudanese scholar and diplomat Francis Deng to Sudan to report.

As a kinsman of many of the displaced people, Francis Deng was uniquely placed to understand their sufferings and aspirations. His report reflects this.

> People at the camps . . . far away from home and evicted from the city, revealed an unmistakable resentment at the inherently degrading conditions of their displacement. Behind the superficially happy faces was a sense of rejection, uprootedness, alienation and anxiety, a suspension between despair and hope, all of which they communicated by various means, mostly in Dinka. One person spoke as the crowd watched approvingly: 'We will not tell you anything; you watch with your own eyes, then go and think for yourself.'[39]

However, given the position already taken by UNDP in Khartoum, there was little that Francis Deng could do other than speak his mind, giving a voice to the displaced people. This he chose not to do, at least in public. One displaced man urged him to do so, repeatedly voicing his complaints:

---

[39] Deng, 1993, p. 76.

'I am speaking my mind because someone must; I know I will not remain free after you go.' I wondered later whether I would protect or expose him if I raised his concern with the authorities. I chose silence.[40]

Deng certainly brought up the cause of the Khartoum displaced with the UN Secretary General and other highly-placed politicians and officials. But his public statements—or rather, lack of them—disappointed the displaced, and his study did not appear to change UN policy.

Meanwhile, the institutional position of OLS had become more complicated. Headed by UNDP in Khartoum and UNICEF in Nairobi, with WFP reserving considerable autonomy in deciding its food deliveries, it was now placed under DHA. In principle, this could have meant that OLS would give itself a wider mandate, to address the range of issues of concern to DHA, such as the displaced. Instead, DHA followed the narrow interpretation of the OLS mandate and only concerned itself with government-approved relief activities in the South.

Throughout, the attitudes of prominent UN staff members has proved crucial to the character of whatever humanitarian activities have been undertaken. Sudan has been unfortunate in having a succession of senior UN staff members who appear to have lacked the insight, integrity or courage required to use their resources and leverage to maximum effect. Michael Priestley never challenged the government, perhaps fearing the fate of his predecessor Winston Prattley. As a former academic and critic of the disaster relief network,[41] Randolph Kent might have been expected to take a challenging approach to the problems faced by the UN in Sudan during his stint in Khartoum as emergencies co-ordinator. He did not: he is recalled as the architect of a policy of compliance. Likewise, Per Janvid proved unwilling to take any institutional risks and was therefore easily manipulated by the government. He sharply differed from some of his more junior staff, who saw the dilemmas

---

[40] Deng, 1993, p. 76.
[41] See: Randolph Kent, *The Anatomy of Disaster Relief,* London, Pinter, 1987.

more clearly and could mitigate some of the most undesirable effects of this policy, but who could do little to influence the overall policy direction. Having signally failed to stop the demolitions, Janvid proposed Project Amal—a modest attempt to make the process more humane, including providing expertise to the Ministry of Housing and Public Utilities. The government took this as an endorsement of its plan.

In 1995, the newly-appointed UNDP Resident Representative, Christoph Jaeger, took an even more pro-government line than his predecessor. One international NGO director described his approach:

> Jaeger believes that to do business here is non-confrontational. It is like talking to people at dinner or tea, calling at offices, drip drip drip. He thinks the confrontational approach was tried and failed: this can't do any worse.[42]

On one occasion—the forced relocation of nearly 10,000 people from the Angola settlement in December 1995—Jaeger did protest, and try to create a common front with the NGOs. (Ironically, the NGOs took the lead in continuing to co-operate with government policy.) But in general he has accepted the case for 'development' and attributed abuses to managerial failings. Several remarkable verbatim quotations from Mr Jaeger can be found in the *OLS Review*. One of them is:

> There is no [Government] strategy for the displaced and therefore no systematic approach. . . this results in things like the destruction of UNICEF's water pumps and other assets. It is not a deliberate policy of the Government; these things happen because of administrative problems. . . I really feel that it is an organisational problem. . . If we want to make changes they have to come from within the Government.[43]

This thinking was echoed by a senior international NGO field director, who said: 'The problem may be the personality of Minister

---

[42] Interviewed in Khartoum, February 1996.

[43] *OLS Review*, p. 89.

Bannaga. Some organised a trip for [Minister] Mohamed Omer Khalifa. It was a good thing; he is a decent man.'[44] Five years on, such statements require a remarkable act of faith.

The Human Cost

The Sudan Government defends its relocations policy on the grounds that it is providing a permanent and humane solution to the problems faced by the displaced. The UN has essentially accepted this position. However, the facts do not support such a sanguine view.

Some of the malnutrition rates recorded are alarming: above 30% or even 40% of children recorded as malnourished. A consultant to the Adventist Development and Relief Agency (ADRA) examined the evidence for malnutrition rates:

> On the one hand MoH [Ministry of Health] records show a gradual improvement in nutritional status while a much lengthier survey by SCC shows a gradual worsening of nutritional status.
>
> Perhaps the most important factor pertaining to malnutrition is the continuous uprooting of the already displaced and once again dispossessed through the ongoing demolitions.[45]

At the minimum, it is certain that the demolition have not improved the material condition of the displaced. What appears to be happening is not that nutritional status is increasing, but that the Sudan Government— and the UN agencies—are growing more tolerant of poor nutrition. Whereas official RRC standards put a ten per cent rate of child malnutrition,[46] a 1996 UN report referred to 'acceptable' rates ranging from 13.7% to 16.1%.[47] The *OLS Review* argued against reducing food rations, concluding:

---

[44] Interviewed in Khartoum, February 1996.
[45] M. Pearson, 'The Nutritional Impact of Food Aid on the Displaced in greater Khartoum,' ADRA, May 1995.
[46] Less than 80% standard weight for height.
[47] *OLS Review*, pp. 126-7.

In this regard, the Review Team was especially alarmed at the way in which standards for what constitutes a nutritional crisis appear to have eroded. In effect, it appears that OLS agencies are accepting ever higher levels of malnutrition as acceptable among war-displaced populations.[48]

THE NUBA MOUNTAINS

The war in the Nuba Mountains arises from a long history of discrimination against the Nuba peoples and their political, economic and social marginalisation. The term 'Nuba' carries two very different sets of connotations: to the people themselves, it refers to the myriad cultures and traditions of the more than fifty different tribal groups in the Nuba Mountains. The music, dance, body art and wrestling of the Nuba peoples have been made rightly famous by some western photographers and anthropologists, and most Nuba people are proud of their distinctive traditions. But, for the dominant class in Sudan, and in particular the NIF, 'Nuba' refers to second class citizens—'primitive' black people, servants and labourers. The Nuba, along with Southerners, are the victims of a racism that pervades life in Northern Sudan. In an important sense, the war is a struggle for who has the right to define Nuba identity.

Discrimination has been a constant in the Nuba experience. In education, Nuba students were consistently disadvantaged—and many volunteers for the SPLA are frustrated students. Due to lack of economic opportunities at home, many Nuba men were forced to become labour migrants, where they were exposed to discrimination and exploitation. In local government, the Nuba were usually not awarded their fair share of jobs.

There is also an intense struggle for natural resources in the Nuba Mountains. The region is rich in fertile land, and is one of the main areas where mechanised farming can be expanded. The issue of land ownership was the most explosive question in the pre-war Nuba Mountains, as merchant farmers, under the aegis of the MFC,

---

[48] *OLS Review*, p. 152.

expropriated smallholders' land. For many farmers, the fight for land eventually turned into a guerrilla war against the government.

The struggle over land sharpened the other areas of dispute in the Nuba Mountains. The Baggara Arab herders who share the plains with the Nuba also lost grasslands to the big farms, and were pushed to pasture their animals on Nuba farms. Farmer-nomad relations always have the potential for friction, and by the 1980s acrimonious and bloody disputes were becoming common. Increasingly, the Nuba would not get a fair hearing in the courts or the inter-tribal conferences convened by the government. One of the tragedies of the Nuba Mountains is the way that the Baggara, themselves a poor and deprived group, were manipulated by politicians to be the vanguard of the attack on the Nuba.

Since independence, the Nuba have struggled to achieve political representation in Khartoum. Despite winning seats in general elections, and forming coalitions with parties representing other marginalised areas of Sudan, the Nuba political agenda has consistently been blocked. This is due not only to the northern elites' stranglehold on power, but also due to infighting within the Nuba political parties. From the late 1970s, a more radical Nuba youth movement, Komolo, became influential. Headed by Yousif Kuwa Mekki, now SPLA Governor of the Nuba Mountains, Komolo aimed to recreate Nuba identity, and made it clear that it was prepared to resort to armed struggle to achieve its aims.

War and Famine

The war in the Nuba Mountains began in July 1985.[49] There were two events: an isolated raid by an SPLA unit on a cattle camp for Baggara Arab nomads close to the north-south internal boundary, and the government decision to arm the Baggara as a militia to fight the SPLA and the civilian population thought to be sympathetic to it. While the SPLA was not present in force until 1989, militia attacks became routine and an army crackdown became intense.

---

[49] African Rights, *Facing Genocide: The Nuba of Sudan*, London, July 1995.

The first stage of the war was marked by militia raids, to loot cattle, kill and occasionally to burn villages. In areas where SPLA units penetrated, the army also undertook mass reprisals, always targeted at villages and civilians. Military intelligence also began a crackdown on chiefs it suspected of sympathising with the SPLA, culminating in 1988 with mass arrests of suspected opposition sympathisers in the towns.

The war intensified with the arrival of the SPLA New Kush Division in 1989. It quickly overran large areas of the Nuba Mountains, and unleashed a ferocious response from the militia and army. Between 1989 and 1991 scores of villages were burned and thousands of villagers killed in joint army and militia assaults. The crackdown on educated Nuba intensified, culminating in wholesale arrests, executions and 'disappearances' in 1991. In its initial entry into the mountains, the SPLA was also abusive; many soldiers went on the rampage and killed and looted. However, while the government policy was to encourage its forces to violate rights, the SPLA command took firm action and reduced the excesses of its troops.

By 1991, repeated raids and the destruction of villages, and the economic disruption due to lack of trade and the collapse of employment caused the beginning of a severe man-made famine in the Nuba Mountains. This famine passed without any comment at all, let alone relief. There is no estimate for the numbers who died, but it undoubtedly ran into the tens of thousands. Between late-1991 and 1993, the Nuba Mountains suffered the most severe famine in Sudan. Over the subsequent years, famine has remained an intrinsic part of the government strategy to force the Nuba to submit.

Jihad and Peace Camps

Government assaults on the Nuba reached a new peak with the *Jihad* declared in January 1992. This involved a military offensive of an unprecedented scale and nature. Over 40,000 troops were deployed against SPLA positions, principally in Jebel Tullishi, together with air support. Continuous attacks went on for six months, but the SPLA remained undefeated.

177

The *Jihad* coincided with the start of a massive programme of forced relocation. Some of the most hard-line members of the Kordofan administration appeared to aim at depopulating the Nuba Mountains altogether, but in fact a rather different plan of relocating the whole Nuba population in militarised peace camps within South Kordofan emerged as the master plan. In February 1992, the head of the Peace and Resettlement Administration for South Kordofan said that 22 'peace camps' had been set up to cope with 70,000 so-called 'returnees' from the SPLA. Between June and September, about 40,000 people were moved by force from around Kadugli, in appalling conditions, to ill-prepared sites in North Kordofan. Many died. Larger numbers of people were relocated over shorter distances within South Kordofan, and some of those taken north were moved back south. In September, the government claimed to have 167,000 people living in 91 peace camps in the region.

The 1992 campaign failed: despite overwhelming numerical superiority, the army failed to capture its main targets and the programme of removing the Nuba from South Kordofan had to be abandoned. But similar if smaller-scale military strategies have continued since. Under the name 'combing', the army and militias engage in wholesale destruction or removal of everything in the rural Nuba Mountains. Villages are burned. Furniture, clothes and household goods are destroyed or taken off. Food stocks are burned or looted. Livestock are raided. People are now relocated more locally (and indeed displaced Nuba from elsewhere are brought back to South Kordofan).

The destruction of the rural Nuba serves two main purposes: it creates hunger, destitution and demoralisation, thus encouraging villagers to come to government-controlled centres to obtain relief and thereby submit to the government; and it enables soldiers and officers to enrich themselves. For the rural population, the result is often famine. Many people have been killed or injured in 'combing' operations. The army kills with complete impunity. Old or disabled people who cannot run away are often killed, by shooting or burning to death inside houses. Others are killed in the shelling of villages, mountainsides and caves, shot down while running away, or executed after capture.

178

The Sudan Government is forcibly abducting rural Nuba people. Groups of soldiers also ambush villagers as they come to collect water or mangoes, herd their animals, or walk to market or health centres. Those who have taken refuge in caves are attacked there, sometimes using tear gas to force them out into the open so they can be captured. It is a strategy designed to depopulate the rural areas and provide a captive civilian population for the garrisons and attached 'peace camps.' Women are raped as they are abducted, raped on arrival in garrisons, repeatedly raped in peace camps or labour camps, or forcibly 'married' to soldiers for the duration of the soldiers' tours of duty. The aim of the policy is to destroy the social fabric of Nuba society by raping every single woman.

The innocuously-named 'peace camps' have three principal functions. One is as 'protected hamlets' in a counter-insurgency strategy. They are concentration camps in the true sense of the word, where the rural population is forcibly concentrated so they can be placed under surveillance and control. A second role is as labour camps. Some of the camps are located close to large commercial farms, which required a docile labour force. All camps are attached to garrisons, where soldiers exploit the internees for cheap labour in their houses and barracks and for tasks such as carrying water and collecting firewood. Thirdly, peace camps are part of the NIF's grand strategy of transforming Sudanese society. Nuba villagers are taken there so that their political and cultural identity can be changed. Children are separated from their parents and 'educated' to become extremist Moslems in the mould of the NIF, in a process of forced acculturation. All able-bodied men are forcibly conscripted to join the Popular Defence Force militia, to become accomplices in the destruction of their own communities.

The South Kordofan peace camps are integrated into the government's agenda of extremist Islamic humanitarian action, social transformation and economic development. Islamic parastatals control key resources that can be used to compel the inhabitants of peace camps to submit to the government's agenda. Control over relief also gives immense power to soldiers and civil servants, which can be used in an arbitrary and cruel manner.

179

A number of Islamic NGOs operate in the peace camps in the Nuba Mountains. Muwafaq al Khairiya has a 'social welfare centre' and at least four peace villages in the region. There are also Islamic parastatals, including the National Development Foundation and the Nuba Mountains Islamic Development and Guidance Authority (NMIDGA), founded in 1994. At its inaugural meeting, Ali Osman Mohamed Taha, then Minister of Social Planning called on the Authority:[50]

> to work for the unification of the ranks, opinion and contradictions of the Moslems in the region and establish unity in place of tribal allegiance.
>
> The Minister urged the Authority to get involved in rehabilitation and reconstruction and stop war and destruction which are expressions of ignorance and lack of awareness. He said that colonial policies were bent on obliterating the region's Islamic identity, stressing that the Authority will represent a model of brotherhood and equality . . . as Islam calls for tolerance and altruism.
>
> He said that the main domain of the Authority's work will be *irshad* [guidance] and *hidayah* [Islamisation].

The roles of Islamic agencies will be examined further in the next chapter.

The Sudan Government has presented peace camps as a 'developmental' initiative: a means of increasing food production and putting displaced people to productive work. Some peace camps have been provided with tractors—or, to be precise, the commercial farms they service have been capitalised at state expense. Farm labour is often carried out under armed guard, ostensibly to guard the workers from rebel attack, but in reality to enforce discipline and prevent escape. Should there be a future food crisis in Sudan's cities, this military control over food production will prove a key asset in the government's efforts to obtain the necessary supplies.

---

[50] 'Minister of Social Planning calls for the Development of the Region and Discarding of Divisions', *Al Sudan al Hadith*, 12 April 1994.

Peace camps therefore combine all the elements of NIF social transformation: the dominance of political Islam, the militarisation of food supply, and the exploitation of cheap labour.

Humanitarian Embargo

The war is fought using basic commodities. The government tries to entice rural people into the peace camps by providing basic relief, such as food rations and clothes. For people who are absolutely destitute, even the offer of one meal can sometimes be enough to coerce them into forfeiting their freedom. Nakedness has driven some Nuba into the towns to look for clothes. Some young men have gone in search of an education. In order to maintain this strategy of emptying the rural areas, the government enforces a strict blockade of the SPLA-held areas. No trade is permitted. The only permitted assistance programmes are on the government side, and these are largely confined to major garrisons.

The Sudan Government has been consistently more sensitive on the Nuba issue than any other question associated with war and relief.[51] Government spokesmen and diplomats have striven to keep the Nuba off the agenda for peace talks and humanitarian access. For the most part they have succeeded. UN agencies including OLS and other humanitarian organisations have failed to challenge this exclusion. The mandate of OLS includes all war-affected areas and also refers to the North-South transitional zone, either of which could be interpreted to include the Nuba Mountains. But the government has consistently vetoed any involvement. UNICEF is also in a unique position among UN agencies on two counts: one, it can operate in a country without agreement from the government, and two, it has a human rights mandate (based on the rights of the child). Either of these reasons could be used to justify UNICEF working in SPLA-held areas without government approval. The 1994 OLS assessment mission included visits to the government-held Nuba towns of Kadugli and Rashad, for which it provided summary

---

[51] Excepting the 1997 escalation of the war in eastern Sudan.

overviews of need[52]—a tacit UN and government admission that the region falls under OLS. In government-held areas of the North, UNICEF implements its own programmes outside the OLS agreement; in principle there is no reason why it should not do the same in SPLA-held areas. But UNICEF has decided to restrict its Southern Sector activities to what is permitted under OLS, in effect sharply delimiting its mandate. The rationale was that UNICEF did not want to endanger OLS. It was implicitly trading its continued access in the South for subservience to the government in the North. The same trade-off was then to prevent any initiative by DHA.

In September 1992 the head of the DHA, Jan Eliasson, visited Sudan. Human rights organisations released evidence for serious abuses in the Nuba Mountains, including mass deportation, to coincide with his visit.[53] Eliasson responded by asking for a special mission by a member of his staff, Charles LeMunière, to Sudan in the coming months. This coincided with growing pressure on Sudan from the U.S. and UN. The outcome of these pressures was a reinvigoration of OLS in December 1992, but no initiatives for the Nuba Mountains: once again, the Nuba were bargained away. Such was the consequence of their national and international invisibility.

This international publicity may have also played a role in the slackening of the relocations programme at the same time, but internal factors were probably more important, namely the defeat of the government's military offensive by the SPLA and the high cost of the removals to North Kordofan.

In August 1993, the UN Special Envoy Vieri Traxler again raised the Nuba issue.[54] The government refused to respond, insisting that the entire region was under government control. In 1994, it was again raised in the context of the IGADD-sponsored 'peace' process. This time the government insisted that the area had not been specifically mentioned in the OLS agreement.

---

[52] Operation Lifeline Sudan, Northern Sector, '1994 Assessments in Southern Sudan, the Transitional Zone and the Khartoum Displaced Camps,' Khartoum, January 1995, pp. 11-13.
[53] Africa Watch, 'Sudan: Eradicating the Nuba,' News from Africa Watch, 7 September 1992.
[54] OLS Review, p. 34.

In July 1995 the Nuba were put back on the international agenda through the initiative of African Rights (the publication of *Facing Genocide*) and the BBC (the release of a documentary film, *Sudan's Secret War*). This time, the issue would not go away: a coalition had been built that ensured that the Nuba remained on the map. The coalition included the Nuba Mountains Solidarity Abroad, publisher of a quarterly newsletter *NAFIR*, and the Nuba Relief, Rehabilitation and Development Society (NRRDS), an indigenous relief agency which became active in the SPLA-held areas of the Nuba Mountains with the support of some international NGOs. The activities of these two Nuba organisations also gave the SPLM Governor, Yousif Kuwa Mekki, the confidence to take a higher profile within the SPLA.

The publicity over the Nuba coincided with a new assertiveness by the SPLA *vis-à-vis* OLS. At the SPLA-convened humanitarian conference in New Kush on 21-23 September 1995, both the SRRA and the NRRDS challenged the UN over its absence from the Nuba Mountains. The challenge was repeated in November. While it became increasingly difficult for the UN to refuse to acknowledge the humanitarian needs in the Nuba Mountains, the wider considerations that dictated UN compliance with government demands did not change. In November 1995, the UN Special Envoy again raised the issue in Khartoum. Despite the evidence to the contrary, the government insisted that it had total control of the Nuba Mountains, a position that it repeated in April 1996. As of the time of writing, no official relief of any kind has been delivered to the non-government held areas of Kordofan.

Co-opting the UN and NGOs

For most of the war, the only international NGO operational in the Nuba Mountains was Save the Children Federation (US), which had programmes in Dilling and Abu Jibeha. UNICEF then opened a programme giving support to health services in Kadugli. In 1995, the Sudan Government tried to entice more agencies into the region. Although it is a war-affected area and hence theoretically subject to the principles governing OLS—i.e. the neutrality of relief—the invitations were made and accepted without consulting the SPLA or invoking any of the OLS principles.

Agencies that operate in peace camps do so under the auspices of the Peace and Development Administration—an institution described by one aid worker as 'the humanitarian branch of security.'[55] Peace camps are given priority for all assistance—the principle that humanitarian agencies should target civilians on the basis of need is not applied. The military authorities have seized NGO supplies, including on one occasion in 1995 more than 500 tonnes of food. Accountability is meagre. The same aid worker described one incident:

> They told us there were 30,000 refugees where you aren't going— where you can't go for security reasons. We asked for the distribution list. They couldn't give it. We asked for the waybills. They were still making them up.

Despite this record, the Sudan Government has been able to exploit the readiness of international agencies to operate in *de facto* war zones, outside OLS, and entice them to open programmes in the government-held areas of the Nuba Mountains. Each of UNICEF, WFP and UNDP has begun to provide assistance, facilitating the government's programme without imposing any of the conditionalities inherent in OLS.

The UNDP Area Rehabilitation Scheme (ARS) in Kadugli is a derivative of UNDP's Area Development Schemes, implemented since 1988 in non-war areas of the north. These claim to be 'designed as an alternative to the conventional "top-down" approach [and] place the community in the forefront of project activities by making villagers the key decision makers.'[56] In Kadugli, the ARS consists largely of funding the government's own strategy for 'development', supporting the Peace and Development Administration to 'resettle returnees in peace villages and then promote agricultural development to strengthen their attachment to land.'[57] The *OLS*

---

[55] Interviewed in Khartoum, February 1996.
[56] UNDP, *Sudan: Seeds for the Future*, 1994, p. 3.
[57] UNDP, 1996, quoted in: *OLS Review*, p. 217.

Review commented that, 'Given that the Nuba [in peace villages] have been dispossessed of their land, this statement suggests a disturbing ignorance of local realities.' UNICEF is also supporting 29 'child friendly villages' in Southern Kordofan. In short, the Sudan Government is in the process of implementing its comprehensive counter-insurgency and social transformation strategy, courtesy of UN funds. As one aid worker put it, 'I know what we are doing is supporting a government programme, building up peace villages and supporting the Popular Defence Forces. There has to be a balance on the other side. We are doing good work, but there are bigger political issues that need addressing.'[58]

MILITARISATION OF FOOD SUPPLY

From the analysis of the NIF's social engineering in the midst of war, two themes stand out. One is the integral nature of the strategy: no one element can be taken in isolation. The way in which the war is fought, the manner in which the NIF and its supporters pursue their economic interests, and the manipulation and denial of humanitarian assistance are all part of a wider plan. The following chapter will examine that plan in greater detail, focusing on the Islamic humanitarian agencies and the way they co-operate under the 'Comprehensive Call.'

The second theme is the militarisation of food supply. The sharpest legacy of the 1990/91 famine is the close control of food supply exercised by the Sudanese army and its ancillaries. Although the urban rationing system was relaxed as the famine waned, the control systems were maintained, even intensified, in displaced camps and throughout the war areas. Chapter 10 looks at how this militarisation is taken to its extreme in the garrison towns of the South.

---

[58] Quoted in: *OLS Review*, p. 216.

9.

THE 'COMPREHENSIVE CALL'

The Comprehensive Call [aims at combating] rebellion of all types and forms of conspiracy targeting the Umma and its religion. . . [It aims at] the termination of wrong and the propagation of Islam . . . the consolidation and entrenchment of religious values in the lives of individuals and societies. . . [and] harnessing the monotheistic values of Islam [and] worship of Allah and construction and development of the land.

Abdel Gadir Mohamed Zein, Secretary General of Nidaa al Jihad organisation

The National Islamic Front is using Islam as a tool of power, in a remarkably comprehensive and sophisticated manner. The focus of this chapter is Islamic humanitarianism, one of the main components of this strategy. Islamic humanitarianism has progressive elements— it is comprehensive, it explicitly engages with politics, and (particularly in the area of small-scale credit), it meets a number of poor people's specific needs. There are genuine Islamic humanitarians in Sudan. But the NIF's political Islam is mostly enacted in the service of a dictatorial, exclusivist and warlike political project, allied to the political and commercial interests of a small but powerful class of people. It is opposed to democratic political mobilisation, pluralism and accountability. Throughout this chapter, Islamic humanitarian ideals that are appealing in theory have become debased and abusive in practice in Sudan today: it is a political-Islam*ist* version of humanitarianism. For these reasons the NIF project makes Sudan more vulnerable to famine, not less.

186

WHAT IS ISLAMIC RELIEF?

Islam has a long tradition of charitable action. Important sections of the Koran are devoted to the Moslem's duty to care for the poor and infirm, and the Koran specifies that certain proportions of the *zakat* (Islamic tithe) are to be donated to various categories of needy people. Giving *zakat* is one of the five pillars of Islam: it is envisaged as a religious and civic duty rather than a discretionary gift. One scholar of Islamic humanitarianism has put it thus:[1]

> Unlike other great sacred books, the Qu'ran sets out the basic headings of the budget and expenses of the state, and historically anticipated by some 12 centuries the principle of what we call social security.
>
> . . .
>
> Some ideologues such as Sayyid Qutb claim that *zakat* is a specifically Islamic concept superior to Christian charity because, being in principle mandatory, it neither exalts the giver nor demeans the recipient.

In Sudan, in common with most Islamic countries, mosques and Islamic institutions such as Sufi lodges have long been centres of charitable endeavour. Islamic principles have informed relief policies down the centuries, at village or province level and in the pre-colonial kingdoms and sultanates and the Mahdist state. What is relatively novel in contemporary Sudan is the way in which systematic humanitarian action has become part of a comprehensive social and above all *political* strategy adopted by a vanguard party, the NIF, which is determined to create an Islamic state. In the circumstances of ascendant political Islam and a civil war, interpreted as a *Jihad*, Islamic humanitarianism has taken on a radically different aspect.

---

[1] Jonathan Benthall, 'The Qu'ran's Call to Alms,' *Times Higher Education Supplement*, 3 January 1997, pp. 15-16.

Contemporary Islamic relief in Sudan cannot be understood outside the context of the NIF's goal of an Islamic State. Dr Hassan al Turabi is the most influential exponent of this particular vision of political Islam. He has written:

> An Islamic state cannot be isolated from society because Islam is a comprehensive, integrated way of life. The division between private and public, the state and society, that is familiar in Western culture, has not been known in Islam. The state is only the political expression of an Islamic society. . . .
>
> The ideological foundation of an Islamic state lies in the doctrine of *tawhid*—the unity of God and human life—as a comprehensive and exclusive program of worship. This fundamental principle of belief has many consequences for an Islamic state: first, it is not secular. All public life in Islam is religious, being permeated by the experience of the divine. Its function is to pursue the service of God as expressed in a concrete way through the *shariah*, the religious law.[2]

Dr Turabi's vision goes far beyond the role of the government as such, to encompass all significant elements of social, economic and political life:

> [A]n Islamic state is not primordia; the primary institution in Islam is the *ummah* [community of all believers]. The phrase 'Islamic state' itself is a misnomer. The state is only the political dimension of the collective endeavor of Muslims.[3]

By implication, the boundaries between government and other institutions set up by the *ummah* in accordance with the *sharia* are dissolved. It makes no sense to speak of 'governmental' and 'non-governmental' organisations: all are together in the collective enterprise of establishing a truly Islamic community and state.

Dr Turabi and his followers fervently believe that they represent the majority in Sudan, and that they have popular legitimacy. The

---

[2] Hassan al Turabi, 'The Islamic State,' in John L. Esposito (ed.), *Voices of Resurgent Islam*, New York, Oxford University Press, 1983, pp. 241-2.
[3] Turabi, 1983, p. 243.

modest share of the NIF vote in the 1986 election (eight per cent) does not deter them: ignoring the many Moslems who oppose the NIF, they hold that all genuine Moslems really want an Islamic state, and that a secular state disenfranchises them. This religious determinism also pervades the Islamic humanitarians: they hold that God and history are on their side.

Implementation of the Islamist project began many years before the 1989 coup: Islamic banking was established in Sudan as early as 1978; in the same year a government committee was established to ensure that the legal system was in conformity with Islam, Islamic penal law was introduced in 1983; the taxation system was gradually Islamised, and professional associations and universities were gradually penetrated by NIF cadres.

Islamic humanitarianism is another component, developed from the 1970s. Unsurprisingly, conventional western categories do not fit (although many of the relief and development activities of Islamic agencies are modelled on western NGOs). In Sudan today, Islamic agencies are often linked to government, the army, commerce and religious proselytisation. This has caused some concern among western humanitarians. In fact, it is questionable whether western ideals of humanitarianism actually fit the practices of most western relief agencies. In Europe and north America, charities are theoretically required to be non-military, non-commercial and non-governmental. Reality is more complicated. In the decades after its foundation in 1863 and the First World War, the ideals of the Red Cross movement also became a tool of nationalism and militarism in Europe, as nurses enlisted in national societies from patriotic fervour and went to the warfront.[4] Today, the activities of western humanitarian institutions often converge with their governments' foreign policies. Many are run on business principles: although they do not turn a profit, some run trading subsidiaries, and their staff may be paid handsomely. Though it has strong roots in Christian theology, most western humanitarianism also avows secular principles. For example, mainstream church-related agencies aspire

---

[4] Geoffrey Best, 'An Enduring Symbol: the Stubborn Survival of the Red Cross,' *Times Literary Supplement*, 14 March 1997, p. 12.

to help people of all religions and do directly not engage in missionary activity. But an ecclesiastical agenda is often smuggled in to a 'pure' humanitarian one. And there are assertive evangelical church agencies with a straightforward religious agenda (see chapter 12). Governmental and UN donors also pursue their own political and economic interests under the guise of humanitarian action. Therefore, it is arguable that Islamic agencies are simply more straightforward about their cultural, political and religious assumptions than their Euro-American counterparts.

But, the fact that some critics are hypocrites should not prevent criticism. One of the arguments of this book is that western relief agencies are commonly the witting or unwitting tools of other agendas. For Sudan's Islamic agencies, the same is true, *a fortiori*. Many of them combine support to the war effort, proselytisation, furthering government policies and engaging in profitable trade. In many places, Islamic agencies effectively represent the government.

The Comprehensive Call

The growth of Islamic relief agencies in contemporary Sudan is related to the overall Islamisation of the economy and government finance, to the declaration of *Jihad*, to the concept of Islamic Social Planning, and to an Islamist internationalism that seeks to build a network of Islamic countries that can collectively break their dependence on the secular-Christian West. Above all, Islamic humanitarianism operates within the compass of the *Da'awa al Shamla* or Comprehensive Call to God.

Like many of the central concepts used by the NIF, the Comprehensive Call does not have a single, precise, readily-available definition, other than the straightforward statement that Islam is being used as a fundamental means of creating and implementing policy and that Islam should become a guiding element in all aspects of every citizen's life. Rather, the Call is akin to a set of principles that can be adapted to particular circumstances. The NIF does not need to have a completely centralised and hierarchical decision-making structure. It can operate as a more devolved network, all parts of which enjoy some operational

190

autonomy but act in accordance with a basic set of principles. There may be lack of co-ordination at a low level, but by the same token the system gives legitimacy and encouragement to zealous junior officials, provided they act in accordance with the basic principles. This chimes with Turabi's wide-ranging interpretation of an Islamic state and society.

When we move from the theory to the practice, a different and less attractive side to the Comprehensive Call appears. One formulation was made in an internal NIF document for the launch of the Nuba Mountains *Jihad* in January 1992. In this instance, the Comprehensive Call had six main components:[5]

(1) religious indoctrination and the imposition of Islam on non-Moslems;
(2) political, social and economic favouritism for Nuba Moslems and their instigation to head the campaign;
(3) *Jihad* against all those who defy the Call, whether Moslems or non-Moslems;
(4) isolation of Nuba Christians and intimidation of church leaders, also isolation of the region from international human rights, humanitarian or solidarity organisations;
(5) resettlement in peace villages to help achieve objectives (1) and (2);
(6) crackdown on all Nuba, inside or outside the Nuba Mountains, who oppose the campaign.

The call for *Jihad* was reaffirmed with a *Fatwa* (an authorised religious opinion) which stressed that any Moslems co-operating with the SPLA should be regarded as infidels. The *Fatwa* reads:

An insurgent who was previously a Moslem is now an apostate; and a non-Moslem is a non-believer standing as a bulwark against the

---

5 Quoted in: Mohamed A. M. Salih, 'Resistance and response: Ethnocide and genocide in the Nuba Mountains, Sudan,' *GeoJournal*, 36, 1995, pp. 71-8, at p. 75.

spread of Islam, and Islam has granted the freedom of killing both of them.[6]

Among other abuses, government troops engaged in the Nuba Mountains *jihad* desecrated at least eight mosques, covering them with graffiti (telling the Moslems to come and pray in the government garrisons), destroying *zakat* grain and tearing up copies of the Koran.[7] Imam Adam Tutu Atrun, one of the most prominent Moslem leaders in the region, commented 'Islam does not allow Moslems to do this.'[8] Imam Adam and other Nuba Moslems would find it hard to recognise the benign descriptions of the Comprehensive Call put forward by the NIF and some Islamic agencies.

The Comprehensive Call has social, political, military, economic and humanitarian components. At the time of its formulation, the second most influential member of the NIF, Ali Osman Mohamed Taha, held the post of Minister of Social Planning. He established the Ministry in its new, expanded form and ran it for several years, before moving to become Foreign Minister. Under Ali Osman, the Ministry of Social Planning developed the concepts of Comprehensive Da'awa and Islamic *Inqilab* (revolution or total social transformation) in accordance with the NIF interpretation of the *Sharia*. During Ali Osman's tenure, a Department of Da'awa was established, and the 'Comprehensive Da'awa Funds' association was formed (initially named the Social and Charitable Funds Co-ordination Council). The latter brings together most of the Jihadist and Da'awa organisations active in Sudan, both parastatals and NGOs.

The Comprehensive Da'awa has been implemented most thoroughly in Blue Nile, an area lying within Northern Sudan whose inhabitants include a large minority of non-Arabs, members of ethnic groups such as the Ingessena, Burun, Gumuz, Koma, Uduk and a

---

[6] *Fatwa* issued by religious leaders, Imams of mosques and Sufists of Kordofan State, 27 April 1992.

[7] African Rights, *Facing Genocide: The Nuba of Sudan*, July 1995, pp. 292-5.

[8] Interviewed in Kauda, Nuba Mountains, 11 May 1995.

number of other small groups, and including many Christians and followers of traditional beliefs. Other areas of major emphasis for the programme include the Nuba Mountains and northern Upper Nile, plus the environs of major towns in the South such as Juba and Wau.

Islamic Social Planning

Islamic Social Planning is part of the Comprehensive Call focused on the core areas of the North which have been Moslem for centuries, but where the NIF believes that Islamic values have lapsed.

For example, a particular focus of Islamic social planning has been the Beja people of north-east Sudan—concern began well before the Beja Congress took up armed opposition to the government. The Da'awa-ist agency al Ithar al Khairiya ('Altruism' or 'Purity') is active in the region, among other things promoting mass circumcision ceremonies. The rationale for this is to 'cure social cavities'—social behaviour that is considered incompatible with the NIF project.[9]

Professor Zakaria Bashir Imam, of the International African University in Khartoum and a veteran NIF activist, has written authoritatively on the subject.[10]

> The idea of Islamic Social Planning means a continuing revolution for the remoulding of the human being and the institutions in society, in accordance with Koranic guidance. . . .
> Islamic Social Planning aims to achieve:
>
> 1. A complete and comprehensive remoulding of the Islamic personality with a view to making it a living, honest and

---

[9] *Al Inqaz al Watani*, 13 February 1996, p. 6.
[10] Zakaria Bashir Imam, 'From the Laws of Dynamism in the Holy Koran: Social and Economic Planning' (in Arabic), *Al Ingaz al Watani*, 30 May 1996, p. 3. The paragraphs cited exclude quotations from the Koran and Hadith.

conscious characterisation of Islamic concepts, values and teachings.

2. Build and reconstruct all state institutions on principles derived from the Koran.
3. Establish an Islamic society formed on the basis of Islamic principles and rules without coercion.
4. Establish an Islamic state to propagate right, justice, spread peace and security on all fields and actualised solidarity, compassion and support among all people, especially Moslems.
5. Establish an international Islamic civilisation and a new international order based on justice and fairness and the recognition of the cultures of others and their cultural, religious and ethnic distinctions.

The Professor outlines the means whereby these goals are to be attained, including 'a revolution in our understanding of the Koran,'[11] revision of all laws, and a huge programme of education and training that involves mobilising all religious, cultural and educational institutions in the country.

Another important principle is *Tamkiin*, which means empowering Moslems who form a weak minority and enabling them to take a dominant position in their society. This has particular relevance to Southern Sudan (and indeed neighbouring African countries), but is also applied in the North, where it entails establishing NIF dominance over key commercial and social sectors. The religious and humanitarian language masks the cynical pursuit of power.

Islam and Humanity in Warfare

The West is rightly proud of the Geneva Conventions and other international humanitarian law that restrains inhumanity in war. This includes strong prohibitions on inflicting starvation and destroying items indispensable to the survival of the civilian population.[12] The

---

[11] *Ibid.*

[12] 1977 Protocols Additional to the Geneva Conventions, Protocol I, Article 54 and Protocol II, Article 14.

Caliph Abu Bakr's instructions to soldiers also demonstrate that these principles are found in Islam:

> Remember that you are always in the sight of God and on the eve of your deaths; that you will give an account on the Last Day. . . . When you fight for the glory of God, behave like men, without turning your backs, but do not let the blood of women or of children and old people stain your victory. Do not destroy palm trees, do not burn down dwellings or corn fields, never cut fruit trees, and only kill cattle when you are obliged to eat them.[13]

The actual behaviour of the Sudan Armed Forces, the PDF and the various pro-government militias is very different. For them, the war areas have become ethics-free zones where any abuses are permitted, and all the crimes prohibited by Caliph Abu Bakr are committed with impunity. Many western relief agencies have a sad record of tolerating human rights abuses, usually tacitly justifying this on the grounds that to speak out would endanger their programmes. African Rights has no evidence that Islamic agencies have exposed or condemned abuses by the Sudan Government.

Islam and the Opposition

In general, the opposition to the NIF has not systematically challenged the NIF's claim to Islam, and nor has it constructed an alternative form of Islamic humanitarianism. For example, the SPLA has not publicised the burning of mosques in the Nuba Mountains, and the New Sudan Islamic Council (set up by the SPLA) has been small and not well-organised. The Northern opposition is fond of contrasting the NIF's claim to Islam with its actual practice, but only with the flight abroad of Sadiq el Mahdi at the end of 1996 did it systematically begin to contest the Islamic legitimacy of the government, making representations in Cairo and Jeddah. Very recently, senior members of the Umma Party have also begun to set up the Sudanese Community Islamic Relief Organisation, based in

---

[13] Marcel A. Boisard, *L'Humanisme de L'Islam*, Paris, Albin Michel, 1985, p. 259. We are indebted to Jonathan Benthall for this insight and quotation.

Saudi Arabia.[14] This has the aim of trying to re-direct some of the *zakat* contributions made by Sudanese expatriates away from the Islamic agencies working in NIF-controlled areas of Sudan. Others in the opposition have also been studying elements of the Comprehensive Call (particularly its micro-credit), with a view to trying to separate the developmental aspects of the model from its political colour. If successful, this may lead to the renewal of a non-extremist Islamic humanitarianism.

ELEMENTS OF A COMPREHENSIVE RELIEF STRATEGY

Modern Islamic humanitarianism in Sudan began in the late 1970s, with the re-entry of the NIF into government. Islamic agencies were part of the wider strategy of Islamising all aspects of society and entrenching the NIF so that it could withstand purges and changes in government. A prominent Islamist and former diplomat, Abdelwahab El-Affendi, explains:

> Shortly after the NR [National Reconciliation of 1977] deal a drive to increase membership ten-fold was launched, coupled with complete decentral-ization within the movement to make the organization more efficient and resistant to crackdowns. Decentralization was enhanced by setting up numerous autonomous sattelite [sic] organizations loosely affiliated to the group. The late seventies and early eighties saw the emergence of the Society of Women Vanguards of Renaissance, the Youth Society for Construction, the Association of Southern Muslims, the Association of Sudanese Ulama, the Islamic Da'wa (Missionary) Organization (and its offshoot, the Islamic African Relief Agency), the Namariq Literary and Artist Society, and the Union of Muslim Literary Men, to mention only the most prominent. Although most of these groups were not directly controlled by the Ikhwan [Moslem Brothers, NIF], Ikhwan could count on support from most of them in crucial moments.[15]

---

[14] Nasr el Din el Hadi el Mahdi, interviewed in March 1997.
[15] Abdelwahab El-Affendi, *Turabi's Revolution: Islam and Power in Sudan*, London, Grey Seal, 1991, p. 115.

The first Islamic agencies (such as IARA) were broadly similar to western NGOs in the activities they undertook and the governmental context in which they operated. Some other international Islamic agencies are similar. Since the NIF took power, and especially since Ali Osman Mohamed Taha became Minister of Social Planning, the activities of Islamic agencies have hugely expanded. They are subject to the government's relief regulations of 1992 and 1993, which, in the words of the *OLS Review*, leaves NGOs as 'little more than an extension of the state in Northern Sudan.'[16] Some of them are more akin to Iranian Islamic foundations.[17] The following discussion charts the Islamic agencies' rise from obscurity to dominance.

Operationality: Being Present 'On the Ground'

The first substantial Islamic relief NGO in Sudan was the Saudi-based Islamic African Relief Agency (IARA), originally an offshoot of the Da'awa al Islamiya (Islamic Call) organisation. It remains among the largest: in 1996 it had a budget for Sudan estimated at $2 million and 500 employees.[18] In its earliest days, IARA began contacting the much neglected Moslem enclaves in sub-Saharan Africa, and was particularly active in Idi Amin's Uganda until Amin's fall in 1979. IARA then formed the Islamic Relief Agency (ISRA: its name '*isra* also means 'ascension to heaven') which became active in Afghanistan and elsewhere.

In 1984-5, IARA was one of the Islamic NGOs that seized the opportunity presented by USAID's insistence on the privatisation of relief operations. Transport contracts were awarded to private

---

[16] *OLS Review*, p. 60.
[17] These foundations have wide autonomy and privileges; their ultimate aim is usually couched in religious or humanitarian terms, but some are powerful political and commercial organisations in their own right. They have become one of the major instruments of Iran's Islamic revolution.
[18] *OLS Review*, p. 96. By comparison the largest international NGO operations in Sudan are CARE with a $3.5 million budget and 160 employees and Oxfam-UK with $3 million and 200 employees.

companies (notably the U.S.-Sudanese Arkel-Talab haulage firm) and distribution contracts to international NGOs (notably CARE, SCF-UK and World Vision). It was an instance of the linkage between neo-liberal economics and international humanitarianism. The aim was leaner government and greater efficiency. But in Sudan as elsewhere capitalists have their own political leanings. Arkel-Talab had NIF links. Islamic NGOs such as IARA also seized the opportunity. After 1986, the government began to 'twin' indigenous and Islamic agencies with foreign ones. (IARA was briefly twinned with Oxfam.) In January 1993, the twinning system was revived (though it proved inoperable)[19], together with a new system of tight regulation of (read: restrictions upon) international agencies. One of these was the requirement that any available staff positions in international agencies be preferentially filled by Sudanese candidates nominated by the Ministry of Labour. While the principle of employing Sudanese in preference to expatriates with similar qualifications is laudable, the powers given to the Ministry in fact meant that NIF cadres or members of security services could be forced on NGOs.[20]

The Islamic NGOs had a longer-term agenda than the international NGOs. During the 1984-6 relief operation, foreign NGOs created distributional structures which supplanted the former SSU and native administration. The Sudanese staff of international NGOs gained a crucial role as interlocutors between rural communities and the authorities and relief providers: another step in the ascendancy of the educated over traditional rural structures. NGOs' activities gained enormous prestige in the eyes of the local populace. Comments such as the following, from a resident of the Red Sea Hills, were common up to 1991:

> There was no benefit [famine relief] from the government, no help. They didn't give us even a single date. No-one gave us anything apart from the *khawaja* [white man]. The government says it is

---

[19] Only four twinning arrangements operated, briefly, among the 54 registered international NGOs.

[20] 'Agreements Adopted by the Joint GOS/INGO/UN Meeting of 24-28 January 1993,' Khartoum.

responsible for the country, and that we are all Muslims, but no benefit can be expected from them. The *khawaja*, whatever he is, non-Muslim (*kafir*) [sic] or whatever, is more beneficial and helpful than our government.[21]

The 1986 elections coincided with continuing relief distributions, and there were many jokes in rural Sudan that people would prefer to vote for the *khawaja*, for *hesb al 'esh* ('the party of bread') or even Ronald Reagan (USAID sorghum was nicknamed *Reagan* after the man who had supposedly donated it). Restoring lost prestige to Islamic philanthropy was a challenge to the NIF. Local relief committees also presented an opportunity for reaching a wide spectrum of rural people. Western agencies scaled down their relief activities in Darfur and Kordofan in the late 1980s, and World Vision was expelled from Blue Nile in 1987. This left an opening for the NIF, which promptly moved in as patron; many relief committees were taken over. As a Sudanese businessman commented: 'These people [foreign NGOs] don't understand fundamentalists: they move like camels, but they are moving. They prepare groundswells for two years, five years.'[22]

The foreign-provided food aid of the mid-1980s encouraged the Islamists in two other ways. One, in some areas such as the Red Sea Hills, Koranic schools (*khalwas*) were entitled to relief allocations. In Sinkat, for example, their number tripled during this period.[23] Two, many Islamists worked as staff members for international agencies, learning their techniques and in some cases setting up programmes that were consonant with the Islamist agenda.

While learning from the international NGOs, the Islamic agencies and their patrons were active in finding ways to reduce the foreigners' operations. A number of means were employed. One was to criticise methods of fundraising such as child sponsorship,

---

[21] Quoted in Leif Manger *et al.*, *Survival on Meagre Resources: Hadendowa Pastoralism in the Red Sea Hills*, Uppsala, Nordiska Afrikainstitutet, 1996, p. 132. More precisely, *kafir* means non-believer, i.e. not a 'person of the book.'
[22] Interviewed in Khartoum, February 1996.
[23] Manger, 1996, p. 191.

condemning them as humiliating and creating a link of dependency between Moslem children and western Christian sponsors. PLAN Sudan Kassala had its child sponsorship programme halted on these grounds. Another method is to whip up local feeling against a foreign NGO. The NGO Christian Outreach was the victim of such a campaign in the Girba area in 1991-2. Christian Outreach was attempting to implement an income-generating programme; it was accused of charging *riba* usury on Moslems, and was ultimately forced to consider using an Islamic model of credit. The government has also imposed a range of restrictive regulations on foreign NGOs, governing their registration, employment of staff, foreign currency transactions, and use of vehicles and radios.

The Sudanese Red Crescent Society was a secular humanitarian agency, part of the international Red Cross and Red Crescent movement. The Islamists took it over from within. The SRCS's independence was already jeopardised in the mid-1980s: some of its staff in sensitive areas such as South Kordofan were already under severe pressure to co-operate extremely closely with security officials and army officers. In July 1989, its newly-appointed director, Dr Mansour el Agab, was detained by the al Bashir government, and a more favourably-inclined replacement was imposed on the organisation. Since then, the SRCS has come to operate in a manner similar to other Islamic NGOs, to the extent that it has caused embarrassment to the Federation of Red Cross and Red Crescent Societies. This has had ramifications for funding, which the SRCS claims has helped rather than hindered its mission. Its Secretary General, Dr Omer Osman, argued that this has created an opportunity for a mass-membership, community based organisation:

> We find this [cut in funds] useful as an organisation. We are growing. Now we have enough time to visit places. Now we are caring for our branches.[24]

This points to the greatest strength of the Islamic agencies: they are willing and able to invest in mobilising rural people, utilising the

---

[24] Interviewed in Khartoum, February 1996.

idealism, patience and hard work of many young people. The government slogan of 'returning to the roots' echoes this concern with focussing on the human and material resources of Sudan itself.

This strength is greatly amplified when Islamic NGOs have not only some governmental resources, but also the clear backing of the state behind them. For example in the small town of Bunj in Upper Nile, local people find it difficult to distinguish between Islamic agencies and the NIF government. Bunj is not a 'peace village' but an established rural town, historically on the frontier between Islam and Christianity and traditional religions.

A former accountant from Bunj knew the staff of the Islamic agencies there very well, as many of them were his former classmates, some of them very recent converts to Islam. He described how the NGOs operated:[25]

> Although [one agency][26] did not have a big headquarters in Bunj, the work it carried out was very effective. In the Bunj office it employed local Meban people, and also Arabs. It opened *Khalwas* [Koranic schools]. In Shatta there were three. It used local teachers; many of them were my friends. El Faki was a teacher there. Awad Omer was another; Mohamed was one. One was Chol—he had many colours; when it was the time of democracy, he said 'I am neutral'; he was a Christian before, became a Moslem, converted back to Christianity, and then became a Moslem again. I think his Moslem name is Nasr el Din. All the teachers are Moslems. They are all members of the NIF.
>
> The school opened in 1992. Many Meban were in the SPLA at that time. . . . The main role of the *khalwas* is to Islamise. Their lessons are all about the Koran. There are no academic lessons. Only one school in Bunj gave two or three academic lessons [per week]—the rest was all about the Koran. These schools are still operating now in 1996.[27]
>
> [One agency] was only teaching the Koran. I used to urge them to do other things too. Sometimes I would challenge them, 'what are you doing?' Because the teachers are all my colleagues, so I

---

[25] Interviewed in Ethiopia, August 1996.
[26] The name of the agency has been concealed to protect the informant.
[27] Bunj was overrun by the SPLA in January 1997.

started to challenge them. I said, 'I don't fear if you hand me over [to the security]'. They had all become members of the NIF.

The person in charge at Bunj was Majit. He is a local man. He was one of my best friends; we studied together in school. I used to put it openly to him. [In February 1996] I took tea with him. He was trying to convince me to convert to Islam. He was keen to say that the area needs much work, and we need you to co-operate. He said, 'you have to come over to us.' I said, 'I can co-operate but I am a Christian. I cannot change the belief I have because of work.'

Majit was originally called Mange Biki. He became a Moslem and went to Khartoum for a short course. That was in November 1995; the course lasted fifteen days. The course was run by [one agency]: they paid, they put him up, and the whole course was about the agency. He had joined them back in 1991. Before then he was a supporter of the Umma Party, then he became NIF. I don't know how he was recruited, because I was in Khartoum at the time.

The most active member of [the agency] there was al Sirr. He was always a Moslem and a member of the NIF from 1985 or 1986. All their people are one hundred per cent NIF.

[The agency] members have their guns. They collaborate with security. One called el Amin Tom (formerly Luma Tuwawa) is the chief officer of the *Mujahidiin* in Bunj. He is an NIF member; he also has a position in [the agency], '*Amin amanat al mutamar*'— they had an assembly in Bunj and he was the speaker. This assembly is a combination of the different governmental sectors, even the army. The assembly is the government's institution. El Amin is '*muhtadi*' [a convert] [and] a *mawlana* who leads the prayers. His role is to convert people; he is working for Islamising people. When he succeeds to convert someone, he gets a reward from [the agency]. The reward is in thousands of dinar.

One of my colleagues in Bunj was a book-keeper. He was Joseph, a Roman Catholic catechist. Now he is dead. He made a girl pregnant. The court charged him LS 1500. He had no money. So [the agency] intervened and told him, 'we can pay you this money, provided you convert.' Security was threatening him on one side, the agency was offering on the other. So he converted. That was about the time of Christmas 1994.

The security and [the agencies] collaborate closely. Security always provides [the agencies] with protection, and [an agency] also pays the security. The security committee of Bunj has members of [an agency]: one is Filel, a security man, another is

Tami, also a member [of the agency] and an officer in internal security.

This testimony brings to life many of the aspects of the work of some Islamic agencies: their intimate collaboration with the government, their close identification with the political aims of the NIF, and the various methods they use to obtain converts and support.

Funding Islamic Humanitarianism

Fundraising is the heartbeat of institutional humanitarianism. The NIF's brand of political Islam is also based on a vision of an Islamic economic system. In theory this rejects extremes of wealth and calls for equity and social justice. In practice, it entails NIF control of key economic sectors.

The transformation of Islamic charity in Sudan from a modest tradition of local donation into today's array of powerful agencies began with the establishment of Sudan's first Islamic bank, the Faisal Islamic Bank (FIB), in 1978. The Saudi Prince, Faisal al Saud, was behind the bank, and in Sudan its senior figures were NIF members or sympathisers. Like many aspects of the Islamist project, the idea of Islamic banking was borrowed from elsewhere—the Khatmiya sect (the basis of the DUP) had come up with the idea first. Islamic banks do not charge interest (*riba*), in conformity with the Koranic prohibition, but enter into a partnership with those in need of capital. There are four main kinds of partnership: *musharaka* (a joint venture, with the respective shares negotiated in advance), *mudharaba* (a joint venture in which the bank provides the full finance), *murabaha* (a form of trade credit) and a straightforward interest-free loan.[28]

Two years after its establishment in Sudan, the FIB made the important and innovative shift into small-scale loans to carefully

---

[28] Richard Brown and Elfatih Shaaeldin, 'Towards an Understanding of Islamic Banking: The Case of the Faisal Islamic Bank,' University of Khartoum, Development Studies Research Centre, 1982,

targetted clients. This contrasted with the continuing focus of the state-owned Agricultural Bank of Sudan on mechanised farms, which has been widely criticised as socially regressive, developmentally ineffective and environmentally damaging. The state-owned Industrial Bank of Sudan concentrated on large industries and the commercial banks chiefly lent for import-export trade. Attempts by international NGOs to fill the gap of supporting small farmers and artisans also largely failed to achieve adequate results. Their high failure rate has been attributed to the unfamiliarity of their institutions to the social and economic environment and their limited capacity, skills and experience. The field was therefore open for the Islamic banks.[29]

The FIB and its successors have achieved markedly more success than others in small-scale loans. In addition, they have always carried their political agenda with them: they are selective in deciding who they will support. NIF supporters are prime recipients of the banks' services, and they can also recommend and guarantee new applicants through a process known as *el tazkeya*. Bank services are also offered to new converts. FIB loans to small producers grew from LS 1.2 million in 1981 to LS 31.4 million in 1990.[30]

Among the statutes of the FIB—alongside its exemption from tax and its requirement not to pay interest—was an obligation to pay a certain proportion of its profits as *zakat*, the Islamic tithe. In the FIB's first year of operation, 1979, it paid something over ten per cent of its profit, amounting to LS 125,000, in *zakat*.[31] This was to provide the first major source of funds for specifically Islamic relief agencies. The *zakat* contributions of the FIB and other Islamic banks grew rapidly.

---

[29] Hamdan Mohamed Goumaa, 'Micro-Credit and Islamic Finance: A Measure for Reaching the Poor Majority,' unpublished paper, February 1997.

[30] Hamdan Mohamed Goumaa, 1997.

[31] Elfatih Shaaeldin and Richard Brown, 'Towards an Understanding of Islamic Banking: The Case of the Faisal Islamic Bank,' in Tony Barnett and Abbas Abdelkarim (eds.) *Sudan: State, Capital and Transformation*, London, Croom Helm, 1988, p. 135.

In Sudan and abroad, President Nimeiri's 1983 imposition of Islamic law was widely criticised on human rights grounds. But its social and economic implications went far wider. Economic advisors to the government were particularly alarmed at the implications of the 1984 Zakat and Taxation Act, which abolished all existing forms of secular taxation and mechanisms for determining government expenditure in favour of an Islamic system based on the provisions in the Koran, including the *zakat*. Under Nimeiri's version of *sharia*, *zakat* became a state tax, and—controversially for Sunni Moslems—the state took over authority for dispensing Islamic charity. Meanwhile a study commissioned by USAID found that the projections for *zakat* income were exaggerated and fanciful: the state would quickly become bankrupt were it not for external aid.[32] Even prominent Islamist economists such as Professor Mohamed Hashim Awad obliquely criticised the implications of the Act, arguing that *zakat* could not replace other taxes such as the business tax, and that as it had been passed at a time of drought and a budget deficit of over LS1 billion, the government would still be compelled to take measures 'incompatible with the objectives of the Islamic economic system.'[33] At this time, the NIF had the privilege of applauding Nimeiri's Islamisation measures, while disclaiming responsibility for the consequences.

The provisions of the Zakat and Taxation Act were first implemented only in 1986, and then on a relatively modest basis, when the Diwan al Zakat (Zakat Taxation Chamber) was formed to take charge of both levying the *zakat* taxes and dispensing the proceeds. Initially, the Diwan al Zakat operated only at a regional level. Economic Islamisation was piecemeal during the parliamentary period: Islamic banking expanded and the NIF

---

[32] A. E. Mayer, 'Sudanese Laws Affecting the Private Sector and the Economy: Assessment of Legal Developments From 1983 to Mid-1985,' USAID, Khartoum, 1985, cited in Richard Brown, *Public Debt and Private Wealth: Debt, Capital Flight and the IMF in Sudan*, London, MacMillan, 1992.
[33] Mohamed Hashim Awad, 'Economic Islamisation in the Sudan: A Review,' University of Khartoum, Development Studies Research Centre, Seminar no. 50, October 1984, p. 29.

domination of key economic sectors (including building materials and the private media) was entrenched.

On seizing power, the NIF had to face a complicated reality. The country was aboyut $13 billion in debt and hence had to deal with western creditors and the IMF, and the remittance economy and the tax privileges of Islamic banks and charities undermined the fiscal base of the state. Moreover the commitment to the war was massively expensive: in 1990, the defence budget was $956 million, almost exactly double the level of 1988.[34] These contradictions were hard to reconcile.

According to Islamic economic theory, the state is obliged to store grain against times of scarcity and famine.[35] Yet in 1990 the government put control of grain reserves in the hands of Islamist banks and businessmen, who exported most of them. One rationale for this was the need to normalise relations with the IMF and Paris Club, so as to break the intimate dependence on them that had bedevilled previous regimes. Hence successive ministers of finance implemented stringent measures that previous governments had shied away from, such as mass privatisation, cutting the bread subsidy, floating the currency and exporting grain to earn hard currency. These measures gained some sympathy in the IMF and among other western financiers. In addition, the government tried to capture as much of the remittances from Sudanese expatrites as possible, by taking harsh measures against businessmen caught with illegal hard currency. Two were executed. This did not work, and in time the government had to liberalise foreign exchange dealing. Meanwhile, the IMF also began to rewrite its rules so that default by a debtor such as Sudan would no longer pose the same threat to the institution. (The collapse of central governments in Liberia in 1990 and Somalia in 1991 could thus be borne.) However, the sheer amount that Sudan owed made normalisation all-but-impossible, and the government's plight was worsened by the drying up in western economic assistance. The U.S. and Europeans cut off aid, for a mixture of reasons including loan defaults, the overthrow of an

---

[34] Economist Intelligence Unity, *Sudan Country Report*, 1990, no. 4.
[35] Mohamed Hashim Awad, 1984, pp. 36-8.

elected government, and human rights abuses. By 1993 almost all official development assistance had been halted. Sudan teetered on the edge of expulsion from the IMF. In 1997 it was saved only when Malaysia provided finance to cover some of its arrears with the IMF.

However, while the state remained bankrupt, economic Islamistion proceeded. This was possible partly because much of the Islamist finance was private: Islamic banks based abroad and Islamic agencies could directly fund the Islamisation process. And, in 1990, the government moved towards the logical conclusion of Islamising the state finances, and centralised both *zakat* collection and allocation. By replacing secular taxes with religious ones whose allocation is governed by Islamic principles alone, the fiscal strength and independence of local government is eroded (contradicting the principle of devolution of powers supposedly found in the federal system).

The *zakat* now became the cornerstone of Islamist humanitarianism. Traditionally, the *zakat* can be used for a range of purposes including supporting religious schools and mosques, aid to the poor and pilgrims, converting non-Moslems and support for *jihad*. Islamic NGOs became the favoured intermediary for these activities, and the Diwan al Zakat came to play a crucial co-ordinating role.

At its first conference, held under the patronship of the President of the Republic, the Secretary General of Diwan al Zakat explained:

> We co-operate with the Da'awa organisations responsible for the Da'awa and the defence of the land and honour, like Nidaa al Jihad organisation and the Islamic Da'awa Authority. We also provide funding for more than 3,000 *khalwas*.[36]

In 1992-3, the Diwan al Zakat supported the *Jihad* in the South and Nuba Mountains.

The growth of Islamic NGOs runs in parallel to the Islamisation of state finance. The combined budgets of the organisations operating within the Comprehensive Da'awa are not known, but it is

---

[36] Quoted in: *al Sudan al Hadith*, 28 April 1994, p. 6.

probable that they run into billions of Sudanese pounds. As well as direct government expenditure on the national Da'awa programme, the Diwan al Zakat sets aside 21% of its annual revenue, estimated at LS35 billion in 1996, for the Da'awa campaigns under a chapter called *Fi Sabeel Allah* ('For the sake of Allah', also a reference to the Koranic verse which elaborates on how the *zakat* is to be dispensed).

Another fiscal instrument for Islamic humanitarianism is the Sharia Support Fund, established by Presidential decree in March 1991.[37] Though formally non-governmental, its trustees are appointed by the President of the Republic, who is its patron. It receives money from the Diwan al Zakat as well as tax-exempt donations from individuals and companies. Among its stated aims, the Sharia Support Fund:

- supports the institutions, organisations and projects aiming to carry out Islamic missionary action;
- constructs mosques and Koranic schools, and encourages the worship of Allah;
- supports Sharia research, education, information and publication and;
- mobilises and provides military training for the PDF and cares for the *Shuhadah* [martyrs].

Al Awqaf al Islamiya (Islamic Pious Endowments) Authority is another quasi-governmental Da'awa-ist organisation. First established in the Central State in 1991, it branched out to other regions in 1993. A senior government figure described Al Awqaf's philosophy as the 'emancipation of ourselves from the supremacy of materialism so as to actualise solidarity and compassion'.[38] It is primarily a vehicle for mobilising funds which can then be allocated to other institutions. For example, the government of Central State allocates five per cent of the money accrued from the licenses on commercial land and investment to finance Al Awqaf al Islamiya, plus another five per cent for general Comprehensive Da'awa

---

[37] *Al Inqaz al Watani*, 24 March 1991.

[38] Ibrahim Nayil Eidam, member of the Revolutionary Command Council, quoted in: *Al Quwat al Musallaha*, 10 January 1993, p. 2.

programmes and projects in the region. It was planning to place levies on banks and financial institutions, also obliging them to provide funding for Al Awqaf al Islamiya. These resources are then used to support the Sharia Support Fund, the Students' Support Fund, and specific Da'awa projects.

As well as receiving money directly or indirectly from taxes, many Islamic humanitarian organisations also engage in trade in their own right. In this they are similar to the Iranian Islamic foundations (most famously Bonyad-i Mostazefin), which have become giant commercial enterprises virtually autonomous from the formal state machinery. Da'awa al Islamiya has significant commercial involvement in construction. Al Takaful al Ijtima'i (Social Solidarity) Fund is one example. Al Takaful's literature claims that it is geared towards the service of the poor and the needy in a way that secures a decent life for them, by means of rekindling social solidarity as believed to have been practised in the early days of Islam. In addition, al Takaful is a commercial enterprise dealing in basic commodities. In several large cities it has held a large share in the distribution of essential commodities, including meat, sorghum, edible oil, lentils and charcoal. The rationale for charitable organisations to be commercially active in this way is that the profits that accrue can then be used for humanitarian purposes. Unfortunately, there can also be an incompatibility—illustrated by the well-documented case of the hoarding of grain by the FIB during the 1984-5 famine. There have been allegations that al Takaful has similarly engaged in racketeering—unusually for a Da'awa-ist organisation, it has been criticised in the highly-controlled Sudanese press, for its commercial activities.[39]

Apart from the profits obtained from its commercial activities, Al Takaful is funded by Diwan al Zakat and receives grants and endowments. Al Takaful also obtains money by levies raised on the salaries of state employees.

Al Takaful's humanitarian activities involve operating health centres in Khartoum, helping to establish 'integrated service centres' (that include Islamic schools, mosques and grain mills) in the

---

[39] *Al Inqaz al Watani*, 10 May 1996, p. 6.

regions and running agricultural investment schemes, to 'support poor families in the least developed States'.[40] Al Takaful's work in the construction of mosques in Gedaref was praised by the Vice-President, Al Zubeir Mohamed Saleh, as a model to be emulated. It has also established Takaful Committees in different parts of the country, which gather information on aspects of family life and monitor poor families.

Recently, the extent of commercial activities by Islamic humanitarian foundations has come under sharp criticism from the Minister of Finance, Abdel Wahab Osman, who accused them of exploiting tax concessions and operating as trading firms. He accused the organisations of trading on the black market and costing the treasury some LS 60 million in lost revenues. He received the support of President Omer al Bashir.[41]

Small Scale Enterprises and Credit

Professor Mohamed Hashim Awad is renowned for his statement that 'I am convinced that the Islamisation process must start in the economic sphere.'[42] This approach has been influential. For example, Dr Sulaf al Din Saleh, an Islamist who holds a PhD in food science from British universities, is well-known for arguing that their aims can be achieved primarily by economic means. One example he has reportedly cited at discussions in the University of Khartoum is providing economic incentives to abandon pig-keeping in favour of rearing goats and sheep. Dr Sulaf has pioneered this economic approach through Islamic NGOs.

A large body of development research indicates that poor people's greatest demand is for credit. The FIB has been joined by a number of other NIF-related banks in providing small-scale credit. The Sudanese Islamic Bank established a specialised branch known as the 'Productive Families Branch' in a poor area of Omdurman in

---

[40] *Al Sudan al Hadith*, 8 February 1992, p. 1.
[41] 'Sudanese President Wants Tax Exemptions for NGOs Cancelled,' PANA, 24 December 1996.
[42] Mohamed Hashim Awad, 1984, p. ii.

1992, with the aim of extending Islamic credit to the urban poor.[43] This proved successful and the SIB has opened another branch in Wad Medani and plans further expansion. It has also experimented with group-based intermediary informal savings and credit organisations. Islamic NGOs have followed these banks' lead and focussed on providing credit to artisans and farmers.[44] As well as filling a key developmental niche, and enabling some farmers to free themselves from the extortionate traditional *shayl* system whereby they were obliged to mortgage their crops to creditors, this has helped to build up the Islamists' political base in rural areas. In February 1993, a workshop was held in Khartoum that, among other things, proposed adopting the model of the extremely successful Grameen Bank in Bangladesh, and extending *murabaha* Islamic credit to small farmers and artisans.[45]

The Sudanese Small Industries Development Company (SSIDC) illustrates another aspect of this approach. It was founded as an NGO by Dr Sulaf al Din Saleh in the 1980s, focussing on a combination of appropriate technology and credit, then became a commercial company and finally went bankrupt. In its early days it copied foreign NGOs' methods of 'grassroots' development and modest technology and gathered admiration from European advocates of appropriate technology. It obtained aid from international donors as well as selling its own products. The precise reasons for its demise remain uncertain, but public discussion in Khartoum in 1992 attributed it to financial mismanagement.

More widely, the model of Islamic credit has attracted interest from international agencies. The World Bank has referred to Islamic credit systems as 'an interesting contrast' to traditional banking.[46] In 1987-88 the Netherlands provided LS 1.1 million in aid to a project by the Sudanese Islamic Bank for buying chicks and incubators to be

---

[43] Hamdan Mohamed Goumaa, 1997.

[44] Hamdan Mohamed Goumaa, 'Islamic Modes of Finance: Prospects for Application in Small Enterprise Programmes,' Discussion Paper presented to ACORD programme meeting, London, 1992.

[45] Naglaa Sadiq Ahmed, 'A Bank for Financing the Poor,' *Sudanow*, July 1993, 24-5.

[46] World Bank, '1989 Development Report,' Washington D.C., 1989, p. 88.

lent out to poor families on a *murabaha* basis.[47] NGOs including SCF-US and ACORD and specialist consultants have also been attracted by 'a rather different and rather unfamiliar approach to financial systems which may at least have the potential to be applied to small enterprise'.[48]

The effectiveness of Islamic forms of credit is reflected in the success of the NIF's mobilisation among important sections of Sudanese society: it is part of the project of *tamkiin*, and will continue to have an impact on Sudan even if the NIF government is removed from power.

Islamist Internationalism

The 1990-1 famine was a shock to the government that accelerated the government's determination to break its dependence for relief resources on western agencies. Henceforth, Islamic agencies were to be the favoured intermediaries, giving the government greater control and more capacity to portray the situation in its own terms. A select group of international Islamic came to channel resources to Sudan from the Islamic world, and some can implement programmes on behalf of multilateral agencies such as UNDP and UNICEF. (IARA falls in the latter group.) Many of them are also a means whereby the Da'awa-ist agenda can be disseminated widely in the Islamic world.

The International Islamic Relief Organisation (IIRO) is an example of an Islamic agency that undertakes conventional relief work, providing an alternative to western NGOs. It is part of the Jeddah-based *Rabitat al Aalam al Islami* (Islamic World League). Founded in 1978, the IIRO provides aid for 'the needy, *muhajiriin* [pilgrims] and refugees, the poor and dispossessed, and deprived

---

[47] Salah el Din al Shazali and Mohamed Osman Khalifa, 'The Experience of the Sudanese Islamic Bank in Musharaka Financing as a Tool for Development Intervention among Small Farmers,' Khartoum, Sudanese Islamic Bank, 1988.

[48] Malcolm Harper, '"Musharaka" Partnership Financing,' Cranfield School of Management, UK, unpublished article, 1994.

Islamic minorities in the world.'[49] The IIRO operates in ninety countries. It started its operations in Sudan in 1989. Working in co-operation with other Islamic relief organisations, the IIRO has been particularly active among the displaced in Khartoum, and Ethiopian and Eritrean refugees in eastern Sudan.

Da'awa al Islamiya is one of the oldest and largest Islamic NGOs in Sudan, with a budget of over $6 million and 500 staff.[50] It was founded in Sudan in 1980, first working with refugees from Ethiopia and Eritrea and building schools. It is politically well-connected: in 1986, Gen. Abdel Rahman Suwar el Dahab, former head of state, became its patron. Da'awa al Islamiya is the implementing partner for a number of UN programmes. The agency's English language publicity is reticent about its Islamist leanings, not going further than statements about 'encouraging dialogue between Islam and different religions', 'socio-economic development of poor communities to combat the prevailing triad of ill health, lack of education and poverty' and 'addressing the needs of people during disaster situations.'[51] Such statements could come from a western secular NGO.

Meanwhile, Da'awa al Islamiya's aspirations range well beyond Sudan. Its literature says it is operational in seventeen other African countries,[52] it spends about two-thirds of its budget elsewhere in Africa, and half its board members are from outside Sudan. In its fifteenth board meeting in April 1996, its trustees discussed 'Towards a globalisation of Da'awa' with representatives from a range of countries.[53] They sent messages of concern to Afghanistan and solidarity to Bosnia-Hercegovina. According to Sudanese Arabic press reports, the board also took a strong stand in support of 'the Islamic civilisational orientation' of the Sudan Government, in opposition to the UN Security Council (then about to impose

---

[49] *Al Quwat al Musallaha*, 12 August 1990, p. 8

[50] *OLS Review*, p. 96.

[51] Islamic Dawa Organization, 'A Statement of Philosophy and Work,' paper for GOS, NGOs and UN meeting, January 1993.

[52] *Ibid.*

[53] *Al Sudan al Hadith*, 7 April 1996, p. 5.

sanctions on Sudan) and other 'malicious campaigns that target [Sudan's] orientation with a view to obstructing its progress.'

The roles of other Islamic agencies are less clear. Their philosophies and agendas appear to be close to the NIF, but their exact status is shrouded in ambiguity.

Al Birr ('Benevolence') International Organisation began its operations in Sudan in early 1991. In common with many other Islamic humanitarian agencies, its precise origins and scope of activities are difficult to determine. Its convergence with government policy appears close. According to its Director General, Ahmad Abdalla Ahmad, it aims to 'participate in boosting development and construction for the consolidation of the pillars of peace.'[54] In 1994, Al Birr signed eighteen agreements with state governments in Southern Sudan, the Nuba Mountains and Blue Nile, which gave the agency responsibilities for rehabilitation and development, maintaining schools, and the operation of hospitals, health centres and mobile clinics.

According to its literature[55] Muwafaq al Khairiya is an international organisation with branches in Sudan, Somalia, Eritrea, Ethiopia, Pakistan, Afghanistan, Lebanon, Bosnia-Hercegovina, the USA and the UK. (Its Eritrean and Ethiopian offices were subsequently closed by the respective governments.) It claims to have been founded in 1991, and to have set up its Sudan programme in October of that year. At that time, Dr Sulaf al Din Saleh left the SSIDC to become director of Muwafaq. In 1992, a former IARA staff member, Ansari Abdullahi became director in Khartoum, while Sulaf al Din oversaw the agency's work in Ethiopia and Somalia. As with a number of other international Islamic agencies, Sudanese professional staff play a prominent role: Sudanese are the pioneers of Islamic relief. The official *OLS Review* team estimated that its 1995 budget for Sudan was $1 million and it employed 200 staff.[56] Some reports indicate that these are conservative figures. Other reports in

---

[54] *Al Nasr*, 19 August 1994, p. 1.
[55] 'Muwaffaq Foundation (MF) (Sudan), From Dependency to Self Reliance,' Khartoum, leaflet.
[56] *OLS Review*, p. 96.

1996 suggested that Muwafaq was in the process of closing its operations in Sudan, but this had not yet occurred at the time of writing.

One of the internationalist activities of some Islamic agencies is supporting the political mobilisation of Eritrean and Ethiopian refugees in Sudan. An example of this is the refugee settlement at Qala en Nahal, established in 1970 south-east of Gedaref. NIF personnel in local government, COR and some Islamic agencies, including Da'awa al Islamiya, paid particular attention to these 30,000 or so refugees, who are Moslems from the lowlands of Eritrea. Educational opportunities were selectively provided for them, and mosques and Koranic schools established. By the late 1980s, the militant Eritrean Jihad organisation had emerged from the Reform Committee (*Lejnat al Islah*) in the settlement. The initial concerns of the Reform Committee were opposition to the EPLF's gender policy, notably the recruitment of female fighters into mixed units (men and women, Christian and Moslem) and the practice of 'battlefield marriage', a simplified marriage, which they considered contrary to the *Sharia*.[57] The Reform Committee also alleged that the EPLF was exploiting a land dispute at Sana Degley in the Eritrean highlands as a means of establishing Christian dominance of that area, and claimed that the EPLF's policy on nationalities was aimed at disrupting the unity of Eritrean Moslems.[58] Anti-EPLF propaganda in Qala en Nahal became extremely virulent.

After the NIF seized power, the Eritrean Jihad movement was called upon to represent Eritrea at a meeting of the International Popular Islamic Conference Organisation in Khartoum hosted by Dr Hassan al Turabi (who founded the organisation). By 1993, Eritrean Jihad members were receiving military training in PDF camps within Qala en Nahal (contrary to international refugee law). Throughout this period, Islamic agencies maintained active offices in the

---

[57] Information from Osman Ibrahim, representative of the militants in Qala en Nahal, November 1994.

[58] Al Amin Mohamed Saeed, *The Eritrean Revolution: Thrust and Regression* (in Arabic), Asmara, 1992, p. 336. The Sana Degley dispute was resolved by the Eritrean Government in 1995.

settlement.[59] In January 1994, Eritrean Jihad participated in a military attack on Eritrea from Sudanese territory, contributing to the breakdown in relations between Sudan and Eritrea. Cross-border incursions have continued since.

Further afield, the NIF and some Islamic agencies are active in Somalia and Uganda. In Somalia, the collapse of central government has provided them with an opportunity for mobilising support, by providing an alternative to the clan-based factional politics that has disillusioned many Somalis, and because they are one of the few Somali movements that has set up schools. The Ethiopian government has launched cross-border raids on Islamic extremist military centres, on the grounds that they have been destabilising Ethiopia. In Uganda, Islamic agencies are active promoting the Moslem minority there, but some have also been allegedly implicated in anti-government activity.

Jihad: Struggle and Holy War

Perhaps the most sensitive area for Islamic humanitarian activity is support for the Sudan Government's war effort. In all humanitarian traditions, there is an element of providing solace to wounded soldiers— this is how the Red Cross movement and British nursing began in the nineteenth century. Similarly, some Islamic agencies, primarily concerned with social action away from the war zones, have lent support to health care for soldiers. Al Ithar Charitable Organisation is one: it was founded in March 1991 to promote education and Da'awa, and gives assistance in the form of mass meals in the month of Ramadan and provision of relief food and clothing for poor families.[60] It also initiated the blood donation project in Gedaref, in which citizens are encouraged to donate blood for the army's emergency supplies. Others were set up specifically to

---

[59] Idris Mohamed Omer, 'Before the Fall: The Eritrean Jihad Movement [is] a Real Challenge that Dictates Decisive Action,' *Al Ittihadi*, 11 January 1997, p. 3. Also information from el Hadi Abdalla, member of ACORD staff at Qala en Nahal, 1990-95.
[60] *Al Ingaz al Watani*, 13 February 1996, p. 8.

care for the widows and orphans of soldiers killed at the front: Al Shaheed (Martyrs) Organisation was established in 1990 for this function.[61]

At Ithar has also publicly proclaimed its support for *Jihad*: Holy War. This has to be interpreted with caution. *Jihad* is both the government's military effort against the SPLA and the non-violent struggle for an Islamic state (more widely, *Jihad* can be 'equality, freedom and struggle in the path of God'[62]). The NIF exploits the ambiguity in the term, but *Jihad* normally entails support for the war effort.

The links between humanitarianism and war are particularly clear in the case of two organisations: the NGO Nidaa al Jihad and the parastatal National Development Foundation. One jihadist women's organisation will also be discussed.

Nidaa al Jihad (Call of Jihad) describes itself as a 'popular voluntary organisation' established with the main objective of promoting and propagating the philosophy of Popular Defence, the mobilisation of volunteers for war efforts, and fighting along the armed forces in their war against the 'enemies of Sharia'.[63] Its Secretary General, Abdel Gadir Mohamed Zein, defines *Jihad* as 'a comprehensive call' aimed at combating

> rebellion of all types and forms of conspiracy targeting the Umma and its religion. . . [It aims at] the termination of wrong and the propagation of Islam . . . the consolidation and entrenchment of religious values in the lives of individuals and societies. . . [and] harnessing the monotheistic values of Islam [and] worship of Allah and construction and development of the land.[64]

According to its own statements, the cardinal philosophy of Nidaa al Jihad is based on the virtue of fighting and conquering the land of the enemies of Islam. *Jihad* is valued both as a moral and

---

[61] *Al Sudan al Hadith,* 26 June 1994, p. 12.

[62] Gudrun Krämer, 'Islamist Notions of Democracy,' in J. Beinin and J. Stork (eds.) *Political Islam*, London, I. B. Tauris, 1997, p. 74.

[63] *Al Ingaz al Watani*, 15 April 1992, p. 4.

[64] *ibid.*

religious duty. According to this philosophy, *Mujahadah* (fighting the enemy of Islam and self restraint through the worship of Allah) can be fulfilled either through direct participation in fighting, or through fund-raising, providing food and logistics, or supporting the families of *mujahidiin* or *shuhadah* (martyrs). A statement by a subsidiary organisation, the Abdel Rahman Ibn Awf Charitable Endowment Foundation, also stresses the aim of:

> Transforming *jihad* from the *'jihad* through the gun' to another *jihad* in the field on investment through training and equipment of *mujahadiin* for the reconstruction of the land.[65]

Nidaa al Jihad has its headquarters in Khartoum and branches in all parts of Sudan and a sizeable number of volunteers. It has tax-free status and can raise funds and run investment endowments (i.e. operate commercially). It has made particular efforts to target businessmen for fundraising, taking them to special training camps for sessions at which they learn about the agency and, according to Abdel Gadir Mohamed Zein, leave 'most enthusiastic about raising funds for the sake of *Jihad'*.[66] The practical activities of Nidaa al Jihad focus on providing logistics and equipment for the *mujahidiin* fighting the SPLA, caring for and ensuring the welfare of the families of the *mujahidiin* and the *shuhadah* and supporting and providing training for the Popular Defence Forces. It also provides assistance to 'returnees' from the SPLA as a gesture of Islam's 'tolerance and sympathy' towards the enemy and supports 'protected settlements' around Juba.[67]

There is a significant media and public relations component to much of Nidaa al Jihad's activities. For example, when it sends missions to the military operations zones to provide assistance such as food and clothes to the *Mujahidiin* and to communicate messages between them and their families, are well publicised.[68] *Sahat al Fidaa* (Fields of Sacrifice) a flagship Jihadist programme broadcast

---

[65] *Al Sudan al Hadith*, 19 December 1992, p. 11.
[66] *Al Ingaz al Watani*, 15 April 1992, p. 4.
[67] *ibid.*
[68] *ibid.*

by the national television, shows citizen-donors visiting the front with gifts and the devout and patriotic feelings of the *Mujahidiin*. Nidaa al Jihad also has its own radio broadcasts, which began in Kadugli in the Nuba Mountains, which aim to rekindle the 'spirit of *Jihad'*. It organises entertainment ceremonies with the objective of promoting 'values of martyrdom', and takes active part in the government's propaganda aimed at the Northern population, including the encouragement and sponsorship of Jihadist music and songs.

The National Development Foundation (NDF) is a rather different but equally Jihadist organisation. Initially called the Peace and Development Foundation, it was set up by the government in March 1992 under the Chairmanship of the then-Minister, Fadl al Seed Abdel Gadir Abu Gisaisa. It is a governmental Da'awa-ist institution with close links to the Ministry of Social Planning and the Ministry of Peace and Reconstruction. Both the NDF and the Ministry of Peace and Reconstruction were established, according to the Minister, Abdalla Deng Nial, 'to repulse the falsehood and gossip about the lack of seriousness on the part of the Revolution concerning the issue of peace.'[69] Other NDF statements speak of the aim of 'bringing peace to the South through development'.[70] Both institutions were set up as the army made major military gains in the South, resulting in a need to consolidate the re-taken areas with assistance programmes. In a press conference announcing its formation, the Director

> outlined the objectives of the Foundation and said that the Revolution had supported the Foundation with LS 1 billion, and authorised it to contact foreign quarters with a view of getting necessary aid. The Foundation is exempt from taxes and custom duties, and free to collect donations.[71]

According to the NDF's Damazin Branch Director, Ahmad Karamno, the NDF also has investment projects to generate income,

---

[69] *Al Sudan al Hadith*, 15 October 1993, p. 5.
[70] *Al Sudan al Hadith,* 9 March 1992, p. 1.
[71] *ibid.*

and provides services with the monies raised. The NDF's investments are chiefly in agriculture, providing seeds, agricultural machinery and tractors to farmers.[72] In 1993 it established an agricultural scheme for the benefit of the families of the former NDF chairman Abu Gisaisa and his colleagues, who had recently been killed in a plane crash. In total, it has been leased some 600,000 hectares.[73]

Its services include the provision of education and vocational training (especially in Da'awa camps) and establishing 'peace villages' and other centres of Islamisation in Blue Nile State and Southern Sudan. One of its major roles is to co-ordinate the work of governmental and non-governmental Da'awa-ist organisations in these regions.

The close integration of the NDF into the war effort is indicated by a remark made by Al Dau Mohamed al Mahi, Director of the Damazin Branch monitoring department, who said that the NDF puts a premium on development, because, 'if the citizen doesn't find development accompanying his return, he shall be tempted to surrender to rebellion.'[74] The word 'return' refers to the surrender or capture of civilians formerly living in SPLA-held areas. Development and counter-insurgency are two sides of the same coin.

Salaam al Izzah (Peace with Pride, PWP) is a women's organisation whose main project is called *Zad al Mujahid* (Food for the Holy Warrior). According to the Secretary-General of PWP, Engineer Widad Yaqoub Ibrahim, the main objective for embarking on *Zad al Mujahid* project was to provide the *Mujahidiin* and soldiers in the war zones with an appropriate type of food which is cost-effective and easy to transport. The PWP claims to have prepared eleven thousand packs of food for soldiers shortly after its establishment in 1996.

In common with other NIF-associated women's organisations, PWP is intended to provide Islamist women with a role in the *Jihad* comparable to that of the male fighters who serve in the front line.

---

[72] *Al Sudan al Hadith*, 15 October 1993, p. 5.
[73] *OLS Review*, p. 87.
[74] *Al Sudan al Hadith*, 15 October 1993, p. 5.

This Islamic philosophy of war can be traced back to the early days of Islam when women were designated the role of providing food for the *Mujahidiin* and caring for the wounded: according to the Prophet Mohamed's *Hadith*, those who cater for the needs of an Islamic conqueror are conquerors themselves.

Peace With Pride is supported from state funds and is personally sponsored by the Vice-President of the Republic, Brigadier Al Zubeir Mohamed Saleh. The Khartoum State Minister of Finance and Economic Development, Al Haj Atta al Mannan praised PWP's activities as 'a major civilised work on the part of the Sudanese women'.[75]

Encouraging the Spread of Islam

There is overwhelming evidence that Islamic NGOs are part of a comprehensive strategy that involves encouraging, and occasionally enforcing, the spread of Islam. The aim is to obtain *Muhtadiin* (new converts). *Muhtadiin* are defined as 'those who have converted to Islam recently, voluntarily and without coercion, and with complete conviction. They have pronounced their conversion to Islam in front of a *Sharia* judge, where all procedures were made and their names changed [to Moslem names].'[76] Some of the methods of rewarding conversion have been mentioned: the question of 'voluntariness' is open to varying interpretations.

Some international Islamic agencies are extremely sensitive to any suggestion of supporting Islamisation, and deny it strongly. For example, the U.K.-based Islamic Relief runs a community centre in el Obeid and medical complexes in Khartoum. It also had a centre in Upper Nile. One of its staff members said: 'Accusation of religious discrimination is never levelled: anyone found guilty would not continue [in employment].'[77] The Executive Director of Muwafaq al Khairiya, Siraj el Din Abdel Bary was also anxious to rebut the

---

[75] *Al Ingaz al Watani*, 16 May 1996, p. 8.
[76] Quoted in: *Al Inqaz al Watani*, 26 August 1994, p. 8.
[77] Interviewed in Khartoum, February 1996.

221

charge that his organisation required people to convert to Islam as a precondition for giving relief:

> These accusations, we heard about them. They are like the accusations for Sudan as a whole. The evidence should be offered. We just wait for one single evidence. We very strongly deny that accusation. In fact, we are not a Moslem organisation. We are a secular organisation. And we also accuse the international organisations as missionaries. Aren't they trying at least to forbid people to become Moslems?

Many Islamic NGOs compare themselves to the Red Cross, and insist that they treat members of all faiths alike. Certainly, some (including IARA and IIRO) operate in non-Moslem countries (for example Rwanda), assisting Christians.

However, there is little doubt that for the major Da'awa-ist agencies, promoting Islam is integral to their mission. Almost every Islamic agency mentioned in this chapter is active in supporting the building of mosques or Islamic schools. They particularly target children; a patient process of persuasion and education is most common. A medical assistant from Upper Nile reported how the agencies in his home town operated:

> The Islamic agencies were there. They used to collect children at night, take firewood and make a fire, and teach children about the Koran. Every night, from 7 until 8 at night. To teach them how to pray. They don't ask questions about who you are. They can let Christians go and pray [as Christians] but they cannot let you teach your children [Christianity]. They asked me to go and also to be a Moslem. I said I cannot change my life. I can work with you, but I will stand on the side of the church. I was baptised and I cannot change it.[78]

Providing an education for non-Moslem children can be the first stage in a process of conversion to Islam. One example of this comes from the Nuba Mountains, where the government uses offers of food

---

[78] Interviewed in Ethiopia, August 1996.

and clothes to lure rural children to schools in government-controlled towns. One escapee from the towns reported:[79]

> For those children staying in Um Dorein and al Atmur [peace camps], now they have schools for them. These are *khalwas*, and they are only taught Arabic and the Koran. At the beginning, the parents of children refused to allow them to go to the school, because they were only Islamic schools, but the authorities decided to cook *zelabiya* [cake/bread] for them, and also provide tea, so the children began to go of their own accord. After some time, the parents were told, 'We are taking the children to Um Ruwaba [in North Kordofan] for further education so that they can return and take positions of responsibility in the Nuba Mountains.'

The removal of over one hundred children from these towns in March 1995 was confirmed by other internees. Most were reportedly aged fifteen or sixteen. They were not seen subsequently by their parents. However, residents of North Kordofan reported the children's arrival in Um Ruwaba on 13 April 1995, at about the same as another similar group from Buram district in the south of the Nuba Mountains arrived. The children had been told they were going for three years' education. On 21 April the Ministry of Social Affairs held a well-publicised ceremony to inaugurate a new *khalwa* in the town, where the children were required to study.

Most of the Nuba around Um Dorein and al Atmur are Christians. After removal, the children were seen by some people who knew them, who reported that many were Christians and they were objecting to their coerced conversion to Islam. The role of Islamic agencies in this incident is not clear, but it is probable that the Um Ruwaba *khalwa* was supported by Da'awa-ist organisations.

In Khartoum, the government has launched several campaigns to remove vagrant children, most of them displaced Southerners and Nuba, from the streets, presenting these as a social welfare measure.[80] One campaign was begun in September 1992. As well as

---

[79] Interviewed in Um Dulu, Nuba Mountains, 18 May 1995.
[80] African Rights, *Sudan's Invisible Citizens: The Policy of Abuse Against the Displaced People in the North*, London, February 1995, pp. 17-20.

223

unaccompanied children, the sweeps caught up substantial numbers of children who were living with their parents, and who had merely been sent out on errands, or were in the market or attending cinemas. Another major sweep was carried out in November 1994, and over three thousand children detained. Most are boys.

The children are removed—usually in secrecy—to 'rehabilitation' camps in various locations across Northern Sudan. Seven camps were set up between 1992 and 1994, and it is likely that more have been established since. According to the meagre information that has been obtained on these camps, their size ranges from about eighty to 1250 inmates aged from five up to about fifteen. In the camps, the children's identities are changed: they are obliged to wear simple cotton clothes bearing the legend *Abna'a al Sudan* (Children of Sudan). Their heads are shaved. They are taught the Koran and how to pray; they are pressured to become Moslems and adopt Islamic names. Prominent among the 're-education' is military drill, taught by PDF instructors. Substantial numbers of children have been subsequently recruited into the army. The Durdeib camp graduated at least forty boys from its 1992 intake straight into the army, and at least sixty boys from Ebeid Katim camp became *Mujahidiin*.

Similar policies are seen at the Dar Tarbiat al Ashbal (Youth Education Centre) reformatory school for juvenile delinquents. This is a well-established institution, now under the Department of Prisons. It takes in juvenile offenders convicted by the Public Order Courts, most of whom are displaced people, many of them non-Moslems convicted of minor offences against the *Sharia*. Increasingly, Dar Tarbia al Ashbal is taking on the character of an institution for Islamising young offenders.

The Comprehensive Da'awa entails encouraging adult *Muhtadiin* also. A number of Islamic Da'awa organisations sponsor Islamic missionary work among the displaced Southerners and Nuba in the north. It appears that the overwhelming majority of *muhtadiin* are people who have been given social and economic encouragement to convert by the government or Islamic agencies, who often exploit the desperate circumstances that these people find themselves in. The country director of one western NGO remarked that 'most alleged incidents of *forcible* conversion' were in fact, on examination, 'cases of expedient conversion.' 'Credible incidents' of coerced conversion were few, he said.[81] But western NGOs are not present in many of the places where Da'awa-ist organisations are active.

Prisoners are a particular target for Islamic missionary programmes, financed and co-ordinated by Diwan al Zakat and implemented by organisations such as the Holy Koran Society and the Sudanese Organisation for the Care of Prisoners. The Director of Prisons, Brigadier al Sheikh al Rayah, has said that 'prisons . . . have become minarets of guidance, castles of reformation and harbours of repentance' through the work of Da'awa agencies.[82] Another senior prison officer explained that 'The prisons have based their policies towards the prisoners on promoting the sense of discipline and national loyalty, along with the provision of intensive courses of Koranic recitation and reading in addition to literacy classes.'[83]

Southern and Nuba prisoners are doubly attractive to the Islamist missionaries: they are captive and vulnerable, and many have been convicted of offences (such as brewing alcohol, prostitution or illicit trading) that the Islamists see as a blot on the social landscape and wish to stamp out. Poor prisoners, especially women, are under enormous stress. Prison conditions are appalling, food and health care is poor (a particular concern for women with young children), physical and sexual abuse is common, and prisoners' families have to bear the double burden of feeding the prisoner and getting by without his or her income. Hence it is not difficult for Islamic humanitarian organisations to bring pressure to bear on prisoners to become *Muhtadiin*, and obtain preferential treatment or early release. For the Da'awa missionaries, converting prisoners is also a programme of moral reform and crime prevention: NIF-style Moslems will no longer commit offences against the Sharia such as prostitution and brewing alcohol.

---

[81] Interviewed in Khartoum, February 1996.
[82] Quoted in: *Al Sudan al Hadith*, 16 August 1996, p. 8.
[83] Lt.-Col. Isam Eisa al Fadil, Khartoum State Director of Prisons, quoted in: *Al Inqaz al Watani*, 26 August 1996, p. 8.

After agreeing to convert to Islam, male prisoners are given a basic education and 'rehabilitated' in Al Huda (The Right Path) Camps. These are operated by the PDF, together with the Department of Prisons and Da'awa-ist agencies. In June 1994, fifty *Muhtadiin* prisoners were released from Al Gireif prison in Khartoum after attending an Islamic re-education programme in the Khartoum Centre for Al Muhtadiin. This was the fifth group of converts to graduate from the Centre. The Secretary-General of Diwan al Zakat, Mohamed Ibrahim Mohamed, addressed the *Muhtadiin* and spoke of what he called the 'breakdown of barriers between the South and the North and the massive conversion of people to Islam.'[84] In August 1996, 500 prisoners were released after the same process. The same month, the Sudanese Organisation for the Care of Prisoners celebrated the 'graduation' of the first group of *Muhtadiin* from the Al Huda Camp in Dabak prison north of Khartoum. One hundred prisoners were then released after they had been converted to Islam 'inundated with piety, with Koranic illumination radiating from their faces, and their hearts filled with the values of righteousness.'[85] As the camp is run by the PDF, it is probable that many subsequently became *Mujahidiin*.

'Repentance Camps', also known as Biyut al Nur (Houses of Light), are designated for female *Ta'ibat* prisoners, where they undergo a variant of the re-education programme.[86] First, the women are required to join the Al Zahra Camp, a training camp specifically for female recruits to the PDF. After graduation, they attend the 'Repentance Camps' or Biyut al Nur camps themselves. One of these camps is situated in Soba, near Khartoum. Accompanied by their small children, the women are taught literacy and other skills, and inculcated with the moral and social values of the Da'awa. According to the Director of Biyut al Nur, Thurayia Taha, the project is intended to 'inculcate the Islamic Sharia in the personalities' of the

---

[84] *Al Sudan al Hadith*, 20 June 1994, p. 3.
[85] *Al Sudan al Hadith*, 16 August 1996, p. 8.
[86] A. Z. Hamad, 'Sudan,' in WUS, *Academic Freedom 3: Education and Human Rights*, London, Zed Press, 1995, pp. 76-7.

repentants through recital and memorisation of the Koran.[87] This project is run by the Da'awa Society of the International African University and financed by the Sharia Support Fund.

Displaced people in general are a major target for incremental Islamisation by Da'awa-ist organisations. One of these is the Moslem Women of Southern Sudan Association (MWSSA), which was formally launched in the wake of the announcement by President Omer al Bashir that the wearing of the Islamic veil (*hijab*—not a traditional Sudanese Moslem dress) was to be compulsory for women in public places (though the organisation had already been in informal existence for some time). Founded by women sympathisers of the Islamist project, it was registered as a voluntary organisation in June 1992, is based in Khartoum and has branches in Southern Sudan. The first objective of the MWSSA was the adoption of the *hijab* by Southern Sudanese women in Khartoum. Using a donation of LS5 million from government ministers, subsidised Islamic dresses were distributed among Southern Sudanese women 'without discrimination between Christians and Moslems.'[88] Subsequently, supported by the NDF and other Islamist financial organs, the MWSSA has been active promoting the Da'awa, especially in the displaced camps around Khartoum, organising campaigns of religious education, rallies and the *Ma'idat al Salam* (Banquet of Peace) in Ramadan—the offer of food is presented as a concrete example of Islam's magnanimity. The MWSSA hopes to expand: 'We in the Association aim to realise the grand objectives of peace and Islamic missionary activity in Southern Sudan.'[89]

In Khartoum and the major cities, Islamisation is backed by the powerful weapons of the mass media, Da'awa-ist organisations and material incentives. In remote rural areas, it can be much cruder. In the Nuba Mountains peace camps, there is a policy of forcible conversion, though it is unevenly implemented. Al Atmur is a peace camp in the Nuba Mountains. One former internee there, Rachel

---

[87] *Al Sudan al Hadith*, 20 May 1992, p. 5.
[88] Iqbal Mahmoud Abdalla, MWSSA, quoted in: *Al Quwat al Musallaha*, 19 May 1993, p. 8.
[89] *Ibid.*

227

Kuku (a pseudonym) described her reception after being abducted by soldiers in February 1995:[90]

> In al Atmur we were put in a hall which happens to be an old school dormitory. All looked quiet and normal that day. We were given clothes, cooking oil, flour and one piece of washing soap.
> The following day we were separated from each other, Christians on one side and Moslems on the other side. We Christians were asked to renounce Christianity and convert to Islam, or they said we would be dealt with accordingly as wives of rebels. Most of us were frightened and kept silent. Islamic preaching started immediately.

Soldiers and PDF were in charge: Rachel made no mention of Islamic agencies. Like many other abducted women, she was raped by the soldiers. She later escaped.

SOUTHERN BLUE NILE: THE MODEL FOR ISLAMIC AGENCIES

Southern Blue Nile or Damazin State has been in the vanguard of the development of the Comprehensive Da'awa. Honouring some prominent Islamists who were killed in a plane crash, a leading member of the NDF spoke of Damazin as 'where the Comprehensive Da'awa has changed the face of the land.'[91] The prominence of the region has been due to a combination of factors, including the activism of the deputy governor and the fact that it is an area of Northern Sudan that has a large 'African' indigenous population including many non-Moslems. It has many similarities with the Nuba Mountains.

Although the area was not severely affected by the famine of 1984-5, it did suffer drought and western relief agencies began to

---

[90] Interviewed in Eri, Nuba Mountains, 3 March 1995.
[91] 'A Martyr Lives, So Springs up a Flour Mill, a School and a Battalion of Mujahidiin along the Path of Peace, However Great are the Human and Financial Sacrifices,' *Al Sudan al Hadith*, 15 October 1993, p. 5.

become operational there. The most prominent ones were World Vision and Fellowship for African Relief (FAR), both of which have strong evangelical Christian leanings. On several occasions World Vision appeared to give priority in food distributions to Christian populations, creating hostility among some Moslems. Just before the 1986 elections, a World Vision truck was stoned when delivering food to communities along the Blue Nile in Gezira, with people rejecting the 'food of the *kufaar*' (non-Moslems). Meanwhile, in southern Blue Nile itself, military intelligence increasingly accused the relief agencies and the Christian churches of passing food to the SPLA, which was beginning recruitment in the area. Tensions culminated in the expulsion of World Vision in late 1986.

The NIF recognised the significance of Southern Blue Nile and made a major effort to mobilise there for the 1986 elections. To the surprise of many, the NIF captured the Kurmuk constituency, defeating the candidate from the local party, the Union of the Southern and Northern Funj.

The SPLA mounted major incursions into Southern Blue Nile in the late 1980s, overrunning the small towns of Kurmuk and Geissan, and prompting major government efforts to recapture them. Popular reaction in the northern cities verged on hysteria: the SPLA was not only coming North, but was threatening the strategically and economically vital Roseires Dam. The second government counter-offensive, in November-December 1989, was highly successful. Not only did the army and militia recapture all the territory of southern Blue Nile, but a subsequent joint military operation by the EPLF and Oromo Liberation Front (OLF) drove the Ethiopian forces and SPLA back from the border. The SPLA, which had co-operated with the Ethiopian government in its counter-insurgency operations against the OLF, was thereby denied use of the strategic border area.

The overthrow of the Mengistu government in Ethiopia in May 1991 and its replacement by a Transitional Government more friendly to the Sudan Government prevented any possibility of resurgent SPLA activity. From 1991 until early 1996 the area was peaceful. Only when the Sudan Government had so antagonised the new Ethiopian Government—the attempted assassination of Egyptian President Hosni Mubarak in Addis Ababa in June 1995 was the spark for a major breakdown in relations—did the situation change. In February 1996, the SPLA re-entered Southern Blue Nile from Ethiopian territory and in January 1997, as part of a co-ordinated offensive together with the Northern opposition parties, the SPLA captured a string of towns including Kurmuk, Geissan and Chali, and threatened Damazin.

From 1991, the 'pacification' of Southern Blue Nile included a major effort by Islamic agencies. Visiting Damazin in October 1993, members of the Transitional National Assembly agreed to call it 'The Model Province' and 'beacon to guide the people of Sudan.'[92] The deputy Wali of Damazin State, Ibrahim Abdel Hafiz, has been one of the masterminds of the Comprehensive Da'awa. He summed up the overall objective of the project as:

> the consolidation of religious values in society and effecting a comprehensive departure from the [present] reality of ignorance and illiteracy and the actualisation of total interaction with the Islamic project. . . which must engulf all sections and denominations of society.[93]

One of the earliest Da'awa programmes in the region was called *Mawakib al Nur* (Processions of Light) and executed under Abdel Hafiz's personal supervision. It comprised Koranic recital and memorisation, literacy classes, military service in the PDF camps, construction of mosques, and building of schools and health centres.

Particular attention has been paid to Kurmuk district, the southernmost part of the State, and the area that has the largest proportion of non-Moslems. In earlier decades, the district was heavily evangelised by the Sudan Interior Mission. The main centre of the Uduk people, Chali el Fil, has been officially renamed Chali el Arab by the government. A new road from Damazin to Kurmuk has been constructed as part of Da'awa al Islamiya's development efforts. 'Peace from Within' delegations were sent to the dispersed Uduk

---

[92] *Al Sudan al Hadith*, 15 October 1993.

[93] Cited in Ordesse Hamad, 'On NIF Ideological Indoctrination and Islamist Education Programmes', (in Arabic) *Alwah*, journal of Sudanese Writers and Journalists Association (UK), May 1995, London.

people in Southern Sudan and Ethiopia, which succeeded in bringing some of them back home. Chali el Fil/Arab is dominated by a large *Khalwa* named Hamesh Koreb, after a well-known centre of Islamic learning in Gezira. A former teacher in Chali described how the state schools were very poorly-equipped in comparison with the Hamesh Koreb *Khalwa*. Although the *Khalwa* was run by an Islamic NGO, to the inhabitants it appeared to be the school really supported by the state authorities. The teacher, a Christian, joined the staff of Chali school in 1994.[94]

In [our] school there were no books and no exercise books. When we ask the students to buy [supplies], they say, 'my father has no money.' For me, I always insist they need books, so some come to their parents and after a long struggle, come with the books. I insist they must learn how to write. There were no stools, no desks for the children to write on. They sat on the ground and their clothes became dirty.

We were five teachers, three of us Christians. When we planned the timetable, the non-Moslems were given most of the workload. The two Moslems were to teach only religion. No Christian religion could be taught; when we asked to teach the Christian religion, they said there was no time, and we could only teach it in the evening—but they knew we were busy with many other things in the evening. So the students went without Christian teaching. Also there were no books. We asked Damazin to send us Christian books, but there was no reply at all.

By comparison, the *Khalwa* was well-financed and well-supported by a prominent Islamic NGO.

They opened a big *Khalwa* in Chali, intended to have over one thousand children from the area. But they didn't get the number they wanted. When they failed to get the number, they came to us in the school and took children, saying they were going to give them intensive language courses. So we talked to the children who were not Moslems and persuaded them not to go. Only the Moslems went.

---

[94] Interviewed in Ethiopia, August 1996.

231

The head of [the NGO][95] in Damazin came. The head of the *Khalwa* was Ishaq, from Hamesh Koreb [in Gezira]. Even the *Khalwa* was called Hamesh Koreb. This Ishaq didn't greet women—he was probably Ansar al Sunna.

In addition, the *Khalwa* was closely identified with the real power in town: the army garrison.

There was close cooperation between [the NGO] and military intelligence. All the army officers spent their time in the place of Ishaq. Either Ishaq goes to the garrison or they come to him. If you don't get Ishaq in his place, he is in the barracks, and vice versa for the army officers. When Yabus was attacked [by the SPLA in February 1996], Ishaq and all the things belonging to the *Khalwa* went to the barracks. Every day, the army sent a guard to the *Khalwa*. Ishaq moved inside the barracks.

The Sudan Government does not conceal the links between the Comprehensive Call and military mobilisation in the region. *Al Sudan al Hadith* reported on the high-level governmental visit to Damazin in October 1993:[96]

In al Hussein ibn Ali camp which we visited just after 3 a.m. in the morning, we saw them reciting the Koran and in the Mosque and preparing for studying after prayers. They were attired in white *Jihad* garments and on them was written '*Al Da'awa al Shamla*'.
. . .
The women . . . were in Um al Mujahidat camp in Damazin. They recite the Koran and study, and them hurry for military training, filled with determination and resilience.
They spoke to the commissioner, Ibrahim Abdel Hafiz [and other officials]. These women are the ones that Prof. Al Bashir, deputy leader of the Transitional National Assembly, has described as 'those who, if men die, are capable of cutting off the hands of the traitors and aggressors even before they could reach them [the women], in defence of their faith, homeland and themselves.'

---

[95] Its identity has been concealed to protect the informant.
[96] *Al Sudan al Hadith*, 15 October 1993, p. 5.

In Bagis area we saw a small school and a Koranic class under a big tree. We saw a military march and the chanting of *Tahleel* ['There is no god except Allah'] and *Takbeer* ['Allah is the most great']. We saw sweating [hard work] in *Al Da'awa al Shamla* camps. The whole of Damazin has turned into a cell of gratitude, administered by the Commissioner and the Peace and Development Foundation.

In Suhaib al Rumi camp there were groups of children who woke up early, finished marching and reading the Koran. They have become friends of the Peace and Development Foundation, which is taking care of them.

The Peace and Development Foundation has bought a carpentry workshop in the centre of Damazin. Ahmad Karamno, director of Damazin branch of Peace and Development Foundation says that the workshop has two functions: investment and use of revenues for the Foundations development goals and; training and education on all types of carpentry.

Ahmad Karamno states that the Foundation has numerous development and agricultural projects in different areas of the South 'because real peace can't be established without development'.

He says: 'we have visited areas like Fashimi which hasn't been reached by a government official for forty years. We have got acquainted with its citizens and their conditions, and it is now enjoying security and stability, and we will be seeking to direct development projects to this area. . . in accordance with the goals for which the Foundation was established in March 1992.'

The director of the Foundation's monitoring department, Al Daw Mohamed al Mahi says . . .: 'The role of the Foundation is the boosting of peace efforts with significant development in support of stability, because if the citizen doesn't get development that accompanies his return to his homeland, remains vulnerable to capitulation to the rebellion. Citizens are fleeing from areas where war is raging, and our duty is to help them find secure and stable areas.'

The Foundation has set aside an agricultural scheme for the families of the martyrs which it operates on their behalf.

Damazin has more than 120 camps for *Al Da'awa al Shamla* and is getting ready at present for the graduation of more than 40,000 recruits.

233

In 1995-6, the Sharia Support Fund became particularly active in Blue Nile State. Among its major projects are the 'Koranic Towns,' new centres of Islamist proselytisation in the region. These were under construction in co-operation with Diwan al Zakat in Damazin, Geissan, Kadalo, Yabus, Bausi, Chali and Bote. According to the Secretary General of the Fund in the Blue Nile State, Yusuf Abdel Rahman Osman, this project aims 'to eradicate illiteracy, alleviate suffering and promote the spirit of piety in [these] societies'.[97]

The Fund also opened a *Dar al Tawbah* (Repentance Centre) and appointed sheikhs in the State's prisons to oversee religious re-education (including obtaining *Muhtadiin*)—for example it has paid off the fines for 500 prisoners. It sponsors the adoption of Islamic dress among women. The Fund also directs resources to Da'awa-ist organisations and the PDF, the police, public order, peace and student organisations.

The intimate relations between Islamic NGOs, quasi-governmental agencies (NDF and Sharia Support Fund), a fiscal institution (Diwan al Zakat) and military institutions (PDF and military intelligence), under the aegis of a prominent NIF cadre in a senior government post, is characteristic of the Comprehensive Da'awa. Elements of this pattern are repeated in the operations of Islamic agencies throughout Sudan.

IMPLICATIONS

The Islamic humanitarian agencies operating within the Comprehensive Call are one of the most significant developments in contemporary Sudan. They are at the vanguard of the NIF project for the social and political transformation of Sudan to a 'prophetic society' and an Islamic state. They are a novel variant of humanitarian practice. In many ways Islamic agencies depart from the contemporary western tradition of humanitarian action. Theirs is an integral social, political and humanitarian mission that is remarkably far-reaching and energetic. In other ways, the power and

---

[97] *Al Sudan al Hadith*, 22 April 1996, p. 5.

influence of Sudan's Islamic humanitarians is comparable to some major western relief agencies, which have assumed mandates that empower them to call for western military intervention in Africa: they merely use a different language to express their agenda than western humanitarians.

The Comprehensive Call Islamic agencies are not neutral in Sudan's war: they are on the side of the government, and many are explicitly engaged in supporting the *Jihad*. This is fundamentally incompatible with the principles of Operation Lifeline Sudan, especially as they have recently been developed under the rubric of humanitarian principles, and other basic UN principles.

The Islamic NGOs in Sudan are not simple instruments of the NIF agenda: they are too varied and their activities too complex to claim that. But most of them work very closely with the government and with government-established agencies: they are part of the NIF project.

One of the main arguments of this book is that political action is central to the conquest of famine, with technical proficiency and diplomatic principle secondary. How do the Islamic agencies stand on this score? Their frank engagement with the political process is encouraging: there is no pretence that the problems of war and famine can be solved except by a comprehensive process. They have a social agenda that they are pursuing with remarkable determination, and that will have a lasting impact on Sudanese society. The problem is: what are the politics of that process? The Comprehensive Call is driven by the authoritarian and warlike leanings of the Sudan Government. It is antithetical to popular political mobilisation and democratic accountability that are at the root of the politics of famine prevention. Under the NIF, the Sudan Government is accountable in principle to God, and in practice to those who control the interpretation of Islam, and those who are not first-class citizens will have at best a weak voice, and at worst be subjected to *Jihad*. The Comprehensive Call leaves Sudan more vulnerable to famine, not less.

10.

FOOD AND SECURITY IN THE GARRISON TOWNS

[We have] very little control. We know all this food is going somewhere. Very little is going to the intended beneficiaries. WFP is turning a blind eye.

Relief official, Juba

In the South, the Sudan Government has been less able to exercise unchallenged control over relief programmes. The NIF government inherited OLS and other international relief programmes in the South, including an ICRC airlift, the Lutheran World Federation/Sudan Emergency Operations Consortium (LWF/SEOC) airlift, primarily to Juba, and the Combined Agencies Relief Team (CART) within Juba. Also, of course, it did not control most of the Southern countryside. Given the international presence and the concession on sovereignty represented by OLS, the Sudan Government cannot exercise total control of relief operations in the name of state sovereignty in the garrison towns of the South. Instead, negotiation is more important. But it has still achieved most of its ends. This entails tight control of information and a gradual process of taking control of major relief operations. The ultimate end is, without doubt, the end of OLS—as the Sudan Government has often promised—and a return to the pre-1989 days whereby the Khartoum government exercised sovereign authority over all relief programmes on Sudanese territory.

INFORMATION CONTROL FROM KHARTOUM

In theory, there is a basic ideological incompatibility between the government and the aid agencies: the concepts of the Comprehensive Call contrast sharply with the precepts of the humanitarian international. There should be a conflict. Nonetheless, the Sudan Government has proved itself adept at getting its way. The basis of this is controlling information and analysis. It does this by restricting access and debate, and by playing the sovereignty card.

The Southern Sector of OLS has developed elaborate rules on neutrality and adherence to humanitarian principles, which it has tried to apply to operations mounted out of Kenya (see chapter 12). These rules are virtually unknown in the Northern Sector.[1] In place of a process of negotiation, based on a set of principles, the Sudan Government simply regulates, and out of respect for sovereignty and a general aversion to any form of confrontation, the UN in Khartoum has almost always complied.

What passes for 'needs assessment' in the Northern Sector is merely recycling elementary and unchecked figures for numbers of people 'in need' obtained from local government officers. The official *OLS Review* was severely critical of the low quality of such assessments, which it argued were too often 'purely on the basis of speculation'.[2] Similarly, the Review Team regarded numbers for 'beneficiaries' in official reports as 'unreliable, even fictitious', noting that the figures were produced in response to donor demands for them.[3] (Many of the 'recipient' figures are in fact higher than the 'in need' figures!)

The issue of information control will recur in the three case studies presented, in summary form, below.

---

[1] Department of Humanitarian Affairs, 'Terms of Reference for an Operation Lifeline Sudan (OLS) Review,' 18 August 1995, cited in Ataul Karim, Mark Duffield *et al. OLS: Operation Lifeline: A Review*, University of Birmingham, July 1996, p. 99.

[2] *OLS Review*, pp. 117-25, 132-3, 233, quote from p. 133.

[3] *OLS Review*, p. 230.

HUMANITARIANISM UNDER SIEGE IN JUBA

As the largest town in the South and the regional capital, Juba has immense political significance: its capture would be symbolic of SPLA victory, and might create a political momentum leading to Southern secession, the fall of the government in Khartoum, or both. Hence, maintaining control of Juba, and by implication securing its food supply, is an imperative for the government.

Food aid has kept Juba alive for over eight years. In mid-1988, the SPLA noose around the city tightened. The last overland relief convoy arrived in September: one convoy on the road from Yei was attacked by the SPLA and eleven Kenyan drivers were killed. Since then, the city has been an enclave, fed by what can be produced within the secure perimeter and what can be flown in by the government and (mostly) international agencies. Between November 1988 and 1995, LWF/SEOC under the command of Bob Koepp mounted one of the world's largest and longest relief airlifts, providing over 60,000 tonnes of food to the city with scarcely a break. It was a tremendous logistical achievement, against formidable difficulties. But some profound questions need to be asked about the impact of the food provided.

Since 1988, aid agency reports on the situation in Juba have been remarkably uniform. They have presented a picture of a large (and often expanding) displaced and 'in need' population, low food stocks, and a food delivery operation struggling to catch up, hobbled by late and inadequate donor funding.[4] Though there is no doubt that major human needs have existed, these reports have rarely been backed by well-substantiated evidence. Doubts have been cast on the 'in need' population figures, which have probably been subject to the common agency tendency to exaggerate.[5] The total population of Juba and its environs has been claimed at about 250,000-300,000 over the last ten years, with up to two-thirds of this number displaced. Sometimes,

---

[4] Mark Duffield, Helen Young, John Ryle and Ian Henderson, *Sudan Emergency Operations Consortium (SEOC): A Review*, University of Birmingham, February 1995, p. 152.
[5] *SEOC Review*, p. 146.

CART agencies have disagreed among themselves, and in 1986 the EC publicly cast doubt on the existence of widespread hunger.[6] At one point, shortly after a donor-WFP estimate put the numbers of displaced at 150,000, CART made a distribution based on a figure of 250,000—much to the donors' annoyance. 'But we also have to be humane,' remarked one of the CART members involved.[7]

There has been uneven monitoring of food stocks and little analysis of the food economy of the city, a notable omission especially for the period since 1993 when the secure perimeter has expanded and local food production has increased. Most significantly, relief reporting from Juba appears to have paid little heed to the rapidly changing military and political situation, which is essential for understanding and predicting relief needs.

An End to Neutrality

The LWF/SEOC airlift, and its less regular companion, the WFP/OLS airlift, have been essentially logistical supply operations. They deliver food and hand it over for distribution. The main distributor has been CART.

As discussed in chapter 5, CART was the first and most sustained attempt to achieve neutrality and accountability in the provision of relief in the Sudanese civil war. At its inception in 1986, it offered a positive model for relief operations. Although formally envisaged as a logistical co-ordination body, its ambitions ranged wider: CART would be collaborative, deliver food on the basis of need, account for it, wholly independently of the military, and might even be able to reach an accommodation with the SPLA. CART and its members also became public advocates for the victims of the disaster in Equatoria.

It did not prevail. Before it was a year old, CART became a battleground in which the government and military contested for

---

[6] Richard Graham and John Borton, 'A Preliminary Review of the Combined Agencies Relief Team (CART), Juba 1986-91,' London, Overseas Development Institute, March 1992, p. 43.

[7] Interviewed in Khartoum, February 1996.

control of aid resources with relief agencies and their donors. Over the years, the government won. The first decisive victory was scored in late 1986, when the donors acceded to the government's definition of the programme, and failed to prevent (or even protest against) the expulsion of the UN Resident Representative. Two expatriate aid workers in Juba were also expelled. Thereafter, the links between the local (implementing) agencies and the international NGOs were systematically put under pressure. CART's major donor, the EC, provided funds only on a month-by-month basis, which made planning extremely difficult (operations continued because Oxfam guaranteed the cash flow). As the SPLA advanced, displaced people poured into Juba and rural areas reachable by CART contracted. The hopes for promoting self-reliant development collapsed into mere emergency feeding programmes, and the prospects for cross-line supplies to SPLA-held areas vanished. In January 1988, the army commandeered ten trucks—the nine that remained intact were returned only after considerable donor pressure. From March, CART's own vehicles moved out of Juba under military escort. In Terakeka, supplies were consigned to the only 'trusted' senior figure in the town—who also happened to be the garrison commander.[8] 'Neutrality' was beginning to wear thin.

Hence by the time of the most serious famine in Juba, between August and October 1988, CART had already become seriously emasculated. The LWF airlift (taken over by SEOC in 1991) did not help it to reassert its neutrality. It appears that LWF proposed the airlift partly as a means of re-entering Sudan (it had been expelled the year before), so it was not in a strong position to strike a favourable deal. LWF/SEOC had no staff inside Juba. Its first ground visit was in 1991, the second and last in 1993.[9]

In February 1989, the Governor proposed that CART be taken over by the government. He backed down after representations from local leaders and donors. In October that year, CART had its most serious confrontation with the government, following its support for a UN-proposed plan to assist displaced people in Juba to return home

---

[8] *CART Review*, p. 28.
[9] *SEOC Review*, p. 154.

(implicitly to SPLA-controlled areas), together with a reduction in supplies to Juba. The military governor accused CART of 'gross interference in state policy'[10] and demanded that the RRC chair the consortium. CART's links with western donors again proved their worth, and the government backed down. It was the last major confrontation that the government lost.

The SPLA again tightened its siege of Juba in January 1990, culminating in an attack on the city and indiscriminate shelling that killed at least nine people. This was the second major humanitarian crisis in Juba. Thousands more displaced people crowded in. It followed a suspension of WFP flights the previous November (LWF flights stopped for only eighteen days, and WFP flights resumed with OLS II in March). In early 1991, security tightened its grip on CART, confiscating NGO radios and insisting that a security representative sit in on committee meetings.[11] Later in the year, CART briefly allowed its food to travel on military trucks.

The SPLA's June and July 1992 attacks on Juba again worsened the situation in the city. A mutiny by Southern army units in the garrison was timed to coincide with a major SPLA assault. The SPLA briefly overran the military headquarters, but its assault troops were then obliged to withdraw. In retaliation, government forces destroyed a large part of the town and killed large numbers of residents and displaced people. Hundreds were arrested and scores executed, among them two Sudanese employees of the EC and one of USAID. It used an aeroplane with UN insignia (that had earlier been flying WFP food) to transport arms to the city. But the sting of international protest was drawn when, a few weeks later, the SPLA murdered four expatriates (three aid workers and a journalist). The outrage and energies of most international agencies were directed into trying to decide how to respond to the SPLA killings, and the opportunity for a reappraisal of feeding Juba was lost.

The Sudan Government exploited its opportunity. The regional government finally succeeded in imposing the RRC Chairman as CART chairman, formally ending the neutrality of the consortium.

---

[10] *CART Review*, p. 36.
[11] *CART Review*, p. 21.

One Sudanese aid official said, 'The original idea of CART is being violated by the Government.' He explained how this worked in practice:

They [the RRC] said, whenever food is sent from Nairobi, information should come to the RRC first, two weeks ahead. Otherwise they have no right [i.e. obligation] to release it. They also need to know about the programme, why the food is needed. [They said] there is a need to follow RRC guidelines.[12]

In short, unless there was a specific request to do otherwise and formal advance warning, the RRC took automatic control over any relief delivered to Juba.

An End to Accountability

The first major questions about the accountability of CART were raised in 1989 when a stockcheck found 700 tons of food missing.[13] Meanwhile, LWF/SEOC never raised any serious questions about accountability, and—until the commissioning of an independent review in 1994—neither did its donors. The Northern Sector of OLS, under UNDP, was also loath to ask hard questions or push for a deeper analysis.

Mounting pressure from the government and security (especially in the wake of the 1992 battles and killings), the expanding role of the Comprehensive Call agencies, and influence from the commercial-military cartel that profited from speculation in the food market, all eroded the accountability of CART. The consortium structure now became a point where the government could exert pressure: CART could not say no when the RRC, under government or military direction, demanded access to the CART stores for unauthorised withdrawals. There were no serious countervailing pressures. One Juba resident complained:

---

[12] Interviewed in Khartoum, February 1996.
[13] *SEOC Review*, p. 154. This may have been due to control errors and underweight bags, see: *CART Review*, p. 19.

242

There was military pressure. The stores were controlled by CART. The government through the RRC used this loophole. A poor civilian like Dr William [Mogga, former CART secretary] would not have the power to say no. . . . The NGOs should have said to WFP to control the store. That would have been good; WFP can say no to the government.[14]

Questioned on some food that disappeared, one Sudanese relief official illustrated how the 'loophole' worked:

We don't know how it was used. If it was taken to the CART stores there would be a record. But they [Security] can release it. They use other NGOs to hide the facts. Most Islamic NGOs will do that for them. [These releases don't need the authorisation of the CART Steering Committee because] the Islamic agencies come with tissues proposals. They say there are people there when really there are not. When you want to send something [i.e. relief] with a third party, Security will not allow it. The Steering Committee is intimidated. Before the meetings, usually the Security and the RRC Chairman and the WFP man meet first. We are powerless. No matter how we go upwards, we can do nothing.

They [the Government] do everything under the cover of CART. Decisions are made by the Chairman of CART, who is the Chairman of the RRC. Whatever decision he is taking is with the backing of Sudan Public Security for NGOs, who fully protect this man and protect all Islamic NGOs. The Chairman dismissed the Acting Administrative Manager, Guido Lolik [in November 1995]. He did it alone.[15]

Hence, the food supply and distribution operation in Juba, of which CART was the largest element, was essentially in government hands and was serving government strategy, but had an independent international facade.

International aid agency staff also began to complain, for example saying, 'There is no control of CART. Nobody can control

---

[14] Interviewed in Khartoum, February 1996. WFP was in fact given control of the CART store.

[15] Interviewed in Khartoum, February 1996.

it. . . . They cannot prove that all the food has been distributed.'[16] In particular, WFP (which stations a food monitor in Juba), was increasingly unhappy; it found that individual agencies were more accountable than CART itself. In 1994, the CART accounts were audited for the first time, and the accountants declined to certify. Some relief workers alleged that this was a conspiracy, that the accounting firm was Islamist and influenced by the government. True or not, the CART management had exposed itself to profound and genuine criticism, and had to take the consequences, including a far-reaching management review.[17] The government took the opportunity to promote the role of the RRC and selected Islamic agencies.

Food and Control

After 1992, Islamic NGOs came to play a prominent role in the city. IARA had been admitted to CART in 1987, and in 1993 three more joined: Da'awa al Islamiya, IIRO and Muwafaq al Khairiya. Other NGOs such as al Birr International and Nidaa al Jihad also began programmes. The Comprehensive Call began to be implemented, coinciding with successful military efforts to expand the 'secure zone' around the city in the wake of the SPLA attacks. As elsewhere, the Islamic agencies are dedicated to ideas of self-reliance and agricultural development. The UNDP Area Rehabilitation Scheme in Juba feeds into this model, by giving material support to projects developed under the auspices of the Comprehensive Call. WFP food policy has also concurred. General food rations to displaced people have been withdrawn, to be replaced by food-for-work programmes, school feeding projects, and programmes for 'self-reliance' in peace camps—with only small free allocations of food to disabled people and malnourished children.

International relief agencies in Juba have been trapped by their own rhetoric into giving support to the NIF strategy in the enclave.

---

[16] Interviewed in Khartoum, February 1996.
[17] Hassabo and Company, 'Combined Agencies Relief Team (CART), Juba: Administrative and Management Review,' July 1995.

244

Following the battles of 1992, foreign NGOs including Oxfam and ACORD began to put emphasis on food security through local production. In 1994, a report indicated that about forty per cent of the food grains and over sixty per cent of the vegetables grown within Juba and the peace camps were produced with the assistance (ploughing services, seeds, irrigation, credit and extension) of one NGO—the ACORD Juba Multisectoral Programme.[18] The government was a keen supporter of this programme, and readily provided land for seed multiplication and facilitated the import and transport of necessary inputs. On one occasion, the government exceptionally offered the NGO the use of a radio (it declined the privilege).

This degree of government co-operation with a foreign NGO is highly unusual. It reflects a high degree of confidence in the ACORD programme and staff. It also reflects the failure of favoured Islamic NGOs to deliver on their promises of food security. An agriculturalist who visited farms run by two Islamic NGOs in 1994 reported that they were far less successful than their public claims had indicated:

These Islamic NGOs are really funny. Despite the fact that their staff are not agriculturalists, they have never been to Juba nor [do] they know about farming practices and requirements in [this] farming zone, and they refuse to consult us on these issues. Their only qualifications are that they are NIF supporters. They believe that they know everything, and now you see how they mess with everything, they are using the wrong varieties of seeds, wrong cultural practices. In Khartoum they are talking big about their achievements in food production, just to raise more funds. Even their photos on their last annual reports on the crops, I am dead sure they were taken from [another NGO's] farm.

The beneficiaries of the foreign NGOs' food security programmes have not necessarily been poor farmers. The productive land around Juba and its peace camps is highly prized, and much of it has been allocated to medium-scale farmers from inside the city,

18 El Hadi Abdalla, 'Juba Visit Report,' August 1994.

245

many of whom are Northerners and affiliated to the NIF. The food produced within the enclave is also distributed through government-controlled channels. This state of affairs has led NGO workers to question whether the programmes are benefiting the government more than the poor people of the area.

But there is no doubt that Islamic agencies remain the government's favoured intermediaries in the Juba enclave. Relief, military control and social transformation are intimately linked under the principle of *tamkiin*: awarding dominance to the NIF-affiliated Moslem minority. *Tamkiin* in practice is illustrated by the Abdel Rahman ibn Awf al Waqfiya al Khairiya (Charitable Endowment Foundation). This runs *mahmiyat* or 'protectorates' around Juba. The Foundation was officially inaugurated in October 1993, with the main objective of supporting *Jihad* and providing funding for Nidaa al Jihad.[19] According to its executive director, Ibrahim Mohammed Ahmad Hasan:

> Ibn Awf al Khairiya has sought to establish investment bodies in the form of protected settlements, and the development of the friction regions in the northern, western, eastern and southern borders. This is a direct call for the sons of Southern and Northern states to migrate to the South for ethnic cross-breeding of the *Umma* and through intermarriage and blood relations.[20]

'Investment bodies' refers to agricultural or other 'developmental' projects that can attract private finance. Sudanese newspaper reports indicate that the Foundation has taken over some loss-making formerly state-run enterprises.

'Protected settlements' has the ring of counter-insurgency. Some Islamic agencies are known to co-operate closely with the military in Juba. They have privileges such as two-way radios and ready availability of travel permits.

But the most remarkable aspect of the Ibn Awf al Khairiya policy is the reference to systematic inter-marriage between Moslem men and non-Moslem Southern women. This is confirmed by other

---

[19] *Al Inqaz al Watani*, 5 October 1993, p. 6
[20] *ibid.*

statements by the agency.[21] As the children of Moslem men are required to be Moslem, and the 'protectorates' are run by Islamic agencies, this would have the implication of bringing a new Islamised generation of Southerners into being. The existence of marriage schemes is not in doubt. Reports indicate that eligible men are given financial incentives to participate. Lubaba al Fadl, a leading NIF women functionary and Secretary-General of the World Association of Moslem Women, reportedly stated in a women's' conference in Khartoum in 1992, that she endorsed marriage schemes in Southern Sudan as a means of solving the political and social problems of the region and that she would allow her 'husband to marry even two from the region'. However, other details of marriage schemes (for example the voluntary nature of the unions and the extent of government involvement) remain obscure.

FOOD SUPPLIES, PROFITS AND PEACE CAMPS IN WAU

Relief manipulation has been more blatant in Wau than in Juba. Three reasons are particularly important.

One is that there was no CART-type structure in Wau (the first attempts to start one in 1986 were aborted by the SPLA shooting down of an airliner at Malakal and the government's hard-line reaction). Wau was left without any substantial relief during the height of the Bahr el Ghazal famine. Both sides blocked access, and overland food convoys were looted. Only in December 1988 did the ICRC begin a small feeding programme in the town, and the following year other agencies began to return.

Second, Wau is divided between a mainly Dinka part and a Fertit-dominated part, with a precarious balance between the two groups in allocation of supplies and jobs. In 1987, the army, under the control of General Abu Gurun, and supported by Fertit militia, waged war on the inhabitants of the Dinka part of town, alleging that they were supporters of the SPLA. A series of massacres culminated on 11-12 August with the killing of several hundred Dinkas, and

---

[21] Advertisement in *Al Sudan al Hadith*, 19 December 1992, p. 11.

perhaps more than one thousand on 6 September.[22] The atrocities abated at the end of the year, with the transfer of General Abu Gurun, but tensions have remained high. One factor that contributed to the fighting was the influx of Dinka displaced people, fleeing *Murahaliin* raids, who were portrayed as a security threat. The large and constantly-growing displaced population has been a challenge to the authorities in Wau ever since.

Three, the food supply cartel has been virtually unchallenged. During the period of mass killing, the army maintained artificially high prices in the Dinka part of town, ensuring that the inhabitants were impoverished while merchant-officer partnerships made handsome profits. While the internal fighting has stopped, exploitation has continued.

The Crisis in Wau

The crisis in Wau is a political one. There are over 100,000 people in and around Wau town, perhaps three quarters of them displaced. The displaced have fled raiding and fighting in rural Bahr el Ghazal. They are in a hopeless situation until the war ends or an intermediate solution is found that enables them to return to their homes with a reasonable degree of safety. But international agencies have been loath to recognise this: instead they have always sought a ray of optimism, envisaging some prospects of rehabilitation within the environs of Wau. At the same time, they have approached the situation with an emergency mindset, with year-by-year proposals and programmes. The result has been a curious amalgam of a commitment to moving along the 'relief-to-development continuum' and a short-sighted incapacity to plan strategically. The government, which has (at least since 1992) had a strategic plan, has readily exploited the international agencies' gullibility.

Since 1989, the government has presented the protracted crisis in the town as a problem of 'development' and lack of 'self-reliance'. From the same date, UN plans for the displaced envisaged their return home. There were no immediate prospects for this, given the

---

[22] 'Sudan's Secret Slaughter,' anonymous report, 1988.

248

devastation in rural areas. By 1990, when *Murahaliin* raids had subsided and rural Bahr el Ghazal was beginning to recover, the prospects of return looked much brighter. The SPLA was also beginning to tighten its siege. In 1991, as conditions worsened in the town, while they improved in rural areas, people began to leave. The Government, which had tolerated discussion of return when it was not a realistic option, now began to look for alternatives. It was saved by the split in the SPLA, which provided the military opportunity for the army to retake the offensive. In the dry season of early 1992, the army and PDF relieved the military pressure on Wau, opening supply roads to north and south, expanding the secure perimeter, and seizing large herds of cattle in raids.

At the same time, the government came up with a strategy that would, in the UN's phrase, put the 'displaced citizens back into the mainstream development process of the country.'[23] This was the creation of peace camps and agricultural schemes.

Government Strategy since 1992

Following the SPLA split of 1991 and the dry season offensive of early 1992, the Sudan Government was optimistic that the SPLA could be militarily defeated. The attack on Juba shattered that confidence, but the Sudan army continued to make substantial gains. One of the aims of military action was mass displacement, to provide human fodder for the Comprehensive Call, which began to be implemented in 1992.

In late 1995, a new variant on government strategy emerged in response to new military threats in eastern Sudan. This was based upon securing key strategic areas of the South (the oilfields, the Ethiopian border and the three main towns), and hence confining the SPLA to an area south of nine degrees north. Proxy forces (the South Sudan Independence Army led by Riek Machar and Kerubino Kuanyin) and the *Murahaliin*-PDF were to be used to destabilise a swathe of Southern countryside, to prevent the SPLA gaining a

---

[23] UNDP Project SUD/032/88, p. 8; Mark Bradbury, 'Wau Case Study: Notes for Official OLS Review,' 26 May 1996, p. 3.

significant military presence in these areas. Meanwhile, the government envisaged an 'oil spot' pattern of secured areas spreading out from the major towns, based upon peace camps, agricultural development schemes and major lines of communication (such as the railway).[24] International assistance has been used to support the 'developmental' aspects of the Comprehensive Call.

The policy of establishing peace camps began in Wau in March 1992. Displaced people in the town relocated to three newly-set up peace camps within the secure perimeter. The decision to do this was not taken in consultation with relief agencies or even the government-headed Local Relief Committee. By 1996, three additional 'peace villages' and three camps along the railway line had been set up.

Islamic NGOs have been given preferential access to work in the peace camps. They are also given privileges such as the use of radios and ready access to government officers. Local Christian NGOs were not permitted to work in the peace camps

Profiteering

A merchant-officer cartel in Wau has exercised tight control over all food supplies to the town, and distributions. Unlike Juba, Wau is not an enclave: it can be fed by overland convoys from Kordofan and Darfur (by rail and road), and the Bagari Loop of Fertit villages to the west of the town also produces marketable surpluses. During the late 1980s famine, the army ensured that food was sold in Wau markets at a price equivalent to three times purchase price and transport costs. Such high prices would normally have attracted more traders, whose supplies would have brought the price down. By regulating the military escorts that made commercial access possible, the army maintained an artificial scarcity. An attempt to provide 8,800 tonnes of relief via Raga in 1987 foundered. Only 131 tonnes reached Wau; the remainder, stored in Raga army compound 'for

---

[24] The 'oil spot' strategy and metaphor was used by French military commanders during the occupation of Morocco in the early 20th century.

security', was stolen with the active connivance of the soldiers.[25] The army dismantled an important bridge on the Raga-Wau road, making wet season deliveries impossible. Only 200 tonnes of relief food reached Wau in the first eleven months of 1988, when the ICRC was finally given permission to begin a relief airlift.

The army also controlled the food supplies from the Bagari Loop, at one point prompting a suggestion that aid agencies supply local people with bicycles so that they could reach Wau market independently of army-escorted lorries.

The ICRC operation was meagre compared to need, but still faced consistent obstruction from the authorities. This culminated on 2 September 1991, when a land mine placed on Wau airport runway blew up an ICRC plane, abruptly halting the airlift. The mine was planted in one of the most securely guarded parts of Wau, casting suspicion on the army as the culprit. Within days, the price of sorghum in Wau rose three-fold. The government also actively discouraged LWF/SEOC from initiating a relief airlift to Wau along the lines of its Juba airlift. In January 1992, the army withheld permission for a food convoy to travel to Wau, and it was widely speculated that this was related to the cartel's efforts to keep food prices high.

Humanitarian Compliance

The military in Wau was the first beneficiary of the western donors' policy of compliance, adopted in late 1986. After the proposed 'mini-CART' for Wau was abandoned in August, the European Community began consigning food directly to the military authorities in Bahr el Ghazal. Since then, the government and army have handled relief with near-total impunity.

The donors, including OLS-Northern Sector, have failed to challenge the government's version of events. There has been a near-complete failure of independent assessment and monitoring, and very little analysis of the food economy or the reasons for the

---

[25] Paul Symonds, 'A Report on the Situation in Raga, Western Bahr el Ghazal Province, June-August 1987,' Khartoum, September 1987.

enduring crisis.[26] Instead, the UN has been willing to accept government's definition of the problem, requiring only (semi-)independent estimates of the numbers of people in need. The result has been that the UN is ready to negotiate programmes based on access (usually through implementing organisations designated by the government), rather than an independent assessment of the nature of the problem. Neutrality and accountability have not been undermined: they never entered the picture.

The first formal relief co-ordinating body in Wau was the Local Relief Committee (LRC), set up in 1991. It is chaired by the RRC, includes security, members of the state relief commission, UN, ICRC, church organisations and Sudanese NGOs. Like CART since 1992, it is a tool of the government. But no more than a year after the LRC's establishment, the government had the confidence to go further. The state commissioner for relief was made chairman of the LRC, giving direct executive control to the Governor's representative. Following the adoption of the Comprehensive Call and the establishment of peace camps, the government has often dealt directly with its favoured Islamic NGOs, including Da'awa al Islamiya, IARA, Muwafaq al Khairiya and IIRO. There are varied and contradictory reports on the effectiveness of these agencies. Muwafaq has at least three peace villages in the region.[27] The OLS Review team reports that official government meetings were held in the Muwafaq offices in Wau.[28] The Ministry of Peace and Reconstruction has begun to work with the National Development Foundation to assist 'returnees' (i.e. people displaced to Wau from SPLA-held areas).

Rather than challenging the co-option of relief into counter-insurgency and the Comprehensive Call, the UN has actively co-operated, by setting up an Area Development Scheme. In March 1994, UNDP sent a mission to Wau to assess the prospects for such a project. The mission reported that 'it is possible to resume normal economic activities within the region close to Wau particularly in

---

[26] Bradbury, 1996.
[27] Siraj el Din Abdel Bagi, interviewed in Khartoum, February 1996.
[28] *OLS Review*, p. 98.

crop production.'[29] UNDP justified its resumption of 'development' activities by referring to continuities with its post-1972 rehabilitation activities, as though there were no war at all. The UNDP project proposal combines conventional aims such as improving self-sufficiency in food production with reference to participation and bottom-up methods of implementation. The project began in April 1995. UNDP's partner in this enterprise is the state government, and its intervention is aimed at three peace villages and three 'indigenous' villages, totalling 20,000 people. While wholly consonant with the Comprehensive Call model of agricultural development, it appears oblivious to how the displaced actually survive (chiefly by providing the town with cheap goods services such as firewood and fodder).

It is clear that the UN accepted, wholly and uncritically, the government's definition of the problem and proposed solution. While supporting the government's counter-insurgency strategy, UNDP appears to believe that this form of development will contribute to peace.

UPPER NILE: AN OIL SPOT

Upper Nile is the most strategic region of the South, because of the Jonglei Canal project, the river Nile, land suitable for mechanised farming, and above all the oilfields. The Sudan Government has invested more political, military and humanitarian resources in Upper Nile than elsewhere in the South. This approach culminated in the signing of the April 1996 Charter, in which Commander Riek Machar's South Sudan Independence Movement joined the government. Malakal is now the government's favoured base for a relocated OLS.

Until 1991, Malakal was the most cut-off major garrison in Sudan. Famine conditions were reported as early as 1984. It was supplied by Nile barges, extremely irregularly. Government-imposed delays of three months or more were common, and no relief at all was available in the town between March 1988 and February 1989.

---

[29] Bradbury, 1996, p. 41.

On arrival, the security services and local church agencies contested for control of relief supplies. On one occasion, food remained in store for nine months until the issue was resolved. At times, food prices in Malakal were the highest in Sudan. The situation was only mildly alleviated when more relief agencies arrived under the auspices of OLS. As late as 1995, the government authorities were able to confiscate about 600 sacks of relief from a local NGO with impunity.

The major change in government policy in Malakal came in the wake of the August 1991 split in the SPLA, which reduced and finally removed rebel military pressure on the city. Around the town and in the northern parts of Upper Nile, the Comprehensive Call agencies became active.

The Da'awa-ist agencies' activities reflect the article of faith among NIF hard-liners that the SPLA is historically doomed. The idea that Southerners traditionally have 'no culture' is axiomatic to them; the destruction of war has only reinforced such views. An advisor to the NIF wrote:

> [The South] is a wasteland . . . it has been a free-for-all—a place of starvation and disease. Young kids roam the bush with automatic weapons. Rail lines have been destroyed, bridges burned. Violence can explode anywhere between anybody.[30]

In the late 1980s, it was fashionable for NIF members to compare the SPLA with RENAMO,[31] with the implication that no negotiation was possible: without external support, the rebel army would collapse under the weight of its own internal contradictions.

---

[30] T. Abdou Maliqalim Simone, *In Whose Image? Political Islam and Urban Practices in Sudan*, University of Chicago Press, 1994, p. 117. In fairness, note that Simone also points out and criticises many Northerners' failure to understand Southerners' 'Africanity', p. 190.

[31] Abdel Wahab el Effendi, 'Discovering the South: Sudanese Dilemmas for Islam in Africa,' *African Affairs*, 89, 1990, pp. 371-89 at p. 386. This comparison has not been heard since RENAMO began talks with the Mozambique Government and contested elections in 1992.

Therefore, government strategy should be to introduce 'civilised' values, laden with material benefits, to bring the population round. The Peace and Development Foundation (since renamed the National Development Foundation) was created with this philosophy in mind in early 1992, as the last sentence of the following quotation from its inaugural press conference makes clear:[32]

The Peace and Development Foundation has set up comprehensive development programmes to rehabilitate and reconstruct war-torn areas in Southern Sudan, starting with the areas where peace had already been established.

The Director General of the Peace and Development Foundation, Fadl Al Seed Abu Gisaisa, said in a press conference yesterday that development programmes will expand in the areas which enjoy peace in the South.

He said that they will depend on local materials in boosting agricultural and pastoral development, in addition to the rehabilitation of the citizens civilisationally and culturally.

The 'Peace from Within' strategy accompanies this: individual rebel leaders are enticed to join the government fold, weakening the SPLA and allowing the government to claim that peace is spreading more widely: another pacified 'oil spot'.

Muwafaq al Khairiya is prominent among the Islamic agencies in Upper Nile. In an interview, its Executive Director, Siraj el Din Abdel Bary, spoke about the agency's role.[33]

There is a lot of suffering caused by war. The war is affecting people negatively. . . . Our understanding is that everybody should try to play a role in recovering the situation.

Nowadays, peace and stability is dominating the South. Most parts are out of the war zone.

Faced with evidence that the SPLA controls significant areas in the South, Siraj el Din said: 'Well, there are some areas [outside

---

[32] *Al Sudan al Hadith*, 9 March 1992, p. 1.
[33] Interviewed in Khartoum, February 1996.

255

government control]. But generally it is stable.' He went on to describe how Muwafaq works:

You may know about the government campaign of Peace from Within.
It is a project led by the government. It is to convince the rebels that it is better for them and their kind to live in peace. We thought that there would be a way to take part and rebuild the country. We as an organisation offer development, not relief; and this is especially in emergencies. We play a role in teaching people how to cultivate, not teaching them to be dependent.

Siraj el Din was underplaying his agency's role: Muwafaq is also involved in relief distributions in the region.

A major shock to the Da'awa-ist programme in the region came in October 1992, when a neo-traditional Nuer religious leader, Wutnyang Gatakek (who is widely referred to as a *Kujur* or 'witchdoctor') rallied a substantial army and launched a surprise attack on Malakal, which he briefly overran. This was a serious military crisis and embarrassment to the government. Members of the supposedly pro-government Anyanya II joined Wutnyang's assault, as a result of which Anyanya II was disbanded and the local militia policy was reviewed. The attack was also a blow for Muwafaq al Khairiya, two of whose workers were killed in the fighting.

Some of the implications of the attack are evident from subsequent official press coverage:[34]

The Governor of Upper Nile, Colonel Paul Reith Kwanj,[35] met yesterday morning at the headquarters of Muwafaq al Khairiya in Khartoum with its workers and managers, in the presence of the deputy leader of the Popular Committee for Salvation in the Upper Nile and the State ministers.
The Director General of Muwafaq, Dr Sulaf al Din Saleh, presented a report on the programmes and activities of the

---

[34] 'The Governor of Upper Nile Praises the Efforts of Muwafaq al Khairiya,' *Al Quwat al Musallaha*, 10 January 1993, p. 2.
[35] He was subsequently killed in a plane crash.

256

Foundation in the region. He stressed that the humanitarian services will continue in the region, despite the latest events which the Foundation has faced as a result of the treacherous *Kujur* attack and its killing of two of the Foundation's employees.

He announced that the Foundation had opened a wireless radio system in Banjila area to connect the north of Upper Nile with Khartoum, in the framework of a radio network that would be set up in peace villages in the Upper Nile this year.

The Director General enumerated the services offered by the Foundation in the fields of health, education, culture, media and agriculture in the peace villages in the State.

He said that the Foundation in co-operation with the Peace and Development Foundation had sent a caravan to Burun, Bunj and Meban areas so as to provide clothing, medicine and food. He said Muwafaq teams will be sent to Malakal to train women in the neighbourhoods in handicrafts. These are in addition to the environment programmes and encouragement of 'productive families' [projects] in Malakal. The Director General indicated that the Foundation will work towards making local citizens get involved in agricultural investment.

The Governor welcomed those services and praised the administration of Muwafaq al Khairiya. He re-iterated his government's total support for all the activities and programmes of Muwafaq in the State, explaining that the citizens had felt for the first time that there was a government [in the region] when Muwafaq al Khairiya brought social services and mills to Upper Nile.

Muwafaq al Khairiya is not only delivering the Da'awa, but, in the words of the Governor, government itself.

RESTRICTING ACCESS TO SPLA-CONTROLLED AREAS

The Sudan Government has never accepted the compromise to its sovereignty represented by OLS: not only does it deliver the largest amounts of material assistance to SPLA-held areas, but it enjoys the diplomatic privileges and recognition of being a UN operation.

257

Indirectly, OLS extends recognition to the SPLA. The Sudan Government has rarely concealed its long-term aim of closing down OLS. It has been deterred by the diplomatic embarrassment this would cause (allowing OLS to continue is one way the Sudan Government uses to deflect human rights criticism) and by the resources it gains (especially valuable since the ban on development assistance). But since the UN has adopted the 'relief to development' model, the government believes (probably correctly) that the UN and other agencies would continue to operate in its territory if OLS were closed down, while the SPLA-held areas would lose out.

Occasionally there are threats to close down OLS altogether and bring the entire operation under government control. These were made in 1989 and 1990. They were dropped when OLS formalised its procedures for gaining access in 1993-4, but more recently have been revived. The Acting Commissioner of the RRC said in early 1996:

> There is a committee in progress to end OLS. The Chairman is Awad Khalifa, the former RRC Commissioner. It reports to the State Minister of Social Welfare.[36]

In 1995 a marginally less extreme version of this was proposed, namely the relocation of the logistical base for the Southern Sector from Lokichoggio in northern Kenya to Malakal, where the government would be able to exercise a great deal more *de facto* control. So far, the western donors have resisted these threats.

In the meantime, the Sudan Government has used a number of stratagems to control and restrict relief moving to Southern Sudan. The most common method is to refuse to issue permission for flights. There is a long history of failing to grant fight permissions, or granting them only at the last minute. Under the more assertive leadership of Philip O'Brien from early 1993, OLS Southern Sector took the attitude that locations not expressly forbidden were permitted, provided that the government was notified, and succeeded in increasing the number of locations where OLS was present

---

[36] Interviewed in Khartoum, February 1996.

258

tenfold. In 1995-6, the government had more success once again in restricting Southern Sector access. First, it used the pretext of an unauthorised flight by the agency CCM to Pariang in Upper Nile, and the capture of two relief workers by the army, to pressure OLS. In 1996, it succeeded in withholding permission to fly to flood-stricken Pochala for several key months. The government has proved more patient and persistent than most of its humanitarian adversaries.

A more imaginative initiative was made in 1995, when the Sudan Government introduced the concept of 'war zones', to be distinguished from 'war-affected areas.' The OLS mandate is to concern itself with 'war-affected areas'; the government defined 'war zones' locations with active hostilities. The Sudan Government proposed that OLS should have access to the latter but not the former.[37] The UN agreed: it ceded the authority to define 'war zones' to the Government. Following this, parts of Eastern Equatoria were declared off-limits to OLS operations, while the government mounted an offensive there. The full ramifications of this innovation have yet to be seen, but if the government exploits this UN concession, it could strangle much of the Southern Sector activity.

The new-found government confidence of 1995-6 unpicked many of the gains made by Philip O'Brien's earlier assertiveness. The head of OLS-Southern Sector found himself trying to explain and justify the UN's apparent policy of compliance in the face of government obstructionism.

The government has repeatedly used the argument of cost to try to shut down the Southern Sector. It has pointed out that delivery by air is many times more expensive than delivery overland, and has proposed using road, rail and barge deliveries from the North to replace air deliveries from Lokichoggio. The counter-argument from the Southern Sector has been that cross-border road deliveries would be a cheaper alternative, and that there could be delivery across the front line to government-controlled towns. But cross-line access would entail drawing a map of government-controlled and SPLA-controlled areas, and the government conceding that it controlled

---

[37] *OLS Review*, p. 28.

rather less territory than its propaganda claims. When cross-line access was proposed, the government quietly toned down its complaints about cost.

Another government strategy has been to deny that significant numbers of people are living outside areas of government control. It has repeatedly disputed population figures produced by the SPLA or by relief agencies. This has yet to convince any major donors.

A final, oft-repeated strategy, is to accuse the OLS Southern Sector and European or American NGOs of supplying the SPLA with war materials. The suspicions run deep. One government official said:

> We discovered that some NGOs illegally entered Sudan, with heavy trucks and big aircraft. They bought some non-food items—we understand what that means. . . . There were seventy trucks carrying parts for a barge.[38]

This was the pretext for shutting off operations in late 1989 and again in late 1990, and the accusation has been made periodically ever since. Another official spoke in these terms:

> The SPLA first depended on native possessions, on looting from the natives. Suddenly that has been stopped as other sources came. If it is only for the needy people, then what about the armed people? How do they get it? If I depend on a source and it stops, it means I found an alternative.[39]

In November 1996, the Sudan Government accused the ICRC of providing military support to the SPLA, and closed its operations.

The UN in Khartoum seems to share much the same opinion, justifying its tolerance of government abuse on the grounds that they suspect the same thing is going on with the SPLA. One senior UN official said:

---

[38] Interviewed in Khartoum, February 1996.
[39] Interviewed in Khartoum, February 1996.

[When] the rebels saw they were the beneficiaries [of OLS] there was a lot of motivation to kiss ass. They formed their humanitarian wings and co-operated with the agencies. Here we have the Government Relief Act of 1992, which says that the government owns the property [of relief agencies]. But when it comes to distribution, it's not that different [with the SPLA]. In some ways the government is more up-front.[40]

This may be true. But in the Southern Sector, the humanitarian agencies have been able to collect a great deal more evidence about relief needs and the effectiveness of programmes, and have engaged in programmes that, whatever their success, have genuinely attempted to introduce transparency and humanitarian principles into relief operations. In the Northern Sector, the UN has simply surrendered: it has not even tried to contest.

IMPLICATIONS

The Sudan Government is interested in the resources unlocked by OLS, and is determined to subvert the principle of a negotiated breach of sovereignty. It can do this in two ways: either by exercising direct operational control of OLS (for example by relocating the Lokichoggio base to Malakal, as it has proposed) or by closing down OLS altogether. It has kept both options open. It aims to capture the resources currently channelled through OLS into its 'developmental' programmes in the South, by tying the major donors, UN agencies and international NGOs into long-term rehabilitation and development programmes that function independently of the OLS infrastructure. To a large extent the government has succeeded: most UNDP and UNICEF programmes in the South would probably continue even if OLS were closed down (and especially if the closure were not seen as the work of the government, but blame could be placed on the SPLA). In the meantime, the Islamic agencies are progressing with the Comprehensive Call agenda.

---

[40] Interviewed in Khartoum, February 1996.

261

11.

AID RESOURCES AND DISUNITY IN THE SPLA

This relief has destroyed our relationship with the Dinka and other groups.

Nuer Prophet Wutnyang Gatakek

The Sudan Government's humanitarian strategy is thorough and sophisticated. But its successes have been greatly facilitated by shortcomings on the other side: the SPLA, SRRA and international relief agencies working alongside them have not developed an approach of comparable sophistication. On the contrary, relief has exposed the political weaknesses of the Southern rebel movement, and may even have deepened them. The central reason for this is that control of aid resources is seen as an end in itself, rather than a means to a set of social and political goals.

The creation of OLS was tribute to the SPLA's military success. It extended an unprecedented recognition to a rebel organisation, both in Sudan and internationally, and provided aid resources into the heart of SPLA-held Sudan (while aid to the camps in Ethiopia was also increasing). Because the world overwhelmingly blamed Khartoum for the famine, OLS was a propaganda coup for the SPLA, and a vehicle for much more favourable publicity, as journalists and diplomats could now visit most parts of the SPLA-held areas in relative comfort and safety. It was an opportunity that previous liberation movements had only dreamed of.

Internally the SPLA was still weak. Its massive battlefield victories and huge field army were not matched by a functioning civil administration, a practical social agenda, a humanitarian capacity, or a diplomatic strategy. OLS brought resources and opportunities that could have helped the SPLA address these weaknesses. This could have entailed either liberalisation (as most aid workers would have preferred) or a more sophisticated and effective but still authoritarian kind of political mobilisation (perhaps a mirror image of the NIF's Comprehensive Call). OLS certainly helped many Southerners, both ordinary rural people and commanders. Overall, however, the coming of OLS probably did more harm than good for the SPLA.

1989-91: A MISSED OPPORTUNITY?

OLS arrived as a new phase in the war got underway. The SPLA was for the first time faced with the challenge of administering substantial amounts of territory. It is true that it had claimed to control vast areas long before that, but 'control' meant little more than rendering a place unsafe for the Sudan Government, and making it available to rebel fighters for movement, recruitment and requisitioning. It had not, on the whole, established steady relations with the civilian populations. However, in the space of a few months in late 1988 and early 1989, the SPLA captured many towns, giving the movement uninterrupted dominion over a wide swathe of land, which it faced no immediate prospect of losing.

In retrospect, it is tempting to identify the two years from 1989 to 1991 as providing a vital missed opportunity for the SPLA to transform itself. Whether that entailed democratisation or not, the essential component would have been to adopt a practical social and political programme for the areas it controlled. That in turn would have required defining the mutual responsibilities of soldiers and civilians, in which the former would protect and respect the latter in turn for recruits, food and other forms of support. There was some progress, notably on trade policies in Upper Nile. But no big initiative was made to reform the governance of the SPLA until the end of 1991, by which time it was too late.

While it is easy with hindsight to suggest such a reform, there were many practical difficulties. The culture of the SPLA would have had to be changed, to limit or control the ruthlessness that had been instilled in the soldiers. A new understanding of army discipline was required. The inter-tribal animosities that had been exacerbated needed to be soothed again; a task that would take months or years under the most favourable conditions. And for John Garang to have encouraged the High Command openly to discuss policy issues would have risked reviving elements of disunity and factionalism that Southern leaders had shown in the past.

These were hard problems, but urgent ones. The delay in tackling social policy can be attributed partly to the exceptionally fluid military and political conditions, and the expectation that the end of the war was at hand. Between the 1988 November Accords and the June 1989 coup, a negotiated peace was in prospect; and in the early days of the Omer al Bashir government, the opposition universally predicted that it would collapse. Meanwhile the SPLA had to learn fast how to deal with international relief. OLS was negotiated and re-negotiated in these volatile circumstances. From November 1989 onwards, the chronically undefined status and character of OLS created uncertainty within the SPLA. The movement's political agenda was set by the diplomacy of responding to the changing politics of the North and trying to obtain a favourable deal with the humanitarian agencies, rather developing social priorities for Southern Sudan itself. The leadership also had absolute faith in the Mengistu regime, which led to the unquestioning reproduction of the relief model of the Gambela refugee camps wherever possible (it also led to the SPLA continuing to fight for Mengistu inside Ethiopia for some weeks even after the Ethiopian army had surrendered in May 1991).

If there existed in the SPLA any beginnings of a debate about the need for civil administration, they were swept up in the hasty new relief programme. For example, Lam Akol has since claimed that he wanted to use the relief operation to lay some foundations of civil society. At the centre of his plans was the humanitarian face of the movement, the SRRA.

> [W]e came with the idea that SRRA should be expanded. First to adapt to a bigger organisation like OLS. Second to train people to establish civil institutions.[1]

---

[1] Interviewed on 4 April 1996.

But the SPLA's militaristic ethos was a bigger obstacle than the shortage of trained people per se, as pointed out, among others, by Bona Malwal, editor of the *Sudan Democratic Gazette*:

> Is it really necessary to insist that all recruits to the movement should still undergo extensive military training? Surely the needs of the liberated areas have moved beyond those of the purely military? There are many teachers, doctors and other professionals who would dearly love to return to liberated areas of Southern Sudan to do the jobs for which they have been trained. However, they have refrained from doing so because of the thought of military training and the uncertainty of being able to pursue their professions. There is a vast untapped personnel resource waiting to be utilised by the SPLA which is going to waste for want of a clearly defined political policy in the liberated areas.[2]

Leaving aside the political motives of John Garang in maintaining militaristic centralism, and those of Lam Akol and Bona Malwal in criticising it, the question arises: in practice, how could a humanitarian wing of the SPLA established some autonomy from the military? The most effective way of reconciling humanitarian and military interests is if both are based on a shared, practical social agenda in the liberated areas. Absent this, SRRA staff would either have to be subservient to the military, or in confrontation with it. To win any confrontations would have required some courage and determination by SRRA field staff, clear directives from the top of the SPLA and a capacity to enforce them, and some independent communications and resource flows.

These conditions were absent. All long-distance communication, especially by radio, was subject to military control in the name of security, so there was very little opportunity for SRRA secretaries to use an external resource as a way of changing the balance of power in their areas. Officials were often appointed by local commanders, and always dependent on their goodwill; they remained as the instruments of the military, rather than those of any humanitarian

---

[2] *Sudan Democratic Gazette*, June 1991, pp. 2, 4-5, 8.

organisation. This meant that they would try to obtain relief, but remain answerable primarily to the commander for the distribution of the supplies. Some commodities might go to needy civilians, some to soldiers, and some for serving the enrichment of relatively powerful individuals.

Most of the foreign aid agencies were committed to the idea that relief should feed civilians rather than soldiers, and should be distributed according to their own criteria of humanitarian need, rather than through a local network of patronage. The relationship between SRRA field staff and the military was not one that they could condone, so any frank discussion of the link would have been dangerous for the SPLA. The SRRA head office was thus continually making assurances that it could not substantiate. It was unable to explain credibly the way the organisation worked, or to convince agencies that it was fit to manage relief projects by itself. Its role became fixed as one of a minder and intermediary for the foreigners.

This role was less about facilitating contacts than limiting them. The SPLA had inherited from Mengistu's Ethiopia an attitude of deep suspicion towards people from western countries. When Lam Akol briefed commanders on the coming of OLS, '[they] were very apprehensive. They always think of NGOs as spies. At one meeting in Kapoeta I said: Yes, let us assume they are spies. But countries do not stop spies from coming. It is up to you to safeguard your information.'[3] The SRRA naturally became part of the mechanism for controlling and manipulating information. As the recognised counterpart of the foreigners, it needed to be staffed with intelligence personnel and others directly reporting to the military authorities. And it had to conceal this. The basic techniques of deception were already well-practised; they were similar to those that had been used in the refugee camps in Ethiopia: exaggerate the numbers of accessible people in need; make up ambiguous and false distribution reports; strictly limit the movements of the foreigners; do not let them talk to anyone without security clearance; use interpreters to censor the information from innocent interviewees; punish SPLA

---

[3] Interviewed on 4 April 1996.

officials who are indiscreet. But inside Sudan the scope of operations was more fluid and more widespread than in the refugee situation. The SPLA and SRRA quickly needed to gain a capacity to implement these techniques in many new locations.

Three factors assisted this task. One was the war itself, which meant that the SPLA had to be given the responsibility for the personal safety of foreigners; so it could generally limit their movements on grounds of security. Secondly, the situation was a novel one for most of the foreigners concerned; there was little experience of working in the middle of a war, or working in Southern Sudan. The third factor was the focus of OLS I on delivery targets and sensational publicity.

The architects of OLS, notably James Grant of UNICEF, were highly conscious of the possible historic status of the agreement, and were determined that the operation should be widely recognised as a great success, largely in order to win the support of donors for further big humanitarian initiatives in future. The Sudan Government's concession on sovereignty was an important one, but it was not set out in any document with legal validity. It was only implied in an informally-agreed 'Plan of Action', undertaking to serve 'all civilian non-combatant populations in need of emergency relief throughout the Sudan'[4]. The plan gained an air of definition not by signatures but by numbers. Like many other big humanitarian programmes, its delivery targets were not based on a detailed evaluation of the human needs, since to do so required time, access and expertise that was unavailable. Instead the needs were determined by a common-sense view of the problem: they were set high enough to show a dramatic increase on what had gone before, but low enough to be logistically and financially conceivable.

> Compiled hurriedly in the interests of speeding the relief task, the UN figures proved not altogether reliable. For the UN no less than for governments, insurgent-held territory had been terra incognita. . . . Moreover, the data were used to frame objectives primarily in

---

4 'Plan of Action—Sudan Emergency Operations', High Level Meeting, Government of the Sudan and the United Nations, Khartoum, 8-9 March 1989.

terms of tonnages and transport. The ton soon took on a life of its own. . . .[5]

In maximising the OLS delivery figures, the UN counted quantities that were moved before the beginning of OLS or by agencies who considered themselves to be working outside OLS. In the field, the UN's preoccupation was with managing a large throughput in a short period: insufficient resources were available for monitoring or for trying to understand local communities and institutions. Indeed, the hectic demands of OLS I killed off some more patient and sensitive approaches to the business of humanitarian work in Southern Sudan, such as the SRRA capacity-building process that had begun in Nairobi in July 1988.[6]

Under the pressure of OLS, then, SRRA could not be a good foundation for civil administration. More fundamentally, the very existence of an erratic but significant flow of relief commodities from outside made it more difficult for SRRA secretaries or local people to appreciate what was their entitlement and demand it, or for SPLA commanders to establish an enduring system of local provisioning. To put it plainly: with the promise of relief supplies, commanders had even less need to gain the willing acceptance of the populace. Meanwhile the presence of foreigners gave legitimacy to the heavy involvement of the military-based security service in matters of civilian welfare.

Again we must state the main limitation of this argument: in 1989-91 the SPLA lacked a strong concept of civil administration anyway. The impact of relief did not destroy an enlightened policy; it only helped to retard the formation of one. At the same time, relief did not make the SPLA more authoritarian—or rather, as it could scarcely have become so, relief did not help the SPLA to entrench its political power and ideological hegemony. This was because the SPLA took a straightforward militaristic view of relief as a welcome

---

[5] L. Minear, *Humanitarianism Under Siege: A Critical Review of Operation Lifeline Sudan*, Trenton, N.J., Red Sea Press, 1991, p. 39

[6] 'Report on an assignment carried out by Anthony Ratter of ERDA Ltd for an with the Sudan Relief and Rehabilitation Association August 1988-March 1989.'

flow of resources but a potential security threat. A more politically adept movement would have integrated external relief into a practical social and political programme, and strengthened its domestic legitimacy and capacity to mobilise resources. A big opportunity was missed. In the two years after the launch of OLS, therefore, the SPLA neither moved towards liberalisation nor a more politically effective authoritarianism. Despite its military successes, it was politically fragile, and that fragility was exposed in the catastrophe which hit it in 1991.

THE 1991 SPLIT IN THE SPLA

On 28 August 1991, three members of the SPLA High Command— Riek Machar, Lam Akol and Gordon Koang Chol—issued their 'Nasir Declaration', announcing that John Garang was removed as leader of the SPLM/A. Garang was not removed; the Movement was split. To date it has recovered neither its unity nor the military strength it possessed at that time. The Sudan Government exploited the initial weakness and disarray to recapture a number of garrison posts, which were then used for intelligence work and for supplying anti-SPLA militias and new factions. It managed to ensure the survival of the Riek faction and to encourage further splits. The divisions weakened the rebel cause as a whole, since the factions often fought against each other.

The peoples of Southern Sudan are diverse and have never succeeded in forming a united front in pursuit of their common interests. Even in times of relative peace, their leaders tended to manoeuvre against each other for lucrative positions in the state, while building up their personal support along tribal lines, and securing it by patronage. The SPLA from 1983 attempted to solve this problem by waging war to gain power, and unifying its politics by means of military authority. Its campaign made progress up to 1991, but some of the methods used to achieve battlefield success began to seem misguided, even to some of John Garang's immediate subordinates. In 1990, Commanders Riek Machar and Lam Akol informally canvassed other members of the SPLA about the desirability of policies that were more liberal, democratic and humanitarian.

John Garang, as Chairman of the Movement, had from the early years of the SPLA deliberately prevented the emergence of free debate about policy. Civilians and soldiers—even members of the High Command—were given no forum for an open airing of their views. This created a risk that the most able officers—those with strong ideas of their own—would feel misused and rebellious. Garang's solution for this involved promoting talented people rapidly, and giving them a lot of freedom within their own sphere. Riek and Lam were both prime examples. (Their advancement had caused some grumbling among colleagues who considered themselves to have a stronger right to seniority, on grounds of political and military experience.) But Garang's system of promotion failed to secure their personal loyalty to himself.

The fall-back option was to punish disloyalty harshly. Garang had already had imprisoned or killed several senior colleagues who opposed him. His ability to do so in the past had rested largely on the support of Colonel Mengistu in Ethiopia, who had steadily backed him as leader. Previous appeals by dissident commanders, including Kerubino Kuanyin, to Mengistu to overrule or depose Garang had backfired. But in May 1991 the Mengistu regime collapsed. The SPLA was forced to move out of Ethiopia; it lost its training camps, its main immediate source of military hardware and other supplies, and its radio station. Garang's personal control was weakened. At the same time, he was released from the need to conform with Mengistu-ite policies.

This change in the situation was by itself enough to open up a prospect of liberalisation in the SPLA. Sympathisers sensed the opportunity and made some frank criticisms. The prominent journalist and politician Bona Malwal, published an influential article called 'Questions the SPLA can no longer ignore'.[7]

Very important questions have been raised as a result of success on the battlefield, which the SPLA can no longer afford to ignore.

---

[7] *Sudan Democratic Gazette*, June 1991, pp. 2, 4-5, 8.

Some of these questions are so pressing that the SPLA needs to formulate practical solutions as a matter of urgency. . . .

One of the issues was the question of independence for the South, a taboo subject while the SPLA enjoyed Mengistu's patronage.

'From the initial organisation of the SPLA in 1983, its philosophy has always been clear to the leadership, if not always quite as clear to the movement's rank and file. Put simply, the SPLA wanted nothing to do with separatist issues . . . . Many Southern Sudanese have felt that the SPLA should liberate the South and establish a separate Southern state.

Another set of questions related to the dominance of the army and the neglect of civil administration and a range of practical social, economic and political programmes.

[T]he question of whether the SPLA can continue adding territory to the liberated areas without first consolidating its gains by setting up an alternative civilian administration in the areas under its control. For a movement which professes the principles of democracy and representative government as one of its policy objectives, the SPLA can no longer ignore the question of political administration in the areas under its control. . . .

[T]he SPLA leadership needs to break away from the political slogans of the past, which served their purpose when the guerrilla army was in its infancy, but which are now largely irrelevant to the administration of the liberated areas. The old mentality of soldiering on steadfastly to the ultimate military victory can no longer be allowed to reign supreme if it is at the expense of everything else that the movement has gained so far. . . . The main issue now would be the removal of the military blinkers in favour of a clearsighted political approach to the administration of the liberated areas by a newly created civilian body.

. . .

The people of Sudan . . . have responded favourably to the SPLA's ideology of militarising society in order to mobilise its forces for the struggle against a despot. However, the Sudanese public does not expect the militarisation to remain forever. . . .

271

[T]he SPLA needs to show the way, by expanding upon its previously limited political philosophy, by developing a political culture through the creation of a civil society progressing side by side with the continuing military struggle.

In other words, it is time that the SPLA's political wing, the Sudan People's Liberation Movement (SPLM) came out of the shadows of subordination to exert its influence in the liberated areas.

Reflecting the unspoken consensus among Southerners, the weakness of the SRRA came in for particular criticism:

It has become evident that the humanitarian wing of the SPLA, the Sudan Relief and Rehabilitation Association (SRRA) has failed to achieve much of its agenda primarily because of its close attachment to the military aspects of the SPLA. It has always been known that the SRRA was part of the SPLA but most observers would have preferred that it remained distinct and operated on a purely humanitarian basis. Unfortunately, military considerations have regularly hampered the SRRA's ability to provide relief to the needy civilians behind SPLA lines. . . . As things stand today, the SRRA does not help either the SPLA or the would-be donors to the cause by continually referring even the most insignificant of decisions to the SPLA leadership.

Expressing a widely-felt view among Southerners, this persuasive article concluded that

there is a pressing need for the SPLA to practice the democratic ideals it has been preaching for so long. It is impossible to speak of democracy whilst every aspect of life is being subordinated to the military cause.

This challenge to the SPLA's approach came from a journalist living in exile in Oxford. Published in June 1991, within three months it was echoed by a more practical challenge, in the 'Nasir Declaration' of Commanders Riek, Lam and Koang. The commanders called for democratisation of the movement and an agenda of self-determination for Southern Sudan. The main

272

difference was that they identified the root cause of the problem as being the leadership of John Garang. In the end they had almost no option but to assert their independence from him. They were already under strong suspicion of disloyalty. When Garang called a meeting of the whole High Command (the first one ever) in Kapoeta,[8] they knew that if they attended it they would probably be arrested.

RELIEF AS A CAUSE OF DIVISION IN THE SPLA

How big a part did relief operations play in making the rift between Riek/Lam and Garang? A simple link was alleged by the SPLA Mainstream in its 'Torit Resolutions' of 12 September 1991 (Paragraph 10)[9].

> There is sufficient documented evidence that individuals within the NGO relief community were deeply and actively involved in the recent Nasir theoretical abortive coup by Commander Riak and Commander Lam. Relief planes, relief radios and foreign relief personnel were the main agents used in the abortive coup. . . .

A great many foreign aid workers were present in Upper Nile (where Riek was the senior SPLA commander) between the months of May and August 1991, because of the return of refugees from the camps in Ethiopia. The available evidence fails to show that any of them knew in advance of a specific plan to overthrow Garang. However, several weaker links between the SPLA split and the relief programme can be made.

Many if not most of the aid workers were impressed with the affable personality of Commander Riek; the kind of co-operation that he seemed to give to their work was in contrast with what they met in other areas. Some of them came to regard themselves as his personal friends, and one of them, Emma McCune, married him during that period. Although such people were probably not privy to his exact plans, they were aware that his views were importantly

---

[8] In the event, the meeting was actually held in Torit.
[9] Interviewed on 14 April 1996.

different from those of John Garang. They expressed their support for these views, and rendered small services such as carrying messages to other parts of Sudan and the outside world. (Relief personnel are constantly exchanging favours with local commanders in all parts of Southern Sudan.) In this case, their derogation from strict political neutrality may have encouraged Riek to think that aid agencies and the countries of the West would look favourably upon his cause, if he should break away. The 'Nasir Declaration' seems to have been angled towards this kind of constituency; five of its thirteen 'immediate steps' are about promoting relief. The new faction rapidly set up its own relief administration, the Relief Association of Southern Sudan (RASS), which received recognition, co-operation and assistance immediately from OLS and various NGOs. Though relief resources were not mentioned in the SPLA-Nasir's attack on the alleged conspiracy, the food, money and transport unlocked by RASS undoubtedly proved the most significant humanitarian contribution the split and its aftermath.

The changing pattern of relief delivery was important. As described in Chapter 4, international provision for refugees had supported the SPLA's centralist strategy, which was based on training camps and bases in Ethiopia. It was therefore partly responsible for the crisis which occurred when this strategy fell apart, on the fall of Mengistu. About 200,000 refugees returned to Southern Sudan. The great majority belonged to Upper Nile, and most of these passed through Nasir, where Riek had his headquarters. The UN mounted a relief operation centred on Nasir, involving deliveries by barge from Northern Sudan, and air drops. This was the first time that significant quantities of relief were arriving here without having to come through places controlled by Garang. It gave Riek and Lam more independence from him. Despite their supposedly humane agenda, they and their subordinates continued to manipulate the relief system in much the same way as Garang's SPLA.

The first clear example of their willingness to do this came shortly before the split, during the crisis of returning refugees.

It was . . . with the arrival of 3,000 Uduk and Maban families, originally from Blue Nile, that it became clear that there was a significant element of SPLA control in the choices that at least some of the returnees were making. The Blue Nile group arrived at Nasir two weeks after the first returnees. They had walked to Maiwut, a location en route to their home territory, and had been turned around by the SPLA and brought to Nasir. By this time many of the first wave of returnees had left Nasir in search of food, and the arrival of a second major wave assisted the SPLA authorities to keep pressure on the UN and international community for assistance . . . . And these Uduk and Maban people stayed in their camp, without permission from the SPLA to leave, until May 1992.[10]

It must have been apparent by mid-1991 that relief could be a useful resource for a splinter movement. Examples of the ways in which it was used in military tactics are given later.

The August 1991 split would have been less devastating for the rebel movement as a whole, had it not led into a cycle of inter-factional fighting. One catastrophic event in particular started the chain of retaliation: the Bor Massacre, a massive series of raids against the Dinka areas of Kongor and Bor, from September to November 1991. Hundreds, probably thousands, of civilians were slaughtered; many women were raped or abducted; the countryside was stripped of cattle and other property; thousands more people died of hunger and disease as a direct result.

Riek, Lam, Koang and their commanders must take the main responsibility for the Bor Massacre, although they probably did not plan it in the form it took. To a great extent they were carried along on a tide of popular feeling which they had unleashed by their Nasir Declaration, and which they tried to incorporate into a military operation, but failed to control.

---

[10] Alastair Scott-Villiers, Patta Scott-Villiers and Cole P. Dodge, 'Repatriation of 150,000 Sudanese refugees from Ethiopia: The Manipulation of Civilians in a Situation of Conflict,' *Disasters* 17, 1993, 202-17.

Many Nuer had long felt themselves to be oppressed by the Dinka in the SPLA. Unsurprisingly, they interpreted the revolt by the leading Nuer commander in their area to be (among other things) an act of ethnic liberation. The hostility of the southern Nuer to the Bor Dinka was exacerbated by jealousies arising from the 1991 OLS relief programme. One of the Lau section chiefs who led his people to Bor was later asked to explain the causes of the fighting:[11]

> When we were rebels against the Sudan Government, all the assistance donated by foreign governments was converted by Garang to particular benefit. Secondly, all military assistance was diverted or given to his own tribe, and leaving the other tribes. Thirdly, when the UN tried to assist the population because of hunger and war, all the relief aid was diverted to a particular area, the area of Bor.

In the dry season of 1991, the UN World Food Programme had managed to deliver food by road to Jonglei province. Most of the relief that was sent to the Nuer centres of Waat and Ayod was first stockpiled at Kongor (in the Dinka area). Since the quantities delivered were always very small compared with the perceived needs, Nuer people thought that supplies were being intercepted on the way. To make matters worse, many of the SPLA administrators posted in Lau country were Dinka officers who were suspected of using the relief to enrich themselves at the expense of the locals. But the fact that the whole Bor population was assumed to have benefited unjustly from relief may help to explain why many Nuer went on to treat women, children and elderly people as legitimate targets of vengeance.

The potential of relief to create divisions was routinely recognised by the Nuer prophet Wutnyang Gatakek, for example at a public speech in Nasir in June 1992.

> This relief has destroyed our relationship with the Dinka and other groups. People are saying that the relatives of John Garang [i.e. the Dinka] are the ones who received a lot of food over the last nine

---

[11] Interviewed in Waat, December 1994

years. And now that it is also coming to you, it will divide you. The Lau Nuer are saying, 'The [eastern] Jikany are the people who consume this food,' and the Jikany are saying 'This relief operation started in our area and it is ours,' and 'Why should this food be collected by other people?' This [attitude] is very bad indeed.[12]

The Lau and Jikany sections of the Nuer were indeed destined to clash with increasing severity over the following two years, (though the major causes may have been disputes over land and cattle rather than relief). The Bor Massacre provoked counter-attacks and vicious reprisals by the SPLA-Mainstream. A cycle of inter-factional fighting was set in motion, which persisted for many years.

RELIEF AS PART OF INTER-FACTIONAL WARFARE, JONGLEI 1992-3

In the next phase of inter-factional fighting, relief operations enabled and encouraged Riek Machar to mount an offensive that might otherwise not have taken place. Following the Bor Massacre, in early- and mid-1992 the SPLA-Mainstream carried out many reprisal raids on the southern Nuer area around Ayod and west of Waat. They looted the food reserves, and disrupted the planting season. They recaptured some of the cattle taken in the Bor Massacre, but many of these were dying of disease. SPLA-Nasir continued to conduct raids of its own, as far south as Kongor. Sudan Government forces also passed through the area in March 1992, as part of an offensive that recaptured Bor, Torit and Kapoeta. Unsurprisingly, this fighting and insecurity created acute food shortages in the latter part of the year. The area between Ayod, Waat and Kongor was to become known as the 'Hunger Triangle'.

Khartoum's 1992 reconquests had the effect of blocking the overland relief route from Kenya and Uganda to Upper Nile. One alternative was to send supplies to Nasir by barge from northern Sudan. (It is likely that Government intelligence officers were

---

[12] Quoted in: Sharon E. Hutchinson, *Nuer Dilemmas: Coping With Money, War and the State*, Berkeley, University of California Press, 1996, p. 342.

among the barge crews and the relief operation was probably abused to facilitate the arming of the Nasir faction against the SPLA Mainstream.) But the barge operations were rare and erratic. OLS had to resort to airlifting supplies. This was expensive, and hampered by the fighting and the frequent denial of flight clearances by the Government. At one point in 1992, Khartoum restricted OLS air access to six locations, four of them under the SPLA-Nasir faction. These factors kept the relief operation at a low level through most of 1992, although the aid agencies were aware of a gathering crisis of hunger, and of the causes for it.

Their response only acquired a sense of urgency at the end of October. A party of television journalists was taken to Waat to report on the condition of the displaced people there, as an attempt by the UN to rally the commitment of donors to OLS. (The UN's campaign was eventually successful in securing a much higher level of funding for 1993, and in putting pressure on the Khartoum Government to allow greatly increased access to rebel-held areas by air.) From November, the rate of food deliveries to Waat increased dramatically.[13] So did the number of displaced people in the town.[14] The rise in population was mainly due to the usual 'magnet effect' of relief. Many of the arrivals were Dinka people, made destitute by the fighting, who had been faced with little choice but to migrate northwards: the only established relief delivery point in the SPLA-controlled Bor Dinka areas was now at Panyagor, near Kongor; and relief deliveries here had been very infrequent because of insecurity.

Waat was the site of one of the two main garrisons of SPLA-Nasir troops in the area bordering the Bor Dinka. The other was at Ayod, where a UNICEF assessment officer reported that '[s]upport for the fighters of the Nasir faction in terms of cereals and livestock

---

[13] In the seven months from April to October, WFP delivered 463 MT. In just two weeks of November it delivered 120 MT, and in December 273 MT, using daily flights of Buffalo aircraft. Source: OLS situation reports.
[14] On 20 October, the number of people counted as requiring food assistance around Waat was 7,769. By 18 November 14,807 people were registered for relief. By 7 January the figure had risen to 21,916. Source: OLS situation reports.

was taxed from all parts of Ayod [County].'[15] Relief operations tended to back the fighters, whether by increasing the level of contribution that could be raised from the local population, or through direct diversion by some military authorities in centres where there were big distributions.

The relation between relief centres and military bases was most strikingly seen in the creation of Yuai, in January 1993. The Nasir faction persuaded WFP/OLS that a new centre was needed 'to alleviate the pressure on Waat'[16] and that Yuai was a suitable location. Yuai was not marked on the maps at that time; it was a semi-desert area with seasonal water, very sparsely populated. (A UN worker initially reported that the local authorities had managed to register a 'local population of 3,564 subsisting mainly on fruits and fish'.) At the end of the month, about 15,000 displaced people were directed there from Waat. With them went a sizeable contingent of armed forces. The new camp happened to be situated sixty kilometres south-west of Waat, close to the Nuer/Dinka border. As a military position, it was thus admirably placed to protect the permanent Nuer population centres further north. (The village of Pathai, between Ayod and Waat, had been raided by the SPLA-Mainstream on four separate occasions in 1992.[17])

But the garrison was not merely defensive. It was a vital base for Riek Machar's new campaign in the first months of 1993, which resulted in the temporary capture of Kongor. To be more precise, the position that Riek attacked and occupied was not the village of Kongor itself (a former government centre) but a place called Panyagor where there was an established airstrip. During those months, he took it twice and lost it twice. Each time it changed hands, WFP quickly received requests for food assistance. When Riek was there in March, OLS increased its delivery capacity by using C-130 aircraft, and WFP began to make a food stockpile ahead of the rainy season. Riek evidently wanted to use the relief to create

---

[15] Report dated 16 December 1992.
[16] WFP monthly report for December 1992, issued 5 January 1993.
[17] Human Rights Watch/Africa, *Sudan: Civilian Devastation*, New York, 1994.

another population centre and military base. He had seen that many displaced Dinka were willing to go to his Nuer areas to receive supplies: apparently he now hoped to win their allegiance in their own country. It was while he was in Panyagor that Riek hosted a conference with other prominent dissidents from the SPLA, which attempted to pull together a faction with a broader ethnic base, to be known as 'SPLA-United'.

Even while this meeting was taking place, the SPLA-Mainstream counter-attacked, and recaptured Panyagor. It followed this up immediately by devastating Ayod and Yuai. These were the military bases from which the attack on Kongor had been launched, and they were also—not by coincidence—the main relief centres in the area. Many destitute civilians were killed in these attacks, or died soon afterwards.

During and after this time, OLS was heavily criticised by sympathisers of the Mainstream SPLA. They complained that it was guilty of political bias, because a disproportionate amount of relief seemed to be going to Riek's areas, as opposed to Garang's. Often this criticism melodramatically attributed malice to the managers of OLS:

> The aim of this manoeuvring is to subvert the politics of Southern Sudan and place real political power in the hands of the officials responsible for delivering food.[18]

To most aid agency workers, these accusations no doubt seemed unfair. They believed that relief was being sent to places where the need was greatest, and that 'humanitarian neutrality' meant providing supplies according to the needs of the suffering, rather than to a notion of political balance. However, the above narrative suggests that a more active and politically conscious approach was needed. Given that they were unable to prevent relief from supporting soldiers, OLS and donor governments should have refused to begin operations in Yuai, should probably have made it clear to Riek from

---

[18] 'How "Operation Lifeline Sudan" has Turned Relief into Political Bias', *Sudan Democratic Gazette*, August 1993.

the outset that they would not supply him in Panyagor, and should have striven harder to establish a more secure relief-point for displaced Dinka in SPLA-Mainstream areas.

FURTHER SPLITS

After 1991, further splits took place among those who had originally been together in the SPLA. At the end of 1992, some of Garang's long-time political prisoners escaped. One of these, Kerubino Kuanyin Bol was then assisted by the Khartoum Government and by Riek Machar's faction to embark on a career of destruction and looting in Bahr el Ghazal. Shortly after his escape, John Garang's Chief of Staff, William Nyuon, turned round and began harassing the SPLA-Mainstream in Eastern Equatoria; also with the help of the Government and Riek's faction.

Meanwhile, the SPLA-United was proving itself divided. In early 1994, Lam Akol broke with Riek and then withdrew to his home (Shilluk) area, around Tonga. Riek Machar then re-named his group the Southern Sudan Independence Movement (SSIM), while Lam Akol retained the name SPLA-United. SSIM itself was shortly to split.

In each of these cases, the splinter-groups tried to use humanitarian relief to support their new factions. For Lam Akol the international relief operation was of interest in part as a route to political recognition and administrative support. He came to the point of dispute with the managers of OLS in November 1994, when they asserted that the relief wing of his movement, the Fashoda Relief and Rehabilitation Association (FRRA) was not a counterpart organisation of OLS in the same sense as the humanitarian agencies of the Garang and Riek factions (SRRA and RASS respectively), despite the fact that it was the only Sudanese relief organisation working in the SPLA-United area. Lam pressed his point in May 1995 when his forces waylaid and looted a relief barge, holding prisoner a WFP worker for one week. He succeeded in pressing negotiations and winning some concessions.

OLS officials at this time did not want to be seen as encouraging the proliferation of rebel factions. This was partly an intuitive political judgement, and partly a conscious desire to keep humanitarian operations clear of political effects. In particular they felt that Lam wanted a seat at any national or inter-factional peace talks. To grant counterpart status to FRRA would be a step towards UN recognition of the whole faction. This was particularly so because the distinction between humanitarian and political affairs was being blurred by programmes of 'humanitarian principles' and 'capacity-building' (see next chapter).

The UN's fear of faction proliferation looked both to the past and the future. As regards the past:

> We need to bear in mind that we are still blamed by the SPLM/A (Garang) for our position on the [1991] split in which, they argue, our actions—i.e. recognising the new faction without conditions—helped the formation of SPLM/A-United and thereby the splitting of the rebel movement.[19]

For the future, the effect of a precedent was feared:

> According to the best information, there are three other potential figures among the southern Sudanese who are currently considering the possibility of establishing their own (mostly ethnically-based) factions. They are all watching to see how we will react to Lam Akol's various demands before deciding whether or not to establish their own factions.[20]

In July 1996 OLS finally recognised FRRA, but six months later the feared proliferation had not yet occurred.

The factions of Kerubino Kuanyin and William Nyuon were slightly different, in that for most of the time they were officially subordinate to that of Riek Machar. Operationally, however, they

---

[19] Philip D. O'Brien, OLS Co-ordinator and UNICEF Chief of Operations, to Christoph Jaeger, UN Co-ordinator for Emergency Relief Operations in the Sudan, 10 January 1995.
[20] *Ibid.*

were so independent that they can be considered separately. Kerubino (this word is commonly used to designate any forces that the man is presumed to control) makes little pretence of having a serious political programme. He is a warlord who appears to be motivated mainly by a desire for vengeance against John Garang, and by loot. Since 1994 he has been marauding throughout northern Bahr el Ghazal, from his base in the Government enclave of Gogrial. He targets the places that produce most food or hold stocks, stealing what he can and destroying much of what remains. Relief deliveries are prime targets, and the way that OLS works in the region has undergone a progressive change, largely as a result. Before 1994 there existed continuously-staffed relief stations, in places like Akon and Mayen Abun. These were repeatedly raided by Kerubino; the aid agencies lost equipment; the centres were moved; and eventually the concept of a semi-permanent base in the area was abandoned. Airstrips had now been created at a large number of locations; WFP and NGOs would visit one place for up to a week at a time, to organise distributions and other programmes. Often the food would be stockpiled in the open for a few days. Kerubino would learn its location by monitoring the relief radio communications, and sometimes arrive even before the distribution had taken place. So by 1996 the agencies had made the relief procedure much quicker, and were taking precautions against publicising dates and locations. This did not prevent Kerubino kidnapping relief workers at the end of the year, and driving a hard bargain with international mediators to grant their release.

William Nyuon's use of relief was more in the style of Riek Machar. With Riek's help, he established a base in Lafon, north of Torit. Lafon was a relief centre. There, in mid-1994, he sent about 500 Nuer boys aged between eight and sixteen. An OLS feeding centre was set up and WFP increased its dry food distributions. But by the end of the year, the boys were in just as bad a condition as at first. Forty-seven of them had died. It became clear to the UN that the food and other supplies, destined for the children and other civilians, were being stolen by the military. The boys had been brought from their homes in Upper Nile to act as soldiers and assistants to soldiers. At this stage, their main help was taking the form of dying as a way of attracting relief supplies. The survivors were mostly repatriated to Upper Nile by UNICEF in December 1994 and early 1995.

William Nyuon rebelled against Riek Machar in August 1995, and formed an alternative version of Riek's faction (known as SSIM-2), in alliance with Garang's SPLA. William himself was killed in January of the following year, and his group was officially reunited with Garang in May.

The careers of William and Kerubino illustrate how superficial are the political labels attached to many Southern Sudanese rebels. Some local commanders enjoy considerable independence of action. The catalogue of abuses committed by splinter factions should not hide the fact that many of the same crimes are committed by John Garang's own subordinates, and that the perpetrators are seldom disciplined strongly or brought to justice. The spread of relief operations throughout Southern Sudan has contributed to loosening the chain of command; some commanders in remote places are a little less dependent on the central leadership because they can occasionally obtain food, utensils, medicines, radio sets and vehicles by their own enterprise in looting and diverting international aid. The potential divisions in the Southern movement are many, perennial and not very far from the surface. Yet the project of creating a more enlightened, stable and cohesive rebel movement has also advanced in some ways in recent years. Its path forward is the subject of the next chapter.

PEACEMAKING

The issue of peacemaking in Sudan since the 1989 coup deserves a book of its own: there has been a succession of initiatives at various levels, with an extremely complicated history. More than seven different non-governmental institutions have been involved at one time or another in negotiating between government and rebels, or between different Southern factions.[21] This book cannot go into details. Nor is peacemaking a central concern of this book, except insofar as it has an impact on humanitarian programmes and the possibility of building a coalition against famine.

External peacemaking efforts in Sudan have been handicapped by numerous factors. One is the widespread belief among European and north American mediators that getting Sudanese from different political organisations to sit together and talk is itself an achievement. While this may be true elsewhere in the world, it is not the case in Sudan: there has never been a lack of dialogue between political opponents, and politicians on all sides have managed to maintain cordial personal relations despite their deep political differences.

Another difficulty lies with the belligerents themselves. In many ways, peace poses more problems than war to both the NIF and the SPLA and other Southern factions. Providing an opportunity for negotiating peace is not enough even to start a peace process. Instead, a mediator must be in the position of being able to offer genuine inducements to peace and genuine sanctions for not achieving it. Non-governmental mediators are not in a strong position to achieve this.

Thirdly, humanitarian programmes have, on balance, proved more of an obstacle than an asset to mediation. The idea prevalent in the early days of OLS that the existence of a humanitarian operation by itself facilitates a peace process was soon laid to rest. War or ceasefire, OLS continues. Meanwhile, other assistance programmes have grown up on both sides that are based on solidarity: these would not necessarily expand (and might indeed contract) if the war came to an end.

Many mediators have been handicapped by their own interests in the continuation of humanitarian programmes. This has meant that mediators have been unable to use the one real resource at their disposal, namely humanitarian aid. With the exception of the U.S. re-direction of food shipments to Port Sudan in late 1990, no major

---

21 Jan Gruiters and Efrem Tresoldi, *Sudan: A Cry for Peace*, The Hague, Pax Christi, 1994.

285

donor has considered an embargo on humanitarian aid to either side. In addition, donors have generally shown more interest than the belligerents in major international humanitarian programmes (such as OLS). There has always been a bargaining, implicit or explicit, on the terms on which relief programmes can continue. This has put the donors in a very weak position to try to negotiate for any other concessions. Meanwhile, the proliferation of mediators, each one apparently anxious for a share of glory, led Garang to refer to them as 'peace vultures.'

A further problem is that attempts to negotiate for unity between the SPLA factions have been undermined by divide-and-rule tactics from Khartoum. The peace agenda within the South can contradict the agenda for trying to negotiate with the Government.

Government-SPLA Peace Talks

From 1989 until 1993, there was a plethora of international peace initiatives, by former President Jimmy Carter, the Nigerian Government, and others, trying to mediate between the SPLA and the government. There was an apparently endless international circuit of meetings and declarations, which gave the impression that the next one may offer a better deal for any one of the participants. The negotiation process was becoming self-defeating. Finally, the Inter-Governmental Authority on Drought and Development (IGADD) was named as the sole mediator. IGADD includes the governments of Djibouti, Eritrea, Ethiopia, Kenya, Somalia (in theory but not currently in practice), Sudan and Uganda. The Sudan Government initially welcomed this. At last there was a single mediator and the prospect of bringing some discipline and prospect of genuine clarity and even progress to the peace process. In July 1994, the IGADD mediators introduced some basic principles to the negotiations, and achieved some modest but significant progress towards recognising how peace talks could, in principle, proceed.

But by 1994 this time the Sudan Government had also antagonised Eritrea and Ethiopia, and came to regret the prominent role of IGADD. The September 1994 IGADD talks broke down, and the government called for a 'new mechanism' for mediation.[22] But while the Sudan Government publicly rejected IGADD as no longer neutral, the African and western countries involved re-affirmed their commitment to IGADD. The Sudan Government now tried to undermine the IGADD process by bringing in alternative mediators such as President Carter and President Moluzi of Malawi. President Carter's initiative illustrates how humanitarianism can be manipulated for political-military ends. In March 1995, Carter negotiated a two-month ceasefire in order for a Guinea-worm eradication programme to proceed. This suited the government in three respects: (1) it allowed the army to resupply beleaguered Southern garrisons, (2) it did not apply to the Nuba Mountains, where an offensive was in progress and (3) it helped to undermine the IGADD process. The SPLA agreed to the ceasefire simply because rejection would have brought it adverse publicity internationally.

By the end of 1996, the IGADD peace process was frozen and no alternative is in sight. This made clear the true interests and intentions of the Sudan Government: it was seeking a military solution. Only should the military tide turn against it, would the government be likely to revive the negotiations.

What the IGADD process has signally failed to address is internal democracy within the Sudanese opposition. The National Democratic Alliance (NDA) asserts its democratic credentials, which are indeed much more impressive than the government's, as its main parties were elected by popular vote in 1986. But the parliamentary period had serious democratic failings, some of which have been reproduced since the parties went into opposition. Despite the reforms of the 1993-5 period, the SPLA's democratic credentials remain slender. In short, many of the same political players who formed the coalition for famine in the South in the late 1980s are now in the 'democratic' opposition, without having repented or reformed, only this time alongside the SPLA, which was far from innocent in the 1980s famine. Under current circumstances, the NDA does not represent a progressive anti-famine coalition.

---

[22] *Sudan Update*, 30 September 1994, p. 1.

287

Reconciliation in the South

Peacemaking initiatives within the South have been similarly handicapped, and for the most part, similarly unsuccessful. There have been several hopeful initiatives from outside and inside. The first was an attempt by the churches to mediate between the SPLA-Torit and the SPLA-Nasir in 1991. This did not succeed, but it provided at least a forum in which the leaders of the factions could meet. It thereby helped set the stage for the inter-factional agreement at Abuja later in 1992 that they would both support the idea of self-determination for the South. However, there are suspicions that the church mediation also heightened the ambitions of some of the factional leaders, by putting them on an international stage. One of the churchpeople involved in organising the meetings said:

> We got a fantastic lot of [financial and other] support from the donor community. I was very impressed. It was a wonderful feeling that this was for a good cause. But, to me, when I look back, I wonder if this was when we began to give all those warlords a chance. Perhaps we created a monster. Those people got too big for their boots. But it was all in good faith. This was the first time for many of us to be involved in such a thing. Maybe we did the right thing, but we ended up creating something else. With the Riek faction I got the feeling that, now they were out, they got the opportunity to perform. It gave them legitimacy and prestige.[23]

The prominent church role also led to suspicions in the SPLA that church leaders wanted to wrest the political initiative from the Movement itself.

The Washington Declaration of October 1993 was a classic example of failed quick-fix mediation. Congressman Harry Johnston was determined to achieve a settlement, but did not seem aware of the complexities that this entailed. While John Garang and Riek Machar were ready to agree on the substantive points in the draft agreement—and indeed signed documents to this effect—the two

---

[23] Interviewed on 27 February 1995.

288

leaders refused to sign the same piece of paper, failing to agree on the titles they and their factions were given.[24] The agreement collapsed in mutual acrimony.

Externally-sponsored negotiations have several things in common. The meeting places tend to be outside the country, the principal actors are the established political-military leaders and their chosen delegates, and the agenda is influenced by the mediator. They therefore have a tendency to reinforce the external orientation of political processes and the legitimacy (and perhaps material power) of the existing leadership. All negotiations of this kind have a potential for marginalising ordinary citizens, and many mediators have not taken safeguards to mitigate this.

Internal Initiatives

The most significant and promising peace-making initiative was an internal one. In April 1995 at Lafon, junior officers in the SPLA and SSIM agreed not to fight each other, but rather to collaborate against the government. This led directly to Cdr William Nyuon re-allying himself with the SPLA-Mainstream, and a hopeful process of dialogue with wide popular support across the South.

Unfortunately, the opportunity this presented was squandered. There was intransigence on both sides. Riek Machar tried to derail the process, first by dismissing his more conciliatory commanders, and then by assassinating William Nyuon. An equally big obstacle was Garang's determination not to deal with the other factions as political movements, but rather to re-absorb individuals into the SPLA. Later in the year Garang blocked SSIM's attempt to join the NDA, leaving it isolated. He effectively pushed Riek into allying with the government. When individuals did rejoin the Movement, this also did not prove productive. For example John Luk, who took over as commander of William's faction of SSIM, precipitously announced a unity accord with the SPLA shortly after Riek signed the April Charter. He had not sufficiently consulted his people

---

[24] See: *Sudan Update*, 10 November 1993.

beforehand, and many in his faction saw this move as a capitulation to Garang, and preferred instead to join the SSIM of Riek.

Lam Akol of the SPLA-United was more patient, not wanting to be pushed into a corner. But Garang also repeatedly stalled negotiations for political agreement. A high-level delegation from the SPLA-Mainstream met with Lam in July 1996,[25] followed by repeated efforts by regional friends to obtain a formal agreement of co-operation or even unity. However, at the time of writing, these have not come to fruition.

Given its popular support, the 'Lafon Process' could have led to an important realignment of Southern politics. A united leadership of the SPLA, or a strategic alliance between the anti-government factions, would have been just one outcome. A shift in the balance of power away from the leadership towards middle-ranking commanders and other leaders would have been another. Potentially, this could have had positive ramifications for the Movement's readiness to take on board a practical progressive social agenda. But arguably, the prospect of a more democratic process within the Movement was more threatening to the leadership than the implications of reconciling with the rival leaders.

'Peace from Within'

As it became more internationally isolated, the Sudan Government launched its own attempts to win round rebel factions and individuals. Under the name *Salaam min al Dakhal* ('Peace from Within') it set about circumventing the established procedures of IGADD and negotiating directly with rebel commanders, at all levels. The Government offered political concessions (positions in State or Central Government, and some modifications of government policy—usually cosmetic) and financial inducements. Carefully-prepared delegations were sent to talk to SPLA commanders, anti-government politicians and community leaders. Often the delegates

---

[25] SPLM/SPLA United, Press Statement, 'Reconciliation and Unity Talks Between the Two SPLM/A Factions,' 18 July 1996.

included relatives of the targetted individual. Many were rebuffed. Some succeeded.

The most notable success of Peace from Within was the Charter of 10 April 1996, signed by Cdr Riek Machar of SSIM and Cdr Kerubino Kuanyin of SPLA-Bahr el Ghazal Group. Under this agreement, the two factions joined the government. The two commanders have since been promoted to the rank of Major-General. The Charter contained many fine words about respect for human rights and cultural diversity. More tangibly, it promised that 'a referendum shall be conducted by the people of the Southern Sudan to determine their political aspirations.'[26] This apparently-major concession is however hedged by pre-conditions: 'After the full establishment of peace, stability and a reasonable level of social development in the south.' Article 2 also clearly rules out Southern independence, supposedly the political aim of SSIM: 'The unity of the Sudan with its known boundaries shall be preserved.' A number of other disaffected SPLA commanders and some Southern politicians have also signed. The government has targetted individuals who are in financial need and who are frustrated by their failure to advance within the SPLA: some critics have dismissed it as buying loyalty with bribes.

Despite the claims of the Sudan Government and media, and some of its apologists, the April Charter does not promise peace. It is a mechanism for divide-and-rule, not a genuine attempt to reach a negotiated solution to the war. It is a propaganda ploy for trying to conceal the government's rejection of the IGADD process and its principles, and its failure to enter into meaningful dialogue with the SPLA-Mainstream and the NDA. The SPLA-United of Cdr Lam Akol rejected the Charter and entered into dialogue with the SPLA and NDA.

'Peace from Within' is in reality intimately bound up with counter-insurgency and social transformation under the Comprehensive Call. This can be seen clearly in the Nuba Mountains, where it goes hand-in-hand with a programme known as *Nafir al Sha'abi* ('Popular Mobilisation'). *Nafir al Sha'abi* refers to

---

[26] Article 3.

the creation of peace camps and the recruitment of men (often by force) to join the PDF. The Sudanese media refers to the leaders of the *Nafir al Sha'abi* as also the leaders of 'Peace from Within': this is peace by conquest. In the South, the progressive language of the April Charter (for consumption by Southerners and western diplomats) is contradicted by the ongoing Islamist extremist rhetoric and practice of the Comprehensive Call. In early 1997, SSIM and SPLA-Bahr el Ghazal Group forces were despatched to fight against the SPLA in Blue Nile. Clearly, for the Sudan Government, the April Charter is essentially a defence pact, not a political agreement for recognising the aspirations of Southerners.

CONCLUSIONS

The defeat of the Mengistu government revealed the political fragility of the SPLA as it existed then: it was already run as a government rather than a liberation movement, and without the support of Ethiopian state power, its political and military structures were ripe for fragmentation. International relief aid influenced the timing and nature of the crisis that followed and helped make the SPLA-Nasir faction militarily viable. The control and manipulation of aid resources became a key factor in the Southern factional struggles that ensued: aid exacerbated the internal crisis of the SPLA and probably made the internal Southern war more brutal.

OLS, the donors and the NGOs had not, until well after the key moment in 1991, considered how they could be manipulated by the factions in pursuit of such abusive military agendas. Whatever the motives, their responses were often—in the wider context— unhelpful. We now turn to the key question of whether the SPLA and the humanitarians were able to learn the lessons of the post-1991 cataclysm. Verbally, all acknowledged that reform was needed: practically, what was achieved?

12.

TOWARDS A REBEL-HUMANITARIAN COALITION

If our situation is understood, we can expect assistance in this important task of building civil society. It is difficult to do this without external resources.

Dr John Garang[1]

During the dry season of 1992/3, the SPLA-Mainstream was at its lowest point. It had undergone an intensely traumatic period of physical and moral collapse, and many Southerners were at the point of despair. But there were two main reasons for believing that it could recover. One: the Sudan Government and the SPLA-Nasir/United failed to defeat the Movement. Two: the level of human rights abuses and manipulation of humanitarian programmes by the Sudan Government had become so outrageous that foreign donors began to take an unusually assertive line in putting pressure on the Government, while also engaging closely with the internal politics of the SPLA.

As the SPLA regained some of its vigour, it was changed in important ways. In the aftermath of the split, it not only lost territory, but lost its ability to exercise the same level of control over Southern Sudanese society, and to provide unchallenged leadership to educated Southerners living abroad. Foreign donors (especially the U.S.) and humanitarian organisations also took the lead in drawing up an agenda for the South: they pushed concepts such as liberalisation, democratisation, 'civil society' and human rights.

---

[1] Opening address to SPLM Conference on Civil Society and the Organisation of Civil Authority of the New Sudan, New Kush, 30 April 1996.

Gradually, the SPLA and the humanitarians identified areas where their interests overlapped.

This chapter looks at the ways in which the agendas of rebels and humanitarians have seemed to converge, to the point where some aid workers consider themselves to be helping to create an SPLA government in the South, and humanitarian concerns figure large in SPLA diplomacy and rhetoric. It asks whether this trend supports a process of democratisation, and whether it is likely to promote a society in which people are less vulnerable to famine.[2] Or, is it an opportunistic way for both aid institutions and the rebel military command to extend their power?

A set of issues will be examined: humanitarian access to SPLA-held areas; the civil and political institutions of the Movement itself; humanitarian institutions; humanitarian principles; and the roles of the churches. In each case, parallel and related processes have existed within the SPLA and among the humanitarian organisations. The loosening of SPLA political control has also allowed some space for independent initiatives, including the establishment of Sudanese indigenous NGOs (SINGOs) and the activities of the churches. There has been important progress in many areas. But there is a recurring theme throughout: the foreign relief workers have set a narrow and incomplete agenda (following on from their own interests), which the SPLA has partly absorbed. While publicly welcoming the foreign initiatives, SPLA leaders (and Southerners more generally) have had strong private reservations. But they have been unable to mount a coherent critique of foreign humanitarianism, and more seriously, they have failed to develop a practicable alternative. As a result, the rebel-humanitarian coalition has been superficial and fractious. The last section of the chapter looks at some of tensions and potential schisms in this relationship.

---

[2] Much of the material in this chapter is also treated in African Rights Discussion Paper No 7., 'Imposing Empowerment? Aid and Civil Institutions in Southern Sudan', December 1995.

HUMANITARIAN ACCESS

At the end of 1992, OLS-Southern Sector had air access to only seven locations, four of them controlled by SPLA-United. Evidence was emerging of the execution of Sudanese aid workers (one of whom was an employee of USAID) in Juba. There was international outrage at the ethnic cleansing in the Nuba Mountains. OLS was almost moribund, and very few agencies were ready to operate outside OLS. At that moment, Thomas Ekval was replaced by Philip O'Brien as head of OLS-Southern Sector. The change was accompanied by a big effort from donor countries to breathe new life into OLS.

In October, the U.S. Senate condemned Sudan's human rights record. In December the General Assembly of the United Nations did the same. Perhaps more significantly, President Bush's 'New World Order' appeared at last to be gaining some bite. On 3 December 1992, the UN Security Council authorised the use of force to attain humanitarian objectives in Somalia. The Sudanese Government felt under intense pressure and on 5 December, OLS and the warring parties reached a new agreement on relief access in Sudan. This enabled a sharp increase in the number of sites in rebel areas to which aid could be delivered by air; up to 63 within a few months.

Although the Sudan Government still insisted on issuing month-by-month flight permissions, and the majority of relief resources was still channelled through the Northern Sector, the locus of power in OLS had shifted. The Government was no longer having everything its own way. Philip O'Brien took the view that unless a location was expressly forbidden by the Sudan Government, OLS was free to send a mission there, merely following the formal courtesy of informing Khartoum. With the backing of the donors, this meant an unprecedented opening-up of Southern Sudan to relief work. Beyond Equatoria, most road access for Southern Sector aid operations remained blocked: the effectiveness of O'Brien's initiative relied on the donors' readiness to fund flights, which were expensive. The donors were ready.

The character of the relief operation to rebel areas changed rapidly. Most aid workers were now entering and leaving the country by air rather than road. Lokichoggio (often known as 'Loki'), the site of the UN base on the border of Sudan and Kenya, increased greatly in size and importance. Supplies were trucked there and stored, to be airlifted into Sudan. The number of relief staff in the place escalated, with people organising logistics and waiting for planes to the various destinations. The UN camp became much larger; many NGOs and commercial companies established their own compounds. The Southern Sector became more and more formally separate from the Northern, to protect it from government interference. This was reflected in various institutional arrangements: for instance OLS-Southern Sector reported to the Department of Humanitarian Affairs, rather than to the UN in Khartoum.

The Issue of Diversion

The reinvigoration of OLS also came in the wake of a major breakdown of relations between the relief agencies and the SPLA, following the SPLA killing of four expatriates in October 1992. Although the agencies failed to achieve a united position on what measures to take, the shock waves from the killings (and the SPLA's undiplomatic lack of remorse) were felt throughout OLS and the donor community. This led directly to the formation of 'Ground Rules' and later 'humanitarian principles' (see below).

Relief agencies' outrage at the killings also focused attention on the issue of diversion of relief. This had been a concern since foreign agencies began dealing with the SRRA. It had never been faced squarely. In the early years of OLS the SPLA was very much concerned to limit the contacts between local people and foreign relief personnel, but it could not prevent them altogether. Donor agencies insisted that expatriates should be present in the field to monitor, if not manage, the programmes. This superficially provided a guarantee that supplies would be distributed fairly. In fact, the foreigners had a very limited ability to control—or even understand—what happened to the relief. They depended heavily on the local authorities to organise distributions, and were only able to witness directly a small proportion of the process. However, they claimed to discover deliberate diversions, done with the knowledge of local officials, often enough to suggest that the practice of deceiving them was widespread, or even systematic. There were many incidents of relief food being taken to military stores to which relief staff were denied access, foreign NGO evacuations being required shortly after distributions, 'taxes' being levied on recipients of food relief, and other subterfuges. The foreign monitors tried to place limits on the power of the SPLA authorities, and forced them to be crafty and determined in diverting supplies. Methods such as conducting head counts or hut counts, or distributing only to women, proved complicated. Much foreign humanitarian policy in South Sudan consists of attempts to bypass the military authorities, close loopholes that could allow diversion, while trying to maintain a minimal expatriate presence (for reasons of cost and security).

The following internal WFP memorandum (with its names and places obscured) reflects the concern the agency feels about the problem of diversion, as well as the difficulty of actually documenting it (one WFP official was dubious about the veracity of the claims). It also indicates some of the inter-agency jealousies that hamper relief operations.

29th May.

Subject: Diversion of OLS food deliveries to military reportedly alleged by PVOs[3]

1. During [a monitoring visit, a donor representative] reported to [a WFP official] that [a donor] senior official had been informed by PVOs on her return from an air delivery in So. Sudan by WFP that such deliveries were a complete waste, since the food was being diverted to the military. She had also apparently been informed that WFP monitors (from U.K. and U.S.A.) were of the same opinion but closed their eyes to it.

---

[3] Private voluntary organisations, i.e. NGOs.

2. [The WFP officer] replied as follows:

a) WFP/OLS operating policy is that distribution is planned only following an assessment on the ground by WFP international monitors and that the distribution itself must be in the presence of WFP international monitors.

b) Precisely because of such reports of diversion to the military, WFP has increasingly adopted the procedure of actually having monitors follow selected recipients to their homes to ensure that food actually goes there. In addition, WFP also has done follow-up visits to the same homes, to see for themselves (about two weeks after deliveries) how much food still remains.

c) In these latter cases, monitors have, in fact, reported surprisingly little food still in stock after such a short time, but explanations given refer to 'taxes' (varying proportions), trading, etc. and food given to other members of the family not present. No monitor has reported families indicating that food had been taken by the military.

3. Of course, it cannot be determined whether or not the military appropriates food from families when monitors are not there to observe.

4. In evaluating the reported PVO allegations, exaggerations arising out of jealousy ought not to be excluded. PVOs envy the WFP air operations, for which they cannot get funding or authorization for themselves. They may also be overstating the case for the possibility of replacing air deliveries by road: WFP does indeed regularly review the feasibility and cost effectiveness of extending road deliveries into Eastern Equatoria and also to Western Equatoria. WFP is too much aware of funding constraints to deliver by air to any location which is reachable safely and at lower cost by road. Finally, the origin of such comments may be traceable to the very high levels of frustration among PVO personnel deriving from their powerlessness to counteract civil rights abuses of many and varied kinds, which they may attribute to the military.

5. It should also be noted that WFP/OLS has established local relief committees at many delivery sites in order to engage the local populations (as distinct from the civil authorities who may be in

close liaison with the military) in the selection of beneficiaries and in distribution. Such committees do not hesitate to speak of the issue of 'taxes' on the food received. However, in light of the fact that most families in any given area will have members in the military, WFP is not confident that local committees would even want to co-operate in eliminating such taxes.

6.   Finally, the diversion of food to the military is a subject regularly discussed at WFP workshops for monitors and others involved in food assessment/distribution: the monitors are encouraged to report and discuss any instances of such diversion.

In short, every foreign agency speaks of diversion and claims that it is occurring in a widespread manner, but, apart from a few well-publicised incidents of looting (e.g. at Akon, Akot and Labone), none has been willing or able to provide documentation.

SPLA Suspicions of the Humanitarians

As well as minimising diversion, international agencies often believe that the mere presence of outsiders has two other kinds of benefit. Firstly, it may have deterred human rights abuses by soldiers in the relatively peaceful zones, through the threat of bad publicity. Besides the *ad hoc* reports of aid workers themselves, OLS created more opportunities for investigation by human rights researchers. Secondly, the foreigners may have been of some importance as public symbols of the existence of a powers other than the SPLA.

> People were once again able to smile. We had helped to bring a sense of normality and security just by our presence.[4]

Of course it was not as simple as that. At times the behaviour of the foreigners was a poor model, and the arrogance or complacency of some aid workers increased some Sudanese people's hopelessness or cynicism.

---

[4] Larry Minear *et al. Humanitarianism Under Siege: A Critical Review of Operation Lifeline Sudan*, Red Sea Press, 1991, p. 37.

A major source of tension between Southern Sudanese and the foreign humanitarians was the conspicuous difference in lifestyles between them. Foreign aid workers appeared pampered, privileged and opulent. One SPLA commander commented:

> I have been to Lokichoggio. It seemed like an international community. I am sorry to say this. When I saw the UN compound in Loki it was amazing. When people talk about Heaven. . . . Heaven is where you enjoy life. When you want to drink something cold, you go for it. When you want to drink something hot, you go for it. Some people are enjoying Heaven. There are people who are enjoying our war in Southern Sudan, and I was sorry for that because people are dying in their hundreds.[5]

Remarks about 'The Lords of Poverty' and foreign aid workers benefiting financially from the suffering of Sudan recur frequently whenever Southern Sudanese pass comment on international aid agencies. When, in 1994 and afterwards, many SINGOs were heavily criticised by foreign aid workers for allegedly being corrupt or serving personal agendas, SINGO staff justifiably pointed out that the critics were often holding to double standards.

A second main strand of SPLA criticism is that many foreign aid staff are underqualified, and that more experienced and better qualified Sudanese have been passed over in recruiting. There is much truth to this claim. Both NGOs and the UN have often employed inexperienced young volunteers in positions of responsibility, while Sudanese of much greater capacity are unemployed.

A third angle of criticism has been that foreign agencies serve secret political agendas. The allegations about foreign involvement in the 1991 split have been discussed in chapter 11.

Lack of an Alternative SPLA/SRRA Practice

It is unfortunate that the SPLA and SRRA, while echoing many of these criticisms, have not been able to formulate a practicable

---

[5] SPLA Commander, interviewed in May 1995.

alternative model of relief. There is a paradox at the centre of the SPLA's attitude to foreign aid: it argues that relief is wasteful and ineffective, and then continues: we need more of it.

One example of this is the SPLA/SRRA attitude to relief work in the SPLA-held areas of the Nuba Mountains. Should OLS be encouraged to go to the Nuba Mountains or not? The SPLA and SRRA cannot decide.

From the beginning of OLS, the Nuba Mountains were excluded. During the period 1990-94 there was a very severe famine in the region on account of the government's military offensives, economic and aid blockade, and policy of forced relocation (see chapter 8). There was no access to the SPLA-held areas at this time, and although there was an SRRA officer for South Kordofan, the SRRA made no serious efforts to gain access. (The one aeroplane sent by the SRRA, to pick up Cdr Yousif Kuwa Mekki so that he could attend peace talks in mid-1993, was sent empty.) The SRRA only made occasional complaints about the lack of access. Admitting that it had not been effective in the Nuba Mountains, the SRRA signed an agreement delegating its authority in the region to the Nuba Relief, Rehabilitation and Development Society (NRRDS). NRRDS began organising locally in 1993-4 and began providing assistance from outside in 1995, with the support of sympathetic NGOs (and not the UN). It chose not to follow the OLS-SRRA model of inviting in foreign agencies to implement their own programmes, but instead agreed that it would be the sole implementing agency, receiving support and technical assistance from foreign donors. This model has, to date, proved relatively successful.

The SPLA and SRRA have not been quick to learn from the NRRDS experience. Their statements about humanitarian policy in the Nuba Mountains consist largely of a call for OLS to be extended to the region. It is fair to point out the double standards of the UN's continuing exclusion of SPLA-held South Kordofan, but is it really in the SPLA's interests for OLS to become operational there, especially when there is a practicable alternative in place?

More widely, the SPLA and SRRA have not developed a humanitarian supply operation that would overcome their dependence on OLS. In late 1996, in response to the official *OLS*

301

Review, they floated the idea of ending OLS and replacing it with a cross-border operation (see below). A 'Committee of the Way Ahead' was established to look into alternatives, but in the five months after the committee was set up, it met only once and did not even begin to formulate feasible options.

Military Intervention and 'Safe Areas'

A second example of the SPLA failure to articulate its own humanitarian agenda and interests is the issue of military intervention. Some prominent Southerners have called—openly or implicitly—for international (i.e. western-led) military intervention in Sudan, to protect civilians. The *Sudan Democratic Gazette* has pushed the following argument:

> Sovereignty has not prevented the UN from operating in other parts of the world independently of the government when a government has deliberately targeted a community for genocide or ethnic cleansing. Such communities have been afforded international protection from their own governments. Recent examples include Rwanda, Burundi, and Bosnia.[6]

Arguments such as this have been often reproduced.[7] They illustrate several points. One is a naiveté about humanitarian interventions. Rwanda and Bosnia of course prove exactly the opposite: in neither of these cases did the UN troops provide much except fine words of solace to the victims of genocide and ethnic cleansing: their protection was chiefly symbolic rather than practical. No UN protection force was sent to Burundi at all. The author of this article appeared to be making the familiar error of

---

[6] 'Beneficiaries Ignored: What does the OLS Review Team's report contain?' *Sudan Democratic Gazette*, October 1996, p. 6.

[7] E.g., 'International Intervention is Required to Save our People in Juba,' editorial in *SPLM/SPLA Update*, 28 August 1992; Bona Malwal, editorial, *Sudan Democratic Gazette*, September 1993; Steven Wondu, 'Guest Column: The Shield of Sovereignty in Sudan: Should it be penetrated?' *Sudan Democratic Gazette*, August 1995, p. 11.

believing that because the Southern cause is just, an international involvement will *ipso facto* act in support of it.

Secondly, there is a prominent concern with sovereignty, or rather, the alleged lack of a basis for the Sudan Government's claim of sovereignty over Southern Sudan. This argument is advanced on the strong grounds that a government that systematically violates the rights of its citizens can no longer use sovereignty as a defence against others wishing to help those citizens. This is a fair point, but its impact is vitiated by a lack of clarity about what Southern leaders would like the international community to do, and how this relates to the opposition agenda.

One option would be 'safe areas' or 'returnee corridors' set up with the agreement of the belligerents but with the option of being policed by an international force. This idea was floated in February 1993, just after U.S. troops were despatched to Somalia. The U.S. ambassador to Sudan, Donald Petterson, hinted at such a measure: 'If peace talks fail and there's a resumption of hostilities, then the international community would have to consider what could be done to stop the tremendous loss of life.'[8] The U.S. then negotiated the principle of demilitarised 'safe havens' between the two SPLA factions, around the towns of Ayod, Kongor, Waat and Yuai, to allow unhindered relief work. Agreement was reached between the SPLA leaders in May, but the Sudan Government rejected the proposal. In June, each SPLA faction accused the other of violating the safe areas, and the proposal collapsed. By this time, the U.S.-UN intervention in Somalia had gone horribly wrong, and there was no prospect of international troops being sent to enforce the safe areas.

The experience of international interventions, including the forces in Bosnia, Operation Restore Hope in Somalia, and the French Operation Turquoise in Rwanda, is that they reinforce the status quo and freeze political and military processes, which resume when they withdraw. Intervention cannot prevent a determined belligerent from fighting, it can do rather little to protect threatened minorities, and it can make a modest contribution to international humanitarian programmes. What it does is strengthen the external orientation of

---

[8] Quoted in: 'Intervention Pressure Remains,' *Sudan Update*, 21 April 1993.

politics in the affected countries, and in particular to bring benefits to local politicians with good contacts in the diplomatic world. It may be opportunistically used to prevent the military defeat of a client (e.g. the proposed French intervention in Zaire in November 1996): most probably, the initiative for an external intervention in Sudan would come from the government, when it feels militarily threatened. Those in the opposition who have called for an intervention would then find themselves outflanked.

In the meantime, the debate (or rather, lack of it) over intervention indicates the prominent role of some politicians who are externally-oriented, their indifference to local accountability and their failure to develop a domestic coalition that can resolve humanitarian crises. A international military intervention might be a blessing to such politicians, but we would expect to see the general populace greet it with enthusiasm, followed by a rapid disenchantment and bitter criticism as its real nature became clear.

SPLM INSTITUTIONS

For its first ten years, the SPLA never held a congress. The first meeting of its Political-Military High Command was convened only in 1991. It has been dominated by the individual of its Chairman and Commander-in-Chief, Dr John Garang: all major decisions on military affairs, foreign relations and internal policy are made by him, and financial control and supply of armaments remains firmly in his hands. Formal democracy is probably too much to ask from an armed movement waging a war, but the extent of centralisation in the SPLA is remarkable even by the standards of rebel armies. There are no formal channels for self-criticism within the Movement.

Impulses towards Liberalisation in the SPLA

From its inception, the SPLA has always voiced some liberal principles. In 1987, Dr John Garang called upon Southern intellectuals living in Khartoum to join the Movement (a significant number did). At the time of the 1991 split, there was already some serious discussion within the SPLA and among its sympathisers about the need to set up civil and political institutions, and provide a home for skilled civilians who were not ready to join the army.

The creation of OLS was an impulse towards liberalisation. While the SPLA's reasons for letting OLS into its territory in 1989 were mostly to do with external politics, the decision had deep implications for the internal organisation and culture of the Movement. It was inevitable that foreigners would gradually learn more—and gain greater influence—on the way that things were done in rebel-held areas. Foreigners almost invariably pressed for more open and liberal structures, largely because they believed that this would make their aid process more effective, but partly because they sincerely believed that Southern Sudan needed it.

Another impulse for changing the political character of the Movement came from the growing presence of Southerners in East African cities (notably Nairobi). After May 1991, the SPLA could no longer rely on the total support of a neighbouring country ready to allow it to enforce its own internal security with complete autonomy. The pouring of refugees into Kenya and Uganda in 1992, following attacks by the Nasir Faction and the Sudanese Government, had a deep and lasting impact. Kenya and Uganda were very different from Mengistu's Ethiopia. Kenya would not allow the SPLA to operate any administrative system on its territory, let alone carry out political detention and execution. Uganda was more sympathetic to the SPLA, but less able than Kenya to enforce control of its territory. Abductions and killings of possible SPLA dissidents are thought to have taken place from refugee camps in northern Uganda, notably the disappearance of Dr Carlo Madut from Adjumani refugee camp in 1994. SPLA forces have been militarily active in northern Uganda, notably fighting against the Ugandan rebel movement, the Lord's Resistance Army, which operates from bases in Southern Sudan. But the SPLA never recreated the privileged control it had exercised in Gambela.

In addition, the large-scale movement of refugees to Nairobi and other towns in East Africa changed the political climate among Southern intellectuals. They found it easier to live in these towns, where they were free to choose which faction to support, and even to

305

discuss the formation of new factions. In Nairobi especially, Sudan Government agents worked hard to encourage further divisions within the SPLA, and to induce some of the prominent rebels to return to Khartoum. Also, Kenya offered the model of educated people setting up in business or establishing NGOs.

It was the 1991 split, however, that created the strongest impulses towards liberalisation. The human rights record of the Movement was now publicly exposed and heavily criticised. The liberal rhetoric of the Nasir Faction meant that the Mainstream was obliged to compete, if it were not going to lose the support of most educated Southerners. (A common feature of the 1990s has been Garang's readiness to appropriate the slogans of his Southern opponents; another example is the SPLA's adoption of the principle of 'self-determination'.) The actual meeting of the High Command, held in September 1991, issued the 'Torit Resolutions' which declared, among other things, that a system of civil administration would be established, and that military training would no longer be compulsory for members of the Movement.[9] This was a move to attract Southern intellectuals[10] who were needed to help create a new 'civil society' in rebel-held areas. In July 1992, a draft Civil Administration Act for SPLA-held areas was issued by Interim National Executive Committee. This envisaged the setting up of elected councils and commissioners. At the same time, draft proposals to set up a judiciary were formulated.

But unfortunately, the creation of the Nasir Faction also created a strong impetus in an authoritarian direction. Internal and external security had to be tightened. In particular, there was a risk that intellectuals and other prominent individuals would defect to the opposing faction, or act as spies. This was not the moment for them to be given more freedom, especially when inside rebel territory. Despite the new welcome given to civilians, Article 6.2 of the Torit

---

[9] 'The SPLM/SPLA Torit Resolution, 1991' of the SPLM Political Military High Command, 12 September 1991.

[10] In what follows, the category of 'intellectuals' is used to denote people who are apt to look for occupations that require the qualifications of formal education, as opposed to military activity, for instance.

306

Resolutions (withheld from publication by the SPLA-Mainstream but quoted by the Nasir Faction shortly afterwards) ordered a 'general mobilisation and compulsory draft of all adults above the age of 18 and below the age of 45 in all fronts'.[11] This very real security threat meant that tangible moves towards lessening the grip of the military high command remained only promises.

In February 1993, the American Ambassador to Sudan, Donald Petterson, visited rebel-held areas with OLS, and went on to meet John Garang in Kampala. Garang was being encouraged to adopt definite measures of liberalisation. On 20 February, the SPLA issued a press release announcing preparations to convene a National Convention as part of a process of democracy and restructuring.[12] On 2 March, Garang gave approval for the formation of the first secular indigenous NGO to work in SPLA-held territory.

Conferences and Reform in the SPLM/A

The first SPLM National Convention was finally held in March-April 1994. Delegates attended from all parts of SPLA-held Sudan; those who came from the Nuba Mountains had walked for over three months. There was much fine rhetoric. John Garang gave speeches at the beginning and end of the Convention, full of both implicit admissions of past mistakes and grand promises for the future:

> We shall restructure ourselves. Our civilians have suffered a great deal. We have now put the citizen at centre stage. He is the one that liberation should serve, not the one that should suffer from liberation.[13]

---

[11] 'Critique on John Garang's "Torit Resolutions" 1991,' Department of Information and Culture, Interim National Executive Committee of the SPLM, Nasir, 20 October 1991.

[12] SPLM/SPLA Press Release, Kampala, 20 February 1993.

[13] Dr Garang's acceptance speech on his election as the Chairman of the National Liberation Council and National Executive Council by the Convention, 12 April 1994.

The Convention debated a range of issues with vigour and seriousness. It was not stage managed. A blueprint for a radically-reformed SPLA was adopted and the first steps were formally taken to set up the SPLM as a party. A National Liberation Council (NLC) was set up as the legislative organ of the Movement, with smaller liberation councils for each region and smaller administrative division. For the first time, SRRA was made formally independent from the SPLA and placed within a wider political structure. But (as was recognised at the 1996 civil society conference), the SRRA continued in effect to do the work of the civil administration. The 1984 SPLA disciplinary code (which had been widely criticised for its summary procedures and severe penalties) was abolished, and a process of drafting a replacement set in motion. National Executive Council (NEC) secretaries were appointed, and also secretaries in the Chairman's office. For the advocates of a reformed, liberalised and institutionalised SPLA/SPLM, both inside and outside Sudan, it was a fine moment.

Many of the hopes of the Convention have not been realised. The positions in the NEC have been largely nominal. For example, James Wani Igga, the Secretary for Finance and Economic Planning (and also later appointed as Secretary-General), is formally number three in the hierarchy, but has no financial resources to dispense. The only money in the Movement is either in the Chairman's office or the SRRA. Other secretaries have found their functions replicated by secretaries appointed in the Chairman's office, who appear to wield much more real power. Some of the practical measures (such as drafting a new penal code and judicial procedure) were rushed and the results were not always satisfactory.[14]

The 1983 Manifesto was scrapped and a committee for drafting a new version was set up. Three years later, it has not reported. The party has yet to mobilise on the ground. In some respects, the appointments made in the Convention are more akin to filling

---

[14] For example, Article 279, 'drunkenness in a private place' appears to restrict the consumption of alcohol in private, on penalty of a prison sentence. The consumption of alcohol is an important part of Southern culture.

government offices than forming a party (and indeed the NEC is sometimes referred to as a 'cabinet' or even a 'government').

A series of conferences followed, including an Officers Conference and a conference on humanitarian assistance. The latter looked at the role of the SRRA, but did not define it, instead concluding: 'The SRRA will continue to translate its mandate into a concise and published Charter.'[15] Working groups in the conference studied the relationships between the SPLA and communities, the SPLA and NGOs, the SRRA and NGOs and the SPLA and SRRA. Discussions and criticisms were remarkably frank.

Among the items listed as 'problems between the SPLA and the local communities' were the following:[16]

- Some individual members of the SPLA undermine traditional authorities and their administration;
- SPLA seeking for food from the local populations brings them into conflict;
- Lack of control, desertion and disobedience of soldiers causes conflict between the SPLA and the affected communities, e.g. rape, looting, theft, etc.
- Forceful extraction of services from the civil population by SPLA, e.g. transport, buildings, etc.

The list continued. The Conference agreed that the resolutions of the National Convention on the rule of law and the development of institutions should be implemented.

By the time of the April 1996 Conference on Civil Society, Southerners were complaining that the Convention had been a charade, and that there was little point in organising a second Convention (or indeed another conference addressing similar issues) until the resolutions of the First National Convention had actually been implemented. Nonetheless, the civil society conference proceeded, with many foreign observers present. John Garang

---

[15] SPLM/SPLA Conference on Humanitarian Assistance to the New Sudan, 'A Partnership for New Sudan,' Chukudum, 21-23 September 1995, draft report, Item III/C/(i)
[16] Humanitarian conference draft report, Points from Group II, p. 14.

opened the proceedings with a speech that indicated just how far the SPLA's rhetoric had moved from its early days.

> Effective democratic, participatory and accountable civil authority is the most important task and challenge facing the Movement, that must take centre stage as the military problem fades in importance.[17]

The conference was lively and many issues were discussed without evident censorship. Several crucial questions, however, were not addressed. One, can there be democracy without formal voting for leaders? There were no arguments in favour of elections for the senior posts in the SPLM—instead the implicit claim was that a more enlightened leadership or a more broadly-based oligarchy would be good things. Two, is there to be a regular system of taxation, with formal criteria, in order to feed the soldiers? This issue was avoided. It had been addressed in passing at the 1995 humanitarian conference, when it was stated that 'The SPLA will produce their own food to enhance self reliance.'[18] But in both conferences, details were not discussed. Implicitly, participants expected matters to continue as before. In short, basic issues of power and provision were not fully discussed: the conference was more concerned with formal structures and principles than with enforcing change.

The resolutions of the civil society conference were written up in a rough form on a flip-chart during the conference. After that they were processed by the Conference Organising Committee and then sent on to the National Liberation Council, which met (belatedly and without all its members present) in January 1997. There, the resolutions were adopted, with only minor modifications. Neither the draft nor the resolutions were published, however, and members of the NLC reported that further work was needed before the recommendations could be implemented.

---

[17] Opening address to SPLM Conference on Civil Society and the Organisation of Civil Authority of the New Sudan, New Kush, 30 April 1996.
[18] Item III/B/(iii).

The slow progress of the conference resolutions is not surprising. The conference itself was organised more as a seminar, with a range of viewpoints and experiences being presented, rather than as a debate on specific recommendations drawn from preparatory work. Overall it resembled more a piece of theatre than legislative process. Some observers have compared it to the NIF's series of conferences in 1990-91, but the comparison is misleading: the Khartoum conferences were a process of consultation, intended to give an illusion of democracy and at the same time to identify individuals who might be ready to collaborate with the new government. The SPLM conference was not a facade behind which the leadership intended to proceed with its own agenda, for the simple reason that there was very little in the way of an agenda beyond holding the conference itself and seeing what would come out of it. The resolutions of the conference were general, often vague and difficult to implement. The SPLM's consultation process also gave greater confidence and feelings of involvement to foreign representatives. Participants may feel disappointed, but they cannot claim to have been manipulated or misled.

External Orientation

Closing the 1996 conference, John Garang said:

> These conferences are not designed for the international gallery. They are designed so that we put our house in order, so that we develop something of our own.[19]

This is a very optimistic interpretation of the conference process. The 'international gallery' was crucial in setting the agenda of the conference and pushing for it to occur, and the SPLA was moving very slowly towards 'putting its house in order.'

---

[19] Speech at the closing session of SPLM Conference on Civil Society and the Organisation of Civil Authority of the New Sudan, New Kush, 4 May 1996.

A fundamental reason for the disappointing progress of the SPLA's reforms is that the leadership continues to set its agenda with respect to external actors: foreign donors, the UN, neighbouring states, and other parties in the NDA. During the Mengistu period, the locus of authority for the leadership was external, in Ethiopia. In search of a renewed external power base, the SPLA leadership has been extremely sensitive to the needs of neighbouring countries. There are allegations that SPLA troops have fought in the Ugandan civil war, and relations with Eritrea and Ethiopia since 1995 have been handled by the Chairman's office alone. Assistance from friendly states is dispensed by the same office, again alone. One of the main functions of Garang's visits to Europe and (particularly) the U.S. is the meetings with leading politicians and the recycling of bland messages of solidarity and support. The Chairman can thereby reinforce his authority internally. The NDA's choice of John Garang as head of its Military Co-ordination Council serves this purpose, among others.

Earlier chapters have shown how successive Sudanese governments found support from abroad and became less responsive to domestic demands for democracy. Many Southerners fear the same phenomenon within the SPLA: that external patronage and the expectation of military victory will lessen the impetus for reform, and the Movement will find itself reacting to others' agendas rather than setting its own.

Local Institutions in the Nuba Mountains

The SPLA's democratisation actually began in the Nuba Mountains, away from any publicity—in fact unknown even to many in the SPLA high command. On entering South Kordofan in 1989, Cdr Yousif Kuwa Mekki had begun the formation of local committees for administration, established courts and tried to encourage services such as clinics, wholly reliant on local resources. But the key moment was in September 1992: a time when the SPLA forces were completely cut off from resupply, and were facing a huge military offensive combined with a programme of mass forcible relocation. It appeared that the very survival of the Nuba people was in question.

312

At that moment, Yousif Kuwa convened an 'Advisory Council' of two hundred delegates from all parts of the Nuba Mountains, in the village of Debi, to discuss a single question: should they continue the struggle or surrender and take their chances on the mercies of the Sudan government? Yousif Kuwa opened the six-day meeting by saying that he was ready to take responsibility for the current dire crisis of the Nuba, having led the people thus far, but that he felt the issue was now so fundamental that the decision whether to continue the struggle should be a collective one. He made it clear that he was prepared to continue. Over the following days the delegates debated, hearing voices on different sides of the argument, before they voted to maintain the struggle and stay with the SPLA.

The Advisory Council also decided to continue in existence. (It has since become the South Kordofan regional Liberation Council.) It meets annually and decides major matters of policy. For example, it decided to create NRRDS, it asked for a conference on religious tolerance to be convened,[20] it decided that the judiciary should be formally independent of the military,[21] it asked for secondary school leavers to be demobilised from the army to serve as schoolteachers, and it deliberated on a number of pressing social issues such as the level of bridewealth. A smaller council meets more regularly to decide on lesser matters. At County, Payam (sub-district) and village level, elected committees meet and wield real power. Though problems persist (for example many debates and resolutions are not recorded), civic structures and civil administration exist to an extent unequalled elsewhere in SPLA-controlled Sudan.

What are the reasons for this success? Part of it lies with the nature of the leadership in the Nuba Mountains. Yousif Kuwa is a former elected parliamentarian with a constituency in the Nuba Mountains: he began his political mobilisation with a different outlook to the soldiers who set the agenda for the SPLA in the South. Another significant factor is, however, the absence of a foreign agenda and foreign agencies. When the Nuba delegates met in Debi,

---

[20] 'Religious Tolerance in the Nuba Mountains,' *NAFIR*, July 1995, p. 7
[21] 'Strengthening the Rule of Law: A Judicial Conference is Convened,' *NAFIR,* January 1996, p. 12.

they were talking only to each other—the outside world did not even find out about the meeting for another three years. There were no promises or hopes of outside aid or recognition hovering in the background. The leadership needed the support of the people, because it had no alternative. The delegates knew that they could rely only on themselves, and they could bargain with the leadership in the confidence that they knew their respective capacities.

This transparency and frankness is the basis of a democratic contract. Once aid is introduced, with its hard-to-calculate promises, the nature of the democratic encounter is fundamentally changed. Leaders can seek power, resources and legitimacy from outside, and the power of the domestic constituency is eroded. Aid-sponsored democracy may be harder to achieve than democracy in an aid-free zone.

HUMANITARIAN INSTITUTIONS

Though many staff act from genuine and informed concern with suffering people, the basic interest of international humanitarian organisations is their own institutions and programmes. Underlying all their initiatives in Southern Sudan is the need to deliver supplies more efficiently and reliably, or at least to be seen to do so. Fashionable ideas such as 'accountability to beneficiaries', 'building civil society', 'democracy and governance' etc. are all shaped by this demand.

Indigenous NGOs in Rebel Areas

In March 1993, John Garang agreed to grant permission to the first SINGO. The name of this NGO was the Cush Relief and Rehabilitation Society (also known as 'CRRS' or just 'Cush'). The precedent was important, because it established the principle of allowing Sudanese citizens in rebel areas to organise themselves without being under the direct control of the SPLA. (The creation of NSCC, three years earlier, had set a much more limited precedent.) Like NSCC and international NGOs, CRRS was destined to experience practical limits to its independence in the field. But it was still an important step. The link to international donors meant that such organisations would always be subject to countervailing forces against military pressure.

The formation of CRRS was also important because it helped to clarify the position of SRRA. SRRA was still nominally an NGO, even though it had long been known as an instrument of the SPLA, and since 1989 had been playing an important role in regulating contacts with foreign aid agencies. The contrast with CRRS (purely an implementing NGO) helped SRRA to give up its confusing claims of independence, and develop more clearly as an arm of the rebel administration.

The idea for CRRS came from a group of six intellectuals, Dinka from the Lakes area of Bahr el Ghazal. Two of them had previously worked with the Sudan Council of Churches (SCC) in Government-controlled areas before joining the SPLA. Two others had held office with the SRRA. They were people who had some familiarity with the international humanitarian culture, as well as outstanding levels of education. In a time of peace they would have been natural leaders of their communities; perhaps national politicians; in time of war some of them were becoming frustrated. One of them, Dr Achol Marial, had for a while belonged to the break-away Nasir Faction of the SPLA, but became disillusioned and returned to the Mainstream. Being an astute politician, he arranged two personal meetings with John Garang. In the second, he presented the concept of CRRS.

> The SPLA was a tough system. I was putting the SPLA on test. Was it a movement subject to reforms, or just the old order? This was a test case. Thank God that Dr John [Garang] saw the point and encouraged the idea and said 'Go ahead as long as it is to benefit the people either as individuals or groups'. . . Reading between the lines, it was another way of accommodating me as a political animal. I was later elected to the NLC in my absence.[22]

Another of Cush's founder members, John Clement Kuc, saw the creation of the organisation in terms of trying to create a more

---

[22] Interview with Dr Achol Marial, 12 June 1995.

pluralistic, entrepreneurial culture in Southern Sudan, less dependent upon the paternalism of a political authority:

> It was to do with the cultural background of our people in Southern Sudan. They think they will work with the government and at the end they will receive their salary. But it is a business, of course, to run an NGO. People in the North are well aware of this and know this business. Western NGOs will channel through [local] NGOs because of government bureaucracy.
>
> Also there was the culture of the Movement. The SPLA started in Ethiopia. In the Eastern Bloc everything must be done by the government. People are fearing that intellectuals [who show some independence] will be accused of plotting.[23]

But, as Kuc put it, the suspicion of NGOs 'changed when we went to Garang.' The Chairman was co-operative and Cush was permitted to operate.

Did the growth of SINGOs mean that the SPLA was yielding its centralised power? The SINGO phenomenon certainly gave a novel liberal gloss to the SPLA. But it is unlikely that this was the sole motivation. Other likely reasons include pressure from USAID (and the belief that going along with a U.S.-backed initiative might bring other advantages) and the prospect of obtaining more resources for Southern Sudan. And in an important respect, the creation of Cush and other SINGOs was in fact a way of reinforcing centralised power inside the Movement. Some of the people who set up the agencies tended to be independent-minded former commanders and functionaries, who might have been a threat within the SPLA, if their hopes and ambitions had remained thwarted. Allowing them—and others with similar backgrounds and mindsets—to move into the NGO sector can be seen as a way of diverting their energies away from the political sphere into something comparatively harmless.

A number of other Southern intellectuals tried to follow the lead of CRRS. The founder of one SINGO categorised his fellow SINGOs:

---

[23] Interviewed on 12 June 1995.

There are three groups. The first group are the opponents of John Garang, the opponents of the SPLA who happened to be in exile and not participating in the liberation. The second group is of the NGOs established by the Movement. MER[24] was formed by Riek and pushed. WomanAid was formed by Emma [McCune] and pushed. The New Sudan Islamic Council was formed by John Garang and pushed ahead. SMC[25] was originally initiated by Northern Sudanese doctors in Europe and passed to John Garang from Dr Mansour Khalid. John Garang had no way except to pass it to Dr Dau [Alier] who is close to him. The third group is of desperate Sudanese exiles in Nairobi who would like to get a means of living.

(This simplifies the case somewhat. Some senior SRRA staff set up SINGOs, and some SINGOs, such as Cush, were hybrid cases set up by individuals who saw limited options within the SPLA, but wanted to remain close to the Movement.)

Whatever the motives of the SPLA leadership, the creation of SINGOs had wider consequences. One was that, in areas where SINGOs handed significant resources, local people came to see the SRRA and SPLA in a less favourable light. The OLS Capacity Building Officer noted:

SINGOs which have received big funding can really rub it in the noses of the SRRA and [County] Commissioners. It is not so much personally (as a matter of salaries) but in terms of local prestige. [SINGOs say:] 'We are bringing these things to our people.' For example [at a meeting in Akot, where Cush had been working] one woman got up and was very contemptuous about the SRRA. She said they weren't bringing anything. . . . Unless there is some regulation, there will be a backlash.[26]

In addition, the senior staff of SINGOs developed extensive contacts with international donors, who thereby gained a wider perspective on the South and its problems. Individuals with

---

[24] Medical Relief; *mer* also means 'peace' in the Shilluk language.
[25] Sudan Medical Care.
[26] Interviewed on 6 March 1995.

experience of other liberation movements in north-east Africa queried the SPLA's rationale: 'why do they want to jeopardise the armed struggle by supporting intellectuals and elites to be independent?'[27]

By the end of 1994, UNICEF/OLS had listed more than twenty groups calling themselves SINGOs. UNICEF/OLS was itself encouraging the phenomenon: the funding opportunities it opened up played an important role in the creation of SINGOs. With funding from USAID it set up an Institution and Capacity-Building Programme (ICBP) in 1993. The initiative aimed 'to empower Sudanese to co-ordinate the delivery of humanitarian assistance and implement their own programmes'.[28] But it also had more practical aims, in the words of one north American aid worker: 'The initial idea for capacity-building was because the UN does not have field capacity, enough staff on the ground to implement programmes.'[29] OLS was employing very few Sudanese: the obvious choice (already practised to a limited extent by a few international NGOs) was simply to employ more of them in more senior positions. But instead, the ICBP aimed to foster separate Sudanese organisations.

The potential benefits of the indigenised approach to aid work seemed to be great. Sudanese people could be expected to have a better understanding of local needs and conditions than expatriates. Sudanese managers might have stronger contacts with members of community groups, with the intended beneficiaries, and with the authorities of the rebel movements. They would require lower levels of payment for similar work. They would be less likely to evacuate staff and shut down programmes during periods of military insecurity.

These potential benefits were set out in a manifesto of September 1993, called the 'Nairobi Joint Statement'. It purported to speak for 'the Sudanese people' and was signed by individuals who nominally represented the following categories of Sudanese organisation: women's groups, 'grassroots community efforts',

---

[27] Foreign aid worker, interviewed on 6 March 1995.
[28] UNICEF/OLS (Southern Sector), 'Review of 1994 Activities', 1995.
[29] Interviewed on 2 March 1995.

SINGOs, churches, RASS and SRRA. However, the document, and the meeting that it came out of, were largely a product of UNICEF's (and USAID's) initiative. This point is important. It is not that Sudanese intellectuals lacked their own ideas and capabilities; but in the present case they were responding to specific encouragement and opportunities offered by foreigners.

. Supporting SINGOs had the benefit (to foreign agencies) of indigenising the programme without giving power to Sudanese. If OLS and foreign NGOs had taken on more Sudanese staff, some of these individuals would have risen to positions of authority, which could have challenged foreign staff members.

In trying to open up the SINGO sector quickly, UNICEF promoted the idea that donors should channel resources through them. The offer of resources was attractive to many Sudanese, who formed SINGOs and came forward with their names and intended programmes, looking for funding. The idea of capacity building met with problems straight away.

> The SINGOs grew up overnight—all those people in Nairobi with nothing to do. In a few months [January-October 1994] there were 29 'briefcase NGOs'. Out of the 29, there were some people desperately looking for a job to survive, some who saw it as a good opportunity to make extra money, and some genuine people. I'd say the genuine ones were less than ten.[30]

Quite what counts as a 'genuine' humanitarian was not always clear, and depended on the skills and outlook of the aid worker making the judgement. The same NGO worker continued:

> You can spot [the genuine ones] by their attitude. Some people came in with shopping lists, and you could immediately see it was not a real proposal which had been worked out.
> So then we had workshops for setting them up, with constitutions, mission statements and the rest. Some would go away and really try to come up with something. Others would say, 'this is

---

[30] Elizabeth Otieno, interviewed on 27 February 1995.

a waste of time; people are dying.' And these were sometimes exiles who never went home to the village.

Then we really slowed down on the gravy train, and began only considering people who attended meetings and training sessions. Of course there were complaints about that.

An early response by the ICBP Officer to the proliferation of SINGOs, many of which he suspected were not 'genuine', was for UNICEF to authorise the SINGO applicants to use OLS facilities for going and carrying out appraisals on the ground. They were also given $1,500 each for expenses. After that, some of them disappeared. Others came back with assessments of varying quality. The ICBP Officer believes it was a useful exercise:

I think it was money well spent. If they disappeared, or produced something worthless, at least it weeded them out. Some went and came back with a good assessment.[31]

But even those SINGOs that believed they had cleared OLS's hurdle by producing a good assessment found that this did not lead automatically to obtaining funds. The (new) OLS ICBP Officer found herself besieged by SINGO representatives with high expectations of what she could deliver: 'They are on the phone every day. It takes a massive amount of stalling from me.'[32] Many Southern individuals and groups became frustrated by the obstacles with which they were confronted in the culture and procedures of the international aid system. Complaints about the resources that OLS and international NGOs expended on salaries, offices and cars abounded; some SINGO staff attributed their failure to obtain support to the personal antipathy, bias or corruption of international aid workers.

CRRS, on the other hand, got too much funding too quickly and too easily. This was probably because it was the first SINGO and because the personalities of its leaders impressed the foreign donors. In the two years 1993 and 1994 it received more than $200,000 in

---

[31] Iain Levine, interviewed on 28 February 1995.
[32] Alison Ayers, interviewed on 22 March 1995.

cash from seven different donors.[33] This figure does not include equipment and project supplies donated in kind. For instance, CRRS was the nominal consignee of considerable quantities of relief food. Its other activities included cattle vaccination, primary health care, immunisation of children, and agricultural projects.

CRRS and its donors seriously underestimated the difficulties that the new organisation would face. Foremost among these were the implications of opening an office in Nairobi. It suddenly attracted enormous pressures from the community of Sudanese exiles. The managers were not fortified by a lot of relevant experience or a long organisational history. They gave in to the pressures, and diverted money from funds meant to support projects in the field.

> We did not have adequate resources to meet the overwhelming demand in terms of staff stipends, in areas like medical bills for executive staff, and in assistance for urban refugees. People are desperate and if you have an office they will be sitting with you all day. So this was agreed . . . to do this as an internal loan and get donor funding. Precisely I had in mind a project of income generation. I had initiated it, and took off by purchasing a mini-bus. The money was approved from another source.[34]

This desperate remedy only made the problem worse. When the donors discovered that project money had been misspent, they stopped further funding. A management audit and evaluation of CRRS was ordered. The evaluation found serious defects in the organisation's constitution and management systems. Furthermore, the staff had lacked the skills to design and manage relief programmes. Perhaps most disappointingly of all for an indigenous organisation, CRRS's links with the communities of needy people in Sudan were 'very weak indeed'.[35] It had been a creation of foreigners

---

[33] 'Management Audit Report' by Finplan Consultants for Matrix Consultants/Christian Aid.

[34] Dr Achol Marial, interviewed on 12 May 1995.

[35] 'Summary of evaluation findings, conclusions and recommendations,' by Matrix Consultants for Christian Aid.

and Sudanese elites that failed to get close enough to those who were vulnerable.

The donors punished CRRS by making its managing director resign. Most of them cut off their funding. Yet they were blameworthy themselves, for writing cheques naively, and for failing to provide a deeper kind of institutional strengthening.

By the end of 1996 there were five or six secular SINGOs that were delivering services in Southern Sudan in their own right. They included Sudan Medical Care (active in Eastern Equatoria with the support of NPA), Sudan Production Aid (active in Tonj, Bahr el Ghazal, with the support of World Vision), the Mundri Relief and Development Association (active in Mundri with the support of International Aid Sweden) and the Nile Relief and Development Society (present in Bor). They had been formed shortly after CRRS and—like CRRS and many new organisations—were mostly headed by charismatic individuals. How far the organisations were dependent on these individuals had still to be seen. But they had learnt many of the lessons of CRRS. One characteristic of the most steadily successful SINGOs was that the managers came from the same part of the country as the intended beneficiaries. Where this was not the case—as with the initial work of Sudan Production Aid and the Community Development Association (CDA)—they tended to get into trouble with the local people or authorities.

Many of the successful SINGOs began in a kind of partnership with an established international agency. The latter provided initial assistance with logistics and finances. This arrangement seemed to provide a useful way of compensating for the initial lack of institutional skills and individual experience within the new organisations. On the other hand, some potential SINGOs—such as the Nile Relief and Development Society—have found difficulty in avoiding dependence on their international NGO partners. This has not stopped them from often doing good work, delivering goods and services as sub-contractors. Likewise, by 1996, some more Sudanese people were employed as project officers and managerial staff by international agencies.

The Sudanese staff and the Sudanese NGOs have something in common; they all depend on resources from foreign donors.

Although they may subscribe to the briefly-fashionable humanitarian concept of 'accountability to beneficiaries', the effective accountability is to paymasters. The new Sudanese humanitarians are an extension of the international aid system. These capable individuals have taken advantage of a new freedom to engage in relief work and serve their people, and are even expanding that opportunity. But politically they are weak. At particular times and places they can build a domestic constituency with an interest in humanitarian action and a degree of political liberalism. Without international agency patronage, however, these individuals and their constituency will be very vulnerable. The SINGOs are still young. They are learning and advancing, but it is improbable that they will be able to meet the expectations of those who thought they would be a strong element of civil society. This is not a reason to reject them, merely to recognise their limitations.

SRRA and RASS: Ceding Autonomy

One of the reasons for donor enthusiasm for SINGOs was undoubtedly frustration with SRRA (and in SPLA-United areas, RASS). Few donors or international NGOs were impressed with these organisations. But they recognised that the Movements needed their humanitarian wings, and duly continued to support them.

Before 1993, some foreign agencies provided grants for administrative costs to SRRA and RASS. The SPLA portrayed itself as a movement of 'volunteers': its workers did not have a right to formal salaries from the Movement. But 'staff allowances' could be budgeted, and were, for SRRA headquarters staff. The grants tended to be uncoordinated as between the donor agencies, and loosely monitored. In 1992, for instance, SRRA's office rent and phone costs were funded simultaneously by NPA and SEOC/LWF, unknown to each other. Individuals with prominent positions in the factions could also gain special assistance from NGOs for such things as house rent, medical bills and school fees.

Although they were very few in number, the educated Southern Sudanese who gained employment or income from working with aid agencies were influential. Theirs was a model to be followed: all

323

Southerners knew that large amounts of aid money were flowing to Southern Sudan, and all could see that few qualified Southerners were profitably employed in these operations. This was an important impulse to the formation of SINGOs.

From 1993, alongside encouraging SINGOs, the UNICEF capacity-building programme was concerned to encourage reforms in SRRA and RASS. The first step was to take control of their external funding. UNICEF provided substantial grants for the running of the organisations, on the understanding that it would also co-ordinate grants provided by other agencies. It became the lead agency for agreeing and monitoring the annual budgets of SRRA and RASS. This gave it considerable influence in shaping the administration of those agencies, and in turn an intimate involvement with the rebel movements themselves.

UNICEF tried to help SRRA and RASS reorganise themselves by funding workshops on issues of organisational development. The early workshops were very encouraging, in that the representatives of SRRA and RASS often proved much more open to realistic discussion and constructive criticism than had previously been the case. They were even willing to acknowledge problems and mistakes in the running of the rebel movements as a whole. Their staff were encouraged to identify corporate problems, and were guided towards solutions such as: management boards, clear job descriptions, admin-istrative guidelines and strategic plans. In the earlier workshops on matters of organisation, the participants were relatively senior and few. Later the scope was widened to include more field officers. This was no doubt intended as a way of disseminating ideas in progressively wider circles. Unfortunately it meant that the particular circumstances of field workers—especially in relation to military authorities—had less chance of being discussed in detail. The humanitarian and managerial orthodoxies were well-established in advance, as the dominant ideas on the agenda.

This was a serious drawback, in view of the weakness of the links between the central offices and the field stations. The process of liberalisation and spreading humanitarian ideas was more marked among the Nairobi-based personnel of SRRA and RASS than among officers on the ground; it might be said to have widened the gap. The effect was accentuated by the fact that many senior staff were receiving official salaries or allowances funded by aid agencies. UNICEF and SRRA then made some efforts to ease this problem; more workshops were organised for field-workers, in such areas as community development.

When it was founded, RASS appeared more progressive and co-operative to foreign donors than SRRA. By 1995, however, it was facing a crisis because it could not account for large sums of donor money. Compounded by the divisions in SPLA-United and SSIM, and then the SSIM agreement with Khartoum, this spelled the demise of RASS as an effective humanitarian intermediary.

SRRA survives. The foreign agencies' involvement may have increased SRRA's technical proficiency, but it did not address the problem of its lack of a clear agenda. This was clearly expressed at the 1995 humanitarian conference, where participants noted (among other things):

- Despite its insistence on involvement, SRRA lacks [an] overall plan on programming NGOs operations.
- SRRA exhibits a top-down tendency in program planning.
- Unclear working relationship between SRRA/NGOs and SPLM secretaries and Local Civil Administration is creating misunderstandings.
- SRRA mandate not clear to all NGOs or donors.[36]

But defining SRRA's mandate would not solve these problems. A still deeper problem lay with the SPLA: the SRRA's difficulties reflect the SPLA's failure to develop a practical social agenda, into which the SRRA can fit. The SPLA and SRRA saw the latter's task primarily in terms of attracting and channelling resources and co-ordinating foreign agencies, rather than mobilising people in pursuit of a social agenda. Tensions between the SPLA and SRRA inevitably followed (and were detailed at the 1995 humanitarian conference).

---

[36] Humanitarian conference draft report, p. 16.

The SRRA's problems also stem from its readiness to cede such a high degree of control to a foreign agency. Despite the complaints of its staff, SRRA readily submitted to others' agendas. As with many aspects of the Southern Sudanese-international humanitarian coalition, the Southerners had not defined their interests and agenda before entering into an agreement, leading to a situation in which their interests were not well-served in the long run, and creating a relationship fraught with distrust and tension.

The foreign agencies had their own agendas and failings. No critique of Southern Sudanese humanitarian organisations is complete without an analysis of the lack of accountability and professional shortcomings and wastage of resources of the donor agencies, including OLS, SEOC and a range of NGOs. Independent assessments of relief operations increasingly focus on the problems of international agencies, as the root problem.

GROUND RULES AND HUMANITARIAN PRINCIPLES

The beginnings of the evolving rebel-humanitarian coalition coincided with a crisis in the relationship between OLS and the SPLA at the end of 1992. Four OLS-protected expatriates were killed by rebel soldiers during William Nyuon's defection from Garang's SPLA. Two of the expatriates probably died in cross-fire; the other two were apparently executed afterwards. The SPLA did not apologise. Many aid workers demanded punitive sanctions against the rebel movements; and some agencies for a while suspended their relief operations in East Bank Equatoria. The UN sent an investigation team from New York, but its report was not published. The calls for justice instead became a way of exerting political leverage on the rebel leaders.

First the UN put pressure on the leaders of the SPLA factions to sign their acceptance of a set of 'Ground Rules'. The Ground Rules attempted to define the minimum conditions under which relief agencies would work in the rebel areas in future. The process of agreeing the rules was seen by many as rehabilitating the relationship between the aid agencies and the rebels, at a time when the U.S. and UN were putting strong pressure on Khartoum.

The idea of Ground Rules were as practical guides to relief operationality. They were concerned with security, and were their practical counterpart was an extremely elaborate system of ensuring the physical safety and when necessary the emergency evacuation of aid staff. Later, the rules grew into the more ambitious concept of 'humanitarian principles'—an application of human rights. OLS is in the almost unique position among major relief programmes of being formally able to address the issue of humanitarian law and human rights. Not only is the UN the guardian of international law (jointly with the ICRC in the case of the Geneva Conventions), but UNICEF bases its mandate on the Declaration of the Rights of the Child. The incorporation of rights-based principles into a relief programme was both a return to the founding principles of humanitarian action and a contemporary innovation. It promised much—perhaps more than could realistically be delivered.

From the outset, the Ground Rules lacked a clear mechanism of adjudication and enforcement. The rules were frequently violated, and when NGOs suffered, their staff often complained that the OLS Co-ordinator had failed to pursue their case vigorously. They could not see what concessions, if any, were being negotiated behind closed doors. At the same time, the NGOs themselves were seldom prepared to withdraw their programmes, even in the face of repeated abuses, and were also reluctant to publicise documented violations.

It became apparent that the Ground Rules, which had been first conceived by the aid agencies as a clear ultimatum to the armed movements, would not actually be used in this way. In 1994-5 OLS/UNICEF decided to develop the Ground Rules instead as the basis for a programme of education and consensus-building instead. Philip O'Brien explained:

> it should not be for OLS or international humanitarian agencies to enforce these principles. Our role must be to encourage and support

the Movements and civil society to be able to make a reality of these principles.[37]

The Ground Rules were re-drafted and greatly expanded. The eleven plain and pragmatic rules became a little booklet of prescriptions, including declarations of assent to the UN Conventions. Like the original Ground Rules, this was formally endorsed by the leaders of the rebel movements. Great efforts were made to make the new rules widely known and understood.

In doing this, the officer in charge of the programme was particularly concerned to emphasise the links between humanitarian principles, as codified, and the traditional values of Sudanese cultures. Making this connection was an important part of the many workshops that were held in order to disseminate the rules. The argument was used largely in order to prevent giving the impression that alien values were being imposed by foreigners. But it could not go as far as demonstrating that adhering to them would be in everyone's fundamental interest. However, people attending the workshops usually had good reason to profess agreement, whether or not it was out of deep conviction. Iain Levine, humanitarian principles officer, recognised this:

> I'm very aware that people tell me what I want to hear, but I don't think it is necessarily bad. I don't think it invalidates the whole approach.[38]

Some observers have wondered how culturally appropriate it was for relatively young Europeans and north Americans to give lectures to Sudanese bishops and elders about humanitarian principles.

The basic problem was not a cultural one, but a question of enforcement. The UN had clearly disavowed any intention of using the two sanctions it had: public exposure and withdrawal. If the outside agencies were not ready to enforce the principles, who was? The obvious option was an internal judicial system in SPLA-

---

[37] Philip D. O'Brien, letter to Alex de Waal, 23 November 1995.
[38] Iain Levine, UNICEF/OLS Humanitarian Principles Officer, interviewed 10 November 1995.

controlled Southern Sudan. But this system did not exist: the SPLA, despite issuing a disciplinary code in 1984 (revised in 1994), did not set up a functioning judiciary. Most disputes were settled either by chiefs, whose remit was limited, or by commanders, who were scarcely independent. An SPLM official admitted, 'using the courts it is too difficult to clear one's name, even for a Sudanese person.'[39]

The weakness of the judiciary was in turn compounded by the unwillingness of foreign agencies to use it. Complaints by aid agencies (for example of looting or diversion), or complaints by local people against aid agencies (for example personally abusive behaviour or sexual harassment) have very rarely been settled in a public and impartial manner. Instead, there have been private, closed-door discussions between aid agency staff and SPLA commanders. Agencies are unwilling to insist on cases going to court: they prefer quicker and quieter procedures that will not upset their relations with the SPLA. After a raid and looting at Akot, in which Oxfam lost material, the agency tried to insist that the SPLA administrative inquiry be closed to outside observers. Meanwhile, Sudanese are also reluctant to take complaints against NGOs to court, as the same SPLM official quoted above explained, 'It is easier to let the NGO go, because people can always say that the NGO bribed the court to get an acquittal. In Akobo, some NGO was boasting that it had people in its pocket—and very cheaply, for a packet of Omo or something.' In some cases (for example a raid and looting at Labone) the SPLA has identified culprits and punished them, in other cases little or nothing has been done.

A rare, even unique case of a foreign agency resorting to the judiciary occurred with SCF in Akon. Following an incident of looting, SCF alleged that the SPLA authorities had failed to protect an agency truck and other properties that were being used for the good of the people. SRRA responded by setting up an administrative board of inquiry rather than, as SCF proposed, sending the case to court. SCF's intention was less to obtain justice than to raise public awareness in the locality of what had happened and where

---

[39] Interviewed on 22 March 1995.

329

responsibilities lay. After the SCF field officer was transferred, the case was dropped.

An opportunity for supporting an enforcement structure was provided by the formation of the Southern Sudan Law Society by a group of lawyers. This was inaugarated in February 1995, following a meeting between the founding chairman of the Society, John Luk, and John Garang. (Earlier, the SPLA had been suspicious of the Law Society, but the SPLA's own New Sudan Law Association, envisaged at the Convention, had failed to materialise.) The Law Society subsequently undertook research on traditional values in Southern Sudan and the protection of children in customary law, and held workshops to disseminate its principles. It has proposed training chiefs, magistrates and commanders in the law. The OLS Humanitarian Principles section supported some of this work, and incorporated some of the findings into the principles it adopted. But OLS still did not move towards enforcement, as explained by John Luk:

> OLS completely forgot the practical aspects of implementing humanitarian principles. The institutions that exist to implement them, such as the Law Society, they do not cater for them. The Law Society could even act as a monitor, a watchdog, and check up on abuses. OLS only makes its visits, it cannot do the job of monitoring.[40]

The SPLM Attorney General, Peter Nyot Kok, has subsequently adopted a similar programme. For example he has circulated proposals for training of legal officers. But overall, despite much talk about the importance of the judiciary, transparency and accountability, neither relief organisations nor the SPLA have made a serious effort to improve the situation. One observer noted the adverse consequences of this: 'There is an increasingly marked abuse of the property and persons of NGOs. Nothing has ever been done

---

[40] Interviewed on 11 March 1997. John Luk (who has a political career in his own right) has since been replaced as Chairman by Talar Deng.

about it. . . . They put everything under the carpet, and it gets worse and worse.[41]

Given OLS's limitations on mandate and action, the concept of humanitarian principles was innovative. Ultimately, it could deliver little, not because the principles themselves were not appropriate, but because there was no opportunity for enforcing them without taking extreme measures such as withdrawal, or engaging with the judiciary in SPLA-held areas.

THE CHURCHES

The position of the churches illustrates the complicated relationships between the SPLA, foreign institutions with a humanitarian (and in this case religious) agenda, non-SPLA Southern leaders (church-people) and popular social change among ordinary Southern Sudanese. The case of the churches is doubly interesting because some church organisations are ready to get into an uncritical relationship of solidarity with the SPLA, on the grounds that the SPLA is fighting against an Islamic government. In its enthusiasm to welcome such ardent supporters, however, the SPLA has found its cause exploited for other ends.

Christianity Invigorated

The opening-up of relief operations in 1989 brought about an important step in the life of the churches in rebel territory. The Church is a major civil institution in Southern Sudan, and its story, important in its own right, also has lessons for the wider development of civil society.[42]

In the 1980s, many in the Sudan and abroad thought that the SPLA was against the Church, because of its communist ideology and authoritarian methods. In early days, many SPLA soldiers

---

[41] Interviewed on 23 August 1995.
[42] See also: African Rights Discussion Paper No 6, 'Great Expectations: The Civil Roles of the Churches in Southern Sudan,' April 1995.

331

'smoked the Bible'—they used its pages for rolling cigarettes. The impression of hostility was intensified by the vicious treatment of Bishop Paride Taban and other members of the (Roman Catholic) Diocese of Torit, after Torit was captured in February 1989. Bishop Paride has been reluctant to speak publicly of the specific abuses that were committed, presumably in order to demonstrate Christian forgiveness and build a constructive relationship with leaders of the SPLA. Widespread and credible rumours speak of the Bishop's imprisonment and public humiliation, the rape of nuns, and looting of Diocese property.

Despite this history, on 17 January 1990, SPLA Radio announced the formation of the New Sudan Council of Churches (NSCC), with Bishop Paride as its head.[43] This has been viewed as the point at which the SPLA gave Christians official sanction, and freedom to operate. A better way of seeing it is as a new mutual accommodation between the institutional church, and the SPLA. Relief was central in this.

Christianity had not in fact been generally suppressed before 1990, though few clergy chose to work behind SPLA lines. Usually they were free to evangelise, construct church buildings and hold services, though this freedom was partly dependent on the personal attitudes of local army officers. But the circumstances had given the local Christians few opportunities to communicate with their parent churches in government-held areas of Sudan or abroad. They lacked external support, and this limited their work in some respects. But the enforced isolation and poverty probably helped them to win the adherence of ordinary people. It meant that evangelists were less tightly bound to the doctrinal interpretations of their superiors in the church hierarchy. It allowed their teaching to focus on a message of salvation geared to the war situation. It reduced the widespread impression that Christianity essentially belonged to—and was controlled by—educated people in towns and foreign countries. Church membership grew rapidly during this period.

---

[43] Like the Sudan Council of Churches, based in Khartoum, NSCC includes the Roman Catholic Church in addition to several Protestant denominations.

The war period has seen an extraordinary growth in Christianity in Southern Sudan. In 1982 in Bor diocese there were just eighteen small Anglican churches; by 1991 there were 120 with 73 ordained clergy. Mass baptisms and confirmations are the norm: Bishop Nathaniel Garang confirmed 10,000 at Kakuma refugee camp in Kenya in July 1993.[44] Some evangelical groups claim that Southern Sudan is now eighty per cent Christian, representing the fastest-growing Church in the world.[45] Many Southern Sudanese see Christianity as a bulwark against 'the Arabs' and also against some of the supposed shortcomings of traditional culture. Some Biblical passages provide apparent explanations for the woes of the country, others express the longing for peace.

Some of the most spectacular areas of church growth have been where local Protestant pastors have dynamically interpreted church teachings to fit in with local needs. For example Archdeacon Abraham Mayom claimed to have 594 churches by March 1995. He was explicit about how he needed to accommodate Christianity to existing cultural practices:

> There are many changes [to Christianity]. Because when you start to bring the new ideas to the old ideas which were in those societies, you have to start with their own previous society, previous belief. You start there in order to change. You cannot just start in the air. Or you cannot start behind the fence. You come inside the fence and then you change slowly by slowly.[46]

Other churches, notably the Roman Catholics, have been more insistent on maintaining their standards for baptism, but have also succeeded in gaining many new converts.

This apparent success may nevertheless have rested partly on the historical association of Christianity with prosperity and self-advancement. Many Southern Sudanese churchmen affirm that the

---

[44] Figures from: Marc Nikkel, 'Dinka Christianity,' unpublished PhD thesis, University of Edinburgh, 1994.
[45] Peter Hammond, *Faith under Fire in Sudan*, Newlands, South Africa, Frontline Fellowship, 1996, p. 7.
[46] Interviewed on 26 December 1994.

message of salvation cannot be heard indefinitely without material signs of help. Providing education and food relief have become increasingly central to the work of the churches. As one catechist put it succinctly: 'The control of persons without food is too difficult.'[47]

When OLS began bringing relief into Southern Sudan, a joint church committee in Itang refugee camp likewise decided to attempt to serve its people, by appealing for supplies from church-oriented donors in Addis Ababa. It gained some items, but also attracted complaints that it could not account for them. The donors wanted to deal with a legally-constituted relief organisation. In order to form one, the committee members needed to gain a mandate from the leader of the SPLA. John Garang was more than sympathetic. The SPLA's new control of border regions, together with the coming and going of relief agencies, meant that the Christians would in any case make firmer contacts with their partners abroad. Any blatant attempt to control this would have been bad for external relations; it would have diminished the SPLA's attempt to appear liberal in contrast to the newly-installed Islamic extremist regime in Khartoum. But rather than leaving freedom to the churches, Garang was now able actively to encourage their development in a particular way. He arranged for the two bishops in rebel areas to be called to meet one another and form the NSCC. In the public announcement, NSCC was described by the spokesman of the SPLA as 'a spiritual wing of the Movement',[48] suggesting a concern to ensure that churches did not become centres for political dissent.

From the beginning, the 'spiritual wing' was seen very much as a means of obtaining material assistance. NSCC began with a strong relief agenda, which reduced the possible function of the churches as channels through which people could voice their complaints to the secular authorities. It revived the role that they had been given under the British colonialists in Southern Sudan, of taking much of the

---

[47] Interviewed on 2 January 1995.
[48] The phrase invites comparison with the SRRA which came to be known as the 'humanitarian wing of the Movement'. Like NSCC, SRRA began as an independent committee of refugees in Itang, though it was soon incorporated into the command system of the SPLA.

government's responsibility for the provision of social services. Demands which might have been directed to the secular authorities were placed upon the clergy instead, who passed them on to their international donor organisations. This was an acceptable arrangement to the local and foreign Christians, since it seemed to be in accordance with Christ's practice of serving the poor, and at the same time created work which afforded incentives, salaries and other benefits. (A similar trade-off between aid activity and political activism seems to exist among the churches in government-held areas.)

The pressure to provide relief often came from rebel officials themselves. The Church internationally was known to be able to mobilise many resources and allocate them with greater flexibility than official aid channels such as the UN or ICRC. Such relief would not be dependent on the continuance of OLS; and monitoring by foreigners would be less rigorous. Through persuasion of Sudanese church personnel, the SPLA could expect to gain control of a fair proportion of the supplies.

By 1991, when church donations began arriving in significant quantities, the agreement in a number of places was that eighty per cent of the food would be handed over to the SRRA, and the remainder kept by the local church for its own use. Some representatives of the donors failed to see an acceptable rationale for such a deal. They had hoped that the Sudanese church people would work together with the secular authorities in administering relief according to common criteria of basic human need, acting as checks on each other. The Sudanese, in defence of the idea of dividing supplies, sometimes argued that the church was especially suited to serving categories of needy people that might otherwise fall through the relief net, such as orphans and recently-arrived displaced people. But two crucial factors were, first, that the local churches themselves (particularly the Protestants) wanted income to sustain the running of their organisations; and, second, that the secular authorities disliked the prospect of interference from the clergy and their foreign partners in the handling the goods. So it was hard for the churchpeople (in whose names relief was consigned) to report to their donors, either on the supplies that they had turned over to the SRRA, or on those that they had administered themselves.

Where the local church did try to keep control of aid goods, it could run into problems. Its freedom of action and property rights were only provisional. In 1992, during the crisis when the Government recaptured Torit and Kapoeta, the SPLA confiscated a lot of equipment and supplies belonging to the Diocese of Torit, and again imprisoned and abused Bishop Paride Taban and several of his staff. The bishop was accused of diverting or hoarding relief funds that should have served the people of Bor area. The SPLA commander seems to have taken this action on the basis of a mere rumour that the Bishop Paride had received five million Deutschmarks raised by a German television appeal. The bishop was later released, but the SPLA made no public apology.

This incident is an illustration of the perilous situation the churches were entering as they began to handle large consignments of relief, in the context of the desperate poverty of Southern Sudan and the Movement's unending need for resources.

NSCC: A Council of Churches or an Aid Agency?

The New Sudan Council of Churches (NSCC) has a unique role in Southern Sudanese civil society. A Council of Churches is ideally a focal point for moral and spiritual reflection and comment on society; particularly for providing a voice on behalf of the weakest. As discussed, the demand for material relief distracted NSCC from this role in 1989-92. At that time there were no secular SINGOs. But after 1993, indigenous aid organisations were allowed as a general principle, there was an opportunity for NSCC to offload its aid activities to other agencies. In fact it has begun to do so, but the process is slow and painful, and in many respects NSCC still functions as a SINGO.

Why has progress been so slow? There are many reasons, but the main one is that valuable facilities and supplies can be obtained by churches and church people if they present themselves as humanitarian aid agencies and aid workers. These benefits are in two main areas: resources from church-related humanitarian donor organisations; and access to OLS facilities, especially flights in and out of Sudan.

NSCC's constitution is more suited to a Council than an NGO. Instead of a board of governors, it has an Executive Committee. This is made up of the representatives of the various member churches, many of whom urgently want material assistance for their regions and denominations. In formal terms, they have power and ownership of NSCC, but practically they are removed from managerial responsibility, which is delegated to an Executive Secretary. Great pressure has come the Executive Secretary to run the Secretariat in such a way as to satisfy those various needs. This has not always been possible. The Executive Secretary has to meet donor requirements, and manage the workings of a complicated organisation, which are sometimes ill-understood by members of the Executive Committee.

In 1995 a financial crisis emerged, largely as a result of these conflicting pressures. Under the pressure of demands for different kinds of help to the member churches, the Executive Secretary had expanded the secretariat without getting a strong enough foundation of administrative funding (always a problem for NGOs). Other project funds had apparently been diverted in order to pay for it. NSCC then went through more than a year of review and restructuring, with a new Executive Secretary. Donors demanded a review process, as they were being asked to write off old grants, or find extra money.

A decision was then made to cut NSCC's relief activity. Much of this burden was transferred to an international church-related agency called CEAS (Church Ecumenical Action in Sudan, the successor to SEOC, which had been dismantled after an unfavourable review process), which was to work more closely with NSCC. However, NSCC remained involved in service-delivery, in fields like health-care and education. There is still a demand for it to retain its identity as a humanitarian NGO with a wide range of activities. As such, NSCC is a member of OLS, and as a member it can nominate individuals to travel on OLS flights in and out of Sudan. That facility has led to serious disputes between NSCC and the OLS co-ordination office. The latter complains that many church-people have been travelling for purposes that do not count as 'humanitarian'. Some of the clergy would like to say that all church work is humanitarian; people need assistance that is spiritual as well as material. OLS has resisted this argument; opening the door to spiritual ministry would pose great problems to the system of international humanitarianism in general. In Sudan the question is particularly sensitive because of the parallel claims of Islamic agencies. So OLS insisted on screening a list of people eligible to fly in the name of NSCC, month by month, though in practice it is hard to tell whether the journeys have a strictly humanitarian purpose or not. The process results in delays and restrictions that may be hard to predict. It reduces NSCC's ability to work efficiently, either as a Council or an NGO.

Another source of pressure on the NSCC arises from the fact that it is mandated to work anywhere in SPLA-controlled territory, whether or not OLS is present. The NSCC is active in the SPLA-held areas of the Nuba Mountains, for example, and by implication also has the ability to work in SPLA-held parts of Southern Blue Nile. In neither of these regions has SRRA been effective. The NSCC is anxious to serve its churches and their congregations in these areas. The SPLA, which is searching for alternatives to OLS, is also eager to see the NSCC co-operate with providing assistance to these areas .

Leading members of the Southern Sudanese churches have recognised the high and sometimes contradictory expectations upon the NSCC and its member churches. It is expected to provide relief and undertake human rights advocacy and peacemaking in addition to caring for its pastors and congregations. As its experience with these wider civil roles increases, the NSCC is increasingly attracted to a smaller, more focused role as a council for the churches only. Whether or not it can achieve this, given the formidable pressures it is under, is a challenge for the church leadership.

Militant Christian Agendas

The SPLA needed international friends who would respond to its overall agenda rather than just meeting some of its specific needs. Its first such friend was NPA, which played a key role in the pioneering early days. But most foreign aid agencies ended up playing a role of neutral service provision. While some also provided technical assistance to the SRRA and lobbied for greater western attention to Sudan, and some individual agency workers became personally committed to Southern Sudan, none of these agencies provided help on terms immediately attractive to the SPLA.

In the 1990s, some militant Christian organisations have jumped into this vacuum. Among them are Christian Solidarity International (CSI) and the South-African based Frontline Fellowship. The mutual enthusiasm between the SPLA and these organisations masks the extent to which Christian fundamentalists are attempting to use Southern Sudan for their own purposes, and once again the SPLA has failed to set the political and social agenda.

To some extent, fundamentalist Christians are the mirror-image of the NIF's *jihad*. Frontline Fellowship's newsletter has run an article 'The Challenge of the Crusaders'. Adorned by a romantic engraving of Richard Lionheart, it disclaims outright endorsement of Holy War, but argues, 'Yet there is much we can learn from the faith that inspired these epic undertakings. . . .'[49] Frontline Fellowship describes the SPLA as 'the Christian forces' and the Sudan army as 'the Muslim army.'[50] It has provided a chaplaincy service to the SPLA, under the heading 'Soldiers for Christ'.[51]

Some of the militaristic passages from the Old Testament resonate in Southern Sudan, as explained by one Dinka pastor:

> The verses which talk about God's action [i.e. Biblical accounts of God's judgement against oppressors] are really working. [But] I believe that the verses that speak about reconciliation are not active at the present time.[52]

CSI is less extremist, and stresses its sympathy for the Northern parties in the NDA (in particular it has lauded Mubarak el Fadl). It

---

[49] *Frontline Fellowship News*, issue 1, 1995, p. 5.
[50] Peter Hammond, *Faith under Fire in Sudan*, Newlands, South Africa, Frontline Fellowship, 1996, p. 51.
[51] *Ibid*. p. 109.
[52] Quoted in Nikkel, 1994, p. 266.

has been particularly active in providing a platform for international lobby and advocacy, untiringly drawing attention to the crimes of the Sudan Government and the suffering of the Sudanese people. (The material aid that it has given has been rather more modest.) This has been much appreciated by many Southerners, who feel that the depth of their misery and the basic justice of their cause require strident advocacy, and that the Christian West has not been as committed to their cause as the Moslem world has supposedly been to the NIF. A civil official in Bahr el Ghazal said:

> Christianity is needed to stand firm against encroaching civilisations. We need a Christian Fundamentalism. There is an intrinsic feeling that there is something other than Islam.[53]

The activities of the Christian extremists is not, however, a true counterpart to the NIF's Comprehensive Call. While often extremist, it is not based on an all-encompassing practical social philosophy. Reactive propaganda dominates.

Exploiting Slavery

The way in which militant Christian organisations have dealt with the issue of slavery illustrates the problem of how foreign agencies set a partial, incomplete agenda, which is uncritically welcomed by the SPLA, even though it means making the SPLA's own political interests hostage to an issue controlled by outside groups. Sadly for both the slaves and the SPLA, emotive propaganda has dominated, marginalising the search for practical solutions to the crime of enslavement.

In the late 1980s, the Baggara *murahaliin* militia seized thousands of Dinka women and children in northern Bahr el Ghazal as hostages, forced labourers and slaves. This practice was documented by two lecturers at the University of Khartoum, Ushari

---

[53] Quoted in African Rights, 'Great Expectations?', 1995, p. 39.

Mahmoud and Suleiman Baldo,[54] and was taken up by Sudanese newspapers.[55] At one point the Sudan Government agreed to an international inquiry by the Anti-Slavery Society.[56] The UN Human Rights Commission also documented cases.[57] The government of Sadiq el Mahdi, and in particularly a group of Umma Party politicians behind the militia strategy, bore ultimate responsibility for these practices. Although perhaps 10,000 slaves were taken during this period (all figures are highly speculative), the violation gained little attention outside Sudan except in some specialist human rights circles.

Under the NIF government, militia raiding and slaving has continued at a lower level. There were documented instances of large-scale kidnapping in 1995 and 1996. Comparisons with U.S. plantation slavery are misleading: most of those taken can be described as 'smallholder slaves', held in ones and twos by small farmers and herders in the Baggara belt. They are grievously exploited and abused; girls and women are routinely raped, and punishments for attempted escape include mutilation. There are isolated cases of branding and some documented instances of

---

[54] Ushari Mahmoud and Suleiman Baldo, 'El Diein Massacre and Slavery in the Sudan,' pamphlet, 1987.

[55] E.g. 'Escaped Slave Girl Arrives in Khartoum to tell her Story,' *Sudan Times*, 10 September 1987; and other articles on: 20 September 1987, 21 January 1988, 18 February 1988, 9 May 1988, 9 October 1988, and 30 April 1989. Also see, Alan Whittaker, 'Slavery in Sudan,' *The Reporter* (Anti-Slavery Society), 1988, 13.4, pp. 64-71 and Tony Horwitz, 'Dinka Tribes made Slaves in Sudan's Civil War,' *Wall Street Journal*, 11 April 1989.

[56] The oldest human rights organisation in the world, founded in the 1830s, and now known as Anti-Slavery International. The inquiry was aborted by the June 1989 coup d'etat.

[57] E.g., United Nations, 'Human Rights Questions: Human Rights Situations and Reports of Special Rapporteurs and Representatives: Situation of Human Rights in the Sudan,' 16 October 1995, paras. 27-31; United Nations, Commission on Human Rights, 'Situation of Human Rights in The Sudan,' 20 February 1996, paras. 33-40.

341

exchange for money. No cases of chaining have been reliably documented; neither have cases of export been proven.

Many slaves have been released through the intervention of relatives (on payment of a fee of between LS 8,000-13,000, equivalent to US$1-4[58]) or through inter-tribal negotiations. In late 1995, 674 were returned to their families after a Rizeigat-Dinka conference, as part of a general agreement over limiting hostilities and providing access to grazing lands: modest payments were made for expenses for the children's travel. These transactions do not indicate a market in slaves, but neither can the practice be explained as simply 'traditional' inter-tribal raiding and hostage-taking. In 1996, two *Baltimore Sun* journalists, Gilbert Lewthwaite and Gregory Kane, with great publicity, paid $500 each to 'buy back slaves' in the SPLA-controlled market of Manyiel. Not only were they paying well over the odds (with all the dangers that entails); they were almost certainly paying a middleman in a hostage redemption exercise. The middleman had brought the children back to where their families lived, and the SPLA would not have tolerated slave traders or a slave market on its territory.

Slavery is a grotesque abuse: there is no doubt about it. It is also clear that successive governments have turned a blind eye to the excesses of the militia, and that some soldiers have themselves encouraged the practice or even participated. The NIF government knew about the practice (General Omer al Bashir was stationed in el Muglad, a centre of the Misiriya *Murahaliin*, in 1988-9) and took no action to suppress it. Some individual magistrates and tribal leaders in Kordofan and Darfur have co-operated with the families of slaves in obtaining their release. But systematic attempts to release slaves and captives have not been supported by central government. The reason for this is undoubtedly that the government continues to rely on the military forces of the *Murahaliin*—thereby giving indirect but strong support to the institution of slavery. But, compared to many of the other instances of human rights abuse, slavery is neither the largest cause of human suffering, nor it integral to central government policy.

---

[58] Individual payments of up to LS 50,000 have also been reported.

342

Yet slavery has been catapulted to a dominant position in the international agenda of the SPLA and some fundamentalist groups: it has been elevated to a central plank—perhaps the central element—of government policy. Frontline Fellowship claims, 'Tens of thousands of Sudanese Christian men, women and children have been kidnapped and sold as slaves by government soldiers.'[59] CSI claims that 'Government troops and Government-backed Arab militias regularly raid black African communities for slaves and other forms of booty.'[60] The organisation repeatedly uses the term 'slave raids,'[61] implying that taking captives is the aim of government policy and that all captives are automatically slaves. On a visit to the U.S., John Garang made a very similar statement:

> The present fundamentalist Islamic regime in Khartoum is resorting to slavery as part of its declared policy of destroying the African/non-Moslem dimensions of the Sudanese identity. The slave raids into northern Bahr el Ghazal and the Nuba Mountains are being conducted by the Government army and its several paramilitary auxiliary organs. Men and old women are killed. More than one million civilians have been killed in this way in the last ten years. Boys, girls and young women are transported in chains to the North for sale. . . .
> We know of several hundred slaves who have been exported to other countries.[62]

Undoubtedly Dr Garang knew better, but he also knew what his audiences wanted to hear.

The reasons for the hyping of the slavery issue are not difficult to identify. Slavery has deep resonance in the U.S. After Louis Farrakhan, leader of the Nation of Islam, visited Sudan and denounced stories of slavery, Farrakhan's many American critics

---

[59] 'Slave Raiders Return,' *Frontline Fellowship News*, issue 3, 1996, p. 7.
[60] Christian Solidarity International (The Baroness Cox and John Eibner), 'Evidence on Violations of Human Rights in Sudan,' submission to the U.N. Human Rights Commission, Geneva, April 1996, p. 9.
[61] *Ibid*, p. 2.
[62] Statement by the SPLA Leader on Slavery in Sudan, *Sudan Democratic Gazette*, August 1996, p. 3.

were eager to demonstrate just how wrong he was, in a way that would do the most damage to his credentials among African-Americans. Slavery therefore became the locus of a proxy war between political opponents in the U.S. In Sudan, slavery has equally deep historical resonances, and speaking of contemporary slavery is a way of consolidating Southerners' demand for separation from the North. One Southerner commented: 'How can we be in one country when some citizens are buying and selling other citizens?'[63] Slavery has become a shorthand for the South-North problem; a caricature with enough truth to be powerful.

But making the Southern Sudanese problem hostage to this single issue is dangerous for the SPLA. If some of the exaggerated allegations over slavery are disproved, it can only embarrass the Movement. The pro-government Sudan Foundation has recently published an attack on CSI for exaggerating the extent of slavery.[64] It uses the familiar propaganda trick of arguing from a valid premise—that CSI's evidence does not support its claims—to a false conclusion, namely that the Sudan Government is innocent, there is no slavery at all (and that the government is working hard to free slaves), and that it is all a U.S. plot, etc.

The Sudan Foundation's line is easily disproved and discredited. More seriously, slavery obscures a range of other, trickier social and political issues which the Movement needs to address: it is a stick for beating the Sudan Government, not a basis for developing a 'New Sudan'. Critics fear that the slavery issue may be an instance in which the SPLA has reacted to others rather than setting the agenda itself.

STRAINS IN THE REBEL-HUMANITARIAN COALITION

By the mid-1990s, it appeared that the international humanitarians and the SPLA had converged on a set of common principles. They

---

[63] Interviewed in March 1997.
[64] David Hoile, 'Sudan, Propaganda and Distortion: Allegations of Slavery and Slavery-related Practices,' The Sudan Foundation, London, March 1997. Hoile was formerly a outspoken advocate for RENAMO.

used much the same language to describe the needs and aspirations of the people of Southern Sudan, and the oppression of Khartoum. But fundamental points of tension still existed. The relief agencies were concerned, above all, with their own programmes, and continued to distrust the SPLA. The SPLA had deep suspicions about the relief agencies. It came to believe that the continuation of OLS was preventing the emergence of a solidarity-based relief programme. But in practice it had yet to develop this alternative model for relief.

In 1995, there was a significant change in posture by some leading donors. The approach taken by USAID altered following the departure of Gordon Wagner, who had taken an assertive role in formulating an assertive humanitarian policy based on many years' close involvement with Southern Sudan. Around the same time, OLS-Southern Sector became markedly less willing to confront the Sudan Government over restrictions on humanitarian access. In 1996, NPA also backed off from its close engagement with the SPLA, following the removal of Helge Rohn from its Southern Sudan programme. The ensuing, more timid international approach discouraged the SPLA and SRRA and pushed them to be more assertive.

The fragility of the rebel-humanitarian coalition was starkly exposed by one episode that could have helped to restore if not cement it: the official OLS Review. The Review was started just as the SPLA and SRRA were gaining in confidence in their critiques of OLS. At the September 1995 humanitarian conference, the SPLA and SRRA passed a special resolution on OLS. Having recognised that 'OLS has facilitated some useful work for the people of New Sudan' and the constraints on the operation, it concluded:

- At times, OLS operations have worked against the aspirations of the SPLM/SPLA and the people of New Sudan, and
- The constraints and the counter-productive aspects of OLS operations threaten to wreck OLS altogether.[65]

---

[65] SPLM/SPLA humanitarian conference, draft report, Special Resolution A, September 1995.

The OLS Review team largely concurred with these criticisms. Their report was completed in July 1996 and discussed with the SPLA and SRRA the following October.[66] The Review Team created an unprecedented opening for the SPLA and SRRA to turn the international relief effort to their advantage. Many of the criticisms of OLS made by the SRRA and other Southerners over the years were present in the Review, while major criticisms of the SPLA and SRRA were notable by their absence. It echoed, for example, many of the points detailed by the SRRA Secretary General a few months earlier.[67] The SPLA and SRRA could have pressed for a unified programme based on impartiality between the needs of civilians in government- and SPLA-held areas, and the application of 'humanitarian principles' to the Northern Sector. The government would have been in a weak position to resist: its only strategy would have been to challenge OLS itself.

Instead, the SPLA appeared disappointed that the Review team did not propose closing down OLS altogether and replacing it with a programme based on direct cross-border supply to the SRRA. The *SPLM/SPLA Update* wrote:

> It is time for the donors to decide whether to continue giving their money to OLS, which will be part of the NIF war effort, or to seek better and efficient ways to reach the Sudanese people.
>
> It is time for the SPLM and its humanitarian arm, the SRRA, to provide an alternative modality while the OLS is being suffocated from Khartoum. The SRRA may have to shift its priority to encouraging, organizing and facilitating humanitarian assistance outside OLS, away from restrictions, denial of access and extravagant waste of resources in UN paradise-camps like Loki where Lords of Poverty dwell.

---

[66] Ataul Karim, Mark Duffield *et al., OLS: Operation Lifeline Sudan: A Review*, University of Birmingham, July 1996.
[67] Mario Muor Muor, 'SRRA Position Paper on Operation Lifeline Sudan (OLS) Southern Sector,' SRRA, 27 November 1995.

The OLS must extricate itself from the control and dictates of the GOS both in the northern and Southern sectors if it has to continue else it may be better to leave the Sudanese alone.

Lastly, time has come for the review team to stop the OLS from claiming credits for achievements made by the Sudanese people. We need only friends but not masters. No more 'civilization missions.' We are not here for recolonization.[68]

Remarkably, it appeared that the SPLA itself was advocating closing the programme. The Sudan Government, which was facing serious potential embarrassment in the Review, was saved. The SPLA agenda for closing OLS was presumably based on the calculation that it would receive more resources through a cross-border operation. There is no strong evidence to support this. Probably Dr John Garang misread the intentions and capacity of the U.S. Government, believing that the bill approved by the U.S. Congress authorising developmental assistance to SPLA-held areas of Sudan (i.e. waiving the general ban on such aid) indicated a U.S. readiness to mount a major cross-border operation. It did not: the bill was a largely symbolic act; any developmental assistance provided by USAID would have been subject to tedious and slow assessment procedures, the bill was some months away from becoming law, and whatever the intentions of the Congress, it is the State Department (which remains cautious about SPLA capacity[69]) that would make major executive decisions.

Echoing the SPLA editorial, *Sudan Democratic Gazette* ran an outspoken attack on the *OLS Review*, in which it called on the UN to protect the rights of Sudanese citizens against the Sudan Government as (it claimed) the UN had done in Rwanda and Bosnia.[70] The reality of UN actions in these countries has been rather

---

[68] 'Operation Lifeline: Sudan at the Crossroads,' Editorial, *SPLM/SPLA Update*, vol. v/96, issue 15, p. 2.

[69] See. e.g. 'Washington dismisses any attack on Juba,' in 'Garang Announces the Capture of Five Garrisons in Southern Sudan,' *al Hayat*, 12 March 1997, p. 6.

[70] 'Beneficiaries Ignored: What does the OLS Review Team's report contain?' *Sudan Democratic Gazette*, October 1996, p. 6.

different, and the *Sudan Democratic Gazette* seems to have difficulty distinguishing allies from enemies.

If the SPLA agenda was indeed to close down OLS, it would have been more astute to have professed its loyalty to OLS while pressing for the reforms that might have provoked the Sudan Government to close it down. As it was, the SPLA received opprobrium for its hostility to OLS, while in fact it helped the programme continue largely unchanged. The SPLA-SRRA strategy was not well-prepared. Its criticisms appeared as ill-informed, gratuitously aggressive and marked by a lack of constructive alternatives. It squandered the best-ever opportunity for reforming humanitarian assistance to Southern Sudan. The Sudan Government was the principal beneficiary.

IMPLICATIONS: MANAGING FAMINE

Despite its regular hiccups, personal animosities and intermittent infighting, an effective coalition between the SPLA and international humanitarians has emerged, centered on the continuing supply of foreign assistance to SPLA-held Southern Sudan. Its foundation is joint opposition to NIF obstruction of humanitarian access. The Sudan Government will not be able to close down OLS without provoking a strong hostile reaction from this coalition, which would probably set up an alternative relief operation, albeit a smaller one, to service SPLA-held areas. Should the war come to an end, this coalition will be weakened, but some elements will continue and provide some form of international guarantee for the viability of an SPLA-dominated government of Southern Sudan.

But this pro-relief coalition is not the same thing as an anti-famine coalition. It certainly has some elements in common, and the commitment on both sides to relief provision and humanitarian principles means that it is very unlikely that a famine could occur without attracting attention and relief. Assistance is provided and some excesses of human suffering are avoided. But the coalition has the effect of entrenching SPLA power, and that power is currently authoritarian and exercised without the constraints of a civil administration or strong independent civil organisations. Perhaps even more importantly, in Southern Sudan, the issue of famine has become the property of a range of specialised institutions, most of them foreign. If a preventable famine occurs, it will be blamed on technical failings by these institutions, rather than the failings of a political leadership. The coalition is a means for managing human suffering, not preventing it.

13.

CONCLUSIONS

CHALLENGING CHARITY

For most programmes, little is known of programme delivery, let alone impact.

OLS Review[1]

DOES RELIEF WORK?

Nobody knows what the human impact of OLS and other humanitarian programmes in Sudan has been. It is remarkably difficult to find out. No relief programme has included a routine measure of mortality levels. Most of the numbers produced for people 'in need' or those 'reached' are difficult to justify. Some mortality surveys were undertaken in the aftermath of the 1984-5 famine (see chapter 3), but since then the quality of data has deteriorated.

It is notable that the 1996 OLS Review was not given the task of assessing lives lost and saved.

> [T]he team will not be expected to undertake a detailed analysis of the impact of OLS programmes, but rather to review the effectiveness of the *modus operandi* in meeting the needs of war-affected civilians.[2]

---

[1] Ataul Karim, Mark Duffield *et al. OLS: Operation Lifeline: A Review*, University of Birmingham, July 1996, p. 153

[2] Department of Humanitarian Affairs, 'Terms of Reference for an Operation Lifeline Sudan (OLS) Review,' 18 August 1995, cited in *OLS Review*.

Hence, rather than assessing impact, the Review was instructed to concentrate on the internal logic of the operation. With a handful of exceptions, the same holds true for other assessments of relief activities in Sudan. *Access* is the simplest and most elementary proxy that is measured in place of impact.

. This helps to explain why nobody has seriously attempted to prove that OLS has been of net benefit. The impossibility of making a clear case may also explain why OLS has not even been consistent in collecting and analysing the most basic and measurable types of data. There is a remarkable lack of transparency in how the figures are generated. The *OLS Review* concluded that information management within OLS on the whole had been inadequate, so that when UNICEF or other agencies have done useful research, the results tend to be forgotten, lost or ignored.[3]

The same difficulties of assessing impact hold for parallel relief operations. Among the most important are the ICRC relief programme, the Lutheran World Federation/Sudan Emergency Operations Consortium (LWF/SEOC) airlift, and the Combined Agencies Relief Team (CART) in Juba and its environs. The culture of discretion and confidentiality within ICRC makes its programmes singularly difficult to evaluate: they have not been discussed here. After six years of operations, the LWF/SEOC operations (to Juba and elsewhere in the South) were independently reviewed in 1994-5.[4] The review failed to find identifiable benefits from the expenditure of $40 million, as a result of which the consortium was radically changed. Ten years after its formation, CART has not had a thorough independent review—the closest is a desk study conducted in 1992,[5] as the prelude to a field-based main evaluation that was in the event never carried out.

---

[3] *OLS Review,* pp. 221-234

[4] Mark Duffield, Helen Young, John Ryle and Ian Henderson, *Sudan Emergency Operations Consortium (SEOC): A Review,* University of Birmingham, February 1995.

[5] Richard Graham and John Borton, 'A Preliminary Review of the Combined Agencies Relief Team (CART), Juba 1986-91,' London, Overseas Development Institute, March 1992.

These are the better examples. Most relief programmes have never been systematically assessed at all. While some international NGOs carry out internal evaluations (some of which are fairly critical), independent assessments are notably absent.

So, nobody can say, or even forward a realistic guess, how many people have died from famine in Sudan. In 1989 the UN publicly used a figure of 250,000 dead in Southern Sudan, without making it clear which period this referred to, and with the implicit claim that OLS was preventing a similar scale of disaster. This was a shot in the dark. Systematic attempts to calculate mortality levels have been hampered by the very poor quality—or complete absence—of primary data. No matter how good the theoretical model applied, the result is largely guesswork.[6]

This is extraordinary. Relief operations have consumed billions of dollars. All are justified on the grounds that they are saving the lives of ordinary Sudanese people, especially women and children. But they cannot produce systematic evidence that they have succeeded. Relief programmes rest on the logic that by delivering essential supplies to needy areas, and in isolated cases observing a measurable increase in (for example) child nutrition, that they must be doing good. To some extent, this logic holds. Almost for sure, relief programmes have saved some lives and sustained some livelihoods, but on what scale, nobody knows.

What does this extraordinary failure of information mean? It indicates a basic failure of concern for human impact. For all the major relief institutions, other considerations seem to be more important.

HUMANITARIANISM AND ACCOUNTABILITY

Taking a cold, objective look at the effectiveness of humanitarian programmes in Sudan is not an encouraging experience. At a purely technical level, the failures are often shocking enough. Looking at

---

[6] See, e.g., Millard Burr, 'Quantifying Genocide in the Southern Sudan 1983-1993,' Washington D.C., U.S. Committee for Refugees, 1993.

the wider social and political impact of aid leads to a persistent worry: perhaps relief assistance has done more harm than good. Humanitarian aid may be motivated by sympathy and altruism, but it is hard to escape the conclusion that these noble motives are often wasted.

Calling Agencies to Account

The 1990s have seen growing pressure for humanitarian institutions to become more accountable. There has been a succession of reviews of major operations, growing in independence and criticism. The taboo of criticising NGOs was broken in a major way in Rwanda in 1994. The Joint Evaluation of Emergency Operations in Rwanda, commissioned by the Danish Government under the auspices of the OECD[7], went a step further than any previous review. It had a higher profile and was more authoritative, and had one volume dealing with specifically political matters. The volume on emergency relief concentrated on technical and professional shortcomings in the relief operations and was uniquely frank about their extent. The Joint Evaluation team was disturbed by the inflated claims of success made by NGOs, and 'came across examples of agencies telling, if not falsehoods, then certainly half-truths.'[8] It also noted 'a remarkable lack of attempts by agencies to seek the views of beneficiaries on the assistance being provided.'[9] Comparable criticisms were made of the UN, notably its lack of preparedness both for the genocide and the enormous flow of refugees, migrants and fugitives to Goma in Zaire. The UN unconvincingly disputed some of the team's findings.

Pointing out shortcomings is one thing: enforcing change is another. Just a few months after the Joint Evaluation of Emergency Operations in Rwanda, many very similar errors were committed in

---

[7] Joint Evaluation of Emergency Assistance to Rwanda, *The International Response to Conflict and Genocide: Lessons from the Rwanda Experience, Vol. 3, Humanitarian Aid and Effects*, Copenhagen, March 1996.
[8] *Ibid*, pp. 152-4.
[9] *Ibid.*

response to the emergency in eastern Zaire. Toughening up the evaluation process is necessary. One option is an international emergencies commissioner, who would have quasi-judicial powers within the UN-donor system, to investigate humanitarian operations and expose their successes and failures.

The OLS Review is part of the same pressure for accountability. Its conclusions were tough on the Sudan Government and some UN agencies (notably UNDP). In this case, enforcement was hampered by the fact that the main potential beneficiary of the Review, the SPLA-SRRA, chose to attack the review process as a sham. As a result, the Sudan Government strategy of a low-key response paid off handsomely, as operations have continued much as before. Meanwhile, internal discussions continue in the UN and between UN agencies and donors.

Although the *OLS Review* is a public document, the review process has been controlled by governments and the UN, and therefore has remained hostage to their interests. Something more radical is needed: a more public and democratic process that involves a much wider section of Sudanese people.

Calling Donors to Account

Donor governments bear great responsibility for what has happened in Sudan. Many of them have short memories, and regard, for example, the over-generous and uncritical U.S. assistance to President Nimeiri as history, no longer of current relevance.

Western government's strategic and commercial interest in Sudan is now very slender. The prominence of humanitarian assistance in their involvement is a manifestation of this: it is the minimum they are ready to do. Lacking a clear political agenda of their own, donors should be able to adopt policies that will allow the Sudanese people to find peaceful and democratic solutions to their problems. This has not happened: instead, the western agenda has largely been driven by humanitarian agencies, which have their own priorities and institutional interests. As this book has documented, this agenda has readily been manipulated and co-opted by the Sudan Government. Donors bear a responsibility for this.

354

Accountability for Famine Crimes

Sudan has its share of war criminals: individuals responsible for gross violations of the Geneva Conventions and other crimes against humanity. A string of human rights publications has documented these violations, though rarely have the perpetrators been identified by name. The issue of accountability for war crimes is currently not on the political agenda in Sudan. There are several reasons for this, including the culpability of members of previous governments, now in opposition, and the culpability of members of the SPLA. As with the 1972 Addis Ababa Agreement, the belligerents anticipate that a post-war settlement will involve 'reconciliation', taken to include an amnesty for abuses committed during the war. This assumption is deeply problematic. Impunity for those primarily responsible for gross crimes against humanity can only encourage future perpetrators to believe they can do the same thing.

There are clear legal, moral and political arguments for calling war criminals to account. This includes those who have inflicted famine. The Geneva Conventions prohibit the infliction of starvation as an instrument of war.

The political logic of famine prevention is based on deterrence: those who create famine or permit it to happen will pay the price. This same logic applies *a fortiori* to famine crimes committed in wartime. The prosecution of war and famine criminals should prove a deterrent to further such crimes, if not immediately then further into the future.

BUILDING AN ANTI-FAMINE POLITICS

Famine will not be the central political issue in Sudan. Peace, self-determination, economic disarray and the constitutional place of Islam are some of the problems that will preoccupy Sudanese democrats, should they assume power, (assuming they are not wholly preoccupied with competition for office). But famine prevention should be elevated to be one of the central political issues.

Famine-vulnerable people themselves are a large but marginalised constituency. Most of them live in Sudan's peripheries and have historically been neglected by the ruling parties. As the NIF has recognised, food and other forms of assistance (notably micro-credit) can be a means of mobilising poor people. Democrats should recognise this opportunity too: there can be a progressive politics of food.

An anti-famine politics in Sudan needs international allies. For the most part, international relief institutions have been wedded to ideas of political neutrality and technical proficiency, which have obscured the political nature of famine and famine prevention. There are exceptions, and there is a challenge for such international organisations to join a democratic Sudanese anti-famine politics.

Tackling Causes

Democratic process means putting some of the basic causes of famine on the political agenda. Sudanese democrats already have a long list of difficult problems to address, should they have an opportunity. But some relatively neglected questions also need also to be considered:

- Land reform is a fundamental issue. Unjust systems of land ownership are a basic reason for war and famine in the Nuba Mountains and a number of other regions. Equitable rural development in Sudan will remain impossible unless commercial mechanised farming ceases to be given priority over smallholder agriculture.

- Ownership of natural resources is a related but slightly different issue, especially in that it includes the Nile waters and oil reserves. Resolving this issue cannot be separated from the demands for regional autonomy and self-determination, not just for the South but for other marginalised areas.

356

- A democratic planning, development or famine prevention process has never existed in Sudan. Lack of popular consultation in aid programmes has been notorious. If there is only one lesson to be learned from the war, it is that rural Sudanese cannot be governed peaceably without their consent.

- Demilitarisation of rural Sudan will be essential as a prerequisite for establishing rural administration, social services, justice and normal economic activity. This in turn requires settling the disputes and grievances that give people reason to hold arms. It is a much more lengthy process than establishing a national peace accord or electoral framework, but experience demonstrates that unless local peace is guaranteed, national peace will not prevail.

- Challenging the current economic dispensation. The NIF has 'bought' Sudan, and established its economic control through a range of banks, businesses, foundations and charitable organisations, as well as the institutions of central government. The economic interests of substantial sections of the opposition are also tied up in commercial farming, banking and import-export businesses. Constitutional change alone will not affect this economic stranglehold, which underpins many of the forces the promote war and famine.

- A governmental obligation to preventing famine is needed. This is much more than a simple administrative commitment, to be implemented when resources allow: it should have mechanisms for enforcement from the outset. The proposal for a commission of inquiry has been mentioned above: a domestic version, operating within a democratic framework, could prove an effective way of monitoring governmental (and NGO) effectiveness at fighting famine.

One of the challenges of an anti-famine politics in Sudan is to identify and articulate these issues, so that they can be put on the political agenda and pursued at the appropriate moment. This in turn requires building a political coalition ready to do that.

Challenging Humanitarian Power

Foreign relief agencies will continue to play an important role in Sudan for the forseeable future. Their technocratic approach to famine relief has provided a pretext for marginalising the politics of famine, while their resources have supported the authoritarians and encouraged an external orientation. Most insidiously, humanitarian power influences the way that people think: it makes them expect solutions from outside. International aid has *managed* Sudan's political decay rather than *halted* it. By concealing the true nature of the wounds it has prevented correct diagnosis and treatment by Sudanese themselves. It may do so again.

Sudanese democrats need to challenge the power of humanitarian agencies and the ways in which they have dominated the anti-famine agenda. Rhetorical and propaganda challenges are not helpful. An effective alternative anti-famine practice is required, based on a Sudanese agenda for tackling the political and economic causes of famine.

FIGHTING FAMINE DURING WARTIME

Currently, the war is a reality in Sudan. One challenge is to bring it to an end; a second is to minimise its human cost; a third is to try to assist in the moulding of progressive political agendas during wartime. The second and third challenges are linked: effective wartime famine relief depends upon the political colour of the belligerent that controls the area and population.

Despite its impressive ability to mobilise people and resources in pursuit of a comprehensive agenda, the NIF government is perpetuating and deepening conflict and the prospects for famine in Sudan. While it continues to pursue its agenda, including the Comprehensive Call, Sudan will not be free from famine.

After nearly fourteen years of war, the SPLA has failed to forge a democratic contract in Southern Sudan. Despite the avowals of its leadership, and the best efforts of many of its members, the SPLA remains a prisoner of its past—and indeed the previous history of failed attempts to establish a system of government in South Sudan. Since 1993, there has been enormous enthusiasm among Southern Sudanese and foreign friends for promoting an agenda of democratisation, capacity building and civil society. Some efforts have been well-meant, some self-serving, but progress has been disappointingly slow.

The National Democratic Alliance (NDA) also gives little reason for optimism. Among its leaders are many of those who were prominent in the pro-war and pro-famine coalition of 1985-9, and they have not expressed remorse for their crimes during that period nor indicated readiness to learn from their mistakes. Issues such as land reform and accountability for creating famine are not on the NDA agenda. Within the NDA, however, there are many who recognise these failings, and some who are ready to learn from them.

The last constellation of forces is in the marginalised areas— regions neglected by both government and opposition. A new model humanitarianism can be developed in these areas, where the humanitarian international has penetrated least, and there is a degree of popular mobilisation by anti-government forces. This has already occurred to some degree in the Nuba Mountains, and there are possibilities elsewhere, such as southern Blue Nile and the Beja Hills. The obstacles are tremendous, but the tenacity of people such as the Nuba and Beja in the face of threats to their survival should not be underestimated.

If a democratic coalition emerges in Sudan, deeply committed to the fight against famine, there will be an opportunity for a constructive engagement by humanitarian agencies, to support them and their approach, or at the very least to provide the political space for them to pursue their agenda without being derailed by a technocratic, charitable approach. Some NGOs should be able to meet this requirement, and themselves challenge humanitarian power.

The Virtues and Limits of Neutrality

But no such opportunity exists at present. In the absence of tangible democratic options: where does this leave a progressive humanitarianism? Abandoning suffering people to their fate because of unpleasant political authorities is not humane.

The ICRC has long developed rules for operating in such situations, governing its activities by international humanitarian law, and using the utmost discretion and diplomacy. Neutrality is prominent among the ICRC's principles. Neutrality has its virtues. Most importantly, it is a mechanism for providing access. It can also be a lever against the co-option of humanitarian programmes by belligerents with abusive agendas. (In fact, in Sudan the main use to which the concept has been put has been to criticise the government's manipulation of relief, starting with CART and most recently manifest in the *OLS Review*.)

Operation Lifeline Sudan has been derived from broadly the same set of principles, but has been required to adapt them. These adaptations have their perils. The first is publicity: OLS was launched in a blaze of media attention and (at least the Southern Sector) has seen facilitating journalists as one of its tasks. Publicity is important to OLS's ability to attract funds from western governmental donors, and has also been seen as providing a measure of protection for the programme. A second change from the ICRC mode of operation is an unwillingness to withdraw. OLS (again, especially the Southern Sector) has become an institution in its own right, determined to preserve itself. Its donors are also determined to see it continue, for a range of reasons.

OLS, the SRRA and Responsibilities in the South

Perhaps most importantly, OLS makes much larger claims for itself than any ICRC programme, entailing larger responsibilities. The Southern Sector has found itself drawn into a vacuum of quasi-governmental responsibility, that it cannot adequately fill, by the shortcomings of the SPLA and SRRA. To be fair to the SPLA, OLS has also embraced the opportunities for control and programme expansion, leading to some understandable frustrations from the SRRA that it is unable to regulate humanitarian activities. This was not envisaged at the launch of OLS, and reflects the way it has grown in an ad hoc way over the years. The rehabilitation, education, capacity building and humanitarian principles programmes of OLS-Southern Sector are all manifestations of this: while they are the most welcome programmes, they also intrude into the social fabric of the South. OLS's relationship to the SPLA and SRRA has echoes of aid agencies in the South in the 1970s, and reminds many Southerners of the colonial encounter.

International humanitarian law was not set up to deal with such a situation: there are no clear rules for how to operate. The Geneva Conventions deal solely with emergency relief, not with education or capacity building. The latter are essential for maintaining a functioning society, but humanitarian law is concerned with much narrower questions. The legal grounds for sustaining such programmes are uncertain, faced with Sudan Government objections founded on sovereignty. This kind of intimate involvement in a war-stricken society is also best done from a sense of solidarity by organisations and individuals closely committed to the cause.

The Geneva Conventions also bestow primary responsibility for meeting relief needs on the host authority. With this responsibility goes the power to regulate relief activities. This is based on the assumption that the host authority can actually do both of these tasks, which is questionable in the case of the SRRA. If the ICRC had been responsible for the programme, the SPLA's role would have remained clear, but the ICRC would not have moved beyond relief and modest rehabilitation assistance.

The SPLA and SRRA would much prefer an operation that abandoned neutrality and provided them with direct assistance out of solidarity. They have measured OLS against this standard and found it wanting. Mario Muor Muor, SRRA Secretary General had a legitimate point when he contrasted the co-ordination and control role played by the Sudan Government in the Northern Sector, with the much smaller role played by the SRRA—UNICEF has taken on most aspects of co-ordination.[10] He pointed out that the Geneva Conventions bestow this responsibility on the SPLA rather than any international agency. However valid this point, the reality is that the SPLA cannot easily improve its position *vis-à-vis* foreign humanitarian agencies and their donors. First, the legal case remains contentious (sovereignty remains an issue). Second, western donors remain sceptical of the SRRA's capacity for effective co-ordination. Only when the SRRA can prove its ability to do the job as well can it mount an effective challenge to OLS's lead role. Third, agencies and donors are unimpressed by the record of human rights and democratisation within the SPLA. Solidarity assistance springs from admiration for the struggle and how it is conducted. At present, the SPLA can only expect uncritical solidarity from certain small Christian groups which have their own agendas to pursue.

There are understandable reasons why the SRRA and SPLA remain weak, but their weakness is a hard fact. Ultimately it is their challenge to prove to the international humanitarians that they can do the job. They have not yet risen to this challenge. Probably, they would have a better chance if there was less of an international humanitarian intrusion: on these grounds, there is a strong case for making OLS smaller. However, until both capacity and democratic accountability are proven, in the meantime there is little alternative except a relief operation founded on the principle of neutrality. This need not be OLS, at least in its present form, but something designed along similar lines is necessary if significant international relief operations are to continue in Southern Sudan.

Extremist Islam, OLS and Co-option in the North

Perhaps the biggest problem with OLS is the degree to which the Northern Sector has been co-opted and manipulated by the Sudan Government, in pursuit of a systematically abusive military and political agenda, making a nonsense out of neutrality and accountability. There is a very powerful case for demanding that

---

[10] Mario Muor Muor, 'SRRA Position Paper on Operation Lifeline Sudan (OLS) Southern Sector,' SRRA, 27 November 1995.

these principles be enforced, or that OLS drastically cut back on its Northern Sector programmes. In particular, 'development' schemes in the government sector should not receive international support.

The Sudan Government's overarching project is the total transformation of society in the image of extremist Islam. Islamic relief is an integral part of this. Islamic relief has a number of advantages over the Christian tradition and secular humanitarianism. Its emphasis on obligations and justice is a welcome change from western notions of charity that have proved so damaging in Africa. Many of those who criticise Islamic relief—notably some fundament-alist Christians—are hypocritical. But the NIF's project of Islamic relief under the Comprehensive Call is deeply flawed. It furthers the interests of a political and commercial elite drawn from a narrow social class and ethnic group, concentrating power and wealth in their hands. The Comprehensive Call is pursued by exploiting the vulnerability of poor, marginalised and oppressed people, who have little option but to submit to its agenda. It is closely integrated into a military strategy that involves gross and systematic violations of human rights.

Little has been published about Islamic relief in Sudan. One reason is that western relief workers and scholars know rather little about it. Another is that diplomats and senior relief officials, especially at the UN, are reluctant to criticise it from fear of appearing anti-Islamic. A policy of tacit co-operation has been adopted by default. This is not acceptable: the merits and demerits of the Comprehensive Call and Islamic relief in NIF-ruled Sudan must be debated openly. It is important to distinguish between the noble principles of Islamic humanitarianism and its practice in Sudan. The conclusion of this study is that Islamic relief in Sudan is too deeply compromised in abusive and exclusive government policies to be worthy of humanitarian support.

Should OLS Continue?

Another huge problem with OLS is that nobody knows whether it is doing any good, that is, saving any lives. The *OLS Review* did not attempt to address this question. It is difficult to make sensible policy choices about international assistance to Sudan, as humanitarian crises emerge in eastern Sudan, without this information. It would be pointless to maintain OLS if it is not delivering on its basic aim of saving lives, at the price of ignoring suffering elsewhere.

The most precious element of OLS is the principle of a negotiated breach of sovereignty that opens up a 'humanitarian space' in parts of Southern Sudan accessed by OLS Southern Sector. When there is acute famine in the South, this principle is essential. When there is none (which in practice means most of the time), the quantities of aid delivered are much less important than maintaining the principle. This has important implications for OLS's priorities. In particular, the chance to be operational on the ground should not be pursued at the cost of neutrality and accountability.

Internationally, OLS produces the illusion that 'something is being done.' The default option for any foreign initiative to do with Sudan is 'let's maintain OLS.' This leaves other options for action hostage to the fortunes of OLS (as the case of the Nuba in 1992 shows). The OLS budget also swallows up money that could be used elsewhere.

In conclusion, humanitarian neutrality remains an important principle in a war in which no side has the capacity and political agenda to enable an effective struggle against famine. An OLS-type operation will be needed for the forseeable future in Southern Sudan: in practice, this means a continuation of OLS. But in the Northern Sector OLS has become far too compromised. In the Southern Sector, it has raised too many expectations and become too intrusive. A smaller OLS might be a more effective one. In the meantime, the challenge for Sudanese democrats and like-thinking outsiders is to make OLS unnecessary as quickly as possible.

CONCLUSION

It is difficult to end any analysis of contemporary Sudan on an optimistic note. The problems are so huge and the potential solutions—when they can be identified at all—are so difficult, that few pessimists have been proven wrong. The greatest source of hope is the tenacity and resilience of the Sudanese people. They have shown an extraordinary capacity to cope with adversity, and in many cases to work for democratic or peaceable solutions. It is a simple truism that solutions can only lie in the hands of Sudanese people. Measures that lead to greater popular involvement and accountability are the surest way of moving towards solutions.

International aid can do many things, but solving political problems and preventing famine do not figure among them. If there is a domestic political process that has humanitarian objectives, then aid can support that process. Otherwise, the best that aid can do is not to obstruct political processes and not obscure real power relations and the need for accountability, while alleviating some human suffering. Aid is the source of many illusions. Democracy, accountability and the prevention of human tragedies require a freedom from such illusions.

INDEX

Department of Humanitarian Affairs, 296
deregulation of relief, 2, 25, 32, 124, 197
Dima, 71
Dinka, 32, 83, 94, 126, 154, 160, 171, 247, 275, 276, 340
displaced people, 3, 137, 144, 156, 223, 250
Diwan al Zakat, 205, 207, 209, 225, 234
DUP, 113, 115, 203

EC, 59, 96, 106, 107, 108, 133, 135, 239, 241
education, 28, 80, 163, 201, 208, 222
Egypt, 10, 21, 26, 65, 115, 229
Ekval, Thomas, 295
EPLF, 35, 64, 215
Equatoria, 29, 73, 80, 126, 239, 259, 281, 326
Eritrea, 32, 62, 87, 115, 138, 214, 286, 312
Eritrean Jihad, 215
Eritrean Relief Association, 34
Ethiopia, 34, 45, 62, 64, 70, 73, 83, 115, 214, 216, 229, 286, 305, 312

Fadallah Burma Nasir, 107
Faisal Islamic Bank, 54, 196, 203, 209
Falashas, 18, 35, 38, 55
Famine Regulations of 1920, 21
FAO, 40, 45
Farrakhan, Louis 343
Fashoda Relief and Rehabilitation Association, *seeFRRA*
Fellowship for African Relief, 229
Fertit, 247
FIB, *see Faisal Islamic Bank*
floods, 100, 114, 156
forced removal, 32, 43, 99, 137, 141, 156, 157, 162, 174
Francis Deng, 171
Frontline Fellowship, 339

FRRA, 281
Funj, 21

Gambela, 71, 127
Garang, *see John Garang*
Geneva Conventions, 327
Gezira, 22, 147
Gizouli Dafallah, 53
Gogrial, 283
Ground Rules, 326

Hassan al Turabi, 12, 54, 114, 188, 215
Hilary Logali, 28
Holy Koran Society, 225
humanitarian access, 3, 124, 257, 295
humanitarian intervention, 302
humanitarian principles, 3, 125, 237, 327
Hunger Triangle, 277

IARA, 197, 212, 244
Ibrahim Abdel Hafiz, 230
ICRC, 109, 116, 123, 124, 129, 247, 251, 327, 351, 360
IGADD, 286, 290
IMF, 16, 41, 102, 109, 117, 121, 206
Institution and Capacity-Building Programme, 318
International Islamic Relief Organisation, 212, 244
Intifada, *see popular uprising*
Islamic banks, 12, 14, 48, 135, 189, 203
Islamic Da'awa Authority, 207
Islamic law, 12, 188
Islamic relief, 3, 60, 179, 185, 187, 188, 195, 221, 244, 250, 338, 363
Islamic schools, *see khalwas*
Islamic social planning, 144, 190
ISRA, 197
Itang, 67, 71, 76, 77, 87, 334

Jaeger, Christoph 173

367

Sudan Foundation, 344
Sudan Medical Care, 322
Sudan Socialist Union, *see SSU*
Sudanese Islamic Bank, 210, 211
Sudanese Organisation for the Care of Prisoners, 225
Sudanese Small Industries Development Company, 211

TMC, 51, 120
Tonj, 322
Toposa, 89
Torit Resolutions, 273, 306
Torit, 120, 277, 332, 336
TPLF, 35, 36
Trade Union Relief Association, 53
trade unions, 46, 53, 115
Traxler, Vieri, 182
Tsore, 72

Uduk, 230, 275
Uganda, 29, 78, 216, 286, 305, 312
Um Ruwaba, 223
Umma Party, 10, 104, 115, 195, 341
UN Department of Humanitarian Affairs, 3, 123, 170, 182
UN General Assembly, 3, 171, 295
UN Human Rights Commission, 166
UN Security Council, 295
UNDP, 114, 143, 153, 155, 166, 170, 171, 173, 184, 212, 244, 252, 354
UNEOS, 51, 106
UNESCO, 155
UNHCR, 25, 34, 74, 171
UNICEF, 89, 108, 120, 125, 152, 161, 172, 173, 181, 184, 212, 284, 351
Union of the Southern and Northern Funj, 229
University of Juba, 28
University of Khartoum, 27,, 42, 53, 101, 340
Upper Nile, 26, 73, 77, 79, 86, 97, 108, 147, 150, 158, 201, 253, 273

urbanisation, 15, 162
US Congress, 295, 347
US State Department, 17, 41, 45, 347
USAID, 16, 41, 52, 106, 108, 115, 120, 127, 138, 197, 199, 205, 241, 295, 316, 345
USAP, 115

Waat, 276, 277, 279, 303
Wagner, Gordon 345
Wau, 85, 99, 105, 107, 247
Western Relief Operation, 108
WFP, 133, 138, 153, 172, 184, 239, 244, 279, 281, 297
wheat subsidy, 102, 207
William Nyuon, 281, 283, 289, 326
World Association of Moslem Women, 247
World Bank, 103, 148, 149, 161, 120
World Vision, 52, 198, 229, 322
Wutnyang Gatakek, 256, 276

Yousif el Aggab, 21
Yousif Kuwa Mekki, 176, 183, 301, 312
Youth Education Centre, 224
Yuai, 279, 303

zakat, 14, 204

AFRICAN RIGHTS PUBLICATIONS

Books

Rwanda: Death, Despair and Defiance, Second expanded edition August 1995, 1200 pages, price £24.95 or US$40.00.

Facing Genocide: The Nuba of Sudan, July 1995, 358 pages, price £9.95 or US$14.95 (also available in Arabic).

Not So Innocent: When Women Become Killers, August 1995, 284 pages, price £8.95 or US$13.95.

Kenya: Shadow Justice: November 1996, 267 pages, price £9.95 or or US$14.95.

Reports

Somalia: Operation Restore Hope: A Preliminary Assessment, May 1993, 60 pages, price £4.95 or US$7.95.

Somalia: Human Rights Abuses by the United Nations Forces, July 1993, 35 pages, price £3.95 or US$6.95.

The Nightmare Continues... Abuses Against Somali Refugees in Kenya, September 1993, 54 pages, price £4.95 or US$7.95.

Violent Deeds Live On: Landmines in Somalia and Somaliland, December 1993, 82 pages plus 12 photographs, price £5.95 or US$8.95, jointly published with Mines Advisory Group.

Sudan's Invisible Citizens, February 1995, 60 pages, (also available in Arabic) price £5.95 or US$8.95.

Rwanda: A Waste of Hope—The United Nations Human Rights Field Operation, April 1995, 69 pages, price £5.95 or US$8.95.

Justice in Zimbabwe, February 1996, 105 pages,   price £7.95 or US$10.95.

Rwanda - Killing the Evidence: Murder, Attacks, Arrests and Intimidation of Survivors and Witnesses, April 1996, 105 pages, price £7.95 or $10.95.

Discussion Papers

No 1: *Land Tenure, The Creation of Famine and Prospects for Peace in Somalia*, October 1993, price £2.00 or US$3.50.

No 2: *Components of a Lasting Peace in Sudan: First thoughts*, December 1993, 28 pages, price £2.00 or US$3.50.

No 3: *Rwanda, Who is killing; Who is dying; What is to be done*, May 1994, 49 pages, price £5.95 or US$8.95.

No 4: *Crimes Without Punishment: Sexual Harassment and Violence against Female Students in Schools and Universities in Africa*, July 1994, 25 pages, price £3.95 or US$6.95.

No 5: *Humanitarianism Unbound? Current Dilemmas Facing Multi-mandate Relief Operations in Political Emergencies*,   November 1994, 40 pages, price £4.95 or US$7.95.

No 6: *Great Expectations: The Civil Roles of the Churches in Southern Sudan*, April 1995, 43 pages, price £4.95 or US$7.95.

No 7: *Imposing Empowerment: Aid and Civil Institutions in Southern Sudan*, December 1995, 54 pages, price £4.95 or US$7.95.

Journal

Witness to Genocide - Issues 1-5. Also available in French: Témoin du Génocide.

Please indicate if you would like information about subscribing to *Witness to Genocide*.